GACE
081
082

Special Education
General
Curriculum
Teacher Certification Exam

By: Sharon Wynne, M.S.

XAMonline, INC.
Boston

To obtain permission(s) to use the material from this work for any purpose including workshops or seminars, please submit a written request to:

XAMonline, Inc.
25 First Street, Suite 106
Cambridge, MA 02141
Toll Free 1-800-509-4128
E-mail: info@xamonline.com
Web www.xamonline.com
Fax: 1-617-583-5552

Library of Congress Cataloging-in-Publication Data
Wynne, Sharon A.
    Special Education General Curriculum 081, 082 : Teacher Certification / Sharon A. Wynne. -2nd
    ed. ISBN: 978-1-58197-538-3
    1. Special Education General Curriculum 081, 082   2. Study Guides.   3.GACE
    4. Teachers' Certification & Licensure. 5. Careers

Senior Editor   Dr. Harte Weiner, Ph.D.   Production Coordinator
Copy Editor   Tamara Brewer   Dave Aronson

Disclaimer:
The opinions expressed in this publication are the sole works of XAMonline and were created independently from the National Education Association, Educational Testing Service, or any State Department of Education, National Evaluation Systems or other testing affiliates.

Between the time of publication and printing, state specific standards as well as testing formats and website information may change that is not included in part or in whole within this product. Sample test questions are developed by XAMonline and reflect similar content as on real tests; however, they are not former tests. XAMonline assembles content that aligns with state standards but makes no claims nor guarantees teacher candidates a passing score. Numerical scores are determined by testing companies such as NES or ETS and then are compared with individual state standards. A passing score varies from state to state.

Printed in the United States of America   œ-1
GACE: Special Education General Curriculum 081, 082
ISBN: 978-1-58197-610-6

ACKNOWLEDGMENTS
Special Education

Recognizing the hard work in the production of our study guides, we would like to thank those involved. The credentials and experience fulfilling the making of this study guide, aided by the professionalism and insight of those who expressed the subject mastery in specialized fields, is valued and appreciated by XAMonline. It results in a product that upholds the integrity and pride represented by modern educators who bear the name **TEACHER**.

Providers of foundational material

Founding authors 1996	Kathy Schinerman
	Roberta Ramsey
Pre-flight editorial review	Paul Sutliff
Pre-flight construction :	Brittany Good
	Harris
	Brooks
	Hughes
Authors 2006	Paul Sutliff
	Beatrice Jordan
	Marisha Tapera
	Kathy Gibson
	Twya Lavender
	Carol Moore
	Christi Godard
Sample test rational	Sidney Findley

XAMonline Editorial and Production acknowledgements

Project Manager	Sharon Wynne
Managing Editor	Harte Weiner
Project Coordinator	Twya Lavender
Series Editor	Mary Collins
Editorial Assistant	Virginia Finnerty
Marketing Manager	John Wynne
Marketing support	Maria Ciampa
Cover design	Brian Messenger
Sales	Justin Dooley
Production Editor	David Aronson
Typist	Julian German
Manufacturing	Chris Morning/Midland Press
E-Books	Kristy Gipson/Lightningsource

About the test

Georgia has discontinued the Praxis exam as a requirement for future Georgia educators. The new educator assessment program is called the Georgia Assessments for the Certification of Educators® (GACE™). These new Georgia assessments are correlated with national standards, Georgia educator certification requirements, Georgia educator preparation standards, and the new Georgia Performance Standards (GPS) for P-12 students now being put into practice by the Georgia Department of Education.

Test Format

The test format for the Special Education General Curriculum (81 and 82) is two separate tests. Test 1 (code 81) covers the subareas *Understanding Students with Disabilities* and *Assessing Students and Developing Programs*. There are about 22 selected-response questions and 1 constructed response question about the objectives covered under *Understanding Students with Disabilities*. There are about 38 selected-response questions and 1 constructed response question covered under *Assessing Students and Developing Programs*.

Test 2 (code 82) is made up of subareas *Promoting Student Development and Learning* and *Working in a Professional Environment*. There are about 30 selected-response questions and 1 constructed response question about the objectives covered under *Promoting Student Development and Learning* and the same for objectives covered under *Working in a Professional Environment*.

Passing Score

All test results are reported as scaled scores. A scale score of 220 is considered passing. Since the special education test is comprised of two tests, the candidate must pass both tests in order to meet certification requirements.

Location, Cost, Fees

For up to date information about locations, cost, and fees, please go to www.gace.nesinc.com.

Table of Contents

Great Study and Testing Tips!

What to study in order to prepare for the subject assessments is the focus of this study guide, but equally important is *how* you study.

You can increase your chances of truly mastering the information by taking some simple but effective steps.

Study Tips:

1. Some foods aid the learning process. Foods such as milk, nuts, seeds, rice, and oats help your study efforts by releasing natural memory enhancers called CCKs (*cholecystokinin*) composed of *tryptopha*n, *choline*, and *phenylalanine*. All of these chemicals enhance the neurotransmitters associated with memory. Before studying, try a light, protein-rich meal of eggs, turkey, and fish. All of these foods release the memory-enhancing chemicals. The better the connections, the more you comprehend.

Likewise, before you take a test, stick to a light snack of energy boosting and relaxing foods. A glass of milk, a piece of fruit, or some peanuts all release various memory-boosting chemicals and help you to relax and focus on the subject at hand.

2. Learn to take great notes. A by-product of our modern culture is that we have grown accustomed to getting our information in short doses (e.g., television news sound bites or *USA Today*–style newspaper articles).

Consequently, we've subconsciously trained ourselves to assimilate information better in neat little packages. If your notes are scrawled all over the paper, it fragments the flow of the information. Strive for clarity. Newspapers use a standard format to achieve clarity. Your notes can be much clearer through use of proper formatting. A very effective format is called the "Cornell Method."

Take a sheet of loose-leaf lined notebook paper and draw a line all the way down the paper about 1–2" from the left-hand edge.

Draw another line across the width of the paper about 1–2" up from the bottom. Repeat this process on the reverse side of the page.

Look at the highly effective result. You have ample room for notes, a left-hand margin for special emphasis items or inserting supplementary data from the textbook, a large area at the bottom for a brief summary, and a little rectangular space for just about anything you want.

3. Get the concept, then the details. Too often we focus on the details and don't gather an understanding of the concept. However, if you simply memorize only dates, places, or names, you may well miss the whole point of the subject. A key way to understand things is to put them in your own words. If you are working from a textbook, automatically summarize each paragraph in your mind. If you are outlining text, don't simply copy the author's words.

Rephrase them in your own words. You remember your own thoughts and words much better than someone else's and subconsciously tend to associate the important details to the core concepts.

4. Ask why? Pull apart written material paragraph by paragraph and don't forget the captions under the illustrations.

Example: If the heading is "Stream Erosion," flip it around to read, "Why do streams erode?" Then answer the questions.

If you train your mind to think in a series of questions and answers, not only will you learn more, but it also helps to lessen the test anxiety because you are used to answering questions.

5. Read for reinforcement and future needs. Even if you only have 10 minutes, put your notes or a book in your hand. Your mind is similar to a computer; you have to input data in order to have it processed. *By reading, you are creating the neural connections for future retrieval.* The more times you read something, the more you reinforce the learning of ideas.

Even if you don't fully understand something on the first pass, *your mind stores much of the material for later recall.*

6. Relax to learn, so go into exile. Our bodies respond to an inner clock called biorhythms. Burning the midnight oil works well for some people, but not everyone.

If possible, set aside a particular place to study that is free of distractions. Shut off the television, cell phone, and pager, and exile your friends and family during your study period.

If you really are bothered by silence, try background music. Light classical music at a low volume has been shown to aid in concentration over other types.

Music that evokes pleasant emotions without lyrics are highly suggested. Try just about anything by Mozart. It relaxes you.

7. <u>Use arrows not highlighters.</u> At best, it's difficult to read a page full of yellow, pink, blue, and green streaks.

Try staring at a neon sign for a while and you'll soon see my point: the horde of colors obscure the message.

A quick note, a brief dash of color, an underline, or an arrow pointing to a particular passage is much clearer than a horde of highlighted words.

8. <u>Budget your study time</u>. Although you shouldn't ignore any of the material, *allocate your available study time in the same ratio that topics may appear on the test.*

Testing Tips:

1. Get smart, play dumb. *Don't read anything into the question.* Don't make an assumption that the test writer is looking for something other than what is asked. Stick to the question as written and don't read extra things into it.

2. Read the question and all the choices *twice* before answering the question. You may miss something by not carefully reading and then rereading both the question and the answers.

If you really don't have a clue as to the right answer, leave it blank on the first time through. Go on to the other questions, as they may provide a clue as to how to answer the skipped questions.

If later on, you still can't answer the skipped ones . . . *guess.* The only penalty for guessing is that you *might* get it wrong. Only one thing is certain; if you don't put anything down, you will get it wrong!

3. Turn the question into a statement. Look at the way the questions are worded. The syntax of the question usually provides a clue. Does it seem more familiar as a statement rather than as a question? Does it sound strange?

By turning a question into a statement, you may be able to spot if an answer sounds right, and it may also trigger memories of material you have read.

4. Look for hidden clues. It's actually very difficult to compose multiple-foil (choice) questions without giving away part of the answer in the options presented.

In most multiple-choice questions, you can often readily eliminate one or two of the potential answers. This leaves you with only two real possibilities, and automatically your odds go to fifty-fifty for very little work.

5. Trust your instincts. For every fact that you have read, you subconsciously retain something of that knowledge. On questions that you aren't really certain about, go with your basic instincts. *Your first impression on how to answer a question is usually correct.*

6. Mark your answers directly on the test booklet. Don't bother trying to fill in the optical scan sheet on the first pass through the test.

7. Watch the clock! You have a set amount of time to answer the questions. Don't get bogged down trying to answer a single question at the expense of 10 questions you can more readily answer.

Pre-Test

1. Joey is in a mainstreamed preschool program. One of the means his teacher uses in determining growth in adaptive skills is that of observation. Some questions about Joey's behavior that she might ask include the following:
    (Average Rigor) (Skill 1.01)

    a. Is he able to hold a cup?
    b. Can he call the name of any of his toys?
    c. Can he reach for an object and grasp it?
    d. All of the above

Correct answer is "d."
Here are some characteristics of individuals with mental retardation or intellectual disabilities:
*   IQ of 70 or below
*   Limited cognitive ability; delayed academic achievement, particularly in language-related subjects
*   Deficits in memory that often relate to poor initial perception or that relate to a poor inability to apply stored information to relevant situations
*   Impaired formulation of learning strategies
*   Difficulty in attending to relevant aspects of stimuli; slowness in reaction time or in employing alternate strategies.

2. Which of the following statements about children with emotional/behavioral disorders is true?
    (Average Rigor) (Skill 1.01)

    a. They have very high IQs.
    b. They display poor social skills.
    c. They are poor academic achievers.
    d. Both b and c

Correct answer is "d."
Children who exhibit mild behavioral disorders are characterized by:
*   Average or above average scores on intelligence tests
*   Poor academic achievement; learned helplessness
*   Unsatisfactory interpersonal relationships
*   Immaturity; attention seeking
*   Aggressive, acting-out behavior, such as hitting, fighting, teasing, yelling, refusing to comply with requests, excessive attention seeking, poor anger control, temper tantrums, hostile reactions, and defiant use of language
*   Anxious, withdrawn behavior, such as infantile behavior, social isolation, few friends, withdrawal into fantasy, fears, hypochondria, unhappiness, and crying

3. **Which behavior would be expected at the mild level of emotional/behavioral disorders?**
   (Average Rigor) (Skill 1.01)

   a. Attention seeking
   b. Inappropriate affect
   c. Self-injurious actions
   d. Poor sense of identity

Correct answer is "a."
Children who exhibit mild behavioral disorders are characterized by:
- Average or above average scores on intelligence tests
- Poor academic achievement; learned helplessness
- Unsatisfactory interpersonal relationships
- Immaturity; attention seeking
- Aggressive, acting-out behavior, such as hitting, fighting, teasing, yelling, refusing to comply with requests, excessive attention seeking, poor anger control, temper tantrums, hostile reactions, and defiant use of language
- Anxious, withdrawn behavior, such as infantile behavior, social isolation, few friends, withdrawal into fantasy, fears, hypochondria, unhappiness, and crying

4. **Which category of behaviors would most likely be found on a behavior rating scale?**
   (Easy) (Skill 1.01)

   a. Disruptive, acting out
   b. Shy, withdrawn
   c. Aggressive (physical or verbal)
   d. All of the above

Correct answer is "d."
These are all possible problem behaviors that can adversely impact the student or the class, thus they may be found on behavior rating scales.

5. **The social skills of students in mental retardation programs are likely to be appropriate for children of their mental age rather than chronological age. This means that the teacher will need to do all of the following except:**
(Easy) (Skill 1.01)

   a. Model desired behavior
   b. Provide clear instructions
   c. Expect age appropriate behaviors
   d. Adjust the physical environment when necessary

Correct answer is "c."
Age appropriate means mental age appropriate not chronological age appropriate.

6. **Which of the following examples would be considered of highest priority when determining the need for the delivery of appropriate special education and related services?**
(Rigorous) (Skill 1.01)

   a. An eight-year-old boy is repeating first grade for the second time and exhibits problems with toileting, gross motor functions, and remembering number and letter symbols. His regular classroom teacher claims the referral forms are too time-consuming and refuses to complete them. The teacher also refuses to make accommodations because he feels every child should be treated alike.
   b. A six-year-old girl who has been diagnosed as autistic is placed in a special education class within the local school. Her mother wants her to attend residential school next year, even though the girl is showing progress.
   c. A ten-year-old girl with profound mental retardation is receiving education services in a state institution.
   d. A twelve-year-old boy with mild disabilities is placed in a behavior disorders program but displays obvious perceptual deficits (e.g., reversal of letters and symbols, an inability to discriminate sounds). He was originally thought to have a learning disability but did not meet state criteria for this exceptionality category based on results of standard scores. He has always had problems with attending to tasks and is now beginning to get into trouble during seatwork time. His teacher feels that he will eventually become a real behavior problem. He receives social skills training in the resource room one period a day.

Correct answer is "a."
No modifications are being made, so the child is not receiving any services whatsoever.

7. The Carrow Elicited Language Inventory is a test designed to give the examiner diagnostic information about a child's expressive grammatical competence. Which of the following language components is being assessed?
    (Rigorous) (Skill 1.01)

    a. Phonology
    b. Morphology
    c. Syntax
    d. Both b and c

Correct answer is "c."
Although both morphology and syntax refer to understanding the grammatical structure of language in the receptive channel, as well as using the grammatical structure of language in the expressive channel, assessment of morphology refers to linguistic structure of words. Assessment of syntax includes grammatical usage of word classes, word order, and transformational rules for the variance of word order.

8. In the Grammatic Closure subtest of the Illinois Test of Psycholinguistic Abilities, the child is presented with a picture representing statements, such as the following: "Here is one die; here are two ____." This test is essentially a test of:
    (Rigorous) (Skill 1.01)

    a. Phonology
    b. Morphology
    c. Syntax
    d. Semantics

Correct answer is "c."
*   Phonology is the study of significant units of speech sounds.
*   Morphology is the study of the smallest units of language that convey meaning.
*   Syntax is a system of rules for making grammatically correct sentences.
*   Semantics is the study of the relationships between words and grammatical forms in a language, as well as the underlying meaning

9. **Five-year-old Tom continues to substitute the "w" sound for the "r" sound when pronouncing words; therefore, he often distorts words (e.g., "wabbit" for "rabbit" and "wat" for "rat"). His articulation disorder is basically a problem in:**
   (Rigorous) (Skill 1.01)

   a. Phonology
   b. Morphology
   c. Syntax
   d. Semantics

Correct answer is "a."
- Phonology is the study of significant units of speech sounds.
- Morphology is the study of the smallest units of language that convey meaning.
- Syntax is a system of rules for making grammatically correct sentences.
- Semantics is the study of the relationships between words and grammatical forms in a language, as well as the underlying meaning.

10. **Which of the following is untrue about the ending "er?"**
    (Rigorous) (Skill 1.01)

    a. It is an example of a free morpheme.
    b. It represents one of the smallest units of meaning within a word.
    c. It is called an inflectional ending.
    d. When added to a word, it connotes a comparative status

Correct answer is "a."
Morpheme is the smallest unit of meaningful language. "Er" on its own has no meaning.

11. **Which component of language involves language content rather than the form of language?**
    (Rigorous) (Skill 1.01)

    a. Phonology
    b. Morphology
    c. Semantics
    d. Syntax

Correct answer is "c."
Semantics is the study of the relationships between words and grammatical forms in a language, as well as the underlying meaning.

12. **Which is least indicative of a developmental delay?**
(Rigorous) (Skill 1.01)

    a. Language and speech production
    b. Gross motor skills
    c. Self-help skills
    d. Arithmetic computation skills

Correct answer is "d."
In a preschool environment, disabling conditions are manifested as the inability to learn adequate readiness skills; the inability to demonstrate self-help; and adaptive, social-interpersonal communication, or gross motor skills. The most typical symptoms exhibited by school-age students are inattention to tasks; disruptiveness; inability to learn to read, write, spell, or perform mathematical computations; unintelligible speech; an appearance of not being able to see or hear adequately; frequent daydreaming; excessive movement; and, in general, clumsiness and ineptitude in most school-related activities. Even though gross motor skills are exhibited in preschool children, they do not carry over to school-age children.

13. **A child with intellectual disabilities who is fairly clumsy and possesses poor social awareness—but who can be taught to communicate and to perform semiskilled labor and maintains himself under supervision—probably belongs to which level of classification as an adult? (Rigorous) (Skill 1.01)**

    a. Mild
    b. Moderate
    c. Severe
    d. Profound

Correct answer is "b."
Mild (IQ of 50–55 to 70)
- Delays in most areas (communication, motor, academic)
- Often not distinguished from normal children until of school age
- Can acquire both academic and vocational skills; can become self-supporting

Moderate (IQ of 35–40 to 50–55)
- Only fair motor development; clumsy
- Poor social awareness
- Can be taught to communicate
- Can profit from training in social and vocational skills; needs supervision but can perform semiskilled labor as an adult

14. The Behavior Evaluation Scale (BES) put out by Hawthorne Publishers includes behavioral items that can be classified as characteristics of emotional/behavioral disorders. The item "Teases other classmates" would most likely fit under which of the following categories?
(Average Rigor) (Skill 1.01)

   a. Inappropriate behavior under normal circumstances
   b. Learning affected by behavior
   c. Unable to build or maintain appropriate relationships
   d. Recurring fears or anxieties

Correct answer is "c."
Teasing breaks down relationships.

15. All of the following *except* one are characteristics of a student who is emotionally disturbed:
(Average Rigor) (Skill 1.01)

   a. Socially accepted by peers
   b. Highly disruptive to the classroom environment
   c. Academic difficulties
   d. Areas of talent overlooked by a teacher

Correct answer is "a."
While a child may be socially accepted by peers, children who are emotionally disturbed tend to alienate those around them and are often ostracized.

16. Which exceptionality category is least likely to be served at a special school in the public school system?
(Easy) (Skill 1.02)

   a. Severely intellectually disabled
   b. Multiple disabled
   c. Learning disabled
   d. Severely emotionally/behaviorally disordered

Correct answer is "c."
Special schools have been established to serve students with disabilities. They may take the form of day schools or residential centers. They serve the emotionally/behaviorally disordered, severely or profoundly intellectually disabled, physically disabled, deaf, blind, and multiple disabled.

17. Individuals with mental retardation can be characterized as:
(Average Rigor) (Skill 1.02)

    a. Often indistinguishable from normal developing children at an early age
    b. Having a higher than normal rate of motor activity
    c. Displaying significant discrepancies in ability levels
    d. Uneducable in academic skills

Correct answer is "a."
Mental retardation is represented by delayed cognitive functioning and social skills. Students who are mentally impaired may function as children of a much younger age.

18. Which is an educational characteristic common to students with mild intellectual learning and behavioral disabilities?
(Easy) (Skill 2.01)

    a. Show interest in schoolwork
    b. Have intact listening skills
    c. Require modification in classroom instruction
    d. Respond better to passive than to active learning tasks

Correct answer is "c."
Some of the characteristics of students with mild learning and behavioral disabilities are as follows:
- Lack of interest in schoolwork
- Prefer concrete rather than abstract lessons
- Weak listening skills
- Low achievement
- Limited verbal and/or writing skills
- Respond better to active rather than passive learning tasks
- Have areas of talent or ability often overlooked by teachers
- Prefer to receive special help in regular classroom
- Higher dropout rate than regular education students
- Require modification in classroom instruction
- Are easily distracted

19. Michael's teacher complains that he is constantly out of his seat. She also reports that he has trouble paying attention to what is going on in class for more than a couple of minutes at a time. He appears to be trying, but his writing is often illegible, containing many reversals. Although he seems to want to please, he is very impulsive and stays in trouble with his teacher. He is failing reading, and his math grades, though somewhat better, are still below average. Michael's psychometric evaluation should include assessment for: **(Rigorous) (Skill 2.01)**

a. Mild mental retardation
b. Specific learning disabilities
c. Mild behavior disorders
d. Hearing impairment

Correct answer is "b."
Here are some of the characteristics of persons with learning disabilities:
- Hyperactivity: a rate of motor activity higher than normal
- Perceptual difficulties: visual, auditory, and haptic perceptual problems
- Perceptual-motor impairments: poor integration of visual and motor systems, often affecting fine motor coordination
- Disorders of memory and thinking: memory deficits; trouble with problem-solving, concept formation, and association; poor awareness of own metacognitive skills (learning strategies)
- Impulsiveness: acts before considering consequences; poor impulse control, often followed by remorselessness
- Academic problems in reading, math, writing, or spelling; significant discrepancies in ability levels

20. In general, characteristics of the learning disabled include: **(Average Rigor) (Skill 2.01)**

a. A low level of performance in a majority of academic skill areas
b. Limited cognitive ability
c. A discrepancy between achievement and potential
d. A uniform pattern of academic development

Correct answer is "c."
The individual with a specific learning disability exhibits a discrepancy between achievement and potential.

21. **Autism is a condition characterized by:**
    (Average Rigor) (Skill 2.01)

    a. Distorted relationships with others
    b. Perceptual anomalies
    c. Self-stimulation
    d. All of the above

Correct answer is "d."

Smith and Luckasson (1992) describe autism as a severe language disorder that affects thinking, communication, and behavior. They list the following characteristics:

- Absent or distorted relationships with people: inability to relate with people except as objects, inability to express affection, or ability to build and maintain only distant, suspicious, or bizarre relationships
- Extreme or peculiar problems in communication: absence of verbal language or language that is not functional, such as echolalia (parroting what one hears), misuse of pronouns (e.g., "he" for "you" or "I" for "her"), neologisms (made-up meaningless words or sentences), or talk that bears little or no resemblance to reality
- Self-stimulation: repetitive stereotyped behavior that seems to have no purpose other than providing sensory stimulation (this may take a wide variety of forms, such as swishing saliva, twirling objects, patting one's cheeks, flapping one's arms, staring, and so on)
- Self-injury: repeated physical self-abuse, such as biting, scratching, or poking oneself, head banging, etc
- Perceptual anomalies: unusual responses or absence of response to stimuli that seem to indicate sensory impairment or unusual sensitivity

22. **In which of the following exceptionality categories may a student be considered for inclusion if his IQ score falls more than two standard deviations below the mean?**
    (Average Rigor) (Skill 2.01)

    a. Mental retardation
    b. Specific learning disabilities
    c. Emotionally/behaviorally disordered
    d. Gifted

Correct answer is "a."

Only about 1 to 1.5 percent of the population fit the AAMD's definition of mental retardation. They fall outside the two standard deviations limit for special learning disabilities and emotionally/behaviorally disordered.

23. **As a separate exceptionality category in IDEA (Individuals with Disabilities Education Act), autism:**
    (Rigorous) (Skill 3.01)

    a. Includes emotional/behavioral disorders as defined in federal regulations
    b. Adversely affects educational performance
    c. Is thought to be a form of mental illness
    d. Is a developmental disability that affects verbal and nonverbal communication

Correct answer is "d."
Individuals with autism are affected by their symptoms every day—something that sets them apart from unaffected students. Because of problems with receptive language, they can have problems understanding some classroom directions and instruction, along with subtle vocal and facial cues of teachers. This inability to fully decipher the world around them often makes education stressful. Teachers need to be aware of a student's disorder and ideally should have specific training in autism education to be better able to help students get the best out of their classroom experiences.

24. **Which of the following is true about autism?**
    (Rigorous) (Skill 3.02)

    a. It is caused by having cold, aloof, or hostile parents.
    b. Approximately four out of ten people have autism.
    c. It is a separate exceptionality category in IDEA.
    d. It is a form of mental illness.

Correct answer is "c."
In IDEA, the 1990 Amendment to the Education for All Handicapped Children Act, autism was classified as a separate exceptionality category. It is thought to be caused by a neurological or biochemical dysfunction. It generally becomes evident before age three. The condition occurs in about 4 of every 10,000 persons.

25. **Which electronic device can provide assistance by dialing a telephone, turning book pages, and drinking from a cup?**
    (Average Rigor) (Skill 3.02)

    a. Communication boards
    b. Manipulator robots
    c. Electronic switches
    d. Crutches

Correct answer is "b."
As the name implies, a manipulator robot is a moving electronic device that can be manipulated or controlled.

26. **Which of the following manifestations are characteristic of students placed in the exceptionality category of "other health impaired?"**
    (Average Rigor) (Skill 3.02)

    a. Limited strength, vitality, or alertness
    b. Severe communication and developmental problems
    c. Chronic or acute health problems
    d. All of the above

Correct answer is "d."
Other health impaired means having an autistic condition that is manifested by severe communication and other developmental and educational problems; and/or having limited strength, vitality, or alertness due to chronic or acute health problems (such as a heart condition, tuberculosis, rheumatic fever, nephritis, asthma, sickle cell anemia, hemophilia, epilepsy, lead poisoning, leukemia, or diabetes), which adversely affect a child's educational performance.

27. **Television, movies, radio, and newspapers contribute to the public's poor understanding of disabilities by:**
    (Rigorous) (Skill 3.04)

    a. Only portraying those who look normal
    b. Portraying the person with the disability as one with incredible abilities
    c. Showing emotionally disturbed children
    d. Portraying all people in wheel chairs as independent

Correct answer is "b."
Many movies, television shows, and so on only show a person with a disability who has "overcome" his or her disability with a talent. The hype over J-Mac, a student with autism at Greece Athena making several baskets is an example. The media only showed his incredible talent and ignored any struggles he may have had.

28. **What is *not* an example of the use of a punishment procedure?**
   (Rigorous) (Skill 3.07)

   a. Ted quit talking with Jim when Mrs. Green frowned at him.
   b. Timmy stopped getting out of his seat when the teacher scolded him.
   c. Mary completed her math when her teacher told her she would have to miss recess if she wasn't through with the work.
   d. Fred stopped making funny faces when Mrs. Smith placed him in time out.

Correct answer is "c."
A punisher is a consequential stimulus, which has the following characteristics:
   • It decreases the future rate or probability of the occurrence of the behavior.
   • It is administered contingent on the production of an undesired behavior.
   • It is administered immediately following the production of the undesired behavior.
In "c," Mary received a prompt, not a consequential stimulus.

29. **One of the most important goals of the special education teacher is to foster and create with the student:**
   (Easy) (Skill 3.07)

   a. Handwriting skills
   b. Self-advocacy
   c. An increased level of reading
   d. Logical reasoning

Correct answer is "b."
When a student achieves the ability to recognize his or her deficits and knows how to correctly advocate for his or her needs, the child has learned one of the most important life skills.

30. **The most important member of the transition team is the**
    (Easy) (Skill 3.07)

    a. Parent
    b. Student
    c. Secondary personnel
    d. Postsecondary personnel

Correct answer is "b."

Transition planning is a student-centered event that necessitates a collaborative endeavor. Responsibilities are shared by the student, parents, secondary personnel, and postsecondary personnel, who are all members of the transition team; however, it is important that the student play a key role in transition planning. This will entail asking the student to identify preferences and interests and to attend meetings on transition planning. The degree of success experienced by the student in postsecondary educational settings depends on the student's degree of motivation, independence, self-direction, self-advocacy, and academic abilities developed in high school. Student participation in transition activities should be implemented as early as possible and no later than age 16.

31. **The extent to which a test measures what its authors or users claim that it measures is called its:**
    (Average Rigor) (Skill 4.01)

    a. Validity
    b. Reliability
    c. Normality
    d. Acculturation

Correct answer is "a."

Validity is the degree or extent to which a test measures what it was designed or intended to measure. Reliability is the extent to which a test is consistent in its measurements.

32. Which of the following is a factor in determining test validity?
(Rigorous) (Skill 4.01)

 a. The appropriateness of the sample items chosen to measure a criterion
 b. The acculturation of the norm group as compared to that of the population being tested
 c. The reliability of the test
 d. All of the above

Correct answer is "d."
Validity can be affected by:
 - The appropriateness of the sample items chosen to measure a criterion
 - The cultural, environmental, and lingual background of the norm group as compared to that of the population being tested
 - The accuracy with which a person's performance on a criterion can be predicted from his or her test score on that criterion
 - The consistency in administration and scoring of the test
 - The reliability of the test

33. If a scholastic aptitude test is checked against predictive success in academic endeavors, which type of validity is one attempting to establish?
(Rigorous) (Skill 4.01)

 a. Content
 b. Criterion-related
 c. Construct
 d. Confirmation

Correct answer is "b."
There are different kinds of evidence to support a particular judgment. If the purpose of a test is to measure the skills covered in a particular course or unit, then one would hope to see test questions on all the important topics and not on extraneous topics. If this condition is met, then there is content validity. Some tests, like the SAT, are designed to predict outcomes. If SAT scores correlate with academic performance in college, as measured by GPA in the first year, then there is criterion-related validity. Construct validity is probably the most important. It is gathered over many years and is indicated by a pattern of scores (e.g., older children can answer more questions on intelligence tests than younger children). This fits with the construct of intelligence.

34. **Which of the following statements reflects true factors that affect the reliability of a test?**
(Rigorous) (Skill 4.01)

   a. Short tests tend to be more reliable than long tests.
   b. The shorter the time length between two administrations of a test, the greater the possibility that the scores will change.
   c. Even if guessing results in a correct response, it introduces error into a test score and into interpretation of the results.
   d. All of the above

Correct answer is "c."
The reliability of a test is concerned with the extent to which the person tested will receive the same score on repeated administrations of that test. When a person's score fluctuates randomly, the test lacks reliability.

35. **Mrs. Freud administered a personality traits survey to her high school psychology class. She re-administered the same survey two weeks later. The method she used to determine reliability was that of:**
(Rigorous) (Skill 4.01)

   a. Test-retest
   b. Split half
   c. Alternate form
   d. Kuder-Richardson formula

Correct answer is "a."
The test-retest reliability is accomplished by doing the same test on a second occasion.

36. **Bill talks out in class an average of 15 times an hour. Other youngsters sometimes talk out, but Bill does so at a higher:**
(Average Rigor) (Skill 4.01)

   a. Rate
   b. Intensity
   c. Volume
   d. Degree

Correct answer is "a."
Rate or frequency is the number of times the behavior is displayed in a given period.

37. **Target behaviors must be:**
    (Average Rigor) (Skill 4.01)

    a. Observable
    b. Measurable
    c. Definable
    d. All of the above

Correct answer is "d."
Behaviors must be observable, measurable, and definable in order to be assessed and changed.

38. **If the teacher observes Mary to be out of her seat five times for a total of 30 minutes during her resource room period, she has measured the behavior dimension called**
    (Rigorous) (Skill 4.01)

    a. Frequency
    b. Rate
    c. Intensity
    d. Duration

Correct answer is "c."
Frequency refers to how often a behavior occurs in a period of time. Rate is expressed as a ratio of frequency with time. Measurements of frequency and duration convey the intensity of the behavior.

39. **For which of the following purposes is a norm-referenced test least appropriate?**
    (Rigorous) (Skill 4.02)

    a. Screening
    b. Individual program planning
    c. Program evaluation
    d. Making placement decisions

Correct answer is "b."
Norm-referenced tests use normative data (including performance norms by age, gender, or ethnic group) for scoring. Results of norm-referenced achievements tests (e.g., Peabody Individualized Achievement Test (PIAT), Wide Range Achievement Test (WRAT)), though important in making comparisons, may not provide information needed for individual program planning, types of behaviors tests, sub-skill data, or types of scores reported.

40. **Which of the following purposes of testing calls for an informal test?**
    (Rigorous) (Skill 4.02)

    a. Screening a group of children to determine their readiness for the first reader
    b. Measuring the content of a social studies unit prepared by the classroom teacher covering one aspect of the general curriculum
    c. Evaluating the effectiveness of a fourth-grade math program at the end of its first year of use in a specific school
    d. Determining the general level of intellectual functioning of a class of fifth graders

Correct answer is "b."
Formal tests are commercially prepared standardized tests. Formal tests may be categorized as norm-referenced or as criterion-referenced. Informal tests are usually teacher-prepared and are usually criterion-referenced. Answer "b" is the only teacher-made test.

41. **Which of the following is *not* a true statement about informal tests?**
    (Rigorous) (Skill 4.02)

    a. Informal tests are useful in comparing students to others of their age or grade level.
    b. The correlation between curriculum and test criteria is much higher in informal tests.
    c. Informal tests are useful in evaluating an individual's response to instruction.
    d. Informal tests are used to diagnose a student's particular strengths and weaknesses for purposes of planning individual programs.

Correct answer is "a."
Informal or teacher-made tests are usually criterion-referenced. Norm-referenced tests are usually group tests given to large populations rather than individualized, or teacher-made tests.

42. **For which situation might a teacher be apt to select a formal test?**
    (Rigorous) (Skill 4.02)

    a. A pretest for studying world religions
    b. A weekly spelling test
    c. To compare student progress with that of peers of same age or grade level on a national basis
    d. To determine which content objectives outlined on the students' IEPs (Individualized Education Plans) were mastered

Correct answer is "c."
Formal assessments include standardized criterion, norm-referenced instruments, and commercially-prepared inventories, which are developmentally appropriate for students across the spectrum of disabilities. Criterion-referenced tests compare a student's performance to a previously established criterion rather than to other students from a normative sample. Norm-referenced tests use normative data (including performance norms by age, gender, or ethnic group) for scoring.

43. **A test that measures students' skill development in academic content areas is classified as an _____ test.**
    (Easy) (Skill 4.02)

    a. Achievement
    b. Aptitude
    c. Adaptive
    d. Intelligence

Correct answer is "a."
Achievement tests directly assess students' skill development in academic content areas. It measures the degree to which a student has benefited education and/or life experiences compared to others of the same age or grade level. They may be used as diagnostic tests to find strengths and weaknesses of students. They may also be used for screening, placement progress evaluation, and curricular effectiveness.

44. **The Key Math Diagnostic Arithmetic Test is an individually administered test of math skills. It is comprised of 14 subtests that are classified into the major math areas of content, operations, and applications for which subtest scores are reported. The test manual describes the population sample on which the test was normed and reports data pertaining to reliability and validity. In addition, for each item in the test, a behavioral objective is presented. From the description, it can be determined that this achievement test is:**
(Easy) (Skill 4.02)

   a. Individually administered
   b. Criterion-referenced
   c. Diagnostic
   d. All of the above

Correct answer is "d."
The test has a limited content designed to measure to what extent the student has mastered specific areas in math. The expressions "individually administered" and "diagnostic" appear in the description of the test.

45. **The Peabody Individual Achievement Test (PIAT) is an individually administered test. It measures mathematics, reading recognition, reading comprehension, spelling, and general information, and reports results as comparison scores. Technical data is offered in reference to standardization, validity, reliability, and so on. This achievement test has features of a:**
(Rigorous) (Skill 4.02)

   a. Norm-referenced test
   b. Diagnostic test
   c. Screening tool
   d. Both a and c

Correct answer is "d."
Norm-referenced tests compare students with others of the same age or grade. It can be used for screening or placement of students.

46. **Which of these factors relate to eligibility for learning disabilities?** **(Rigorous) (Skill 5.01)**

   a. A discrepancy between potential and performance
   b. Sub-average intellectual functioning
   c. Social deficiencies or learning deficits that are not due to intellectual, sensory, or physical conditions
   d. Documented results of behavior checklists and anecdotal records of aberrant behavior

Correct answer is "a."
Tests need to show a discrepancy between potential and performance. Classroom observations (such as impaired reading ability) and samples of student work also provide indicators of possible learning disabilities. Eligibility for services in behavior disorders requires documented evidence of social deficiencies or learning deficits that are not due to intellectual, sensory, or physical conditions. Any student undergoing multidisciplinary evaluation is usually given an intelligence test, diagnostic achievement tests, and social and/or adaptive inventories. Answers "b," "c," and "d" are symptoms displayed before testing for eligibility. Some students who display these symptoms do fail the tests and are not categorized as eligible to receive services.

47. **When a student is identified as being at-risk academically or socially, what does federal law hope to see happen first?** **(Average Rigor) (Skill 5.01)**

   a. Moving the child quickly to assessment
   b. Placing the child in special education as soon as possible
   c. Observing the child to determine what is wrong
   d. Performing remedial intervention in the classroom

Correct answer is "d."
Once a student is identified as being at-risk academically or socially, remedial interventions are attempted within the regular classroom. Federal legislation requires that sincere efforts be made to help the child learn in the regular classroom.

48. **Safeguards against bias and discrimination in the assessment of children include:**
(Average Rigor) (Skill 5.01)

   a. The testing of a child in standard English
   b. The requirement for the use of one standardized test
   c. The use of evaluative materials in the child's native language or other mode of communication
   d. All testing performed by a certified, licensed psychologist

Correct answer is "c."
The law requires that the child be evaluated in his or her native language or mode of communication. Having a licensed psychologist evaluate the child does not meet the criteria if it is not done in the child's normal mode of communication.

49. **Which of the following types of tests are used to estimate learning potential and to predict academic achievement?**
(Easy) (Skill 5.01)

   a. Intelligence tests
   b. Achievement tests
   c. Adaptive behavior tests
   d. Personality tests

Correct answer is "a."
An intelligence test is designed to measure intellectual abilities like memory, comprehension, and abstract reasoning. IQ is often used to estimate the learning capacity of a student, as well as to predict his or her academic achievement.

50. **Acculturation refers to the individual's:**
(Rigorous) (Skill 5.02)

   a. Gender
   b. Experiential background
   c. Social class
   d. Ethnic background

Correct answer is "b."
Acculturation is the difference in an individual's experiential background. A person's culture has little to do with gender, social class, or ethnicity. A person is the product of his or her experiences.

51. **To which aspect does fair assessment relate?**
    (Average Rigor) (Skill 5.02)

    a. Representation
    b. Acculturation
    c. Language
    d. All of the above

Correct answer is "d."
All three aspects are necessary and vital for assessment to be fair.

52. **Children who write poorly might be given tests that allow oral responses unless the purpose for the test is to:**
    (Easy) (Skill 5.03)

    a. Assess handwriting skills
    b. Test for organization of thoughts
    c. Answer questions pertaining to math reasoning
    d. Assess rote memory

Correct answer is "a."
It is necessary to have the child write if a teacher is assessing his or her skill in that domain.

53. **Which is characteristic of group tests?**
    (Rigorous) (Skill 5.03)

    a. Directions are always read to students.
    b. The examiner monitors several students at the same time.
    c. The teacher is allowed to probe students who almost have the correct answer.
    d. Both quantitative and qualitative information may be gathered.

Correct answer is "b."
In group tests the examiner may provide directions for children up to and
including fou~~~~~~~~~~~~~~~~~~~~~~~~~~~~~~~~~~~~~~. The examiner
monitors the ~~~~~~~~~~~~~~~~~~~~~~~~~~~~~~~~~ she cannot
rephrase qu~~~~~~~~~~~~~~~~~~~~~~~~~~~~~~~lt—almost
impossible—~~~~~~~~~~~~~~~~~~~~~~~~ tests are
appropriate ~~~~~~~~~~~~~~~~~~~~~~~~ program
planning, su~~~~~~~~~~~~~~~~~~~~~~~given if there
are any moti~~~~~~~~~~~~~~~~~~~~~~factors that
might impair~~~~~~~~~~~~~~~~~~~~~ial programs,
individual te~~~~~~~~~~~~~~~~~~~~

[handwritten notes]
GROUP TEST
program ev., Screening, + program planning (tracking)

INDIVIDUAL PROG
use Individual test

SPECIAL E

54. For which of the following uses are individual tests most appropriate?
(Rigorous) (Skill 5.03)

a. Screening students to determine a possible need for special education services
b. Evaluating special education curricula
c. Tracking gifted students
d. Evaluating a student for eligibility and placement, or individualized program planning, in special education

Correct answer is "d."
The choice between group and individual testing should be primarily determined by purpose and efficiency. When testing for program evaluation, screening and some types of program planning (such as tracking) group tests are appropriate. Individual tests could be used but are impractical in terms of time and expense. Special consideration may need to be given if there are any motivational, personality, linguistic, or physically disabling factors that might impair the examinee's performance on group tests. When planning individual programs, individual tests should be used. When a student is being evaluated for placement in a special education program, all areas related to the suspected disability must be assessed. Individual tests should be administered when there is a reason to question the validity of results of group tests, or when an in-depth evaluation of the test taker's performance is needed.

55. Which of the following is an advantage of giving individual, rather than group tests?
(Average Rigor) (Skill 5.03)

a. The test administrator can control the tempo of an individual test, giving breaks when needed.
b. The test administrator can clarify or rephrase questions.
c. Individual tests provide for the gathering of both qualitative and quantitative results.
d. All of the above

ridual test, the tester has the opportunity to
onses and to determine how things like
ished. Within limits, the tester is able to control
sting session and to rephrase and probe
individual's best performance. In short,
liner to encourage best efforts and to observe
skills to answer questions. Thus, individual
of both quantitative and qualitative

56. **Mrs. Stokes has been teaching her third-grade students about mammals during a recent science unit. Which of the following would be true of a criterion-referenced test she might administer at the conclusion of the unit?**
    (Average Rigor) (Skill 5.05)

    a. It will be based on unit objectives.
    b. Derived scores will be used to rank student achievement.
    c. Standardized scores are effective of national performance samples.
    d. All of the above

Correct answer is "a."
Criterion-referenced tests measure the progress made by individuals in mastering specific skills. The content is based on a specific set of objectives rather than on the general curriculum. Criterion-referenced tests provide measurements pertaining to the information a given student needs to know as well as the skills that student needs to master. Norm-referenced tests have a large advantage over criterion-referenced tests when used for screening or program evaluation. Norm-referenced tests provide a means of comparing a student's performance to the performance typically expected of others of his or her age.

57. **Criterion-referenced tests can provide information about:**
    (Rigorous) (Skill 5.05)

    a. Whether a student has mastered prerequisite skills
    b. Whether a student is ready to proceed to the next level of instruction
    c. Which instructional materials might be helpful in covering program objectives
    d. All of the above

Correct answer is "a."
In criterion-referenced testing, the emphasis is on assessing specific and relevant behaviors that have been mastered. Items on criterion-referenced tests are often linked directly to specific instructional objectives.

58. **The best measures of a student's functional capabilities and entry-level skills are:**
   (Rigorous) (Skill 5.05)

   a. Norm-referenced tests
   b. Teacher-made post-tests
   c. Standardized IQ tests
   d. Criterion-referenced measures

Correct answer is "d."
Criterion-referenced measures are useful for assessment of a student's functional capabilities and entry-level skills. Unlike norm-referenced tests, which compare an individual with others of the same grade or age level, criterion-referenced tests measure the level of functions and skills of the individual.

59. **Jane is a third grader. Mrs. Smith, her teacher, noted that Jane was having difficulty with math and reading assignments. The results from recent diagnostic tests showed a strong sight vocabulary, strength in computational skills, but a weakness in comprehending what she read. This weakness was apparent in mathematical word problems as well. The multidisciplinary team recommended placement in a special education resource room for learning disabilities two periods each school day. For the remainder of the school day, her placement will be:**
   (Easy) (Skill 6.01)

   a. In the regular classroom
   b. At a special school
   c. In a self-contained classroom
   d. In a resource room for mental retardation

Correct answer is "a."
The resource room is a special room inside the school environment where the child goes to be taught by a teacher who is certified in the area of disability. It is hoped the accommodations and services provided in the resource room will help Jane to catch up and perform with her peers in the regular classroom.

60. **Bob shows behavior problems, such as lack of attention, out of seat behavior, and talking out. His teacher kept data on these behaviors and found that Bob is showing much better self-control since he has been self-managing himself through a behavior modification program. The most appropriate placement recommendation for Bob at this time is probably:**
(Average Rigor) (Skill 6.01)

   a. Any available part-time special education program
   b. Solely the regular classroom
   c. A behavior disorders resource room for one period a day
   d. A specific learning disabilities resource room for one period a day

Correct answer is "b."
Bob is able to self-manage himself and is very likely to behave like the other children in the regular classroom. The classroom is the least restrictive environment.

61. **The greatest number of students receiving special services are enrolled primarily in:**
(Easy) (Skill 6.01)

   a. The regular classroom
   b. The resource room
   c. Self-contained classrooms
   d. Special schools

Correct answer is "a."
The majority of students receiving special services are enrolled primarily in regular classes. Those with mild learning and behavior problems exhibit academic and/or social interpersonal deficits that are often evident only in a school-related setting. These students appear no different to their peers, physically.

62. **The most restrictive environment in which an individual might be placed and receive instruction is that of:**
(Easy) (Skill 6.01)

   a. Institutional setting
   b. Homebound instruction
   c. Special schools
   d. Self-contained special classes

Correct answer is "a."
Individuals who require significantly modified environments for care treatment and accommodation are usually educated in an institutional setting. They usually have profound and/or multiple disorders.

63. **Placement at a special school is considered to be a less restrictive educational setting than what?**
(Easy) (Skill 6.01)

   a. Regular classroom
   b. Inclusive setting
   c. Self-contained special education setting
   d. Homebound

Correct answer is "d."
A special needs child who is homebound is considered too disabled to benefit from any of the other three educational settings.

64. **There are students who are unmotivated in the learning environment because of learning problems they have experienced in the past. Some effective ways of helping a student become academically motivated include:**
(Average Rigor) (Skill 6.03)

   a. Setting goals for the student and expecting him or her to achieve them
   b. Avoiding giving immediate feedback, as it may be demoralizing
   c. Making sure the academic content relates to personal interests
   d. Planning subject matter based on grade-level placement

Correct answer is "c."
A student who is unmotivated in a conventional setting may become interested in learning through an individualized program. In such a setting, he or she can make choices, learn in accordance with the preferred learning style, participate in pairs or groups, or work by him or herself at a more personal pace.

65. **The effective teacher varies his or her instructional presentations and response requirements depending on:**
    (Easy) (Skill 6.03)

    a. Student needs
    b. The task at hand
    c. The learning situation
    d. All of the above

Correct answer is "d."
Teachers may vary the method of presentation in the areas of content, general structure, and type of presentation. They may vary the response requirements in the areas of type, general structure, and level of response. Effective teachers vary instructional presentations and response requirements based on student needs, the task at hand, and the learning situation.

66. **The work-study movement:**
    (Rigorous) (Skill 7.04)

    a. Evolved primarily during the 1970s
    b. Focused on the delivery of services within a specific type of interagency agreement
    c. Was declared a top priority by the U.S. Office of Education by Sidney Maryland, the Commissioner of Education
    d. Was implemented in both regular and special education settings

Correct answer is "b."
This program was conducted cooperatively between the schools and the local state rehabilitation services when it emerged in the 1960s. The general goal was to create an integrated, academic social and vocational curriculum that included appropriate work experience. Programs were to be designed in such a way that students with mild disabilities would become prepared for eventual community adjustment. Cooperative agreements between the schools and the rehabilitation agencies were made in order to administer these programs.

67. The career education movement:
(Rigorous) (Skill 7.04)

a. Had its inception during the 1960s
b. Maintained a cooperative agreement between schools and rehabilitation agencies
c. Was funded by federal monies generated by rehabilitation agencies
d. Was targeted for the general populace of students but included special education students as well

Correct answer is "d."
This movement had its inception in 1970 and focused on integration and readiness for a life career throughout a student's education, from kindergarten through the 12th grade. It targeted the general populace of students and did not mention students with disabilities. However, when the Career Education Implementation Incentive Act (Public Law 95-207) was passed in 1977, it specifically mentioned people with disabilities as an appropriate target population for services.

68. Vocational training programs are based on all of the following ideas except:
(Easy) (Skill 7.04)

a. Students obtain career training from elementary through high school.
b. Students acquire specific training in job skills prior to exiting school.
c. Students need specific training and supervision in applying skills learned in school to requirements in job situations.
d. Students obtain needed instruction and field-based experiences that help them to work in specific occupations.

Correct answer is "a."
Vocational education programs or transition programs prepare students for entry into the labor force. They are usually incorporated into the work-study at the high school or postsecondary levels. They are usually focused on job skills, job opportunities, skill requirements for specific jobs, personal qualifications in relation to job requirements, work habits, money management, and academic skills needed for specific jobs.

69. **Career-education-specific training and preparation for the world of work occurs during the phase of:**
(Average Rigor) (Skill 7.04)

   a. Career awareness
   b. Career exploration
   c. Career preparation
   d. Daily living and personal-social interaction

Correct answer is "c."
Curricular aspects of career education include:
   - Career awareness: diversity of available jobs
   - Career exploration: skills needed for occupational groups
   - Career preparation: specific training and preparation required for the world of work

70. **Which is most descriptive of vocational training in special education?** *(Easy) (Skill 7.04)*

   a. Trains students in intellectual disabilities solely
   b. Segregates students with and without disabilities in vocational training programs
   c. Only includes students capable of moderate supervision
   d. Instruction focuses on self-help skills, social-interpersonal skills, motor skills, rudimentary academic skills, simple occupational skills, and lifetime leisure and occupational skills

Correct answer is "d."
Persons with disabilities are mainstreamed with nondisabled students where possible. Special sites provide training for those persons with more severe disabilities who are unable to be successfully taught in an integrated setting. Specially trained vocational counselors monitor and supervise student work sites.

71. **Presentation of tasks can be altered to match the student's rate of learning by:**
    (Average Rigor) (Skill 7.07)

    a. Describing how much of a topic is presented in one day and how much practice is assigned, according to the student's abilities and learning style
    b. Using task analysis, assigning a certain number of skills to be mastered in a specific amount of time
    c. Introducing a new task only when the student has demonstrated mastery of the previous task in the learning hierarchy
    d. Both a and c

Correct answer is "d."
Pacing is the term used for altering tasks to match the student's rate of learning. This can be done in two ways: altering the subject content or altering the rate at which tasks are presented.

72. **All of the following are suggestions for altering the presentation of tasks to match the student's rate of learning except:**
    (Average Rigor) (Skill 7.07)

    a. Teach in several shorter segments of time rather than a single, lengthy session
    b. Continue to teach a task until the lesson is completed in order to provide more time on task
    c. Watch for nonverbal cues that indicate students are becoming confused, bored, or restless
    d. Avoid giving students an inappropriate amount of written work

Correct answer is "b."
This action does not alter the subject content; neither does it alter the rate at which tasks are presented.

73. **According to which of the following statements can an effective teacher incorporate pacing as a means of matching a student's rate of learning?**
    (Easy) (Skill 7.07)

    a. Selected content is presented based on prerequisite skills.
    b. Task presentations are paced during optimum time segments.
    c. Special needs students always require smaller steps and learning segments regardless of the activity or content.
    d. Both a and b

Correct answer is "d."
Choice "c" is not a true statement; "a" and "b" are true statements.

74. **In order for a student to function independently in the learning environment, which of the following must be true?**
(Easy) (Skill 7.07)

    a. The learner must understand the nature of the content.
    b. The student must be able to do the assigned task.
    c. The teacher must communicate performance criteria to the learner.
    d. All of the above

Correct answer is "d."
Together with the above, the child must be able to ask for and obtain assistance when necessary.

75. **Alan has failed repeatedly in his academic work. He needs continuous feedback in order to experience small, incremental achievements. What type of instructional material would best meet this need?**
(Average Rigor) (Skill 8.04)

    a. Programmed materials
    b. Audiotapes
    c. Materials with no writing required
    d. Worksheets

Correct answer is "a."
Programmed materials are best suited, as Alan would be able to chart his progress as he achieves each goal. He can monitor himself and take responsibility for his successes.

76. **John learns best through the auditory channel, so his teacher wants to reinforce his listening skills. Through which of the following types of equipment would instruction be most effectively presented?**
(Easy) (Skill 8.04)

    a. Overhead projector
    b. Cassette player
    c. Microcomputer
    d. Opaque projector

Correct answer is "b."
An audio cassette player would help sharpen and further develop his listening skills.

77. **For which stage of learning would computer software that allows for continued drill and practice of a skill to achieve accuracy and speed be utilized?**
    (Average Rigor) (Skill 8.04)

    a. Acquisition
    b. Proficiency
    c. Maintenance
    d. Generalization

Correct answer is "b."
   • Acquisition: introduction of a new skill
   • Maintenance: continued practice without further instruction
   • Proficiency: practice under supervision to achieve accuracy and speed
   • Generalization: application of the new skills in new settings and situations

78. **In which way is a computer like an effective teacher?**
    (Average Rigor) (Skill 8.04)

    a. Provides immediate feedback
    b. Sets the pace at the rate of the average student
    c. Produces records only of errors made
    d. Programs to skill levels at which students at respective chronological ages should be working

Correct answer is "a."

79. **During which written composition stage are students encouraged to read their stories aloud to others?**
    (Average Rigor) (Skill 8.04)

    a. Planning
    b. Drafting
    c. Revising/editing
    d. Sharing/publication

Correct answer is "c."
It is encouraged at this stage, as both the child and the audience will distinguish errors and make corrections. The child also learns to accept constructive criticism.

80. **Immediate feedback is appropriately used when a student is:**
   (Average Rigor) (Skill 8.04)

   a. Demonstrating lack of self-control
   b. Self-motivated and wants to work out his or her own solutions
   c. Making errors practicing a newly introduced skill
   d. Attempting to correct his or her mistakes

Correct answer is "c."
Immediate feedback should not be used when a student is out of control. Immediate feedback increases motivation and reinforces correct learning. Delayed feedback can lead to frustration and can cause an easily frustrated or poorly motivated student to stop performing. However, for students who are self-motivated, delayed feedback can actually encourage learning by giving them an opportunity to correct their own mistakes and discover their own answers. Delayed feedback also provides a good review of previously learned skills.

81. **Some environmental elements that influence learning styles include all except:**
   (Average Rigor) (Skill 9.01)

   a. Light
   b. Temperature
   c. Design
   d. Motivation

Correct answer is "d."
Individual learning styles are influenced by environmental, emotional, sociological, and physical elements. Environmental elements include sound, light, temperature, and design. Emotional elements include motivation, persistence, responsibility, and structure.

82. **Which of the following is descriptive of a good safety precaution when operating equipment?**
   (Easy) (Skill 9.01)

   a. Reporting malfunctioning of a machine to the school's media specialist
   b. Leaving the room while a filmstrip is being shown in class
   c. Operating a machine with frayed cords
   d. Allowing an overhead projector to remain set up and plugged into a wall receptacle so the next class can view the transparencies

Correct answer is "a."
All three others are hazardous practices and should not be allowed to happen.

83. **Appropriate safety features that should be used in learning environments with special needs students include:** *(Average Rigor) (Skill 9.04)*

    a. Physical barriers
    b. Effective procedures to be used in emergencies
    c. Equal treatment for all students to avoid stigma
    d. Multisensory instructional approach

Correct answer is "b."
None of the other three choices is a safety feature.

84. **Which would be least effective as a verbal intervention?** *(Rigorous) (Skill 9.04)*

    a. Praise and encouragement
    b. Reprimands
    c. Sane messages
    d. Hypodermic affection

Correct answer is "b."
Praise and encouragement reinforce positive classroom behavior. Sane messages are descriptive and model classroom behaviors that help students understand how their behaviors affect others. Hypodermic affection is words or other modes of encouragement letting students know they are valued. All three are positive interventions. Reprimands are least effective because they are negative and often hurt students' feelings. They attack the students, rather than their behaviors.

85. **Attention-seeking behaviors can be reduced most effectively by using which of the following nonverbal interventions?** *(Rigorous) (Skill 9.04)*

    a. Planned ignoring
    b. Signal interference
    c. Proximity control
    d. Removal of seductive objects

Correct answer is "a."
Many minor classroom disturbances are best handled through planned ignoring. When teachers ignore attention-seeking behaviors, students often do the same.

86. **When a teacher designs a contract with a student, input from that student may be obtained in:**
    (Average Rigor) (Skill 9.04)

    a. Selecting the target behavior
    b. Choosing the reinforcer
    c. Collecting and evaluating data
    d. All of the above

Correct answer is "d."
Students may be involved in the process of designing, implementing, and evaluating a contingency management plan. They can decide on behaviors that are in need of modification and evaluate the effectiveness of the contingency or treatment plan. The ultimate goal is to encourage their use of the procedures they have been taught to manage their own behavior.

87. **In establishing a behavior management plan with the students, it is best to:**
    (Average Rigor) (Skill 10.04)

    a. Have rules written and in place on day one
    b. Hand out a copy of the rules to the students on day one
    c. Have separate rules for each class on day one
    d. Have students involved in creating the rules on day one

Correct answer is "d."
Rules are easier to follow when students not only know the reason they are in place but also when they took part in creating them. It may be good to already have a few rules pre-written and then to discuss if these ones cover all the rules the students have created. If not, teachers may want to modify their sets of pre-written rules.

88. Donna has been labeled "learning disabled" since second grade and has developed a fear of not being able to keep up with her peers. She has just entered middle school with a poor self-concept and often acts out to cover up her fear of failure. What is the most appropriate action her teacher can take when Donna exhibits minor inappropriate behavior?
    (Rigorous) (Skill 10.04)

    a. Ignore the behavior unless it is too dangerous or distracting
    b. Praise her for her correct behavior and responses
    c. Discuss the inappropriate behavior tactfully and in private
    d. All of the above

Correct answer is "d."

All three of the actions listed will help correct the minor inappropriate behavior while at the same time helping to improve Donna's self-concept.

89. **Behaviorists contend that all behavior is:**
    (Rigorous) (Skill 10.06)

    a. Predictable
    b. Observed
    c. Conditioned
    d. Learned

Correct answer is "d."
Behavior modification is based on the premise that all behavior, regardless of its appropriateness, has been learned and can therefore be changed.

90. **Procedures employed to decrease targeted behaviors include:**
    (Rigorous) (Skill 10.06)

    a. Punishment
    b. Negative reinforcement
    c. Shaping
    d. Both a and b

Correct answer is "a."
Punishment and extinction may be used to decrease target behaviors.

91. . **Which description best characterizes primary reinforcers of an edible nature?**
(Average Rigor) (Skill 10.06)

    a. Natural
    b. Unconditioned
    c. Innately motivating
    d. All of the above

Correct answer is "d."
Primary reinforcers are those stimuli that are of biological importance to an individual. They are natural, unlearned, unconditioned, and innately motivating. The most common and appropriate reinforcer used in the classroom is food.

92. **Mrs. Chang is trying to prevent satiation from occurring so that her reinforcers will be effective, as she is using a continuous reinforcement schedule. Which of the following ideas would be least effective in preventing satiation?**
(Average Rigor) (Skill 10.06)

    a. Using only one type of edible rather than a variety
    b. Asking for 10 vocabulary words rather than 20
    c. Giving pieces of cereal, bits of fruit, or M&Ms rather than large portions of edibles
    d. Administering a peanut then a sip of water

Correct answer is "a."
Here are some suggestions for preventing satiation:
- Vary reinforcers with instructional tasks
- Shorten the instructional sessions (thereby, the presentation of reinforcers will be decreased)
- Alternate reinforcers (e.g., food, then juice)
- Decrease the size of edibles presented
- Have an array of edibles available

93. **Which tangible reinforcer would Mr. Whiting find to be most effective with teenagers?**
(Easy) (Skill 10.06)

    a. Plastic whistle
    b. Winnie-the-Pooh book
    c. Poster of a current rock star
    d. Toy ring

Correct answer is "c."
This tops the list of things that teenagers crave. It is the most desirable.

94. Which is an example of a secondary reinforcer?
(Average Rigor) (Skill 10.06)

    a. Water
    b. Praise
    c. Hug
    d. Both b and c

Correct answer is "d."
Secondary reinforcers are not necessarily naturally reinforcing to most people. Their value is learned or conditioned through an association, or pairing, with primary reinforcers. Secondary reinforcers include social participation in preferred activities, praise, body language, and attention.

95. Which is not a valid reason for using a secondary reinforcer?
(Rigorous) (Skill 10.06)

    a. The possibility of satiation using a primary reinforcer
    b. The pairing of a primary reinforcer with a secondary reinforcer, as it requires too much time and effort
    c. The inability to assure a state of deprivation when using a primary reinforcer
    d. The possibility of student dependency upon the primary reinforcer

Correct answer is "b."
Some reasons for using secondary reinforcers are:
- The student may become temporarily satiated with the primary reinforcer
- The inability to assure a state of deprivation when using a primary reinforcer
- The possibility of student dependency upon the primary reinforcer

96. A positive reinforcer is generally effective if it is desired by the student and:
(Average Rigor) (Skill 10.06)

    a. Is worthwhile in size
    b. Given immediately after the desired behavior
    c. Given only upon the occurrence of the target behavior
    d. All of the above

Correct answer is "d."
Timing and the quality of the reinforcer are key in encouraging the individual to continue the targeted behavior.

97. **Which of the following is a behavioral rule that places emphasis on consequential events?**
    (Average Rigor) (Skill 10.06)

    a. Behavior that is reinforced tends to occur more frequently
    b. Behavior that is no longer reinforced will be extinguished
    c. Behavior that is punished occurs less frequently
    d. All of the above

Correct answer is "d."
The basic rules of behaviorism are stated in "a," "b," and "c."

98. **Dispensing school supplies is a component associated with which type of reinforcement system?**
    (Average Rigor) (Skill 10.06)

    a. Activity reinforcement
    b. Tangible reinforcement
    c. Token reinforcement
    d. Both b and c

Correct answer is "a."
The Premack Principle states that any activity in which a student voluntarily participates on a frequent basis can be used as a reinforcer for any activity in which the student seldom participates. Running errands, decorating bulletin boards, leading group activities, passing out books or papers, collecting materials, or operating equipment all provide activity reinforcement.

99. **Which type of reinforcement system is most easily generalized into other settings?**
    (Rigorous) (Skill 10.06)

    a. Social reinforcement
    b. Activity reinforcement
    c. Tangible reinforcement
    d. Token reinforcement

Correct answer is "a."
There are many advantages to social reinforcement. It is easy to use, takes little of the teacher's time or effort, and is available in any setting. It is always positive, unlikely to satiate, and can be generalized to most situations.

100. The behaviorist approach emphasizes:
   (Rigorous) (Skill 10.06)

   a. Reinforcing appropriate behavior
   b. Teaching students how to manage their own behaviors in school
   c. Heavily structuring the learning environment
   d. Generalizing learning from one setting to another

Correct answer is "a."

Treatment models for learning disabilities have evolved in response to theories about their causes. For example, in the 1940s and 1950s, the **medical approach** was advocated. This approach structured daily schedules; used instructional practices such as study carrels, alternating seated, and active tasks; reduced noise; structured tasks corresponding to attention span; assigned tasks appropriate to functioning levels; structured time; and used tape recorded lessons.

The **psychological processing approach** of the 1960s advocated identifying student learning styles, administering tests orally, and audio taping textbooks. It also advocated activities that included the reproduction of designs; the use of simplified, uncluttered worksheets; the identification of missing objects; attention to detail; discrimination of sounds and symbols; interviews; puppetry; role playing; and referential communication.

The instructional practices of the **behavioral approach** of the 1970s included task analysis; mastery of prerequisite skills; small, sequential learning steps; identification of functioning abilities; use of concrete, hands-on materials; use of oral and written materials simultaneously; use of visual auditory and tactile teaching aids; use of compensatory and supportive aids; error analysis; use of color; use of high interest, low-vocabulary reading materials; and teacher-made or adapted instructional materials.

In the 1980s and 1990s, **strategy approaches** were postulated. The instructional strategies included giving clues to identify important information; encouraging "talking through" problems; setting up homework organizers; teaching how to take notes and organize content read; asking for periodic status reports on long-term assignments; teaching test-taking, study skills, and use of mnemonic cues; use of index cards for review; and instruction in use of calculators, tape recorders, typewriters, and word processors.

At the present time, practices from each of these models are in evidence in special education settings. Most teachers utilize an eclectic approach. The contemporary practice emphasizes cognitive learning strategies in which students are taught how to learn; how to manage their own behaviors in school; and how to generalize information from one setting to another. The ultimate goal is to produce self-sufficient, independent learners with skills to last a lifetime.

101. **The preventive discipline technique of proximity control is characterized by the teacher:**
    (Average Rigor) (Skill 10.07)

    a. Using signals to communicate disapproval to the student
    b. Showing interest in the student at crucial times
    c. Using humor to lessen tension
    d. Moving closer to the student who is showing signs of difficulty

Correct answer is "d."
Proximity control occurs when the teacher stands close to the student having difficulty, thus providing a source of protection, strength, and self-control.

102. **Charise comes into the classroom and seems to know every button to push to get the teacher upset with her. What would be a good intervention?**
    (Rigorous) (Skill 10.07)

    a. Nonverbal interactions
    b. Self-monitoring
    c. Proximity control
    d. Planned ignoring

Correct answer is "d."
Planned ignoring takes control from the student and tends to reduce the irritating behaviors, as the behaviors do not draw the attention they were employed to receive.

103. **After purchasing what seemed to be a very attractive new math kit for use with her SLD (severely learning disabled) students, Ms. Davis discovered her students could not use the kit unless she read the math problems and instructions to them, as the readability level was higher than the majority of the students' functional reading capabilities. Which criterion of the materials selection did Ms. Davis most likely fail to consider when selecting this math kit?**
    (Easy) (Skill 11.02)

    a. Durability
    b. Relevance
    c. Component parts
    d. Price

Correct answer is "b."
Relevance is the only cognitive factor listed above. Since her students were severely learning disabled, she almost certainly would have considered the kit's durability and component parts.

104. Which of the following questions most directly evaluates the utility of instructional material?
(Average Rigor) (Skill 11.02)

a. Is the cost within budgetary means?
b. Can the materials withstand handling by students?
c. Are the materials organized in a useful manner?
d. Are the needs of the students met by the use of the materials?

Correct answer is "c."
It is a question of utility, or usefulness.

105. A money bingo game was designed by Ms Johnson for use with her middle-grade students. Cards were constructed with different combinations of coins pasted on each of the nine spaces. Ms. Johnson called out various amounts of change (e.g., 30 cents), and students were instructed to cover the coin combinations on their cards that equaled the amount of change (e.g., two dimes and two nickels, three dimes, and so on). The student who had the first bingo was required to add the coins in each of the spaces covered and tell the amounts before being declared the winner. Five of Ms. Johnson's sixth graders played the game during the ten minutes of free activity time following math the first day the game was constructed. Which of the following attributes are present in this game in this situation?
(Easy) (Skill 11.02)

a. Accompanied by simple, uncomplicated rules
b. Of brief duration, permitting replay
c. Age appropriateness
d. All of the above

Correct answer is "d."
Games and puzzles should also be colorful and appealing, of relevance to individual students, and appropriate for learners at different skill levels in order to sustain interest and motivational value.

106. One of the passages in the informal reading inventory developed by Mrs. Aultman is a story about a boy whose family buys a monkey from the pet store. The story describes both the pleasures and the problems incurred by his family's choice of pet. If the reader is later asked to elaborate upon whether he would like his family to get a monkey as a pet, this question would be reflective of what type of thinking skill?
(Average Rigor) (Skill 11.02)

a. Literal recall
b. Reorganization
c. Inferential
d. Evaluation

Correct answer is "d."
In this example, the teacher is using an inventory. The student is being asked to evaluate or assess whether or not his family would like to keep a monkey as a pet. In doing so, he will contrast the pleasures and problems to find, in his own opinion, whether the pleasures outweigh the problems (or vice-versa).

107. **Which of the following is a good example of a generalization?**
(Average Rigor) (Skill 11.03)

a. Jim has learned to add and is now ready to subtract.
b. Sarah adds sets of units to obtain a product.
c. Bill recognizes a vocabulary word on a billboard when traveling.
d. Jane can spell the word "net" backwards to get the word "ten."

Correct answer is "c."
Generalization is the occurrence of a learned behavior in the presence of a stimulus other than the one that produced the initial response. It is the expansion of a student's performance beyond the initial setting. Students must be able to expand or transfer what is learned to other settings (e.g., reading to math word problems, resource room to regular classroom). Generalization may be enhanced by the following:

- Use many examples in teaching to deepen application of learned skills.
- Use consistency in initial teaching situations and later introduce variety in format, procedure, and use of examples.
- Have the same information presented by different teachers, in different settings, and under varying conditions.
- Include a continuous reinforcement schedule at first, later changing to delayed and intermittent schedules as instruction progresses.
- Teach students to record instances of generalization and to reward themselves at that time.
- Associate naturally occurring stimuli when possible.

108. **Mrs. West, the learning disabilities teacher, taught her students to use the SLANT technique in the regular classroom in order to help them be perceived by the classroom teacher as having acceptable behaviors. She taught them that each letter in SLANT stands for an action. S stands for "sit up straight"; L stands for "lean forward"; A stands for "attend/pay attention"; N stands for "nod" when you understand or agree with information given; and T stands for "track" the teacher as he or she moves around the classroom. For which of the identified categories of behavior does this technique help students the most?** *(Average Rigor) (Skill 11.04)*

   a. Interact positively with other students
   b. Follow class rules
   c. Display proper work habits
   d. None of the above

Correct answer is "c."
The series of actions in SLANT do not all fit into "a" or "b."

109. **Which is not considered a proper work habit?** *(Easy) (Skill 11.04)*

   a. Seeks assistance when appropriate
   b. Initiates assignments independently
   c. Follows directions
   d. Stops working when tasks become challenging

Correct answer is "d."
The best students are usually those who rise to a challenge.

110. **Normality in child behavior is influenced by which aspect of society?** *(Average Rigor) (Skill 11.08)*

   a. Attitudes and cultural beliefs
   b. Religious beliefs
   c. Religious and cultural beliefs
   d. Attitudes and Victorian era motto

Correct answer is "a."
Normality in child behavior is influenced by society's attitudes and cultural beliefs about what is normal for children (e.g., the motto for the Victorian era was "Children should be seen and not heard").

111. Children with disabilities can be taught social-interpersonal skills by:
(Average Rigor) (Skill 12.03)

    a. Developing sensitivity to other people
    b. Making behavioral choices in social situations
    c. Developing social maturity
    d. All of the above

Correct answer is "d."
Social-interpersonal skills are the ability to build and maintain interdependent relationships between persons. These skills are considered the domain of affective education and classroom management.

112. Children are engaged in a game of charades. Which type of social-interpersonal skill is the teacher most likely attempting to develop?
(Rigorous) (Skill 12.03)

    a. Sensitivity to others
    b. Making behavioral choices in social situations
    c. Social maturity
    d. All of the above

Correct answer is "a."
Children with disabilities often perceive facial expressions and gestures differently than their nondisabled peers. The game of charades, a guessing game, would help them develop sensitivity to others.

113. Social maturity may be evidenced by the students':
(Average Rigor) (Skill 12.03)

    a. Recognition of rights and responsibilities
    b. Display of respect for legitimate authority figures
    c. Formulation of a valid moral judgment
    d. Demonstration of all of the above

Correct answer is "d."
Some additional evidence of social maturity includes:
- The ability to cooperate
- Following procedures formulated by an outside party
- Achieving appropriate levels of independence

114. Mrs. Wright has noticed that Stevie typically plays alone and is seldom seen playing with other children. Today Stevie is one of the last children in the room to be chosen by a team captain as a member of the group. One way in which Mrs. Wright can find out how Stevie is accepted by his peers would be to administer:
(Rigorous) (Skill 12.03)

    a. Burk's Behavior Rating Scale
    b. The Walker Problem Behavior Identification Checklist
    c. A class play
    d. A self-test

Correct answer is "c."
A class play is the best choice, as it gives the teacher a chance to assess the behavior through all of its five phases.

115. Which of the following skills does a test of adaptive behavior measure?
(Average Rigor) (Skill 12.03)

    a. Self-help skills
    b. Communication skills
    c. Social skills
    d. All of the above

Correct answer is "d."
A test of adaptive behavior is used to predict whether or not a person can maintain personal independence in daily living and meet the social expectations of his or her environment. It measures self-help skills (e.g., eating, grooming), communication skills (e.g., following directions), and social skills (e.g., interpersonal relationships).

116. A functional curriculum approach focuses on
(Rigorous) (Skill 12.05)

    a. Remediation of basic academic skills
    b. Preparation for functioning in society as adults
    c. Preparation for the world of work
    d. Daily living and social skills

Correct answer is "b."
A functional curriculum approach focuses on what students need to learn that will be useful to them and prepare them for functioning in society as adults. Life preparation includes not only occupational readiness but also personal-social and daily living skills.

117. Functional skills include _____ skills.
      (Easy) (Skill 12.05)

    a. Personal-social
    b. Daily living
    c. Occupational readiness
    d. All of the above

Correct answer is "d."
A functional curriculum approach focuses on what students need to learn that will be useful to them and prepare them for functioning in society as adults. Life preparation includes not only occupational readiness but also personal-social and daily living skills.

118. **The transition activities that have to be addressed, unless the IEP team finds them uncalled for, are:**
      (Average Rigor) (Skill 12.06)

    a. Instruction
    b. Community experiences
    c. The development of objectives related to employment and other post-school areas
    d. All of the above

Correct answer is "d."

Transition services will be different for each student, but all three aspects must be addressed. Transition services must take into account the student's interests and preferences. Evaluation of career interests, aptitudes, skills, and training may also be considered.

119. **Which of these is the best resource a teacher can have to reach a student?**
      (Rigorous) (Skill 13.02)

    a. Contact with the parents/guardians
    b. A successful behavior modification exam
    c. A listening ear
    d. Gathered scaffold approach to teaching

Correct answer is "a."
Parents are often the best source of information on their children. They generally know if a behavior management technique will be successful.

120. **Which is a less than ideal example of collaboration in successful inclusion?**
(Easy) (Skill 14.01)

 a. Special education teachers are part of the instructional team in a regular classroom.
 b. Special education teachers assist regular education teachers in the classroom.
 c. Teaming approaches are used for problem solving and program implementation.
 d. Regular teachers, special education teachers, and other specialists or support teachers co-teach.

Correct answer is "b."
In a special education setting, the special education teacher should be the lead teacher.

121. **Of the following, who helps students develop motor, perceptual, and self-help skills?**
(Rigorous) (Skill 14.01)

 a. Occupational therapist
 b. Physical therapist
 c. Speech and language pathologist
 d. School psychologist

Correct answer is "a."
Physical therapy includes the use of adaptive equipment and prosthetic and orthotic devices to facilitate independent movement. Occupational therapy involves the development of self-help skills (e.g., self-care, motor, perceptual, and vocational skills).

122. **The role of the speech and language pathologist includes:**
(Average Rigor) (Skill 14.01)

 a. Language instruction in the general classroom
 b. Performing minor corrective surgery on vocal impediments
 c. Diagnosing speech and language impediments
 d. Specializing in cultural language deficits

Correct answer is "c."
The speech and language pathologist assists in the identification and diagnosis of children with speech or language disorders, makes referrals for medical or rehabilitation needs, counsels family members and teachers, and works to prevent communicative disorders. The pathologist concentrates on rehabilitative service delivery and continuing diagnosis.

123. The best way to ensure the success of educational interventions is to:
(Average Rigor) (Skill 14.01)

    a. Give regular education teachers the primary responsibility of teaching special needs students in regular classrooms.
    b. Give special education teachers the primary responsibility of teaching special needs students in special education classrooms.
    c. Promote cooperative teaching efforts between general and special educators.
    d. Have support personnel assume the primary responsibility for the education of special needs students.

Correct answer is "c."
In this situation, both types of teachers can learn from each other, and students can learn from each other and become sensitive to the special needs of each other.

124. Janice requires occupational therapy and speech therapy services. What must be done by her teacher to insure her needs are met? *(Rigorous) (Skill 14.01)*

    a. Watch the services being rendered
    b. Schedule collaboratively
    c. Ask for services to be given in a push-in model
    d. Ask to be trained to give the service him or herself

Correct answer is "b."
Collaborative scheduling of students to receive services is the responsibility of both the teacher and the service provider. Scheduling together allows for the convenience of both. It also will provide the teacher with an opportunity to make sure the student does not miss important information.

125. In successful inclusion:
(Easy) (Skill 14.01)

a. A variety of instructional arrangements are available
b. School personnel shift the responsibility for learning outcomes to the student
c. The physical facilities are used as they are
d. Regular classroom teachers have sole responsibility for evaluating student progress

Correct answer is "a."

Some support systems and activities that are in evidence where successful inclusion has occurred are as follows:

Attitudes and beliefs

- The regular teacher believes the student can succeed.
- School personnel are committed to accepting responsibility for the learning outcomes of students with disabilities.
- School personnel and the students in the class have been prepared to receive a student with disabilities.

Services and physical accommodations

- Services needed by the student are available (e.g., health, physical, occupational, or speech therapy).
- Accommodations to the physical building and equipment are adequate to meet the students' needs (e.g., toys, building and playground facilities, learning materials, assistive devices).

School support

- The principal understands the needs of students with disabilities.
- Adequate numbers of personnel, including aides, are available.
- Adequate staff development and technical assistance, based on the needs of the school personnel, are being provided (e.g., information on disabilities, instructional methods, awareness and acceptance activities for students, and team-building skills).
- Appropriate policies and procedures for monitoring individual student progress, including grading and testing are in place.

Collaboration

- Special educators are part of the instructional or planning team.
- Teaming approaches for program implementation and problem solving.
- Regular teachers, special education teachers, and other specialists collaborate (e.g., co-teach, team teach, work together on teacher assistance teams).

Instructional methods

- Teachers have the knowledge and skills needed to select and adapt curricular and instructional methods according to individual student needs.
- A variety of instructional arrangements are available (e.g., team teaching, cross-grade grouping, peer tutoring, teacher assistance teams).

- Teachers foster a cooperative learning environment and promote socialization.

126. **Students who receive special services in a regular classroom with consultation generally have academic and/or social-interpersonal performance deficits at which level of severity?**
(Easy) (Skill 14.03)

   a. Mild
   b. Moderate
   c. Severe
   d. Profound

Correct answer is "a."
Most students receiving special services are enrolled primarily in regular classes. Individuals with mild learning and behavior problems are those who exhibit academic and/or social interpersonal deficits evident mostly in a school-related setting. These students appear no different to their peers, physically.

127. **What can a teacher do to create a good working environment with a classroom assistant?**
(Rigorous) (Skill 14.05)

   a. Plan lessons with the assistant.
   b. Write a contract that clearly defines his or her responsibilities in the classroom.
   c. Remove previously given responsibilities.
   d. All of the above

Correct answer is "a."
Planning with a classroom assistant demonstrates that the teacher respects his or her input and allows the teacher to see where he or she feels confident.

128. **A paraprofessional has been assigned to assist a teacher in the classroom. What action on the part of the teacher would lead to a poor working relationship?**
(Average Rigor) (Skill 14.05)

    a. Having the paraprofessional lead a small group
    b. Telling the paraprofessional what he or she is expected to do
    c. Defining classroom behavior management as the teacher's responsibility alone
    d. Taking an active role in his or her evaluation

Correct answer is "c."
When a teacher does not allow another adult in the room to enforce the class rules, he or she creates an environment where the other adult is seen as someone not to be respected. Few people want to be in work environments where they do not feel respected.

129. **Mrs. Freud is a consultant teacher. She has two students with Mr. Ricardo. Mrs. Freud should:**
(Rigorous) (Skill 14.05)

    a. Co-teach
    b. Spend two days a week in the classroom helping out
    c. Discuss lessons with the teacher and suggest modifications before class
    d. Pull her students out for instructional modifications

Correct answer is "c."
Consultant teaching provides the least intervention possible for the success of the academic child. Pushing in or pulling out are not essential components. However, an occasional surveillance as a classroom observer who does not single out any students may also be helpful in providing modifications for the student.

130. **Which of the following must be provided in a written notice to parents when proposing a child's educational placement?**
    (Average Rigor) (Skill 14.07)

    a. A list of parental due process safeguards
    b. A list of current test scores
    c. A list of persons responsible for the child's education
    d. A list of academic subjects the child has passed

Correct answer is "a."
Written notice must be provided to parents prior to a proposal or refusal to initiate or make a change in the child's identification, evaluation, or educational placement. Notices must contain:
  - A listing of parental due process safeguards
  - A description and a rationale for the chosen action
  - A detailed listing of components (e.g., tests, records, reports) that were the basis for the decision
  - Assurance that the language and content of the notices were understood by the parents

131. **Teachers must keep meticulous records. They are required to share all of them with the student's parent/guardian *except*:**
    (Rigorous) (Skill 14.07)

    a. Daily attendance records
    b. Grade reports
    c. Teacher's personal notes
    d. Discipline notice placed in cumulative record

Correct answer is "c."
Information on students that a teacher writes down for his or her own reference do not have to be shared with parents. However, the teacher may choose to share these notes with the parent/guardian.

132. **During which time period did the parents, legislature, and courts become very involved in improving education for children and youth with disabilities?**
     (Rigorous) (Skill 15.01)

     a. The 19th century
     b. 1900–1919
     c. 1919–1949
     d. 1950–1969

Correct answer is "d."
In 1950, the National Association of Retarded Children, later renamed the National Association of Retarded Citizens (NARC) was established. In 1954, the court ruling in *Brown v. the Topeka Board of Education* guaranteed equal opportunity rights to free public education for all citizens. The parents of children and youth with disabilities insisted their children were included in this decision. This and the numerous court cases following are known collectively as the Doctrine of Selective Incorporation, under which states are compelled to honor the substantive rights of persons with disabilities under procedural authority of the 14th Amendment.

133. **The early 19th century is considered a period of great importance in the field of special education because principles presently used in working with exceptional students were formulated by Itard. These principles included:** *(Average Rigor) (Skill 15.01)*

     a. Individualized instruction
     b. Sequence of tasks
     c. Functional life-like skills curriculum
     d. All of the above

Correct answer is "d."
A French physician, Jean Marc Itard, found a boy abandoned in the woods of Aveyron, France. His attempts to civilize and educate the boy, Victor, established these principles, including developmental and multisensory approaches. At that time, students with mild intellectual sensory impairments, mild intellectual disabilities, and emotional disorders were referred to as "idiotic" and "insane."

134. Effective transition was included in:
(Rigorous) (Skill 15.01)

    a. President Bush's 1990 State of the Union message
    b. Public Law 101-476
    c. Public Law 95-207
    d. Both a and b

Correct answer is "d."
With the enactment of Public Law 101-476, (IDEA) transition services became a right.

135. Included in data brought to the attention of Congress regarding the evaluation procedures for education of students with disabilities was the fact that:
(Average Rigor) (Skill 15.02)

    a. There were a large number of children and youths with disabilities in the United States
    b. Many children with disabilities were not receiving an appropriate education
    c. Many parents of children with disabilities were forced to seek services outside of the public realm
    d. All of the above

Correct answer is "d."
All three factors, and many more, have driven Congress to act.

136. The Individuals with Disabilities Education Act (IDEA) was signed into law in and later reauthorized through a second revision in what years?
(Rigorous) (Skill 15.02)

    a. 1975 and 2004
    b. 1980 and 1990
    c. 1990 and 2004
    d. 1995 and 2001

Correct answer is "c."
IDEA, Public Law 101-476, is a consolidation and reauthorization of all prior special education mandates, with amendments. It was signed into law by President Bush on October 30, 1990. Revision of IDEA occurred in 2004, when it was re-authorized as the Individuals with Disabilities Education Improvement Act of 2004 (IDEIA 2004). IDEA 2004 became effective on July 1, 2005.

137. **How was the training of special education teachers changed by the No Child Left Behind Act of 2002?**
(Rigorous) (Skill 15.02)

    a. It required all special education teachers to be certified in reading and math.
    b. It required all special education teachers to take the same coursework as general education teachers.
    c. If a special education teacher is teaching a core subject, he or she must meet the standard of a highly qualified teacher in that subject.
    d. All of the above

Correct answer is "c."
In order for a special education teacher to be a student's sole teacher of a core subject, he or she must meet the professional criteria of No Child Left Behind. The teacher must be *highly qualified*—that is, certified or licensed in the appropriate area of special education—and show proof of a specific level of professional development in the core subjects that he or she teaches. As special education teachers receive specific education in the core subject they teach, they will be better prepared to teach to the same level of learning standards as the general education teacher.

138. **Which of the following is a specific change of language in the IDEA?**
(Rigorous) (Skill 15.02)

    a. The term "disorder" changed to "disability"
    b. The term "children" changed to "children and youth"
    c. The term "handicapped" changed to "impairments"
    d. The term "handicapped" changed to "with disabilities"

Correct answer is "d."
"Children" became "individuals," highlighting the fact that some students with special needs were adolescents and not just "children." The word "handicapped" was changed to "with disabilities," denoting the difference between limitations imposed by society (handicap) and an inability to do certain things (disability). "With disabilities" also demonstrates that the person is thought of first, and the disabling condition is but one of the characteristics of the individual.

139. **Which component changed with the reauthorization of the Education for All Handicapped Children Act of 1975 (EHA) amendment in 1990?** *(Rigorous) (Skill 15.02)*

    a. Specific terminology
    b. Due process protections
    c. Nondiscriminatory re-evaluation procedures
    d. Individual education plans

Correct answer is "a."
"Children" became "individuals," highlighting the fact that some students with special needs were adolescents and not just "children." The word "handicapped" was changed to "with disabilities," denoting the difference between limitations imposed by society (handicap) and an inability to do certain things (disability). "With disabilities" also demonstrates that the person is thought of first, and the disabling condition is but one of the characteristics of the individual.

140. **Which is untrue about the Americans with Disabilities Act (ADA)?** *(Rigorous) (Skill 15.02)*

    a. It was signed into law the same year as IDEA by President Bush
    b. It reauthorized the discretionary programs of EHA
    c. It gives protection to all people on the basis of race, sex, national origin, and religion
    d. It guarantees equal opportunities to persons with disabilities in employment, public accommodations, transportation, government services, and telecommunications.

Correct answer is "b."
EHA is the precursor of IDEA. ADA, however, is Public Law 101-336, which gives civil rights protection to all individuals with disabilities in private sector employment, all public services, public accommodations, transportation, and telecommunications. It was patterned after the Rehabilitation Act of 1973.

141. Requirements for evaluations were changed in IDEA 2004 to reflect that no "single" assessment or measurement tool can be used to determine special education qualification, which previously furthered a disproportionate representation of what types of students? *(Average Rigor) (Skill 15.02)*

    a. Disabled
    b. Foreign
    c. Gifted
    d. Minority and bilingual

Correct answer is "d."

IDEA 2004 recognized that there exists a disproportionate representation of minorities and bilingual students and that pre-service interventions that are *scientifically based on early reading programs, positive behavioral interventions, and support,* as well as early intervening services, may prevent some of those children from needing special education services.

142. IEPs continue to have multiple sections; one section, present levels, now addresses what? *(Rigorous) (Skill 15.02)*

    a. Academic achievement and functional performance
    b. English as a second language
    c. Functional performance
    d. Academic achievement

Correct answer is "a."

IEPS continue to have multiple sections. The section of present levels now addresses academic achievement and functional performance. Annual IEP goals must now address the same areas.

143. Which of the following is true about IDEA? In order to be eligible, a student must: *(Easy) (Skill 15.02)*

    a. Have a medical disability
    b. Have a disability that fits into one of the categories listed in the law
    c. Attend a private school
    d. Be a slow learner

Correct answer is "b."

IDEA is a legal instrument, thus it is defined by law. Every aspect in the operation of IDEA is laid out in law.

144. **What determines whether a person is entitled to protection under Section 504?**
    (Average Rigor) (Skill 15.02)

    a. The individual must meet the definition of a person with a disability
    b. The person must be able to meet the requirements of a particular program in spite of his or her disability
    c. The school, business, or other facility must be the recipient of federal funding assistance
    d. All of the above

Correct answer is "d."
To be entitled to protection under Section 504, an individual must meet the definition of a person with a disability, which is: any person who (i) has a physical or mental impairment that substantially limits one or more of that person's major life activities; (ii) has a record of such impairment; or (iii) is regarded as having such an impairment.

Major life activities are defined as: caring for oneself, performing manual tasks, walking, seeing, hearing, speaking, breathing, learning, and working. The person must also be "otherwise qualified," which means that the person must be able to meet the requirements of a particular program in spite of the disability. The person must also be afforded "reasonable accommodations" by recipients of federal financial assistance.

145. **Legislation in Public Law 94-142 attempts to:**
    (Average Rigor) (Skill 15.02)

    a. Match the child's educational needs with appropriate educational services
    b. Include parents in the decisions made about their child's education
    c. Establish a means by which parents can provide input
    d. All of the above

Correct answer is "d."
Much of what was stated in separate court rulings and mandated legislation was brought together into what is now considered to be the "backbone" of special education. Public Law 94-142, (Education for All Handicapped Children Act) was signed into law by President Ford in 1975. It was the culmination of a great deal of litigation and legislation, including decisions supporting the need to assure an appropriate education to all persons regardless of race, creed, or disability, from the late 1960s to the mid-1970s. In 1990, this law was reauthorized and renamed the Individuals with Disabilities Education Act (IDEA).

146. **The law affects required components of the IEP. The elements required by the IEP and the law are:**
    (Easy) (Skill 15.02)

    a. Present level of academic and functional performance; statement of how the disability affects the student's involvement and progress; evaluation criteria and timeliness for instructional objective achievement; modifications of accommodations
    b. Projected dates for services initiation with anticipated frequency, location, and duration; statement of when parent will be notified; statement of annual goals
    c. Extent to which child will not participate in regular education program; transitional needs for students aged 14
    d. All of the above

Correct answer is "d."
IEPs state 14 elements that are required. Educators must keep themselves apprised of the changes and amendments to laws such as IDEA 2004, including the addendums released in October 2006.

147. **The opportunity for persons with disabilities to live as close to the normal as possible describes:**
    (Average Rigor) (Skill 15.02)

    a. Least restrictive environment
    b. Normalization
    c. Mainstreaming
    d. Deinstitutionalization

Correct answer is "b."
The principles of IDEA also incorporate the concept of "normalization." Within this concept, persons with disabilities are allowed access to everyday patterns and conditions of life that are as close as possible or equal to their nondisabled peers.

148. **The IDEA states that child assessment is:**
    (Rigorous) (Skill 15.02)

    a. At intervals with teacher discretion
    b. Continuous on regular basis
    c. Left to the counselor
    d. Conducted annually

Correct answer is "b."
Assessments in special education are continuous and occur on a regular basis.

149. **Which are the most important political forces whose efforts resulted in obtaining the regulations and mandates contained within Public Law 94-142?**
(Rigorous) (Skill 15.02)

a. Action taken by parent and professional support groups
b. Public laws put into effect
c. Rulings put into effect
d. All of the above

Correct answer is "d."
The trio of forces is interdependent. No one force could have worked effectively on its own.

150. **The Free Appropriate Public Education (FAPE) describes special education and related services as:**
(Average Rigor) (Skill 15.06)

a. Public expenditure and standard to the state educational agency
b. Provided in conformity with each student's individualized education program, if the program is developed to meet requirements of the law
c. Inclusive of preschool, elementary, and/or secondary education in the state involved
d. All of the above

Correct answer is "d."
FAPE states that special education and related services are provided at public expense; meet the standards of the state educational agency; include preschool, elementary, and/or secondary education in the state involved; and are provided in conformity with each student's IEP. The program is developed to meet requirements of the law.

Rigor Table

	Easy 20%	Average Rigor 40%	Rigorous 40%
Question	4, 5, 16, 18, 29, 30, 43, 44, 49, 52, 59, 61, 62, 63, 65, 68, 70, 73, 74, 76, 82, 93, 103, 105, 109, 117, 120, 125, 126, 143, 146	1, 2, 3, 14, 15, 17, 20, 21, 22, 25, 26, 31, 36, 37, 47, 48, 51, 55, 56, 60, 64, 69, 71, 72, 75, 77, 78, 79, 80, 81, 83, 86, 87, 91, 92, 94, 96, 97, 98, 101, 104, 106, 107, 108, 110, 111, 113, 115, 118, 122, 123, 128, 130, 133, 135, 141, 144, 145, 147, 150	6, 7, 8, 9, 10, 11, 12, 13, 19, 23, 24, 27, 28, 32, 33, 34, 35, 38, 39, 40, 41, 42, 45, 46, 50, 53, 54, 57, 58, 66, 67, 84, 85, 88, 89, 90, 95, 99, 100, 102, 112, 114, 116, 119, 121, 124, 127, 129, 131, 132, 134, 136, 137, 138, 139, 140, 142, 148, 149

DOMAIN I.   UNDERSTANDING STUDENTS WITH DISABILITIES

COMPETENCY 1.0 UNDERSTAND HUMAN DEVELOPMENT

Skill 1.01   **Demonstrates knowledge of typical and atypical human growth and development (e.g., cognitive, linguistic, physical, social, emotional).**

SOCIAL EMOTIONAL

This topic pertains to children whose behavior deviates from society's standards for normal behavior for certain ages and stages of development. Behavioral expectations vary from setting to setting—for example, it is acceptable to yell on the football field but not as the teacher is explaining a lesson to the class. Different cultures have their own standards of behavior, further complicating the question of what constitutes a behavioral problem. People also have their personal opinions and standards for what is tolerable and what is not. Some behavioral problems are openly expressed; others are inwardly directed and not very obvious. As a result of these factors, the terms **behavioral disorders** and **emotional disturbance** have become almost interchangeable.

While almost all children will, at some time, exhibit behaviors that are aggressive, withdrawn, or otherwise inappropriate, the IDEA definition of serious emotional disturbance focuses on behaviors that persist over time, are intense, and impair a child's ability to function in society. The behaviors must not be caused by temporary stressful situations or other causes (e.g., depression over the death of a grandparent or anger over the parents' impending divorce). In order for a child to be considered seriously emotionally disturbed, he or she must exhibit one or more of the following characteristics over a **long period of time** and to a **marked degree** that **adversely affects** a child's educational performance:

- Inability to learn, which cannot be explained by intellectual, sensory, or health factors
- Inability to maintain satisfactory interpersonal relationships
- Inappropriate types of behaviors
- General pervasive mood of unhappiness or depression
- Physical symptoms or fears associated with personal or school problems
- Schizophrenic children are covered under this definition, and social maladjustment by itself does not satisfy this definition unless it is accompanied by one of the other conditions of SED.

The diagnostic categories and definitions used to classify mental disorders come from the American Psychiatric Association's publication *Diagnostic and Statistical Manual of Mental Disorders* (DSM-IV), the handbook that is used by psychiatrists and psychologists. The DSM-IV is a multiaxial classification system consisting of dimensions (axes) coded along with the psychiatric diagnosis. The axes are:

- Axis I   Principal psychiatric diagnosis (e.g., overanxious disorder)
- Axis II   Developmental problems (e.g., developmental reading disorder)
- Axis III   Physical disorders (e.g., allergies)
- Axis IV   Psychosocial stressors (e.g., divorce)
- Axis V   Rating of the highest level of adaptive functioning (includes intellectual and social). Rating is called Global Assessment Functioning (GAF) score.

While the DSM-IV diagnosis is one way of diagnosing serious emotional disturbance, there are other ways of classifying the various forms that behavior disorders manifest themselves. The following tables summarize some of these classifications.

Externalizing Behaviors	Internalizing Behaviors
Aggressive behaviors expressed outwardly toward others	Withdrawing behaviors that are directed inward to oneself
Manifested as hyperactivity, persistent aggression, and irritating behaviors that are impulsive and distractible	Social withdrawal
Examples: hitting, cursing, stealing, arson, cruelty to animals, hyperactivity,	Depression, fears, phobias, elective mutism, withdrawal, anorexia, and bulimia

Well-known instruments used to assess children's behavior have their own categories (scales) to classify behaviors. The following table illustrates the scales used in some of the widely used instruments.

Walker Problem Identification Checklist	Burks' Behavior Rating Scales (BBRS)	Devereux Behavior Rating Scale (adolescent)	Revised Behavior Problem Checklist (Quay & Peterson)
Acting out	Excessive self-blame	Unethical behavior	Major scales
Withdrawal	Excessive anxiety	Defiant-resistive	Conduct Disorder

Distractibility	Excessive withdrawal	Domineering-sadistic	Socialized aggression
Disturbed peer Relations	Excessive dependency	Heterosexual interest	Attention-problems-immaturity
Immaturity	Poor ego strength	Hyperactive expansive	Anxiety-withdrawal
	Poor physical strength	Poor emotional control	
	Poor coordination	Needs approval, dependency	Minor scales
	Poor intellectuality	Emotional disturbance	Psychotic behavior
	Poor academics	Physical inferiority-timidity	Motor excess
	Poor attention	Schizoid withdrawal	
	Poor impulse control	Bizarre speech and cognition	
	Poor reality contact	Bizarre actions	
	Poor sense of identity		
	Excessive suffering		
	Poor anger control		
	Excessive sense of persecution		
	Excessive aggressiveness		
	Excessive resistance		
	Poor social conformity		

Disturbance may also be categorized in degrees: mild, moderate, or severe. The degree of disturbance will affect the type and degree of interventions and services required by emotionally handicapped students. Degree of disturbance must also be considered when determining the least restrictive environment and appropriate education. One example of a set of criteria for determining the degree of disturbance is that developed by P.L. Newcomer:

	DEGREE	OF	DISTURBANCE
CRITERIA	Mild	Moderate	Severe
Precipitating events	Highly stressful	Moderately stressful	Not stressful
Destructiveness	Not destructive	Occasionally destructive	Usually destructive
Maturational appropriateness	Behavior typical for age	Some behavior untypical for age	Behavior too young or too old
Personal functioning	Cares for own needs	Usually cares for own needs	Unable to care for own needs
Social functioning	Usually able to relate to others	Usually unable to relate to others	Unable to relate to others
Reality index	Usually sees events as they are	Occasionally sees events as they are	Little contact with reality
Insight index	Aware of behavior	Usually aware of behavior	Usually not aware of behavior
Conscious control	Usually can control behavior	Occasionally can control behavior	Little control over behavior
Social responsiveness	Usually acts appropriately	Occasionally acts appropriately	Rarely acts appropriately

Source: *Understanding and Teaching Emotionally Disturbed Children and Adolescents*, (2nd ed., p. 139), by P.L. Newcomer, 1993, Austin, TX: Pro-De. Copyright 1993. Reprinted with permission.

LANGUAGE DEVELOPMENT AND BEHAVIOR

Language is the means whereby people communicate their thoughts, make requests, and respond to others. Communication competence is an interaction of cognitive competence, social knowledge, and language competence. Communication problems may result from any or all of these areas that directly impact the student's ability to interact with others. Language consists of several components, each of which follows a sequence of development.

Brown[TAR1] and colleagues were the first to describe language as a function of developmental stages rather than age (Reid 1988 p. 44). Brown developed a formula to group the mean length of utterances (sentences) into stages. Counting the number of morphemes per 100 utterances, one can calculate a mean length of utterance (MLU). Total number of morphemes / 100 = MLU (e.g. 180/100 = 1.8).

Summary of Brown's findings about MLU and language development:

Stage	MLU	Developmental Features
L	1.5–2.0	14 basic morphemes (e.g., in, on, articles, possessives)
LI	2.0–2.5	Beginning of pronoun use, auxiliary verbs
LII	2.5–3.0	Language forms approximate adult forms, beginning of questions and negative statements
Lv	3.0–3.5	Use of complex (embedded) sentences
V	3.5–4.0	Use of compound sentences

COMPONENTS OF LANGUAGE

Language learning is made up of five components. Children progress through developmental stages through each component.

Phonology

Phonology is the system of rules about sounds and sound combinations for a language. A phoneme is the smallest unit of sound that combines with other sounds to make words. A phoneme, by itself, does not have a meaning; it must be combined with other phonemes. Problems in phonology may be manifested as developmental delays in acquiring consonants or as reception problems, such as misinterpreting words because a different consonant was substituted.

Morphology

Morphemes are the smallest units of language that convey meaning. Morphemes are root words—free morphemes that can stand alone (e.g., walk) and affixes (e.g., ed, s, ing). Content words carry the meaning in a sentence, and functional words join phrases and sentences. Generally, students with problems in this area may not use inflectional endings in their words, may not be consistent in their use of certain morphemes, or may be delayed in learning morphemes, such as irregular past tenses.

Syntax

Syntax rules, commonly known as grammar, govern how morphemes and words are correctly combined. Wood[TAR2] (1976) describes six stages of syntax acquisition (Mercer, p. 347):

- **Stages 1 and 2** - Birth to about 2 years: Child is learning the semantic system.

- **Stage 3** - Ages 2 to 3 years: Simple sentences contain subject and predicate.
- **Stage 4** - Ages 2 ½ to 4 years: Elements such as question words are added to basic sentences (e.g., where), and word order is changed to ask questions. The child begins to use "and" to combine simple sentences, and embeds words within the basic sentence.
- **Stage 5** - Ages 3 ½ to 7 years: The child uses complete sentences that include word classes of adult language. The child is becoming aware of appropriate semantic functions of words and differences within the same grammatical classes.
- **Stage 6** - Ages 5 to 20 years: The child begins to learn complex sentences and sentences that imply commands, requests, and promises.

Syntactic deficits are manifested when the child uses sentences that lack length or complexity for a child that age. The child may have problems understanding or creating complex sentences and embedded sentences.

Semantics
Semantics is language content: objects, actions, and relations between objects. As with syntax, Wood (1976) outlines stages of semantic development:

- **Stage 1** - Birth to about 2 years: The child is learning meaning while learning his or her first words. Sentences are one word, but the meaning varies according to the context. Therefore, "doggie" may mean, "This is my dog," or "There is a dog," or "The dog is barking."
- **Stage 2** - About 2 to 8 years: The child progresses to two-word sentences about concrete actions. As more words are learned, the child forms longer sentences; until about age 7, things are defined in terms of visible actions. The child begins to respond to prompts (e.g., pretty/flower). At about age 8, the child can respond to a prompt with an opposite (e.g., pretty/ugly).
- **Stage 3** - Begins at about age 8: The child's word meanings relate directly to experiences, operations, and processes. Vocabulary is defined by the child's experiences, not the adult's. At about age 12, the child begins to give "dictionary" definitions, and the semantic level approaches that of adults.

Semantic problems take the form of:
- Limited vocabulary
- Inability to understand figurative language or idioms; interprets literally
- Failure to perceive multiple meanings of words and changes in word meaning from changes in context, resulting in incomplete understanding of what is read
- Difficulty understanding linguistic concepts (e.g., before/after), verbal analogies, and logical relationships, such as possessives, spatial, and temporal
- Misuse of transitional words such as "although" and "regardless"

Pragmatics

Commonly known as the speaker's intent, pragmatics are used to influence or control the actions or attitudes of others. **Communicative competence** depends on how well one understands the rules of language, as well as the social rules of communication, such as taking turns and using the correct tone of voice.

Pragmatic deficits are manifested by failures to respond properly to indirect requests after age 8 (e.g., "Can't you turn down the TV?" elicits a response of "No" instead of "Yes" when the child turns down the volume). Children with these deficits have trouble reading cues that indicate the listener does not understand them. Whereas a person would usually notice this and adjust his or her speech to the listener's needs, the child with pragmatic problems does not do this. Pragmatic deficits are also characterized by inappropriate social behaviors, such as interrupting or monopolizing conversations. Children may use immature speech and have trouble sticking to a topic. These problems can persist into adulthood, affecting academic, vocational, and social interactions.

Problems in language development often require long-term interventions and can persist into adulthood. Certain problems are associated with different grade levels:

Preschool and kindergarten: The child's speech may sound immature, may not be able to follow simple directions, and often cannot name things such as the days of the week and colors. The child may not be able to discriminate between sounds and the letters associated with the sounds. The child might substitute sounds and have trouble responding accurately to certain types of questions. The child may play less with his or her peers or participate in nonplay or parallel play.

Elementary school: Problems with sound discrimination persist, and the child may have problems with temporal and spatial concepts (e.g., before/after). As the child progresses through school, he or she may have problems making the transition from narrative to expository writing. Word retrieval problems may not be very evident because the child begins to devise strategies (such as talking around the word he or she cannot remember, or using fillers and descriptors). The child might speak more slowly, have problems sounding out words, and get confused with multiple-meaning words. Pragmatic problems—failure to correctly interpret social cues and adjust to appropriate language, inability to predict consequences, and inability to formulate requests to obtain new information—show up in social situations.

Secondary school: At this level, difficulties become more subtle. The child lacks the ability to use and understand higher-level syntax, semantics, and pragmatics. If the child has problems with auditory language, he or she may also have problems with short-term memory. Receptive and/or expressive language delays impair the child's ability to learn effectively. The child often lacks the ability to organize/categorize the information received in school. Problems associated with pragmatic deficiencies persist; because the child is aware of them, he or she becomes inattentive, withdrawn, or frustrated.

Cognitive Development

Children go through patterns of learning, beginning with pre-operational thought processes, and move to concrete operational thoughts. Eventually, they begin to acquire the mental ability to think about and solve problems in their heads because they can manipulate objects symbolically. Children of most ages can use symbols (such as words and numbers) to represent objects and relations, but they need concrete reference points. It is essential children be encouraged to use and develop the thinking skills they possess in solving problems that interest them. The content of the curriculum must be relevant, engaging, and meaningful to the students.

The teacher of special needs students must have a general knowledge of cognitive development. Although children with cognitive development special needs may be different than other children, a teacher needs to be aware of some of the activities of each stage as part of the basis to determine what should be taught and when.

The following information about cognitive development was taken from the Cincinnati Children's Hospital Medical Center at www.cincinnatichildrens.org. Some common features indicating a progression from more simple to more complex cognitive development include the following:

Children (ages 6-12)

- Begin to develop the ability to think in concrete ways. Concrete operations are operations performed in the presence of the object and events that are to be used.

Examples: how to combine (addition), separate (subtract or divide), order (alphabetize and sort/categorize), and transform (25 pennies=1 quarter) objects and actions

Adolescence (ages 12-18)

- Adolescence marks the beginning development of more complex thinking skills, including abstract thinking, the ability to reason from known principles (form own new ideas or questions), the ability to consider many points of view according to varying criteria (compare or debate ideas or opinions), and the ability to think about the process of thinking.

What cognitive developmental changes occur during adolescence?

During adolescence, the developing teenager acquires the ability to think systematically about all logical relationships within a problem. The transition from concrete thinking to formal logical operations occurs over time. Every adolescent progresses at varying rates in developing his or her ability to think in more complex ways. Each adolescent develops his or her own view of the world. Some adolescents may be able to apply logical operations to school work long before they are able to apply them to personal dilemmas. When emotional issues arise, they often interfere with an adolescent's ability to think in more complex ways. The ability to consider possibilities as well as facts may influence decision making in either positive or negative ways.

Here are some common features indicating a progression from more simple to more complex cognitive development:

Early adolescence

During early adolescence, the use of more complex thinking is focused on personal decision making in school and home environments, including the following:

- Begins to demonstrate use of formal logical operations in school work
- Begins to question authority and society standards
- Begins to form and verbalize his or her own thoughts and views on a variety of topics, usually more related to his or her own life:
  - Which sports are better to play
  - Which groups are better to be included in
  - What personal appearances are desirable or attractive
  - What parental rules should be changed

Middle adolescence

With some experience in using more complex thinking processes, the focus of middle adolescence often expands to include more philosophical and futuristic concerns, including the following:

- Often questions more extensively
- Often analyzes more extensively
- Thinks about and begins to form his or her own code of ethics
- Thinks about different possibilities and begins to develop his or her own identity
- Thinks about and begins to systematically consider possible future goals
- Thinks about and begins to make his or her own plans
- Begins to think long-term
- Use of systematic thinking begins to influence relationships with others

Late adolescence

During late adolescence, complex thinking processes are used to focus on less self-centered concepts as well as personal decision making, including the following:

- Develops idealistic views on specific topics or concerns
- Debates and develops intolerance of opposing views
- Begins to focus thinking on making career decisions
- Begins to focus thinking on emerging role in adult society
- Increased thoughts about more global concepts, such as justice, history, politics, and patriotism

What encourages healthy cognitive development during adolescence?

The following suggestions will help to encourage positive and healthy cognitive development in the adolescent:

- Include adolescents in discussions about a variety of topics, issues, and current events.
- Encourage adolescents to share ideas and thoughts with adults.
- Encourage adolescents to think independently and develop their own ideas.
- Assist adolescents in setting their own goals.
- Stimulate adolescents to think about possibilities of the future.
- Compliment and praise adolescents for well-thought-out decisions.
- Assist adolescents in re-evaluating poorly made decisions for themselves.

IDENTIFY MAJOR STAGES OF NORMAL MOTOR AND LANGUAGE DEVELOPMENT

The normal progression of learning demonstrated by a child is related to development growth in the areas of gross and fine motor abilities, as well as language development. This table presents a compilation of development milestones in motor and language skills that are normally achieved by children and youth of various ages.

Age	Motor (gross and fine)	Language (understood and spoken)
0-1 yrs.	<ul><li>Sits without support</li><li>Develops one- and two-arm control crawls</li><li>Stands</li><li>Walks with aid</li><li>Begins to indicate hand preference</li><li>Pincer grasp develops</li><li>Loses sight of object and searches</li><li>Transfers objects from one hand to another</li></ul>	<ul><li>Responds to sound (loud noises, mother's voice)</li><li>Turns to sources of sound</li><li>Babbles vowel and consonant sounds</li><li>Responds with vocalization after adult speaks</li><li>Imitates sounds</li><li>Responds to words such as "up," "hello," "bye-bye," and "no" if adult gestures</li></ul>
1-2 yrs.	<ul><li>Begins scribbling in repetitive, circular motions</li><li>Holds pencil or crayon in fist</li><li>Walks unaided</li><li>Steps up onto or down from low objects</li><li>Seats self</li><li>Turns pages several at a time</li><li>Throws small objects</li><li>Turns doorknobs</li></ul>	<ul><li>Begins to express self with one word and increases to 50 words</li><li>Uses several suggestive words to describe events</li><li>Understands "bring it here," "take this to Daddy"</li><li>Uses "me" or "mine"</li></ul>

2-3 yrs.	• Begins a variety of scribbling patterns • Holds crayon or pencil with fingers and thumbs • Turns pages singly • Demonstrates stronger preference for one hand • Manipulates clay or dough • Runs forward well • Stands on one foot • Kicks • Walks on tiptoe	• Identifies pictures and objects when they are named • Joins words together in several phrases • Asks and answers questions • Enjoys listening to storybooks • Understands and uses "can't," "don't," "no" • Frustrated when spoken language is not understood • Refers to self by name
3-4 yrs.	• Pounds nails or pegs successfully • Copies circles and attempts crosses such as "+" • Runs • Balances and hops on one foot • Pushes, pulls, steers toys • Pedals and steers tricycle • Throws balls overhead • Catches balls that are bounced • Jumps over, runs around objects	• Uses words in simple sentence form, such as "I see my book." • Adds "s" to indicate plural • Relates simple accounts of experiences • Carries out a sequence of simple directions • Begins to understand time concepts • Understands comparatives, such as bigger, smaller, closer • Language (understood and spoken) • Understands relationships indicated by "because" or "if"

4-5 yrs.	• Copies crossed lines or squares • Cuts on a line • Prints a few letters of alphabet • Walks backward • Jumps forward • Walks up and down stairs alternating feet • Draws human figures including head and "stick" arms and legs	• Follows several unrelated commands • Listens to longer stories but often confuses them when re-telling • Asks "why," "how," "what for" questions • Understands comparatives, such as "fast," "faster," and "fastest" • Uses complex sentences such as "I like to play with my tricycle in and out of the house." • Uses relationship words, such as "because" or "so" • General speech is intelligible but may be frequently mispronounced
5-6 yrs.	• Runs on tiptoe • Walks on balance beam • Skips using alternate feet • Jumps rope • May ride two wheel bicycle • Roller skates • Copies triangles, name, numbers • Has firmly established handedness • Cuts and pastes large objects and designs • Includes more detail in drawing humans	• Generally communicates well with family and friends • Spoken language still has errors of subject-tense • Takes turns in conversation • Receives and gives information • With exceptions, use of grammar matches that of adults in family and neighborhood

7-10 yrs.	• Continued development and refinement of small muscles in writing, drawing, handling tools • Masters physical skills for game playing • Physical skills become important with peers and self-concept	• Develops ability to understand that words and pictures are representational of real objects • Understands most vocabulary used • Begins to use language aggressively • Verbalizes similarities and differences • Uses language to exchange ideas • Uses abstract words, slang, and often profanity
11-15 yrs.	• Adolescent growth spurts begin • May experience uneven growth resulting in awkwardness or clumsiness • Continued improvement in motor development and coordination	• Has good command of spoken and written language • Uses language extensively to discuss feelings and other more abstract ideas • Uses abstract words discriminately and selectively • Uses written language extensively

SOURCE: Gearhart, B. R. 1985. Learning disabilities: Educational strategies, (4th ed.), Appendix B: 371-373. Printed with permission of Charles E[TAR3].

Skill 1.02   Demonstrates knowledge of the effects of various disabilities on physical, sensory, motor, cognitive, language, social, and/or emotional development and functioning.

According to IDEA 2004, *student with a disability* means a student with a disability who has not attained the age of 21 prior to September 1st; who is entitled to attend public schools; and who, because of mental, physical, or emotional reasons, has been identified as having a disability that requires special services and programs approved by the department. The terms used in this definition are defined as follows:

1. Autism
2. Deafness
3. Deaf-blindness
4. Emotional disturbance
5. Hearing Impairment
6. Learning disability
7. Mental retardation
8. Multiple disabilities
9. Orthopedic impairment
10. Other health-impairment
11. Speech or language impairment
12. Traumatic brain injury
13. Visual impairment including blindness

The concern of the special educator is how a disability impacts a student's functioning in the education setting. Certainly, having a disability impacts a student socially as he or she learns to interact with others and react to outside responses. General implications of the above disabilities are as follows.

Autism impacts children to a great extent socially, as communication is difficult. Some autistic individuals report that even eye contact is painful. Because of the neurological component of autism, these children have sensory integration difficulties that may even cause an aversion to tags in clothing and a fixation on eating only a few foods. While some children on the Asperger's end of the autism spectrum have average or even above average intelligence, many other autistic children demonstrate below average intellectual functioning.

Deafness creates a language deficit that impacts social interaction, written language, and reading skills. Because vocabulary and sentence structures are not heard with spontaneous repetition, these must be taught in isolation and sequence. Social language expressions must also be taught. Because of the isolation caused by deafness, these children often demonstrate social immaturity in comparison to their hearing peers.

Deaf-blindness influences the child with a disability as deafness does, but with additional implications. The deaf-blind child must be taught specialized mobility skills. Print material must be reformatted into large print or Braille according to the student's level of functional vision.

Emotional disturbance impacts the child's perception of the world and those around him or her. This can result in communication difficulty, inappropriate behavior/language, and possibly physical aggression.

Hearing impairment, although not as severe as deafness, impacts vocabulary and language development, reading skills, and written language. Again, due to limited exposure to social language, behavior can be immature for the chronological age, and communication is difficult.

Learning disability can impact the understanding of spoken and written language. The ability to attend to a speaker or a task may be compromised. In addition, children with learning disabilities may demonstrate inconsistent abilities across subject areas. For example, a student may have a learning disability that affects only math and not the other subject areas.

Mental retardation is represented by delayed cognitive functioning and social skills. Students who are mentally impaired may function as children of a much younger age.

Multiple disabilities are more prevalent with the advancing treatment of premature babies and other newborns with medical conditions. A child with multiple disabilities may display any combination of disabilities and associated educational concerns. For example, a child may have an orthopedic impairment and be deaf; the child's language and communication skills would be affected by the deafness, while, at the same time, the child would likely require physical therapy and appropriate orthopedic equipment.

Orthopedic impairment involves the physical and neurological functioning of the body. A child with an orthopedic impairment may have difficulty with speech articulation, gross motor movements (such as walking or running), and fine motor movements (such as writing or tying shoes). In the case of cerebral palsy, a child may also experience processing delays.

Other health impairment means having limited strength, vitality, or alertness—including a heightened alertness to environmental stimuli—that results in limited alertness with respect to the educational environment, which: (i) is due to chronic or acute health problems such as asthma, attention deficit disorder, attention deficit hyperactivity disorder, diabetes, epilepsy, a heart condition, hemophilia, lead poisoning, leukemia, nephritis, rheumatic fever, sickle cell anemia, and Tourette syndrome; and (ii) adversely affects a child's educational performance.

Speech or language impairment refers to difficulty with pronouncing words (articulation) or communicating through oral language. The language component may be in expressive or receptive language and may, for example, involve forming sentences with appropriate syntax, understanding questions, or being able to comprehend the inferred meaning of a phrase or passage.

Traumatic brain injury refers to injury to the brain from an accident that results in physical impairment, speech and language difficulty, memory deficits, and/or physical disability.

Visual impairment, including blindness impacts a student's mobility and the use of print text. A student may need to have print material formatted in a larger font or typed into Braille. Because of the inability to see themselves or others, instruction may be needed in personal care and physical appearance.

Skill 1.03 **Recognizes the similarities and differences between individuals with and without disabilities in regard to growth and development.**

Please refer to Skill 1.01.

Skill 1.04 **Recognizes the roles families and environment play in the development and learning of individuals with and without disabilities.**

Please refer to Skill 11.08.

COMPETENCY 2.0   UNDERSTAND THE VARIOUS CHARACTERISTICS AND NEEDS OF STUDENTS WITH DISABILITIES

Skill 2.01   Demonstrates knowledge of types, etiologies, and characteristics of various disabilities.

THE CAUSATION AND PREVENTION OF A DISABILITY

No one knows exactly what causes various disabilities. There is a wide range of possibilities that make it almost impossible to pinpoint the exact cause. Listed below are some factors that can attribute to the development of a disability.

Problems in fetal brain development: During pregnancy, things can go wrong in the development of the brain, which alters how the neurons form or interconnect. Throughout pregnancy, brain development is vulnerable to disruptions. If the disruption occurs early, the fetus may die, or the infant may be born with widespread disabilities and possibly mental retardation. If the disruption occurs later, when the cells are becoming specialized and moving into place, it may leave errors in the cell makeup, location, or connections. Some scientists believe that these errors may later show up as learning disorders.

Genetic factors: Learning disabilities can run in families, demonstrating that there may be a genetic link. For example, children who do not have certain reading skills—such as hearing separate sounds of words—are likely to have a parent with a similar problem. A parent's learning disability can take a slightly different form in the child. Due to this, it is unlikely that specific learning disorders are directly inherited.

Environment: Additional reasons for why disabilities appear to run in families stem from the family environment. Parents with expressive language disorders may talk less to their children, or their language may be muffled. In this case, the lack of a proper role model for acquiring good language skills causes the disability.

Tobacco, alcohol, and other drug use: Many drugs taken by the mother pass directly to the fetus during pregnancy. Research shows that a mother's usage of cigarettes, alcohol, or other drugs during pregnancy may have damaging effects on the unborn child. Mothers who smoke during pregnancy are more likely to have smaller birth weight babies. Newborns who weigh less than 5 pounds are more at risk for learning disorders.

Heavy alcohol use during pregnancy has been linked to Fetal Alcohol Syndrome (FAS), a condition resulting in low birth weight, intellectual impairment, hyper-activity, and certain physical defects.

Problems during pregnancy or delivery: Complications during pregnancy can also cause learning disabilities. The mother's immune system can react to the fetus and attack it as if it were an infection. This type of problem appears to cause newly formed brain cells to settle in the wrong part of the brain. In addition, during delivery, the umbilical cord can become twisted and temporarily cut off oxygen to the fetus, resulting in impaired brain functions.

Toxins in the environment: New brain cells and neural networks are produced for a year after the child is born. These cells are vulnerable to certain disruptions. There are certain environmental toxins that may lead to learning disabilities. Cadmium and lead are becoming a leading focus of neurological research. Cadmium is used in making some steel products. It can get into the soil and therefore into the foods we eat. Lead was once common in paint and gasoline and is still present in some water pipes.

Children with cancer who have been treated with chemotherapy or radiation at an early age can also develop learning disabilities. This is very prevalent in children with brain tumors who received radiation to the skull.

In order to prevent disabilities from occurring, information on the causes of disabilities should be widely available so that parents can take the necessary steps to safeguard their children from conception up until the early years of life. While some of the causes of disability are unavoidable or incidental, there are many causes that can be prevented.

CHARACTERISTICS OF CHILDREN WITH EMOTIONAL DISABILITIES

Children with emotional disturbances or behavioral disorders are not always easy to identify. It is usually easy to identify the acting-out child who is constantly fighting, who cannot stay on task for more than a few minutes, or who shouts obscenities when angry. On the other hand, it is not always easy to identify the child who internalizes his or her problems, who may appear to be a "model" student but suffers from depression, shyness, or fears. Unless the problem becomes severe enough to impact school performance, the internalizing child may go for long periods of time without being identified or served.

Studies of children with behavioral and emotional disorders share some general characteristics:

Lower academic performance: While it is true that some emotionally disturbed children have above-average IQ scores, the majority are behind their peers in measures of intelligence and school achievement. Most score in the "slow learner" or "mildly mentally retarded" range on IQ tests, averaging about 90. Many have learning problems that exacerbate their acting out or "giving-up" behavior. As the child enters secondary school, the gap between the child and his or her nondisabled peers widens, often until the child may be as many as 2 to 4 years behind in reading and/or math skills in high school. Children with severe degrees of impairment may be difficult to evaluate.

Social skills deficits: Students with social skills deficits may be uncooperative, selfish in dealing with others, unaware of what to do in social situations, or ignorant of the consequences of their actions. This may be a combination of lack of prior training, lack of opportunities to interact, and dysfunctional value systems and beliefs learned from the family.

Classroom behaviors: Often, emotionally disturbed children display behavior that is highly disruptive to the classroom setting. Emotionally disturbed children may get out of their seats and run around the room; hit, fight, or disturb their classmates; steal or destroy property; or be otherwise defiant, noncompliant, and/or verbally disruptive. They may not follow directions and often do not complete assignments.

Aggressive behaviors: Aggressive children often fight or instigate their peers to strike back at them. Aggressiveness may also take the form of vandalism or destruction of property. Aggressive children also engage in verbal abuse.

Delinquency: As emotionally disturbed, acting-out children enter adolescence, they may become involved in socialized aggression (e.g., gang membership) and delinquency. Delinquency is a legal term, rather than a medical one; it describes truancy and actions that would be criminal if they were committed by adults. Not every delinquent is classified as emotionally disturbed, but children with behavioral and emotional disorders are especially at risk for becoming delinquent because of their problems at school (the primary place for socializing with peers), deficits in social skills that may make them unpopular at school, and/or dysfunctional homes.

Withdrawn behaviors: Children who manifest withdrawn behaviors may consistently act in an immature fashion or prefer to play with younger children. They may daydream or complain of being sick in order to "escape." They may also cry often, cling to the teacher, ignore those who attempt to interact, or suffer from fears or depression.

Schizophrenia and psychotic behaviors: Children may have bizarre delusions, hallucinations, incoherent thoughts, and disconnected thinking. Schizophrenia typically manifests itself between the ages of 15 and 45: the younger the onset, the more severe the disorder. These behaviors usually require intensive treatment beyond the scope of the regular classroom setting.

Gender: Many more boys than girls are identified as having emotional and behavioral problems, especially hyperactivity and attention deficit disorder, autism, childhood psychosis, and problems with under-control (e.g., aggression, socialized aggression). Girls, on the other hand, have more problems with over-control (e.g., withdrawal and phobias). Boys are much more prevalent than girls in problems with mental retardation and language and learning disabilities.

Age characteristics: When they enter adolescence, girls tend to experience affective or emotional disorders such as anorexia, depression, bulimia, and anxiety at twice the rate of boys, which mirrors the adult prevalence pattern.

Family characteristics: Having a child with an emotional or behavioral disorder does not automatically mean that the family is dysfunctional. However, there are family factors that create or contribute to the development of behavior disorders and emotional disturbance.

- Abuse and neglect
- Lack of appropriate supervision
- Lax, punitive, and/or lack of discipline
- High rates of negative types of interaction among family members
- Lack of parental concern and interest
- Negative adult role models
- Lack of proper health care and/or nutrition
- Disruption in the family

Identify children with mild learning, intellectual, and behavioral disabilities:
Some characteristics of students with mild learning and behavioral disabilities are as follows:

- Lack of interest in schoolwork
- Prefer concrete rather than abstract lessons
- Possess weak listening skills
- Low achievement; limited verbal and/or writing skills
- Respond better to active rather than passive learning tasks
- Have areas of talent or ability often overlooked by teachers
- Prefer to receive special help in regular classroom
- Higher dropout rate than regular education students
- Achieve in accordance with teacher expectations
- Require modification in classroom instruction and are easily distracted

Identify characteristics of students who have learning disabilities:

- Hyperactivity - a rate of motor activity higher than normal
- Perceptual difficulties - visual, auditory, and perceptual problems
- Perceptual-motor impairments - poor integration of visual and motor systems, often affecting fine motor coordination.
- Disorders of memory and thinking - memory deficits, trouble with problem-solving, poor concept formation and association, poor awareness of own metacognitive skills (learning strategies)
- Impulsiveness - acts before considering consequences and has poor impulse control, often followed by remorselessness.
- Academic problems in reading, math, writing or spelling, with significant discrepancies in ability levels

Identify characteristics of individuals with mental retardation or intellectual disabilities:

- IQ of 70 or below
- Limited cognitive ability and delayed academic achievement, particularly in language-related subjects
- Deficits in memory that often relate to poor initial perception, or an inability to apply stored information to relevant situations
- Impaired formulation of learning strategies
- Difficulty in attending to relevant aspects of stimuli - slowness in reaction time or in employing alternate strategies

Identify characteristics of individuals with autism: This exceptionality appears very early in childhood. Here are six common features of autism:

- **Apparent sensory deficit** -The child may appear not to see, hear, or react to a stimulus and may then react in an extreme fashion to a seemingly insignificant stimulus.
- **Severe affect isolation** - The child does not respond to the usual signs of affection, such as smiles and hugs.
- **Self-stimulation** - Stereotyped behavior takes the form of repeated or ritualistic actions that make no sense to others, such as hand flapping, rocking, staring at objects, or humming the same sounds for hours at a time.
- **Tantrums and self-injurious behavior (SIB)** - Autistic children may bite themselves, pull their hair, bang their heads, or hit themselves. They can throw severe tantrums or direct aggression and destructive behavior toward others.
- **Echolalia** - Also known as "parrot talk," the autistic child may repeat what is played on television or respond to others by repeating what was already said. Alternatively, he or she may simply not speak at all.
- **Severe deficits in behavior and self-care skills** - Autistic children may behave like children much younger than themselves.

Teachers of special education students should be aware of the similarities as well as the differences between areas of disabilities.

- Students with disabilities (in all areas) may demonstrate difficulties with social skills. For a student with hearing impairment, social skills may be difficult because of not hearing social language. However, the emotionally disturbed student may have difficulty because of a special type of psychological disturbance. An autistic student, as a third example, would be unaware of the social cues given with voice, facial expression, and body language. Each of these students would need social skill instruction, but in a different way.

- Students with disabilities (in all areas) may demonstrate difficulty in academic skills. A student with mental retardation will need special instruction across all areas of academics, while a student with a learning disability may need assistance in only one or two subject areas.

- Students with disabilities may demonstrate difficulty with independence or self-help skills. A student with a visual impairment may need specific mobility training, while a student with a specific learning disability may need a checklist to help in managing materials and assignments.

Special education teachers should be aware that although students across disabilities may demonstrate difficulties in similar ways, the causes may be very different. For example, some disabilities are due to specific sensory impairments (hearing or vision), some to cognitive ability (mental retardation), and some to neurological impairment (autism or some learning disabilities). The reason for the difficulty should be a consideration when planning the program of special education intervention.

Additionally, special education teachers should be aware that each area of disability has a range of involvement. Some students may have minimal disability and require no services. Others may need only a few accommodations and have 504 Plans. Some may need an IEP that outlines a specific special education program to be implemented in an inclusion/resource program, self-contained program, or in a residential setting.

A student with ADD may be able to participate in the regular education program with a 504 Plan that outlines a checklist system to keep the student organized and additional communication between school and home. Other students with ADD may need instruction in a smaller group with fewer distractions and would be better served in a resource room.

When planning an appropriate special education program, special educators should be knowledgeable of the cause and severity of the disability as well as its manifestations in the specific student. Because of the unique needs of the child, such programs are documented in the child's IEP.

Skill 2.02	Demonstrates knowledge of causes and effects of common medical conditions and health impairments affecting students with disabilities (e.g., diabetes, asthma, seizure).

In addition to having a disability that affects learning, students may also have medical conditions and other health impairments that effect the school day. These students may take medications that will cause side effects, impacting behavior and educational development. Teachers should be knowledgeable of these side effects to ensure they don't misperceive the child's behavior.

Some medications may impair concentration, which can lead to poor processing ability, lower alertness, and drowsiness and hyperactivity. Students who take several medications may have an increased risk of behavioral and cognitive side effects.

Students' parents should let the school know when they are beginning or changing medication so they can look out for possible side effects.

Antidepressants
There are three different classes of antidepressants that students can take.

One type is called the selective serotonin-reuptake inhibitors (SSRIs). The SSRIs block certain receptors from absorbing serotonin. Over time, SSRIs may cause changes in brain chemistry. The side effects of SSRIs include dry mouth, insomnia or restless sleep, increased sweating, and nausea. They can also cause mood swings in people with bipolar disorders.

A second type of antidepressants are the tricyclic antidepressants. They are considered good for treating depression and obsessive-compulsive behavior. They cause similar side effects to the SSRIs, such as sedation, tremor, seizures, dry mouth, light sensitivity, and mood swings in people with bipolar disorders.

A third type of antidepressants are the monoamine oxidase inhibitors (MAOIs). They are not as widely used as the other two types because many have unpleasant and life-threatening interactions with other drugs, including common over-the-counter medications. People taking MAOIs must also follow a special diet because these medications interact with many foods. The list of foods to avoid includes chocolate, aged cheeses, and more.

Stimulants

Stimulants are often prescribed to help with attention deficit disorder (ADD) and attention deficit hyperactivity disorder (ADHD). The drugs can have many side effects, including agitation, restlessness, aggressive behavior, dizziness, insomnia, headache, or tremors.

In severe cases of anxiety, an anti-anxiety medication (tranquilizer) may be prescribed. Most tranquilizers have a potential for addiction and abuse. They tend to be sedating and can cause a variety of unpleasant side effects, including blurred vision, confusion, sleepiness, and tremors.

WHAT EDUCATORS SHOULD KNOW

If educators are aware of the types of medication that their students are taking, along with the myriad of side effects, they will be able to respond more positively when some of the side effects of the medication change their students' behaviors, response rates, and attention spans.

Medical complications must be considered when developing schedules and curricular plans. Students may miss school due to medical conditions that require extensive rest or hospital-based intervention. Cooperative programs with home and hospital teachers can decrease the impact of such absences.

Also of considerable concern is the tendency to overcompensate. Teachers should try not to focus too much on the medical implications of a student's handicap. Interruptions for suctioning, medication, or other medical interventions should not be disruptive to the classroom and learning atmosphere. Focus should be on maximizing opportunities for educational success and social interaction, not on limitations and isolation. For example, class parties can include food treats that meet a student's dietary restrictions, or medical intervention can be completed during individual work times rather than during group learning activity periods.

Students with seizures will require considerable medical support. A seizure is an abnormal electrical discharge in the brain. Incidences and behaviors range from experiencing odd tastes or smells to jerking and spasms throughout the body. The individual may experience altered consciousness or the loss of consciousness, muscle control, or bladder control. Seizures may be triggered by repetitive sounds, flashing lights, video games, touching certain parts of the body, certain drugs, low sugar level, or low oxygen levels in the blood.

Asthma is another well-known condition found in students with and without disabilities. Asthma is a condition in which the person's airway becomes inflamed. The inflammation may cause coughing, wheezing, tightness of chest, and shortness of breath. The cause of asthma is not completely known, but research indicates that if children are exposed to tobacco smoke, infections, and some allergens early in life, it will increase their chances of developing asthma. Research also indicates there may be a family connection; in many cases, children who have asthma have other family members with this condition. Short-acting inhaled beta-agonists are the preferred quick-relief medicine. The most common side effects of beta-agonists inhalers are rapid heartbeat, headache, nervousness, and trembling.

Juvenile diabetes (type 1) is another condition that may affect students. Those with juvenile diabetes are typically under the age of 30. It is a condition in which the pancreas cannot produce insulin, or insulin is produced in extremely small amounts. People with type 1 need to take insulin injections in order to live. A student with diabetes should be allowed to eat snacks during the day, monitor blood sugar level, and take insulin shots.

Some students may also require tube feeding. Tube feeding is a method of providing nutrition to people who cannot sufficiently obtain calories by eating or to those who cannot eat because they have difficulty swallowing. Tubes that transport nutritional formulas can be inserted into the stomach (G tubes), through the nose and into the stomach (NG tubes), or through the nose and into the small intestine (NJ tubes). The NG and NJ tubes are considered to be temporary; the G tube is considered more permanent, but it can be removed. Tube feeding is common among students with dysphagia, a condition that hampers swallowing.

Other students may need to use catheters. A catheter is a thin, flexible, hollow plastic tube that can be used to perform various diagnostic and/or therapeutic procedures. They are designed to gain access to the body with as little trauma as possible.

Skill 2.03   Recognizes the educational implications of various types of disabilities (e.g., emotional/behavioral disorders, learning disabilities, physical disabilities).

Please refer to the common educational definitions of various disabilities used in Skill 1.01.

Skill 2.04 Demonstrates knowledge of transfers (e.g., floor to sitting, wheelchair to stander, chair to chair) and safe, appropriate procedures for transferring and positioning students with physical disabilities.

Rationale for Student Transfer

Students with physical disabilities range from those with mild impairments to those in wheelchairs. There are times that the physical transfer of a student is necessary. Common reasons for student transfer include the following:

- Movement to another chair, therapy table, or swing
- Assistance with toilet skills
- Transfer of student to bus seat
- Emergency evacuation of bus or school building

On rare occasions, students with visual impairments or other disabilities may need to be physically transported (e.g., emergency evacuations).

Additionally, any student may need to be transported if injured.

Safety Considerations in Student Transfer

When transferring a student, safety must always be the primary consideration. Proper training by a nurse or physical therapist ensures that this is done correctly.

Staff safety should also be a consideration. Again, proper training will address this issue. Staff may also be directed to wear a lifting and back belt. It is crucial that a special educator or other staff member not attempt to lift someone who is heavier than he or she can easily handle.

General Positioning for Student Transfer

In general, the legs should be bent in preparation to lift. The back should be straight, and the weight of the person to be carried should be close to the body. The lifting movement should be from the legs—not the back.

Respect for Student Dignity

The personal dignity of the special needs student should be considered in all transfers and transports.

Common Methods of Student Transfer

- **Single person transport** is a means of lifting the student over the shoulder and carrying him or her.

- **The seat-carry method** can be used if two people are moving a student from one point to another (not just transferring from a wheelchair to a toilet or another chair). In this method, each of the individuals places an arm behind the back and one under the thighs of the student being transported. With their hands clasping at the wrists, a type of seat is formed.

- **Transfer to another seat** can be accomplished by giving support under the arm pits with the adult's forearms while the student places his or her arms around the adult's neck.

COMPETENCY 3.0 UNDERSTAND FACTORS AFFECTING LEARNING AND DEVELOPMENT OF STUDENTS WITH DISABILITIES

Skill 3.01 Demonstrate knowledge of the effects (e.g., on education, career, vocation, recreation) of various disabilities on learning and behavior throughout an individual's lifespan.

Deaf-Blindness

The loss of vision and hearing cause more challenges when combined than individually.

Deaf-blindness impacts motor skills, such as the ability to walk and move. It also impacts communication skills, including the ability to request things and to let others know feelings or expressions of displeasure. It also effects general development, such as the possibility of low muscle tone and development.

Deaf-blindness impacts sensory information access. Taste, touch, and smell are impacted, since people can only taste what they put in their mouths, touch only as far as they can reach, and smell things only when the odor reaches the nose.

The access to information for learning can also be impacted, as information is not learned incidentally. Information is learned through direct one-on-one instruction. The information received through distance senses can vary; for some, vision and hearing are progressively lost, while for others, it is a life-long disability.

Motivation to interact with the environment can be reduced due to the effect of vision and hearing loss. This will impact the individual throughout his or her life and career choices and may make the individual more solitary (although he or she will need help and support to function effectively in society).

Impaired vision and hearing interfere with the individual's ability to understand and respond to the communication and movement of others in the environment.

The impact on recreation is also very high, as many sporting activities require the use of sight (although there are numerous sporting events in which individuals with low vision can safely participate). When choosing a career, individuals with deaf-blindness have a limited number of professions they can go into, as their disabilities impact their abilities to see and communicate.

Attention Deficit Disorder

A person with ADD or ADHD is at an increased risk of having brain malfunctions that can lead to lack of insight and foresight, lack of fear and remorse, impulsivity, poor abstract thinking and social skills, low anger threshold, an inability to realize the consequences of actions or to learn from experience, and a lack of empathy for animals and people.

ADD has a clear impact on the learning and behavior of individuals throughout life. In the school setting, ADD can render an individual unable to pay attention to details, or give him or her a tendency to make careless errors in school or other activities. The individual may also have difficulty sustaining attention in task or play activities. This will impact individuals in school and when they get jobs, as they may not be able to focus on tasks and complete them satisfactorily. They have problems following instructions and problems with organization. Individuals with ADD have a tendency to lose things like homework, keys, or work assignments. They are also distractible and can be very forgetful.

About half of all children with ADHD also have a specific **learning disability**. The most common learning problems are reading dyslexia and difficulty with handwriting. Although ADHD isn't categorized as a learning disability, its interference with concentration and attention can make it even more difficult for a child to perform well in school.

Autism

Individuals with autism are affected by their symptoms every day; this sets them apart from unaffected students. Because of problems with receptive language, they can have problems understanding some classroom directions and instruction, along with subtle vocal and facial cues from teachers. This inability to fully decipher the world around them often makes education stressful. Teachers need to be aware of a student's disorder and should ideally have specific training in autism education. This will enable them to better help the student get the best out of his or her classroom experiences.

Individuals with autism spectrum disorders sometimes have high levels of anxiety and stress, particularly in social environments like school and work. If an individual shows aggressive or explosive behavior, it is important for educational teams to recognize the impact of stress and anxiety.

Skill 3.02   Recognizes the impact of physical and health-related disabilities on individuals, their families, and society.

Children with physical impairments possess a variety of disabling conditions. Although there are significant differences among these conditions, similarities also exist. Each condition usually affects one particular system of the body: the cardiopulmonary system (i.e., blood vessels, heart, and lungs), the neurological system (i.e., spinal cord, brain nerves), or the musculoskeletal system (i.e., muscles, bones). Some conditions develop during pregnancy, birth, or infancy. Other conditions occur later due to injury (trauma), disease, or factors not fully understood.

In addition to motor disorders, individuals with physical disabilities may have multi-disabling conditions, such as concomitant hearing impairments, visual impairments, perceptual disorders, speech defects, behavior disorders, mental handicaps, or difficulties with performance and emotional responsiveness.

Some characteristics of individuals with physical disabilities and other health impairments include the following:

1. Lack of physical stamina; fatigue
2. Chronic illness; poor endurance
3. Deficient motor skills; normal movement may be prevented
4. Physical limitations or impeded motor development; a prosthesis or an orthosis may be required.
5. Limited mobility or inability to explore one's environment
6. Limited self-care abilities
7. Progressive weakening and degeneration of muscles
8. Frequent speech and language defects; communication may be prevented; echolatia orthosis may be present
9. May experience pain and discomfort throughout the body
10. May display emotional (psychological) problems, which require treatment
11. Social adjustments may be needed; may display maladaptive social behavior
12. May necessitate long-term medical treatment, which can become a financial burden on the family
13. May have embarrassing side effects from certain diseases or treatment
14. May exhibit erratic or poor attendance patterns, which leads to the child missing many skills and the parent or caregiver to miss days of work

Related Technology

Technology has helped individuals with physical and health impairments to gain access to and control of the environments around them, to communicate with others, and to take advantage of health care. In addition to high-tech devices such as computers, there are low-tech devices like built-up spoons and crutches. Computers, spell checkers, and automated language boards provide means for communication to occur.

Mobility has been assisted by use of lightweight or electric specialized wheelchairs. These include motorized chairs, computerized chairs, chairs in which it is possible to rise, wilderness sports chairs, and racing chairs (Smith & Luckasson, 1992). Electronic switches allow persons with only partial movement (e.g., head, neck, fingers, toes) to be more mobile. Even driving a car is possible.

Mobility is also enhanced by the use of artificial limbs, personalized equipped vans, and electrical walking machines. Myoelectric (or bionic) limbs contain a sensor that picks up electric signals transmitted from the person's brain through the limb. Robotic arms can manipulate objects by at least three directional movements: extension/retraction, swinging/rotating, and elevation/depression. Manipulator robots can assist by dialing a telephone, turning book pages, and drinking from a cup.

Skill 3.03 **Demonstrate familiarity with the uses and possible effects of various types of medications (e.g., stimulant, antidepressant, seizure) in relation to students' learning, development, and functioning.**

Please refer to Skill 2.02.

Skill 3.04 **Demonstrate knowledge of the effects of cultural, linguistic, and socioeconomic differences on learning and development and strategies for addressing such differences.**

Different cultures place varying values on education and the role of genders. As a result, different views may be taken regarding individuals with disabilities, as well as their appropriate education, career goals, and roles in society. Special educators must become familiar with the cultural representations of their students and the communities in which they teach. Educators who demonstrate respect for different students' cultures will build the rapport necessary to work with the student, family, and community to prepare him or her for future, productive work, independence, and possible postsecondary education or training (IDEA 2004).

While society has progressed, and many things are more acceptable today than they were years ago, having a disability still carries a stigma. Historically, people with disabilities have been ostracized from their communities. Up until the 1970s, a large number of people with special needs were institutionalized at birth because relatives either did not know what to do, felt embarrassed to admit they had a child with a disability, or gave into the cultural peer pressure to put their "problem" away. Sometimes, this meant hiding a child's disability, which may even have meant locking a child in a room in the house. Perhaps the worst viewpoint of society, largely expressed up to the 1970s and still prevalent in some cultures today, is that the person with "special needs" is unable to contribute to society.

Today American society has eliminated the "must institutionalize" method in favor of a "normalize" concept. Houses in local communities have been purchased for the purpose of providing supervision and/or nursing care that allows for people with disabilities to have "normal" social living arrangements. Congress passed laws that have allowed those with disabilities to access public facilities. American society has widened doorways, added special bathrooms, and undergone other useful physical transformations. The regular education classroom teacher is now learning to accept and teach students with special needs. America's media today has provided education and frequent exposure of people with special needs. The concept of acceptance appears to be occurring for those with physically noticeable handicaps.

However, the appearance of those with special needs in media (such as television and movies) are generally those who rise above their "label" as disabled because of an extraordinary skill. Most people in the community are portrayed as accepting the "disabled" person when that special skill is noted. In addition, those who continue to express revulsion or prejudice towards the person with a disability often express remorse when the special skill is noted or when peer pressure becomes too intense. This portrayal often ignores those who appear normal by appearance with learning and emotional disabilities, who often feel and suffer from the same prejudices.

The most significant group any individual faces is that of his or her peers. Pressure to appear normal and not "needy" in any area is still intense from early childhood to adulthood. During teen years, when young people are beginning to express their individuality, the very appearance of walking into a special education classroom can bring feelings of inadequacy, as well as labeling by peers that the student is "special." Being considered normal is the desire of almost all individuals with disabilities, regardless of the age or disability. People with disabilities today, as many years ago, still measure their successes by how their achievements mask or hide their disabilities.

The most difficult cultural/community outlook on those who are disabled comes in the adult work world, where disabilities of persons can become highly evident—often causing those with special needs to have difficulties in finding work and keeping their jobs. This is particularly difficult for those who have not learned to self-advocate or accommodate for their area/s of special needs.

Skill 3.05 Recognize the impact of language development and listening comprehension on students' learning.

Please refer to the Language Development and Behavior section of Skill 1.01.

Skill 3.06 Recognize the impact of various disabilities on auditory and information-processing skills and on expressive language skills.

Language development begins from the moment of birth. Children develop receptive language (their ability to understand language) skills first. Students can typically understand things well above their age level. When something interferes with that naturally developing skill, many different things are impacted beyond the language skill itself. Children often become frustrated because they misunderstood someone, or they may complete an activity inappropriately. This may then lead to a correction, which the student does not understand. Imagine being told to go close your closet door, and when you do, someone corrects you and tells you it was wrong. All you know is that you were told to close your closet door: that's what you understood. It becomes a very frustrating experience for both the child and adult.

Additionally, receptive language skills develop to include the ability to process and follow more than one direction at a time. Some students with deficits are unable to do this task. They need directions broken down into one step at a time in order to be successful. Sometimes these misunderstandings lead to behavioral issues, which can usually be solved through improving the receptive language skills of the child, by using different vocabulary, or by using less oral language when communicating with the student.

After receptive language develops, expressive language (oral language) begins. Difficulties here can be just as frustrating for the student. These students are trying their best to communicate and get their points across, but no one seems able to understand what they are saying. Sometimes this is due to an articulation issue—a problem in the way words are pronounced. Other times it is due to the fact that they are unable to put their feelings or thoughts into the appropriate words.

We have all been at the loss to recall a word. Phrases like "it's on the tip of my tongue" have become clichés because it is an occurrence that afflicts everyone once in awhile. For children with expressive language difficulties, it happens much more frequently. Behaviorally, they can become irritated and angry simply because no one understands what they are trying to communicate.

Both expressive and receptive language are integral parts of the learning process. Numerous research studies have been completed, indicating that lecture is still the most used method of delivering information in classrooms. If a child struggles with language, this method is not going to work well for them. In fact, it will probably be one of the least effective methods. Furthermore, in the continuum of learning any skill—from reading to math or science to social studies—the basis for all learning begins with language.

Skill 3.07 **Demonstrate knowledge of the effects of different learning environments, classroom management strategies, and intervention techniques on students' development and learning.**

REVIEW OF STUDENT NEEDS WITH INCLUSION TEACHER AND SUPPORT STAFF

It may be determined at a student's IEP meeting that some time in the general education setting is appropriate. The activities and classes listed for inclusion may be field trips, lunch, recess, physical education, music, library, art, computers, math, science, social studies, spelling, reading, and/or English. The IEP will specify which classes and activities, as well as the amount of time that the student will spend with general education peers. The IEP will also list any modifications or accommodations that will be needed.

Modifications that may be considered for the general education classroom include the amount of work or type of task required. Modifications for a student with a learning disability might include a reduced number of spelling words or a task of writing the vocabulary word that goes with a given definition instead of writing the definition that goes with a given word.

Accommodations are changes made to the school environment or a student's use of necessary equipment to overcome a disability. For example, an accommodation for a student with a hearing impairment might include the use of an auditory trainer or another student to serve as a notetaker.

Prior to the student starting in a general education placement (regardless of the minutes on the IEP), the general education teacher and support staff (if any) should be in-serviced on the student's disability and his or her needs according to the IEP. Sometimes this inservicing happens as the student's IEP is developed. Other times it is done at a later date.

Student expectations in the inclusion setting:

The student with a disability should be well aware of his or her responsibilities in the general education setting ahead of time. These expectations should be a combination of behavior and task performance. Although students should be aware of needed accommodations and modifications, and should be self-advocates for such, they should not use their disabilities as excuses for not fulfilling the expectations.

Students may benefit from previewing material, using a checklist to keep track of materials and assignments, keeping an assignment notebook, reviewing materials after the lesson, and using study aids such as flashcards. Sometimes, a behavior tracking chart may also be used.

Monitoring student progress in the inclusion setting:

Once the student is in the general education setting for the time and activities listed on the IEP, the special education teacher will need to monitor student progress. This can be done through verbal follow-up with the general education teacher or by asking the teacher to complete a progress form periodically. Of course, grades and the student's ability to restate learned information or answer questions are also indicators.

Evaluation of the student's future placement in the inclusion setting:

If the student is successful in the general education activities and classes listed on the IEP, the special education teacher may consider easing back on modifications and accommodations on the next IEP. He or she may also consider adding minutes or classes for student's general education inclusion.

If the student has difficulty in the general education activities and classes, the special educator may consider adding more modifications or accommodations on the next IEP. If the student had significant difficulty, he or she may need to receive more services in the special education classroom.

SELF-ADVOCACY

Learning about one's self involves the identification of learning styles, strengths and weakness, interests, and preferences. For students with mild disabilities, developing an awareness of the accommodations they need will help them ask for necessary accommodations on a job and in postsecondary education. Students can also help identify alternative ways they can learn.

Self-advocacy involves the ability to effectively communicate one's own rights, needs, and desires, and to take responsibility for making decisions that impact one's life.

There are many elements in developing self-advocacy skills in students who are involved in the transition process. Helping the student to identify future goals or desired outcomes in transition planning areas is a good place to start. Self-knowledge is critical for the student in determining the direction that transition planning will take.

The role of the teacher in promoting self-advocacy should include encouraging the student to participate in the IEP process, as well as other key parts of his or her educational development. Self-advocacy issues and lessons are effective when they are incorporated into the student's daily life. Teachers should listen to the student's problems and ask the student for input on possible changes that he or she may need. The teacher should talk with the student about possible solutions, discussing the pros and cons of doing something. A student who self-advocates should feel supported and encouraged. Good self-advocates know how to ask questions and get help from other people. They do not let other people do everything for them.

Students need to practice newly acquired self-advocacy skills. Teachers should have students role play various situations, such as setting up a class schedule, moving out of the home, or asking for accommodations needed for a course.

The impact of transition planning on a student with a disability is very great. The student should be an active member of the transition team, as well as the focus of all activities. Students often think that being passive and relying on others to take care of them is the way to get things done. Students should be encouraged to express their opinions throughout the transition process. They need to learn how to express themselves so that others listen and take them seriously. These skills should be practiced within a supportive and caring environment.

Effective classroom management strategies can impact the learning environment for students with disabilities. There are a number of strategies that can be used to foster an environment for learning.

- Expect the best from all students in the classroom. The positive relationship between high teacher expectations and high student behavior has been demonstrated as an effective classroom management technique. Teachers who expect the best from students and are able to communicate these expectations will receive respect and cooperation from their students. This is the first step to reducing behavior problems.

- Make the behavior expectations clear by spelling out exactly what the rules of the class are at the beginning of the school year in a positive manner. Give examples of a student following the rule and a student not following the rule, so that everyone is clear how the rule is to be carried out. It is a good practice to include the students in the rule-making process, as this will give them ownership of the rules and will make them more likely to follow them.

- Have plenty of rewards in place with minimal punishments. Discipline problems can arise when educators overuse punishment. The use of rewards is a better system of ensuring good behavior, as a reward brings attention to good behaviors and provides models for all students.

- Ensure that any punishment given fits the crime or rule that was broken. If several students were misbehaving, it would not be appropriate to punish the entire class. This approach will anger the students who are not misbehaving and may even cause additional problems. If there is no natural punishment to fit the student's misbehavior, an alternative would be to remove privileges, such as extra computer time, from the student who misbehaves.

- Be consistent with rewards and punishments. If rules and consequences are not done consistently, discipline problems will occur. Teachers should also make sure they get to know each student well so they can modify the punishments and rewards based on the individual student's likes and dislikes. A punishment to one student may be a reward to another.

DOMAIN II.   ASSESSING STUDENTS AND DEVELOPING PROGRAMS

COMPETENCY 4.0   UNDERSTAND TYPES AND CHARACTERISTICS OF VARIOUS ASSESSMENTS

Skill 4.01   Recognize basic concepts and terminology used in assessment (e.g., reliability, validity, basal, ceiling).

RECOGNIZING BASIC CONCEPTS AND TERMINOLOGY USED IN ASSESSMENT

The following terms are frequently used in behavioral as well as academic testing and assessment. They represent basic terminology and not more advanced statistical concepts.

Baseline: This is also known as establishing a baseline. This procedure means collecting data about a target behavior or performance of a skill before certain interventions or teaching procedures are implemented. Establishing a baseline will enable a person to determine if the interventions are effective.

Criterion-referenced test: This is a test in which the individual's performance is measured against mastery of curriculum criteria rather than comparison to the performance of other students. Criterion-referenced tests may be commercially or teacher made. Since these tests measure what a student can or cannot do, results are especially useful for identifying goals and objectives for IEPs and lesson plans.

Curriculum-based assessment: This is an assessment of an individual's performance of objectives of a curriculum, such as a reading or math program. The individual's performance is measured in terms of what objectives were mastered.

Duration recording: This measures the length of time a behavior (e.g., tantrums, time out of class, or crying) lasts.

Error analysis: The mistakes on an individual's test are noted and categorized by type. For example, an error analysis in a reading test could categorize mistakes by miscues, substituting words, omitted words or phrases, and miscues that are self corrected.

Event recording: The number of times a target behavior occurs during an observation period.

Formal assessment: Standardized tests that have specific procedures for administration, norming, scoring, and interpretation. These include intelligence and achievement tests.

Frequency: The number of times a behavior (e.g., out-of-seat behavior, hitting, or temper tantrums) occurs in a time interval.

Frequency distribution: This plotts the scores received on a test and tallies how many individuals received those scores. A frequency distribution is used to visually determine how the group of individuals performed on a test, illustrate extreme scores, and compare the distribution to the mean or other criterion.

Informal assessment: These are nonstandardized tests such as criterion referenced tests and teacher-prepared tests. There are no rigid rules or procedures for administration or scoring.

Intensity: This is the degree of a behavior as measured by its frequency and duration.

Interval recording: This technique involves breaking the observation into an equal number of time intervals, such as 10-second intervals during a 5-minute period. At the end of each interval, the observer notes the presence or absence of the target behavior. The observer can then calculate a percentage by dividing the number of intervals in which the target behavior occurred by the total number of intervals in the observation period. This type of recording works well for behaviors that occur with high frequency or for long periods of time (e.g., on- or off-task behavior, pencil tapping, or stereotyped behaviors). The observer does not have to constantly monitor the student; he or she can simply gather enough data to get an accurate idea of the extent of the behavior.

Latency: This is thee length of time that elapses between the presentation of a stimulus (e.g., a question) and the response (e.g., the student's answer).

Mean: This is thee arithmetic average of a set of scores, calculated by adding the set of scores and dividing the sum by the number of scores. For example, if the sum of a set of 35 scores is 2935, dividing that sum by 35 (the number of scores) yields a mean of 83.9.

Median: This is the middle score. Fifty percent of the scores are above this number and 50 percent of the scores are below this number. In the example above, if the middle score were 72, 17 students would have scored less than 72 and 17 students would have scored more than 72.

Mode: This is the score most frequently tallied in a frequency distribution. In the example above, the most frequently tallied score might be 78. It is possible for a set of scores to have more than one mode.

Momentary time sampling: This is a technique used for measuring behaviors of a group of individuals or several behaviors from the same individual. Time samples are usually brief and may be conducted at fixed or variable intervals. The advantage of using variable intervals is increased reliability, as the students will not be able to predict when the time sample will be taken.

Multiple baseline design: This may be used to test the effectiveness of an intervention in a skill performance, or to determine if the intervention accounted for the observed changes in a target behavior. First, the initial baseline data is collected, followed by the data during the intervention period. To get the second baseline, the intervention is removed for a period of time and data is collected again. The intervention is then reapplied, and data is collected on the target behavior. An example of a multiple baseline design might be ignoring a child who calls out in class without raising his or her hand. Initially, the baseline could involve counting the number of times the child calls out before applying interventions. During the time the teacher ignores the child's call-outs, data is collected. For the second baseline, the teacher would resume the response to the child's call-outs in the way he or she did before ignoring. The child's call-outs would probably increase again if ignoring actually accounted for the decrease. If the teacher reapplies the ignoring strategy, the child's call-outs would probably decrease again.

Multiple baseline designs may also be used with single-subject experiments where the following may occur:

- The same behavior is measured for several students at the same time. An example would be observing off-task or out-of-seat behavior among three students in a classroom.
- Several behaviors may be measured for one student. The teacher may be observing call-outs, off-task, and out-of-seat behavior for a particular child during an observation period.
- Several settings are observed to see if the same behaviors are occurring across settings. A student's aggressive behavior toward his or her classmates may be observed at recess, in class, going to or from class, or in the cafeteria.

Norm-referenced test: An individual's performance is compared to the group that was used to calculate the performance standards in this standardized test. Some examples are the CTBS, WISC-R, and Stanford-Binet.

Operational definition: This is the description of a behavior and its measurable components. In behavioral observations, the description must be specific and measurable so that the observer will know exactly what constitutes instances and noninstances of the target behavior. Otherwise, reliability may be inaccurate.

Pinpoint: This specifies and describes the target behavior for change in measurable and precise terms. "On time for class" may be interpreted as arriving physically in the classroom when the tardy bell has finished ringing, it may mean being at the pencil sharpener, or it may mean being in one's in seat and ready to begin work when the bell has finished ringing. Pinpointing the behavior makes it possible to accurately measure the behavior.

Profile: This is the plotting of an individual's behavioral data on a graph.

Rate: This is the frequency of a behavior over a specified time period, such as 5 talk-outs during a 30-minute period, or typing 85 words per minute.

Raw score: This is the number of correct responses on a test before they have been converted to standard scores. Raw scores are not meaningful because they have no basis of comparison to the performance of other individuals.

Reliability: This is the consistency (stability) of a test over time to measure what it is supposed to measure. Reliability is commonly measured in four ways:

- **Test-retest method:** The test is administered to the same group or individual after a short period of time and the results are compared.
- **Alternate form (equivalent form):** This measures reliability by using alternative forms to measure the same skills. If both forms are administered to the same group within a relatively short period of time, there should be a high correlation between the two sets of scores if the test has a high degree of reliability.
- **Interrater:** This refers to the degree of agreement between two or more individuals observing the same behaviors or observing the same tests.
- **Internal reliability:** This is determined by statistical procedures or by correlating half of the test with the other half of the test.

Standard deviation: The standard deviation is a statistical measure of the variability of the scores. The more closely the scores are clustered around the mean, the smaller the standard deviation will be.

Standard error of measurement: This statistic measures the amount of possible error in a score. If the standard error of measurement for a test is + or - 3, and the individual's score is 35, then, the actual score may be 32 to 35.

Standard score: This is a derived score with a set mean (usually 100) and a standard deviation. Examples are T-scores (mean of 50 and a standard deviation of 10), Z-scores (mean of 0 and standard deviation of 1), and scaled scores. Scaled scores may be given for age groups or grade levels. IQ scores, for instance, use a mean of 100 and a standard deviation of 15.

Task analysis: This breaks an academic or behavioral task down into its sequence of steps. Task analysis is necessary when preparing criterion-referenced tests and performing error analysis. A task analysis for a student learning to do laundry might include the following:

1. Sort the clothes by type (white, permanent press, delicate).
2. Choose a type and select the correct water temperature and setting.
3. If doing a partial load, adjust the water level.
4. Measure the detergent.
5. Turn on the machine.
6. Load the clothes.
7. Add bleach, fabric softener at the correct time.
8. Wait for the machine to stop spinning completely before opening it.
9. Remove the clothes from the machine and place in a dryer (a task analysis could be done for drying and folding, as well).

Validity: This is the degree to which a test measures what it claims to measure, such as reading readiness, self-concept, or math achievement. A test may be highly reliable, but it will be useless if it is not valid. There are several types of validity to examine when selecting or constructing an assessment instrument.

- ***Content:*** This type of validity examines the question of whether the types of tasks in the test measure the skill or construct the test claims to measure. That is, a test, which claims to measure mastery in algebra would probably not be valid if the majority of the items involved basic operations with fractions and decimals.
- ***Criterion-referenced validity:*** This involves comparing the test results with a valid criterion. For example, a doctoral student preparing a test to measure reading and spelling skills may check the test against an established test such as the WRAT-T or another valid criterion such as school grades.
- ***Predictive validity:*** This refers to how well a test will relate to a future criterion level, such as the ability of a reading test administered to a first-grader to predict that student's performance at third or fifth grade.
- ***Concurrent validity:*** This refers to how well the test relates to a criterion measure given at the same time. For example, a new test that measures reading achievement may be given to a group, which will then also take the WRAR-R (which has established validity). The test results are compared using statistical measures. The recommended coefficient is 80 or better.
- ***Construct validity:*** This refers to the ability of the test to measure a theoretical construct, such as intelligence, self-concept, and other nonobservable behaviors. Factor analysis and correlation studies with other instruments that measure the same construct are ways to determine construct validity.

Skill 4.02 Recognize the uses and limitations of various formal and informal assessments.

Formal assessments include standardized criterion, norm-referenced instruments, and commercially prepared inventories, which are developmentally appropriate for students across the spectrum of disabilities. Criterion-referenced tests compare a student's performance to a previously established criterion rather than to other students from a normative sample. Norm-referenced tests use normative data, including performance norms by age, gender, or ethnic group, for scoring.

Informal assessment strategies include nonstandardized instruments, such as checklists, developmental rating scales, observations, error analysis, interviews, teacher reports, and performance-based assessments that are developmentally appropriate for students across disabilities. Informal evaluation strategies rely upon the knowledge and judgment of the professional and are an integral part of the evaluation. Advantages of using informal assessments are the ease of design and administration, as well as the usefulness of information the teacher can gain about the student's strength and weaknesses.

Some instruments can be both formal and informal tools. For example, observation may incorporate structured observation instruments as well as other informal observation procedures, including professional judgment. When evaluating a child's developmental level, a professional may use a formal adaptive rating scale while simultaneously using professional judgment to assess the child's motivation and behavior during the evaluation process.

Limitations of Assessments

Achievement tests are instruments that directly assess students' skill development in academic content areas. This type of test measures the extent to which a student has profited from educational and/or life experiences compared to others of like ages or grade levels. Emphasis needs to be placed upon the kinds of behaviors each test samples, the adequacy of its norms, the test reliability, and its validity.

An achievement test may be classified as a diagnostic test if strengths and weaknesses in skill development can be delineated. Typically, when used as a diagnostic tool, an achievement test measures one basic skill and its related components. For example, a reading test may measure reading recognition, reading comprehension, reading fluency, decoding skills, and sound discrimination. Each skill measured is reported in sub-classifications.

In order to render pertinent information, achievement tests must reflect the content of the curriculum. Some achievement tests assess skill development in many subject areas, while others focus upon single content areas. Within similar content areas, the particular skills assessed and how they are measured differ from test to test. The more prominent areas assessed by achievement tests include math, reading, and spelling.

Achievement test usages include screening, placement, progress evaluation, and curricula effectiveness. As screening tests, these instruments provide a wide index of academic skill development and may be used to pinpoint students for whom educational interventions may be necessary for purposes of remediation or enrichment. They offer a general idea of where to begin additional diagnostic assessment.

Placement decisions in special education include significant progress, or lack thereof, in academic achievement. It is essential that data from individually administered achievement tests allow the examiner to observe quantitative (i.e., scores) performance as well as to denote specific strengths and weaknesses inherent in qualitative (e.g., attitude, motivation, problem-solving) performance. Knowing how an individual reacts or produces answers during a testing situation is equally relevant to measured skill levels when making placement decisions.

Achievement tests are routinely given in school districts across the nation as a means of evaluating progress. Scores of students can be compared locally, statewide, and with national norms. Accountability and quality controls can be kept in check through the reporting of scores.

Achievement tests may be norm-referenced or criterion-referenced and administered individually or within groups. Results of norm-referenced achievements tests (e.g., Peabody Individualized Achievement Test (PIAT), Wide Range Achievement Test (WRAT)), considered important in making comparisons, may not provide information needed for individual program planning, types of behavior tests, sub-skill data, or types of scores reported. Criterion-referenced achievement tests (e.g., KeyMath Diagnostic Arithmetic Test, Brigance Diagnostic Inventories) contain items that correspond with stated objectives, thus enabling identification of cognitive deficiencies. Knowledge of specific skill deficits is needed for developing individualized education plans.

Teachers can be provided with measures showing the effectiveness of their instruction. Progress reflected by student scores should be used to review, and often revise, instructional techniques and content. Alternative methods of delivery (e.g., presentations, worksheets, tests) can be devised to enhance the instruction provided to students.

Skill 4.03 Demonstrate knowledge of specific assessment instruments used to evaluate students with disabilities.

Four testing methods are used to measure the achievement of students with disabilities for the purpose of determining whether they and their schools have made annual yearly progress. The testing methods are regular assessment, regular assessment with accommodations, alternate assessment judged against grade-level achievement standards, and alternate assessment judged against alternate achievement standards.

The assessment program in the state of Georgia includes customized criterion-referenced tests at the elementary, middle, and high school levels; the National Assessment of Educational Progress in grades 4, 8 and 12; and a norm-referenced test at grades 3, 5, and 8. These mandatory state assessments include the Criterion-Referenced Competency Tests (CRCT), End-of-Course Tests (EOCT), Georgia High School Graduation Tests (GHSGT), Georgia Writing Assessments (above) as well as Georgia Alternate Assessment (GAA), Georgia Kindergarten Assessment Program – Revised (GKAP-R), National Assessment of Educational Progress (NAEP), Norm-Referenced Test (Iowa Tests of Basic Skills), and ACCESS for ELLs Lexile Framework for Reading.

The GAA is a primary element of the Georgia Student Assessment Program. Under the No Child Left Behind Act (NCLB) and the Individuals with Disabilities Education Act (IDEA), states must make sure that all students, including students with significant cognitive disabilities, have access to a general curriculum that includes challenging academic standards. States must also make sure that all students are assessed for their progress toward meeting academic standards.

Beginning in the fall of 2006, a portfolio of student work samples will be used to capture student learning and achievement/progress in the four content areas (English/Language Arts, Mathematics, Science, and Social Studies). The GAA portfolio entries will be scored for four discrete dimensions: fidelity to standard, context, achievement/progress, and generalization. A separate score will be issued for each dimension.

The student's achievement is documented in two collection periods during a school year. The first collection period will give evidence of a student's entry-level performance, while the second collection period will give documentation of a student's progress to date.

Skill 4.04 **Demonstrate knowledge of how to collaborate with parents/guardians, classroom teachers, related service providers, and others to gather background information on students' academic, medical, and family history.**

STRATEGIES FOR COLLABORATING WITH FAMILIES AND OTHER PROFESSIONALS IN THE ASSESSMENT PROCESS

The assessment process is an essential part of developing an individualized program for students. The needs of the whole child must be considered in order to address all the needs of each child. Therefore, information should be gathered by using various sources of information.

Besides the general education teacher, a vital person or persons in the assessment process should be the parent. The parent can provide needed background information on the child, such as a brief medical, physical, and developmental history. Paraprofessionals, doctors, and other professionals are also very helpful in providing necessary information about the child.

The following are ways of gathering information:

Interview: Interviews can be in person or on paper. The related parties can be invited to a meeting to conduct the interview; if the parent does not respond after several attempts, the paper interview may be sent or mailed home.

Questionnaires: Questionnaires are also a good way of gathering information. Some questionnaires may have open-ended questions, and some may have several questions that are to be answered using a rating scale. The answerer is to circle ratings ranging from 1 to 5, or 1 to 7 (Strongly Disagree to Strongly Agree).

Conference/meeting: With parents' permission, it may be useful to conduct a meeting—either one-on-one or in a group setting—to gather information about the child. Everyone who may be able to offer any information about the child and his or her academic progress, physical development, social skills, behavior, medical history, and/or needs should be invited to attend.

HOW TO GATHER BACKGROUND INFORMATION REGARDING ACADEMIC, MEDICAL, AND FAMILY HISTORY; COLLABORATE WITH PARENTS/ GUARDIANS AND WITH OTHER PROFESSIONALS TO CONDUCT ASSESSMENTS AND EVALUATIONS; DOCUMENT ONGOING STUDENT ASSESSMENT; AND MAINTAIN ACCURATE RECORDS

Relevant background information regarding the student's academic, medical, and family history should be used to identify students with disabilities and evaluate their progress.

An evaluation report should include the summary of a comprehensive diagnostic interview by a qualified evaluator. A combination of candidate self-report interviews—with families and others—and historical documentation, such as transcripts and standardized test scores, is recommended.

The evaluator should use professional judgment as to which areas are relevant in determining a student's eligibility for accommodations due to disabilities. In order to properly identify students with disabilities and evaluate their progress, the evaluator should include background information regarding academic, medical, cultural, and family history. The evaluation should include a developmental history; relevant medical history, including the absence of a medical basis for the present symptoms; academic history, including results of prior standardized testing; reports of classroom performance; relevant family history, including primary language of the home and the candidate's current level of fluency of English; relevant psychosocial history; a discussion of dual diagnosis, alternative or co-existing mood, behavioral, neurological, and/or personality disorders along with any history of relevant medication use that may affect the individual's learning; and exploration of possible alternatives that may mimic a learning disability.

By utilizing all possible background information in the assessment, the evaluator can rule out alternative explanations for academic problems (such as poor education, poor motivation and study skills, emotional problems, or cultural and language differences). If the student's entire background and history is not taken into account, it is not always possible to institute the most appropriate educational program for the student with disabilities.

COMPETENCY 5.0 UNDERSTAND PROCEDURES FOR CONDUCTING ASSESSMENT ACTIVITIES TO ADDRESS THE INDIVIDUAL NEEDS OF STUDENTS WITH DISABILITIES

Skill 5.01 Demonstrate knowledge of screening, pre-referral, referral, and classification procedures, including procedures for early identification of young children who may be at risk for disabilities.

The following information maybe helpful to familiarize a new educator with common procedures. State specific information about these procedures can be found at http://public.doe.k12.ga.us/index.aspx.

Referral
Referral is the process through which a teacher, parent, or some other person formally requests an evaluation of a student to determine eligibility for special education services. The decision to refer a student may be influenced by: (1) student characteristics, such as the abilities, behaviors, or skills that students exhibit (or lack of them); (2) individual differences among teachers in their beliefs, expectations, or skill in dealing with specific kinds of problems; (3) expectations for assistance with a student who is exhibiting academic or behavioral learning problems; (4) availability of specific kinds of strategies and materials; (5) parents' demand for referral or opposition to referral; and (6) institutional factors that may facilitate or constrain teachers in making referral decisions. Fewer students are referred when school districts have complex procedures for referral, psychological assessments are backlogged for months, special education classes are filled to capacity, or principals and other administrators do not fully recognize the importance of special services.

It is important that referral procedures be clearly understood and coordinated among all school personnel. All educators need to be able to identify characteristics typically exhibited by special needs students.

The student suspected of having a disability is referred to a multidisciplinary team. This multidisciplinary committee is charged with determining if a student is in need of any special education services. Members of this committee generally include all school members involved in the education of the student; the school psychologist, a special educator, parents, or outside agencies that may be involved with the student; and sometimes the student themselves. This committee also, if appropriate, develops and reviews the Individual Education Program (IEP). From the initial referral, schools districts have 60 calendar days to complete an individual evaluation and then an additional 30 calendar days to complete an eligibility meeting. Reevaluations occur every 3 years, with annual updates to the IEP occurring in between, as well.

Evaluation

The evaluation is comprehensive and includes norm- and criterion-referenced tests (e.g., IQ and diagnostic tests), curriculum-based assessment, systematic teacher observation (e.g., behavior frequency checklist), samples of student work, and parent interviews. The results of the evaluation are twofold: to determined eligibility for special education services and to identify a student's strengths and weaknesses in order to plan an individual education program.

The wording in federal law is very explicit about the manner in which evaluations must be conducted and about the existence of due process procedures that protect against bias and discrimination. Provisions in the law include the following:

1. The testing of children in their native or primary language unless it is clearly not feasible to do so.
2. The use of evaluation procedures selected and administered to prevent cultural or ethnic discrimination.
3. The use of assessment tools validated for the purpose for which they are being used (e.g., achievement levels, IQ scores, adaptive skills).
4. Assessment by a multidisciplinary team utilizing several pieces of information to formulate a placement decision.

Eligibility

Eligibility is based on criteria defined in federal law or state regulations, which vary from state to state. Evaluation methods correspond with eligibility criteria for the special education classifications. For example, a multidisciplinary evaluation for a student being evaluated for intellectual disabilities would include the individual's intellectual functioning, adaptive behavior, and achievement levels. Other tests are based on developmental characteristics exhibited (e.g., social, language, and motor).

A student evaluated for learning disabilities is given reading, math, and/or spelling achievement tests; an intelligence test to confirm average or above average cognitive capabilities; and tests of written and oral language abilities. Tests generally need to show a discrepancy between potential and performance (although new federal guidelines have indicated that the qualifications for learning disabilities may also consider a response to intervention models). Classroom observations and samples of student work (such as impaired reading ability or impaired writing ability) also provide indicators of possible learning disabilities.

The tests used during the evaluation process are typically representative of all academic, cognitive, social, physical, and behavioral functioning. Additional tests may be added or deleted throughout the process alongside the child's response to previously administered assessments.

If considered eligible for special education services, the child's disability should be documented in a written report stating specific reasons for the decision. A CSE meeting to discuss the results should be held, at which time the parent and other professionals must be a part. The status of the child's eligibility will be determined during this meeting. The team will discuss the results of the evaluation and make a determination as to whether or not special education services are warranted. Among students for whom it is warranted, an IEP will be written and services will begin. For students who do not need services, this will be the end of the process, unless new information arises in the future.

If the child qualifies, 3-year re-evaluations of the student's progress are required by law. These serve the purpose of determining the growth and changing needs of the student. During the re-evaluation, continued eligibility for services in special education must be assessed using a range of evaluation tools similar to those used during the initial evaluation. All relevant information about the student is considered when making a decision about continued eligibility, or when the student no longer needs the service and is ready to begin preparing to exit the program.

Skill 5.02 **Demonstrate knowledge of how to develop, select, adapt, and modify assessment instruments and strategies for students with diverse characteristics and needs (e.g., related to culture, language, nature and severity of disabilities, communication, and response modes).**

The term "multicultural" incorporates the idea that all students—regardless of gender, social class, and ethnic, racial, or cultural characteristics—should have an equal opportunity (Banks and Banks 1993). This is as true in the evaluation of students as it is in assuring fairness at the work site.

The issue of fair assessment for individuals from minority groups has a long history in law, philosophy, and education. Slavia and Ysseldyke (1995) point out three aspects of this issue that are particularly relevant to the assessment of students:

Representation
Individuals from diverse backgrounds need to be represented in assessment materials. It is essential that persons from different cultures be represented fairly. Of equal importance is the presentation of individuals from differing genders in nonstereotypical roles and situations.

Acculturation

It is important that individuals from different backgrounds receive opportunities to acquire the tested skills, information, and values. When students are tested with standardization instruments, they are compared to a set of norms in order to gain an index of their relative standing and to make comparisons. We assume that the students we test are similar to those on whom the test was standardized. That is, we assume that their acculturation is comparable. Acculturation is a matter of educational, socioeconomic, and experiential background rather than gender, skin color, race, or ethnic background. When it is said that a child's acculturation differs from that of the group used as a norm, what is really meant is that the experiential background differed, not simply that the child is of a different ethnic origin (Slavia & Ysseldyke, 1991). Differences in experiential background should therefore be accounted for when administering tests.

Language

The language and concepts that comprise test items should be unbiased. Students should be familiar with terminology and references when they are administered tests, especially when the results of the tests are going to be used for decision-making purposes. Many tests given in regular grades relate to decisions about promotion and grouping of students for instructional purposes. Tests and other assessment instruments that relate to special education are generally concerned with two types of decisions: eligibility and program planning for individualized education.

When selecting a test, many factors are considered; perhaps the most important consideration is the purpose for testing. The teacher may be screening a large group of students to determine which students would benefit from further assessment of skills; performing a progress check; diagnosing capabilities or deficiencies; evaluating special placement qualifications or benefits from special programs following a pre-determined period; or determining mastery on criterion objectives. The decision to use a criterion-referenced rather than a norm-referenced test, an informal versus a formal type of test, or an individual rather than a group-administered test may be decided based upon one's reason for testing. Scope and content, as well as the form in which scores are reported, are related to purpose and should be given primary consideration.

Additional evaluative criteria might include the following:

1. **Limitations.** Are there special limitations (e.g., hearing, sight, and physical) present? Are there test norms covering these limitations, or will special adaptations or accommodations be necessary? If norm-referenced measures are used, are the student's characteristics and acculturation similar to those with whom the test was normed? Is the test age or grade appropriate?

2. **Number.** Is individual testing required, or will an entire class or small group of students be tested at one time?

3. **Training.** Has the teacher been fully trained to administer the test, or does the test require administration, scoring, and interpretation of results by a person trained in another specialty area (e.g., speech pathologist, school psychologist)?

4. **Presentation-response modes.** How are the test items presented to the student (e.g., attending to figures, watching demonstrations, reading)? Likewise, what method of response is required of the student? Will enough information be provided by student responses (e.g., pointing to the correct answer, writing the answer on a form) to determine capability versus chance factors?

5. **Format.** Depending on the types of questions-responses selected, what format does the teacher want to use? For example, if written answers are desired for written queries, will true-false, multiple choice, or essay type questions be used?

6. **Time.** Are there specific and required time constraints, or can testing be flexible and open-ended?

7. **Cost.** Is the cost of the test and supplementary materials reasonable in relation to desired results? Are the test items current and sufficiently matched to the curriculum to be worth the investment? How expensive will it be to replace consumable items (e.g., test booklets, answer forms)?

8. **Physical facility.** Are the physical attributes of the room, such as lighting, ventilation, sound reduction, and well-fitting, comfortable furniture, conducive to good testing?

9. **Space considerations.** Is there adequate space for administering the test to a group of students? Does the amount of available room allow for proper spacing of test takers? If one student is to be tested, can suitable provisions be made for any other students for whom the teacher is responsible during that period? (Teachers should never be required to administer an individual test for program or placement purposes while attempting to supervise other students. This invalidates the test results.)

10. **Professional resources.** A teacher may use descriptive materials provided by publishing companies (e.g., test manuals, catalogues) in his or her selection process. However, prior to making final decisions, the teacher should investigate professional reference sources for specific information about potential tests. Has the test user reviewed the *Standards for Educational and Psychological Tests*, a resource cooperatively prepared by the American Psychological Association, the American Educational Research Association, and the National Council on Measurement in Education? Is the teacher familiar with the data compiled by the Buros Institute of Mental Measurements in their publications *Tests in Print* and *Mental Measurement Yearbooks*? Is he or she aware of the computerized data-based serviced offered by this institute?

Skill 5.03 **Demonstrate knowledge of how to administer nonbiased formal and informal assessments, including assessments of students from culturally and linguistically diverse backgrounds.**

Students from culturally and linguistically diverse backgrounds are over-represented in special education programs. Research has been conducted that suggests that the reasons for these over representations is due to a bias against children from different backgrounds as well as a bias against students who come from low-income families. The style and emphasis of the school may be different from those found in the cultures of students who are racially diverse. Because culture and language affect learning and behaviors, the school system may misinterpret what students know, how they behave, and how they learn. Students from diverse backgrounds may also appear less competent than they actually are due to language difficulties.

When assessing students from diverse backgrounds, educators must make sure they test the student in their native language and use culturally sensitive assessment material.

Before performing any formal testing of a student who is a nonnative speaker of English, it is important to determine the student's preferred language and to conduct a comprehensive language assessment in both English and the native language. It is highly inappropriate to evaluate students in English when that is not their dominant language unless the reason for the testing is to assess the student's English language proficiency. The IDEA states that tests and other evaluation materials must be provided and administered in the child's primary language or mode of communication unless it is clearly not feasible to do so. If possible, the evaluator in any testing situation or interview should be familiar to the child and speak the child's language.

When tests or evaluation materials are not available in the student's native language, examiners may find it necessary to use English-language instruments. Because this is a practice fraught with the possibility of misinterpretation, examiners need to be cautious in how they administer the test and interpret results. Alterations may need to be made to the standardized procedures used to administer tests; these can include paraphrasing instructions, providing a demonstration of how test tasks are to be performed, reading test items to the student rather than having him or her read them, allowing the student to respond verbally rather than in writing, or allowing the student to use a dictionary.

IDEA requires that a variety of assessment tools and strategies be utilized when conducting assessments. Before utilizing a formal or informal tool, the practitioner should make sure that the tool is the most appropriate one that can be used for that particular population group. Many assessment tools can be used across disabilities. Dependent upon the disability in question (such as blindness, autism, or hearing impaired), some assessment tools will give more information than others.

Group Tests and Individual Tests

The obvious distinction between a group test and an individual test is that individual tests must be administered to only one person at a time, whereas group tests are administered to several people simultaneously (although they can be administered individually, as well). However, there are several other subtle differences.

When administering an individual test, the tester has the opportunity to observe the individual's responses and to determine how such things as problem solving are accomplished. Within limits, the tester is able to control the pace and tempo of the testing session and to rephrase and probe responses in order to elicit the individual's best performance.

If the child becomes tired, the examiner can break between subtests or end the test; if the child loses his or her place, the tester can help the child to regain it. Likewise, if the child dawdles or loses interest, the tester can encourage or redirect him or her. If the child lacks self-confidence, the examiner can reinforce his or her efforts. In short, individual tests allow the examiner to encourage best efforts and to observe how a student uses his or her skills to answer questions. Thus, individual tests provide for the gathering of both quantitative and qualitative information.

In a group test, the examiner may provide oral directions for younger children, but beyond the fourth grade, directions are usually written. The children write or mark their own responses, and the examiner monitors the progress of several students at the same time. The examiner cannot rephrase questions, or probe or prompt responses. Even when a group test is administered to only one child, qualitative information is very difficult, if not impossible, to obtain.

The choice between group and individual testing should be primarily determined by purpose and efficiency. When testing for program evaluation, screening, and some types of program planning (such as tracking), group tests are appropriate. Individual tests could be used but are impractical in terms of time and expense.

When planning individual programs, individual tests should be used. When a student is being evaluated for placement in a special education program, all areas related to the suspected disability must be assessed. Individual tests should be administered when there is a reason to question the validity of results of group tests, or when an in-depth evaluation of the test taker's performance is needed.

Special consideration may need to be given a particular student who possesses limitations that make a group test inappropriate. Most group tests require that test takers be able to read and select graphic responses (e.g., marking or writing). If a student cannot read the instructions or content (e.g., a math reasoning test), or is unable to perform the type of response required, the test results are then reflecting measured inability to read or write rather than skill or ability in the area of the test content. Children with learning disabilities or physical impediments may know the answers but be unable to deliver them orally.

Skill 5.04 **Demonstrate knowledge of environmental factors (e.g., lighting, noise) that can affect the assessment of students with disabilities.**

The use of appropriate furniture when taking the test can impact the student with disabilities. Dependent upon the nature of the disability, the size of the desk, the shape of the desk and/or chair, and the heights and slopes of the chair/desk can impact the student's ability to concentrate, sit comfortably, or focus on the exam.

Another environmental factor deals with having adequate space for equipment and specific personnel to assist the student. Students who are wheelchair-bound or who require specialized equipment need to have adequate space in the testing area to accommodate their equipment and any additional staff.

Noise can also be a factor that impacts assessments. There is noise created when using equipment such as computers, audio devices, and other assistive technology; these could distract the students or other students in the testing area. A separate examination venue may have to be set aside to ensure that students have sufficient quiet to concentrate. Additional steps may need to be taken to ensure that the least distractive assistive technology is utilized during testing situations to eliminate noise distractions. Flexible time arrangements can be set to prevent overloading the student. A separate examination venue can be set up if students are distracted by other student's movements or noise.

Lighting is another environmental factor that can impact students with disabilities. This is especially important for students with low vision and vision difficulties. The elimination of glare can be very important to students with low vision.

Low vision students are normally print users, and they may need special equipment and materials. The student's vision may fluctuate or may be influenced by factors such as inappropriate lighting, light glare, or fatigue. These factors must be addressed in the testing environment.

Skill 5.05   Demonstrate knowledge of how to use ecological assessments, portfolio assessments, individualized inventories, task analyses, and functional assessments (e.g., behavioral, social, communication) to accommodate the unique strengths and needs of students with disabilities.

Ecological Assessments

Ecological assessments entail assessing students in real-life contexts. This involves comparing the performance of a student with disabilities with a student who does not have disabilities. These assessments can assist teachers in identifying the student's needs. Teachers use discrepancies between the performance of a student with disabilities and that of a student without disabilities as a point of reference for identifying potential instruction and support strategies.

There are numerous types of ecological assessments. These include the following:

1. **Authentic assessment:** A demonstration of a skill or behavior in a real-life context.
2. **Curriculum-vased assessment:** A broad approach of linking assessment to instruction.
3. **Dynamic assessment:** A technique in which the assessor actively engages the student in learning. Interactions between the evaluator and the student reflect upon the world of the student by focusing and feeding back environmental experiences in a manner that produces appropriate learning habits.
4. **Performance assessment:** A demonstration of the behavior that has been outlined by the assessor.
5. **Product assessment:** An analysis of the product of the student's performance.
6. **Portfolio assessment:** A collection of the product of a student's play and work that showcases the student's efforts, progress, and achievements.

Portfolio Assessment

The use of student portfolios for some aspect of assessment has become quite common. The purpose, nature, and policies of portfolio assessment vary greatly from one setting to another. In general, a student's portfolio contains samples of work collected over an extended period of time. The nature of the subject, age of the student, and scope of the portfolio all contribute to the specific mechanics of analyzing, synthesizing, and otherwise evaluating the portfolio contents.

In most cases, the student and teacher make joint decisions as to which work samples go into student portfolios. A collection of work compiled over an extended time period allows teachers, students, and parents to view the student's progress from a unique perspective. Qualitative changes over time can be readily apparent from work samples. Such changes are difficult to establish with strictly quantitative records typical of the scores recorded in the teacher's grade book.

Task Analysis

A teacher can use the set of behavioral specifications that are the result of a task as an analysis to prepare tests to measure the student's ability to meet those specifications. These tests are referred to as "criterion measurements." If task analysis identifies which skills will be needed to perform a task successfully, then the criterion measurements will further identify whether the student possesses the necessary skills or knowledge for that task. The level of performance that is acceptable is the "criterion level."

Criterion measurements must be developed along certain guidelines if they are to accurately measure a task and its sub-skills. Johnson and Morasky (1977) give the following guidelines for establishing criterion measurement:

1. Criterion measurement must directly evaluate a student's ability to perform a task.
2. Criterion measurements should cover the range of possible situations in order to be considered an adequate measure.
3. Criterion measurements should measure whether or not a student can perform the task without additional or outside assistance. They should not give any information that the student is expected to possess.
4. Criterion measurement requires that all responses should be relevant to the task being measured.

Behavioral objectives offer descriptive statements defining the task that the student will perform, state the conditions under which the task will occur, and show the criterion measurement required for mastery. The criterion measurement is the process for evaluating what the student can do. For the instruction to be meaningful, there must be a precise correspondence between the capabilities determined in a criterion measurement and the behavioral demands of the objective.

Functional Assessments

A functional behavioral assessment is a procedure that tries to identify the problem behaviors a student may show in school, to determine the function or purpose of the behaviors, and to develop interventions to teach satisfactory alternatives to the behaviors. The first step in carrying out a functional behavioral assessment is for the school team to identify and agree upon the primary behavior that needs to be changed. The next step is to gather data on the occurrence of the target behavior, identifying frequency, intensity, and where, when, and how the behavior takes place. The third step is to develop a hypothesis about the function or purpose of the student's behavior and to develop an intervention. The last step is to evaluate the effectiveness of the proposed intervention.

Functional assessments have been utilized for students with severe disabilities, to help parents and teachers understand the function of inappropriate behavior, and to plan effective interventions. Functional assessments are also a helpful approach to evaluating the reason for inappropriate behaviors for students who have milder disabilities, especially when their behaviors do not improve with the use of typical school interventions.

COMPETENCY 6.0 UNDERSTAND HOW TO INTERPRET AND COMMUNICATE ASSESSMENT RESULTS

Skill 6.01 Applies knowledge of how to interpret the results of formal and informal assessments and recommend appropriate services and interventions based upon those results.

Each child receiving special education services are to be placed in the least restrictive environment. The placement of the student depends on his or her current functioning level. The student's current functioning level is determined by formal and informal assessments (see definitions below). Assessment information will help determine the child's least restrictive environment and give key information to assist with accommodation decisions.

Placement
Placement of the student could be in a wide range of settings, but the best location for the child is as close as possible to full-time in the general education class, while still providing for the student's weaknesses. (See the cascade of services, also called continuum of services, below.)

Cascade System of Special Education Services

Level 1 Regular classroom, including students with disabilities able to learn with regular class accommodations, with or without medical and counseling services

Level 2 Regular classroom with supportive services (e.g., consultation, inclusion)

Level 3 Regular class with part-time special class (e.g., itinerant services, resource room)

Level 4 Full-time special class (e.g., self-contained)

Level 5 Special stations (e.g., special schools)

Level 6 Homebound

Level 7 Residential (e.g., hospital, institution)

Adapted from 1. Deno. 1970. "Special Education as Developmental Capital." *Exceptional Children.* 37, 239, 237. Copyright 1970 by the Council for Exceptional Children, Reprinted with permission from the Council for Exceptional Children.

The law defines special education and identifies related services that may be required if special education is to be effective. By law, placement in a special education delivery service must be the student's least restrictive environment. Many factors determine least restrictive environment. Assessment has a large weighing on the child's least restrictive environment. If the child functions on a first-grade level in reading, it would be hard for that student to be successful in a fifth-grade class without accommodations and interventions. Through the assessment information, work samples, and input from parents and support service personnel, the child's least restrictive environment will be decided.

Formal and Informal Assessments

Results of formal assessments are given in derived scores, which compare the student's raw score to the performance of a specified group of subjects. Criteria for the selection of the group may be based on characteristics such as age, sex, or geographic area. The test results of formal assessments must always be interpreted in light of what type of tasks the individual was required to perform.

These are the most commonly used derived scores:

A. Age and grade equivalents

These scores are considered developmental scores because they attempt to convert the student's raw score into an average performance of a particular age or grade group.

Age equivalents are expressed in years and months (e.g., 7-3). In the standardization procedure, a mean is calculated for all individuals of the particular age who took the test. If the mean or median number of correct responses for children 7 years and 3 months was 80, then an individual whose raw score was 80 would be assigned an age-equivalent of 7 years and 3 months.

Grade equivalents are written as years and tenths of years (e.g., 6.2 would read sixth grade, second month). Grade equivalents are calculated on the average performance of the group. They have been criticized for their use to measure gains in academic achievement and to identify exceptional students.

Quartiles, deciles, and percentiles indicate the percentage of scores that fall below the individual's raw score. Quartiles divide the score into four equal parts; the first quartile is the point at which 25 percent of the scores fall below the full score. Deciles divide the distribution into ten equal parts; the seventh decile would mark the point below which 70 percent of the scores fall. Percentiles are the most frequently used. A percentile rank of 45 would indicate that the person's raw score was at the point below which 45 percent of the other scores fell.

B. Standard scores

These are raw scores with the same mean (average) and standard deviation (variability of asset of scores). In the standardization of a test, about 68 percent of the scores will fall above or below 1 standard deviation of the mean of 100. About 96 percent of the scores will fall within the range of 2 standard deviations above or below the mean. A standard deviation of 20, for example, will mean that 68 percent of the scores will fall between 80 and 120, with 100 as the mean. The most common are T scores, Z scores, stanines, and scaled scores. Standard scores are useful because they allow for direct comparison of raw scores from different individuals. In interpreting scores, it is important to note what type of standard score is being used.

C. Criterion referenced tests and curriculum-based assessments

These are interpreted on the basis of the individual's performance on the objectives being measured. Such assessments may be commercially prepared or teacher-made and can be designed for a particular curriculum or a scope and sequence. These assessments are made by selecting objectives, task analyzing those objectives, and selecting measures to test the skills necessary to meet those tasks. Results are calculated for each objective; for example, Cindy was able to divide 2-digit numbers by 1-digit numbers 85 percent of the time and was able to divide 2-digit numbers by 2-digit numbers 45 percent of the time.

These tests are useful for gaining insight into the types of error patterns the student makes. Because the student's performance is not compared to others in a group, results are useful for writing IEPs as well as deciding what to teach.

Possible Accommodations

Modifying materials is a great accommodation to use in order to include students in the general education classroom. Materials, usually textbooks, are usually modified because of reading level. The goal of modification is to present the material in manner that the student can better understand while preserving the basic ideas and content. Modifications of course material may take the form of the following:

Simplifying texts

1. Use a highlighter to mark key terms, main ideas, and concepts. In some cases, a marker may be used to delete nonessential content.
2. Cut and paste—the main ideas and specific content are cut and pasted on separate sheets of paper. Additional headings or other graphic aids can be inserted to help the student understand and organize material.
3. Supplement text with graphic aids or tables.
4. Supplement text with study guides, questions, and directed preview.
5. Use self-correcting materials.
6. Allow additional time or break content material into smaller, more manageable units.

Taped textbooks

Textbooks can be taped by the teacher or aide for students to follow along. In some cases, the students may qualify for recordings of textbooks from agencies such as Recordings for the Blind.

Parallel curriculum

Projects such as Parallel Alternative Curriculum (PAC) or Parallel Alternative Strategies for Students (PASS) present the content at a lower-grade reading level and come with tests, study guides, vocabulary activities, and tests.

Supplementary texts

Book publishers, such as Steck-Vaughn, publish series of content-area texts that have been modified for reading level, amount of content presented on pages, highlighted key items, and visual aids.

ACCOMMODATIONS IN TEST-TAKING SITUATIONS

Test taking is not a pleasant experience for many students with behavioral and/or learning problems. They may lack study skills, may experience anxiety before or during a test, or may have problems understanding and differentiating the task requirements for different tests. The skills necessary to be successful vary with the type of test. Certain students have difficulty with writing answers but may be able to express their knowledge of subject matter verbally. Therefore, modifications of content area material may be extended to methods and modifications for evaluation and assessment of student progress.

Some of the ways that teachers can modify assessment for individual needs include the following:

- Help students to get used to timed tests with timed practice tests.
- Provide study guides before tests.
- Make tests easier to read by leaving ample space between the questions.
- Modify multiple choice tests by reducing the number of choices, reforming questions to yes-no, or using matching items.
- Modify short-answer tests with cloze (fill-in) statements, or provide a list of facts or choices that the student can choose from.
- Essay tests can be modified by using partial outlines for the student to complete, allowing additional time, or testing items that do not require extensive writing.

Skill 6.02 **Applies knowledge of strategies for communicating assessment results to all stakeholders (e.g., students with disabilities, their parents/guardians, general education teachers, administrators, service providers).**

ABILITY TO INTERPRET TEST RESULTS INTO LAYMAN'S TERMS

The special educator must be able to communicate assessment results into understandable language for a variety of individuals. These individuals may include parents or guardians, paraprofessionals, professionals in general education, administration, and (in the case of older students) even the student him or herself.

A review of assessment and evaluation results may be done during an IEP meeting in which the formal test lingo is used but paired with an interpretation in layman's terms. Results may also be done in the form of a written report.

ABILITY TO REPRESENT TEST RESULTS AND EDUCATIONAL IMPLICATIONS IN WRITTEN FORMAT

Although the school psychologist often completes student evaluations and writes a report, this may be the task of the special educator when assessment is done in the classroom in preparation for the student's annual review. In this case, the special education teacher will be asked to write a report summarizing assessment findings and educational implications. The teacher should be able to organize the data in a concise, readable format. Some components of such a report include the following:

- Identifying information (student name, age, date of birth, address, gender)
- Reason for assessment
- Test administration information (date, time, duration of test, response of student)
- Test results
- Summary of educational recommendations

Skill 6.03   Demonstrates knowledge of how to use formal and informal assessments to evaluate the effectiveness of instruction and monitor students' ongoing progress.

Please refer to Skill 4.02 for various formal and informal assessments.

Assessment skills should be an integral part of teacher training, where teachers are able to monitor student learning using pre- and postassessments of content areas; analyzing assessment data in terms of individualized support for students and instructional practice for teachers; and designing lesson plans that have measurable outcomes and definitive learning standards. Assessment information should be used to provide performance-based criteria and academic expectations for all students in evaluating whether students have learned the expected skills and content of the subject area.

For example, in an Algebra I class, teachers can use assessments to see whether students have learned the knowledge necessary to engage in the subject area. If the teacher provides students with a preassessment on algebraic expression and ascertains whether the lesson plan should be modified to include a pre-algebraic expression lesson unit to refresh student understanding of the content area, then the teacher can create, if needed, quantifiable data to support the need of additional resources to support student learning. Once the teacher has taught the unit on algebraic expression, a postassessment test can be used to test student learning and a mastery exam can be used to test how well students understand and can apply the knowledge to the next unit of math content learning.

Teachers can use assessment data to inform and impact instructional practices by making inferences on teaching methods and gathering clues for student performance. By analyzing the various types of assessments, teachers can gather more definitive information on projected student academic performance. Instructional strategies for teachers provide learning targets for student behavior, cognitive thinking skills, and processing skills that can be employed to diversify student learning opportunities.

"Learning styles" refer to the ways in which individuals learn best. Physical settings, instructional arrangements, materials available, techniques, and individual preferences are all factors in the teacher's choice of instructional strategies and materials. Information about the student's preference can be done through a direct interview or a Likert-style checklist wherein the student rates his or her preferences.

The assessment information gathered from various sources is key to identify the strengths and the weaknesses of the student. Each test and each person will have something to offer about the child, therefore increasing the possibility of creating a well-developed plan to assist in the success of the student. The special education and general education teacher, along with other professionals, will use the assessment data to make appropriate instructional decisions and to modify the learning environment so that it is conducive to learning.

The information gathered can be used to make some of the following instructional decisions:

I **Classroom organization:** The teacher can vary grouping arrangements (e.g., large group, small group, peer tutoring, or learning centers) and methods of instruction (teacher directed, student directed).

II **Classroom management:** The teacher can vary grading systems, vary reinforcement systems, and vary the rules (differentiated for some students).

III **Methods of presentation/variation of methods included:**
   A. *Content*: amount to be learned, time to learn, and concept level
   B. *General structure*: advance organizers, immediate feedback, memory devices, and active involvement of students.
   C. *Type of presentation*: verbal or written, transparencies, audiovisual

IV **Methods of practice:**
   A. *General structure*: amount to be practiced, time to finish, group, individual or teacher-directed, and varied level of difficulty
   B. *Level of response*: copying, recognition, or recall with and without cues
   C. *Types of materials*: worksheets, audiovisual, texts

V **Methods of testing:**
   A *Type*: verbal, written, or demonstration
   B. *General structure*: time to complete, amount to complete, group or individual testing
   C. *Level of response*: multiple choice, essay, recall of facts

Instructional Decisions

Subject matter should be presented in a fashion that helps students **organize**, **understand,** and **remember** important information. Advance organizers and other instructional devices can help students:

- Connect information to what is already known
- Make abstract ideas more concrete
- Capture students' interest in the material
- Help students to organize the information and visualize the relationships

Organizers can be visual aids like diagrams, tables, charts, guides, or verbal cues that alert students to the nature and content of the lesson. Organizers may be used:

- **Before the lesson** to alert the student to the main point of the lesson, establish a rationale for learning, and activate background information
- **During the lesson** to help students organize information, keep focused on important points, and aid comprehension
- **At the close of the lesson** to summarize and remember important points

Examples of organizers include:

- *Question- and graphic-oriented study guides*
- *Concept diagramming*: Students brainstorm a concept and organize information into three lists (always present, sometimes present, and never present).
- *Semantic feature analysis*: Students construct a table with examples of the concept in one column and important features or characteristics in the opposite column.
- *Semantic webbing*: The concept is placed in the middle of the chart or chalkboard, and relevant information is placed around it. Lines show the relationships.
- *Memory (mnemonic) devices such as diagrams, charts, and tables*.

Instructional modifications should be tried in an attempt to accommodate the student in the regular classroom. Effective instruction is geared toward individual needs and recognizes differences in how students learn. Modifications are tailored to individual student needs. Some strategies for modifying regular classroom instruction shown in the following table are effective with at-risk students with disabilities and students without learning or behavior problems.

Strategies for Modifying Classroom Instruction

Strategy 1   Provide active learning experiences to teach concepts. Student motivation is increased when students can manipulate, weigh, measure, read, or write using materials and skills that relate to their daily lives.

Strategy 2   Provide ample opportunities for guided practice of new skills. Frequent feedback on performance is essential to overcome student feelings of inadequacy. Peer tutoring and cooperative projects provide nonthreatening practice opportunities. Individual student conferences, curriculum-based tests, and small group discussions are three useful methods for checking progress.

Strategy 3   Provide multisensory learning experiences. Students with learning problems sometimes have sensory processing difficulties; for instance, an auditory discrimination problem may cause misunderstanding about teacher expectations. Lessons and directions that include visual, auditory, tactile, and kinesthetic modes are preferable to a single sensory approach.

Strategy 4   Present information in a manner that is relevant to the student. Particular attention to this strategy is needed when there is a cultural or economic gap between the lives of teachers and students. Relate instruction to a youngster's daily experience and interests.

Strategy 5   Provide students with concrete illustrations of their progress. Students with learning problems need frequent reinforcement for their efforts. Charts, graphs, and check sheets provide tangible markers of student achievement.

Skill 6.04 **Applies strategies for recommending modifications and accommodations to curriculum, based upon assessment results**

Please refer to Skill 3.07.

COMPETENCY 7.0   **UNDERSTAND PROCEDURES FOR DEVELOPING, IMPLEMENTING, AND AMENDING INDIVIDUALIZED EDUCATION PROGRAMS (IEPS), INDIVIDUALIZED FAMILY SERVICE PLANS (IFSPS), AND TRANSITION PLANS**

Skill 7.01   **Demonstrates knowledge of the continuum of placement and services available for students with disabilities.**

Please refer to the cascade of student services located in skill 6.01 for state-specific placement and services, or to the Georgia Department of Education Web site http://public.doe.k12.ga.us/index.aspx.

Skill 7.02   **Applies knowledge of how to use assessment information to make appropriate eligibility, program, and placement recommendations for students with disabilities, including those from culturally and linguistically diverse backgrounds.**

Certainly a child with a disability may come from a culturally diverse background. Although special education placement is not made because of a delay due to cultural diversity, if both a disability and a language difference exist, both should be considered when making placement and planning programming. In some instances, an ESL or ELL teacher may be a part of the IEP team and may provide consultation or direct instruction to the special education teacher.

Language Considerations

If the special education student does not speak English as his or her native language, or if English is not used primarily by the family, language consideration will be important in the classroom. Key words and concepts will need to presented in a parallel fashion (in both languages, first explaining in the student's native tongue and then in English).

Classroom Assessments

Not only will the student's needs regarding his or her disability be considered when making assignments and giving tests, his or her language will need to be considered, as well. It is important that the student be tested on his or her knowledge of the subject and not the ability to communicate in English. For example, assessment of a child's understanding of the water cycle may be evaluated by asking the student to draw the sequence and verbally explain it instead of writing a paragraph on the same.

Skill 7.03 **Recognizes strategies for collaborating with students and their families in developing and monitoring progress toward instructional, behavioral, social, career, and independent living goals.**

Involving the special education student (when appropriate) and his or her family in setting instructional goals is necessary to develop a well-rounded IEP. When families help set goals for things that are important to the special education student, subsequent increased family cooperation and involvement are usually evident. Typically, the parent of the child knows the child best, so meshing the school goals and those of the family will provide a program that is most thorough in meeting the student's needs.

Skill 7.04 **Demonstrates knowledge of how to develop and implement comprehensive, longitudinal individualized programs (e.g., IEPs, IFSPs, transition plans) in collaboration with students with disabilities, their parents/guardians, general education teachers, and other professionals.**

APPLIES PROCEDURES FOR DEVELOPING AND USING INDIVIDUAL EDUCATION PROGRAM (IEP) OBJECTIVES TO PLAN INSTRUCTION FOR INDIVIDUALS WITH DISABILITIES

No Child Left Behind, Public Law 107-110, was signed on January 8, 2002. It addresses accountability of school personnel for student achievement with the expectation that every child will demonstrate proficiency in reading, math, and science. For example, all students should know how to read by grade 3.

General education curriculum should reflect state learning standards. Because special educators are responsible for teaching students to a level of comparable proficiency as their nondisabled peers, this curriculum should also be followed closely in the special education program.

Naturally, certain modifications and accommodations will be necessary to meet learning standards. IEP goals and objectives are based on the unique needs of the child with a disability in meeting the curriculum expectations of the school (and the state/nation). Consider some of the following hypothetical cases:

- Teachers in grades K-3 are mandated to teach reading to all students using scientifically based methods with measurable outcomes. Some students (including some with disabilities) will not learn to read successfully unless taught with a phonics approach. It is the responsibility of the general education teacher and special education teacher to incorporate phonics into the reading program.

- Students are expected to learn mathematics. While some students will quickly grasp the mathematical concept of groupings of tens (and further skills of adding and subtracting large numbers), others will need additional practice. Research shows that many students with disabilities need a hands-on approach. Perhaps those students will need additional instruction and practice using snap-together cubes to grasp the grouping-by-tens concept.

School districts, individual general education classrooms, and special education classrooms are no longer functioning independently. Learning standards set forth by the government now hold all education to the same bar and is evidenced in curriculum and related IEP goals and objectives.

KNOWS HOW TO PLAN, FACILITATE, AND IMPLEMENT TRANSITION ACTIVITIES AS DOCUMENTED IN INDIVIDUALIZED FAMILY SERVICES PLANS (IFSPS) AND INDIVIDUAL EDUCATION PROGRAMS (IEPS)

Vocational Training
Vocational education programs prepare students for entry into occupations in the labor force. Through these programs, it is intended that the students become self-sufficient, self-supporting citizens. This training has typically incorporated work-study programs at the high school and postsecondary levels. These programs include training while students are in school and on-the-job training after leaving school. Instruction focuses on particular job skills and on integral activities, such as job opportunities, skill requirements for specific jobs, personal qualifications in relation to job requirements, work habits, money management, and academic skills needed for particular jobs. Such vocational training programs are based on the following 3 main ideas (Blake, 1976):

1. Students need specific training in job skills. They must acquire them prior to exiting school.
2. Students need specific training and supervision in applying skills learned in school to requirements in job situations.
3. Vocational training can provide instruction and field-based experience, which will meet these needs and help the student become able to work in specific occupations.

Career Education
Curricular aspects of career education include the phases of:
1. Career awareness (diversity of available jobs)
2. Career exploration (skills needed for occupational groups)
3. Career preparation (specific training and preparation required for the world of work)

The concept of career education:
1. Extended this training into all levels of public school education (e.g., elementary through high school)
2. Emphasized the importance of acquiring skills in the areas of daily living and personal-social interaction, as well as occupational training and preparation
3. Focused upon integrating these skills into numerous areas of academic and vocational curricula. In general, career education attempts to prepare the individual for all facets of life

Vocational Training in Special Education
Vocational training in special education typically focuses on the exceptionality area of intellectual disabilities. Special guidance and training services are directed toward students with learning disabilities or emotional behavior disorders, or who are physically disabled, visually impaired, or hearing impaired. Individuals with disabilities are mainstreamed with nondisabled students in vocational training programs, when possible. Special sites provide training for those persons with more severe disabilities who are unable to be successfully taught in an integrated setting. Specially trained vocational counselors monitor and supervise student work sites.

Regardless of the disabling condition, aptitude testing is considered an important component in vocational training for the students in a mild or moderate setting. This assessment is necessary in order to identify areas of interest and capability. Attitudes and work habits are deemed important by many prospective employers, and so these competencies are included in the training.

Training provisions for individuals with severe intellectual disabilities are fairly expansive. They include special programs for school-aged children and secondary-level adolescents and sheltered workshop programs for adults. Instruction focuses on self-help skills, social-interpersonal skills, motor skills, rudimentary academic skills, simple occupational skills, and lifetime leisure and recreational skills. In addition, secondary-level programs offer on-the-job supervision, and sheltered workshop programs provide work supervision and pay a small wage for contract labor. Some persons with moderate to severe intellectual disabilities can be trained for employment in supervised unskilled occupations, while others are only able to perform chores and other simple tasks in sheltered workshops.

Skill 7.05   Demonstrates knowledge of how to prioritize goals and objectives within areas of the general curriculum for students with disabilities.

As a special educator, it is imperative to look to the general education curriculum as a means for developing appropriate goals and objectives for Individual Education Plans (IEPs). Since many special education students are unable to complete the general education curriculum to the same level and at the same pace as those students who are not identified as in need of special education, it is necessary to develop appropriate strategies and skills to prioritize the curriculum areas into attainable goals and objectives for the students.

The first step in prioritizing curriculum areas is to look for high stakes areas or those areas that are able to be generalized to others most easily. In this way, the teacher can target these skills with the students and provide the most intense instruction possible in the shortest amount of time. Choosing these types of skills provides the necessary foundational knowledge students need to be successful. There always will be more to learn, but providing students with a solid foundation allows them the opportunity to achieve success in the future.

This is not always an easy process and may require the input of regular education teachers, curriculum specialists, or other district level personnel. It is also helpful to have specific data on the skills and curricular areas students have already mastered. This information, at the beginning, may allow teachers to eliminate portions of the curriculum at the onset. Using the information a student has already mastered is an excellent strategy for determining which curriculum can be eliminated, enhanced, or started at the most basic levels.

Once the curriculum has been prioritized into meaningful areas, a gradation of success can be planned. In this way, students can tackle the skills in smaller, more manageable chunks of information to ensure mastery and success. Just as a car does not go directly from zero to sixty without seeing all the numbers in between, students do not go from not having any knowledge to complete mastery. Taking the time to build in smaller steps, even if they are only on those steps for short periods of time, provides a more realistic path. These paths may be measured in weeks, months, or even years, depending on the abilities of the students, but they should always be making forward progress toward the end goal of mastery of a specific objective.

Sometimes, the curriculum itself is not the issue, but rather the manner in which it is taught. Modification and adaptation to the regular education curriculum and instruction is one of the cornerstones of special education services; it needs to be considered an integral part of this process. When prioritizing and planning appropriate instruction for goals and objectives, it is imperative to keep in mind which areas can be taught with simple modifications or adaptations and still yield student success. This balancing act is ongoing throughout special education.

Skill 7.06   Demonstrates knowledge of national, state, and local content and performance standards (e.g., Georgia Performance Standards).

Please refer to the Georgia department of education Web site (http://public.doe.k12.ga.us/index.aspx) for detailed information.

Skill 7.07   Demonstrates knowledge of how to sequence, implement, and evaluate short- and long-term individualized learning goals.

Effective curriculum design assists the teacher from teacher demonstration to independent practice. Components of curriculum design include the following:

- Quizzes or reviews of the previous lesson
- Step-by-step presentations with multiple examples
- Guided practice and feedback
- Independent practice that requires the student to produce faster responses

The chosen curriculum should introduce information in a cumulative sequence but not introduce too much new information at a time. Review difficult material and practice to aid retention. New vocabulary and symbols should be introduced one at a time, and the relationships of components to the whole should be stressed. Students' background information should be recalled to connect new information to the old. Finally, teach strategies or algorithms first and then move on to tasks that are more difficult.

Course objectives may be obtained from the department head at the local school. The ESE (Exceptional Student Education) coordinator may have copies of objectives for functional courses or applied ESE courses. District program specialists also have lists of objectives for each course provided in the local school system. Additionally, publishers of textbooks will have scope and sequence lists in the teacher's manual.

Addressing Students' Needs
There are a number of procedures teachers can use to address the varying needs of the students. Here are some of the more common procedures:

1. **Vary assignments**
   A variety of assignments on the same content allows students to match learning styles and preferences with the assignment. If all assignments are writing assignments, for example, students who are hands-on or visual learners are at a disadvantage unrelated to the content base itself.

2. **Cooperative learning**
   Cooperative learning activities allow students to share ideas, expertise, and insight in a nonthreatening setting. The focus tends to remain on positive learning rather than competition.

3. **Structure environment**
   Some students need and benefit from a clear structure that defines the expectation and goals of the teacher. The student knows what is expected and when and can work and plan accordingly.

4. Clearly stated assignments

Assignments should be clearly stated, along with the expectation and criteria for completion. Reinforcement and practice activities should not be a guessing game for the students. The exception to this is, of course, those situations in which a discovery method is used.

5. Independent practice

Independent practice involving application and repetition is necessary for thorough learning. Students learn to be independent learners through practicing independent learning. These activities should always be within the student's abilities to perform successfully without assistance.

6. Repetition

Very little learning is successful with a single exposure. Learners generally require multiple exposures to the same information for learning to take place. However, this repetition does not have to be dull and monotonous. In conjunction with No. 1 above, varied assignments can provide repetition of content or skill practiced without repetition of specific activities. This helps keep learning fresh and exciting for the student.

7. Overlearning

As a principle of effective learning, overlearning recommends that students continue to study and review after they have achieved initial mastery. The use of repetition in the context of varied assignments offers the means to help students pursue and achieve overlearning.

Progress on these mutually accepted goals—as well as those initiated by the school—can be charted or measured in a variety of ways. The method used to track the goals should be those indicated in the goals and objectives section of the IEP.

Charting is a formal tracking method of student behavior and progress. Often based on a functional behavioral assessment portion of the IEP, the chart will include behaviors (positive or negative), the time covered, and frequency of the behavior (which is often shown with tally marks).

Anecdotal records are a journaling of behaviors observed in the home or classroom. Such records may be notes kept by the classroom teacher or therapist, or notes from the parent (often literally in the form of paper notes, passbook entries, or e-mails) regarding student success and challenges.

Observations are a more focused form of anecdotal records. They occur when a specific activity, class, or time period is observed and the behaviors and skills of the individual student are recorded. A comparison of student behavior in various settings often gives information needed to write appropriate IEP goals.

Rating scales are frequently used to assess a student's behavior or level of functioning in a particular environment (home, classroom, or playground). These scales are often given to more than one person (parent, teacher, and therapist) to complete so that a more comprehensive picture of the student is obtained.

Commonly used rating scales with a component for professionals and parents include the Conners' Rating Scale, the Vineland Adaptive Behavior Scale, and the Child Development Inventory.

Informal tests are ways of tracking a student's behaviors through the use of classroom tests and assignments in various subject areas.

Formal tests may include standardized tests that are administered to all students at the local and state levels, alternative assessment as indicated on the child's IEP, and tests used by a psychologist or therapist to assess skills and deficiencies. Formal testing results give measurable data, which can be used in school-parent discussions for planning IEP goals and objectives.

COMPETENCY 8.0   UNDERSTAND USES OF INSTRUCTIONAL AND ASSISTIVE TECHNOLOGIES TO SUPPORT THE COMMUNICATION AND LEARNING OF STUDENTS WITH DISABILITIES

Skill 8.01   **Recognizes how to make informed decisions regarding types and levels of assistive technologies, devices, and services needed by students with various strengths and needs.**

EVALUATION OF STUDENT LEARNING ENVIRONMENT AND NEED FOR ASSISTIVE TECHNOLOGY

This is an age of technology; often, the appropriate technology can benefit the efforts of the special needs student.

Consideration of Student Need
What are the expectations of the student in the classroom? Some expectations that may be best address with technology include the following:

- Basic communication of wants and needs
- Books on tape
- Braille typewriters
- Note taking
- Writing assignments
- Math calculations
- Spelling and grammar
- Movement between locations
- Auditory input or processing

Consideration of Existing Technology
At times, the technology used by all students will meet the needs of the student with a disability. An example would be the physically handicapped student who is researching and writing a report about Texas. Like his or her classmates, the student will use the school computers to accomplish this task. He or she may, however, need the keyboard to be adjusted to a certain angle to accommodate physical needs.

In other cases, existing general population technology will not meet student needs, and alternatives will be necessary.

Skill 8.02 **Apply knowledge of procedures for selecting and implementing assistive technologies, devices, and services to facilitate students' educational achievement, communication, mobility, and active participation in educational activities and routines.**

There are many services available to special education students. These include, but are not limited to, those provided by speech pathologists, physical therapists, occupational therapists, behavioral therapists, and trained paraprofessionals. All these services are provided to increase the child's ability to participate in the general education curriculum to the greatest extent.

Please refer to Skill 14.01 for the roles of the IEP members.

Determination of Student Need for Assistive Technology
Oftentimes, the special educator will identify the need for consultation or testing in an area in which a student is having difficulty. Testing or other professional evaluation may result in the trial or ongoing use of some form of assistive technology as listed on the student's IEP.

Development of Student Skill Using Specific Assistive Technology
Students who have been identified as needing assistive technology require training in the use of the equipment. Sometimes, a therapist or consultant will "push in" to the classroom, providing training for the student in the classroom setting. Other times, the student will practice using the assistive technology in a separate setting until a level of experience/expertise is reached. The assistive technology may then be used in the special education or inclusion classroom.

Communication of Expected Skill Level in Classroom
As students begin to use assistive technology in the classroom, the desired use (Including activity, location, and time) should be outlined for the special educator so that misunderstandings do not result in a student misusing or under-using the technology. The student, then, will have a level of accountability and be functioning to the best of his or her abilities.

Training of School Personnel on Use of Assistive Technology
Although special educators are often trained in using a variety of assistive devices, advances in technology make it necessary for professionals to participate in ongoing training for new or unfamiliar equipment. This training may be conducted by a knowledgeable therapist or consultant in the school district, or school personnel may need to attend workshops off campus.

Evaluation of Student Independent Management of Assistive Technology in Various Settings

Ongoing evaluation of the student's use of the equipment is vital. This may be monitored through observation by the therapist or consultant, anecdotal records of the special educator, or some type of checklist. Oftentimes, an IEP goal will address how the use and evaluation of the student's performance with the equipment will be implemented.

Skill 8.03   Demonstrate knowledge of how to incorporate instructional and assistive technologies into IEPs.

Many students with disabilities require assistive technologies in order to be successful within the regular curriculum or environment. As with any form of technology, assistive devices are constantly being changed and updated; therefore, it is important to stay as up-to-date as possible. It is also essential to search out within a district to discover who to contact to provide help in finding the necessary technologies to allow student success.

When considering adding technology for students with special needs, it is important to conduct a multidisciplinary evaluation to ensure that specific student strengths are utilized in providing appropriate technology. This might include consulting such people as an assistive technology specialist, an occupational therapist, a physical therapist, a speech pathologist, or other designated professionals with specific training.

Consider the needs of the student and those working with the device. For instance, an augmentative communication device is only as good as it is easy for the student to use and access. The ease with which the person in school and at home can program it is also a factor. If the device is too complicated to program with phrases or to make changes to when necessary, it will be less than ideal in the school setting.

Also, always start with the least restrictive device. If, for example, a student requires information to be visually presented at the same time it is orally presented, an overhead/smart board might be the best choice. There are other students in the classroom who will benefit from this type of modification, as well, and the student with special needs will not have to be isolated or pointed out to his or her classmates.

If any form of assistive technology (even simply typing assignments instead of handwriting them) is required, it is essential to include it in the child's IEP. While many teachers and parents will follow the special educator's word and implement what is best for the child with no difficulties, it can provide future teachers with beneficial information. While the IEP is legally binding and therefore mandates the users to implement what is written in it, it also contains a wealth of information for people who are working with that child.

Teachers in future years can look back and see what worked in previous years, or if the student moves, the new personnel will understand what specific devices and needs the student has. They will thus be better able service those needs from the beginning. In the end, the IEP is an important document wherein all information pertaining to the student, including assistive technology needs, should be conveyed.

Skill 8.04 Demonstrates knowledge of the use and maintenance of various assistive technology devices.

Physical and Health Impairments
Technology has helped individuals with physical and health impairments to gain access to and control the environment around them, communicate with others, and take advantage of health care. There are high-tech devices, such as computers, but also low-tech devices like built-up spoons and crutches. Electric typewriters, computer keyboards, and automated language boards provide means for communication to occur.

Mobility has been assisted by use of lightweight or electric specialized wheelchairs. These include motorized chairs, computerized chairs, chairs in which it is possible to rise, wilderness sports chairs, and racing chairs (Smith and Luckasson 1992). Electronic switches allow persons with only partial movement (e.g., head, neck, fingers, toes) to be more mobile. Even driving a car is possible.

Mobility is also enhanced by use of artificial limbs, personalized equipped vans, and electrical walking machines. Myoelectric (or bionic) limbs contain a sensor that picks up electric signals transmitted from the person's brain through the limb. Robotic arms can manipulate objects by at least three directional movements: extension/retraction, swinging/rotating, and elevation/depression. Manipulator robots can assist in making a phone call, turning book pages, and drinking from a cup.

Speech/Communication
A communication board is a flat surface on which words, pictures, or both can be placed. The student is encouraged to point to the symbols of what he or she wants to communicate. Simple boards can be made from magazine or newspaper pictures. Others can be written onto display messages. More sophisticated boards incorporate an attachment that synthesizes a "voice." Communication books function like a board and assist communication.

Media Equipment
Many types of media equipment are available for use in the classroom. Multidimensional teaching approaches are possible with machines that provide instruction through various sensory modality channels. Individual receptive strengths can be matched with equipment, directing learning through visual, auditory, haptic, or multidimensional input channels.

The CD player is particularly of benefit to students who learn best by auditory input. CDs frequently accompany commercial instructional programs (e.g., reading kits, programmed workbooks) and can be operated by students trained to do so. A CD player can accommodate earphones or headsets for single or group listening opportunities.

CD players offer the additional benefit of being lightweight for easy transport, relatively inexpensive, and adaptable for recording information or responses by teachers or students. Teacher-recorded CDs offer the opportunity for students to read along with or follow story sequences with accompanying pictures, listen to stories for pleasure, practice spelling words, and learn to follow instructions. They can also be used to answer comprehension questions, discriminate auditory sounds, perform word study exercises, and, in general, maintain and motivate student interest.

Media such as VCRs, DVDs, and television provide unlimited opportunities for visual and auditory input. Equipment of this type offers the capability of presenting instructional content to individuals or groups of students in a format that readers and nonreaders alike can understand. Special effects (e.g., flashbacks, fades, close-ups, quick and slow pans) can be obtained by use of most DVD players. Selected pauses and review of material are also easily achieved.

CCTV, special television programs, and VHS and DVDs are often used to supplement and enhance instructional material already introduced. On occasion, instructional material is introduced by these means. Reinforcement may also be delivered through the showing of entertaining visual material.

Dependent on your schools policies, students may be allowed to go to a media center and view a video for pleasure. Another alternative is to show a part of a selected video and ask students to hypothesize what preceded the viewed portion, or what followed the action they saw. Students can be asked to write a narrative for a film they have only seen in silence. A video dealing with a social problem can be stopped before the solutions are offered; students may offer their own solutions. A video portraying a dramatic story can be ended prematurely; students can then be directed to write endings and act them out.

The overhead projector is an easy to use and maintain visual communication device. A bright lamp source transmits light through the translucent material to a screen close to the machine. Transparencies can be purchased commercially or made from clear photocopies of materials.

Computers and Software

PCs are valuable teaching tools. Software programs and adaptations enable learners with disabilities (e.g., physical, cognitive, and sensory) to profit from instruction in the classroom they might not be able to receive otherwise. For example, tutorial programs simulate the teaching function of presentations, questions, and feedback. By this means, children are provided learning exercises on an appropriate level of difficulty and in an interesting manner. Other programs can be used to allow drill and practice (with correct answers shown) over previously learned material. Games are effective as motivators and reinforcers. In addition, use of computer software provides a way of testing students that is more appealing to many than a written test.

Teachers can acquire the skills needed to program the computer so that tasks provided by software correspond with students' individualized education programs. Teaching students to program will develop problem solving and discovery skills, as well as also foster reasoning comprehension skills.

Stages of Learning

Suggestions about selecting and using software are given by Male (1994). First, make sure there is a curriculum correspondence between what students are working on at their desks and what they do at the computers. This should follow what Male calls stages of learning. Then, make certain the students proceed through the five stages. Software should be selected with these stages in mind:

1. **Acquisition:** Introduction of a new skill
2. **Proficiency:** Practice under supervision to achieve accuracy and speed
3. **Maintenance:** Continued practice without further instruction
4. **Generalization:** Application of new skills in new settings and situations
5. **Adaptation:** Modifications of the task to meet new needs and demands of varying situations

Computer-Assisted Instruction

Computers are used to provide a safe, stimulating learning environment for many youth. The computer does not evaluate or offer subjective opinions about the student's work. It merely provides feedback about the correctness or incorrectness of each answer in a series. The computer is like an effective teacher by the way in which it does the following (Smith and Luckasson 1992):

1. Provides immediate attention and feedback
2. Individualizes to the particular skill level
3. Allows students to work at their own paces
4. Makes corrections quickly
5. Produces a professional-looking product
6. Keeps accurate records on correct and error rates
7. Ignores inappropriate behavior
8. Focuses on the particular response
9. Is nonjudgmental

Computers are useful in helping to teach traditional academic subjects like math, reading, spelling, geography, and science. Effective teachers allow for drill and practice on the computer, monitor student progress, and reinforce appropriately. When students have mastered a particular level, these teachers help them to progress to another level. Reasoning and problem solving are other skill areas that teachers have discovered can be taught using computers.

One type of newly developed computer software is the program Hypertext. It enables further explanation of textbook material. This is accessed by a simple press of a key while the student is working on the learning material. For example, by a single press of a key, students can access definitions of difficult vocabulary words, reworded complicated text, additional detailed maps, and further information about concepts being introduced in the text. Teachers can help students by creating individualized lessons, and students with learning disabilities can especially benefit.

Computer games can enhance learning skills and provide a highly desired reinforcement opportunity. When played alone, the games serve as leisure activities for the individual. When played with classmates, the games can help develop interpersonal relationships. This is particularly applicable to youngsters with behavioral disorders and learning and intellectual disabilities, as well as those without any identified disability.

Word Processors

Word processors are used to assist students with written composition. Students with learning disabilities often have difficulty organizing thoughts. Problems with writing are compounded by handwriting difficulties. Many teachers report that use of a word processor has enabled them to motivate students to write. Most are less resistant to rewriting texts when they can do it on a word processing program that erases and replaces text quickly. Printed texts in typewritten form are easier to read. Spelling checkers, built into many word processing programs, assist those who may not be able to spell words correctly. Another option is a thesaurus, which provides synonyms (in so doing, it helps to build vocabulary). The overall quantity and quality of written work improves when word processing programs are used in conjunction with computers.

When working on a word processor program, each student needs a storage disc, preferably a jump drive, so that his or her work can be evaluated over time and stored electronically. Having a portfolio of printouts enables students to take work home to show parents.

Process Approach

The process approach to writing is encouraged, especially when using a word processor (Male 1994). These stages include planning/prewriting, drafting, revising/editing, and sharing/publication. Progressing through these stages is particularly helpful to developing writers.

The **planning stage** is characterized by written outlines; brainstorming; clustering or mind mapping; and lists of ideas, themes, or key words. These activities are ideally suited to a classroom that has a large television monitor or a computer projection device that will allow the teacher to list, group, revise, and expand ideas as students share them. Printed copies of what was generated by the group can be distributed at the end of the class session.

In the **drafting stage**, individuals can do draft work at a computer by themselves, or they can collaborate as a group on the work. Some students may choose to use pencil and paper to do initial draft work, or they may want to dictate stories to the teacher or another student who can write it down for them.

Students share their work during the **revising/editing stage**. Students read their stories aloud to a partner, a small group, or the whole class. Classmates are instructed to ask questions and give feedback that will help the writer make revisions to his or her work. After the story has been completed as far as content, attention is given to mechanics and writing conventions.

The **sharing/publication stage** enables students to experience being authors responding to an audience. Students are encouraged to share their work by reading it aloud and in printed form. They can do this with or without graphics or illustrations.

Skill 8.05   Demonstrates knowledge of how to collaborate with families, colleagues, and other professionals to facilitate students' use and independent management of assistive technologies in various settings (e.g., school, home, work).

Please refer to Skill 8.02.

| DOMAIN III. | PROMOTING STUDENT DEVELOPMENT AND LEARNING |

COMPETENCY 9.0 UNDERSTAND STRATEGIES FOR MANAGING THE LEARNING ENVIRONMENT TO CREATE A SAFE, SUPPORTIVE, AND INCLUSIVE CLASSROOM CLIMATE THAT PROMOTES THE DEVELOPMENT AND LEARNING OF STUDENTS WITH DISABILITIES

Skill 9.01   Applies knowledge of strategies for creating a safe, supportive, and positive classroom climate that fosters respect for diversity and positive interactions among all students.

Awareness of cultural diversity and beliefs will help the special educator understand how best to communicate school goals with his or her students' families. As understanding and communication grow, family support will help the student become more successful in academics.

Classroom Climate

Learning styles refer to the ways in which individuals learn best. Physical settings, instructional arrangements, available materials, techniques, and individual preferences are all factors in the teacher's choice of instructional strategies. Information about the student's preference can be done through a direct interview or a Likert-style checklist where the student rates his or preferences.

Physical Environment (Spatial Arrangements)

The physical setting of the classroom contributes a great deal to the propensity for students to learn. An adequate, well built, and well-equipped classroom will invite students to learn. This has been called "invitational learning." Among the important factors to consider in the physical setting of the classroom are the following:

1. **Adequate physical space**
   A classroom must have adequate physical space so students can conduct themselves comfortably. Some students are distracted by windows, pencil sharpeners, doors, and so on. Some students prefer the front, middle, or back rows.

2. **Repair status**
   The teacher has the responsibility to report any items of classroom disrepair to maintenance staff. Broken windows, falling plaster, exposed sharp surfaces, leaks in ceiling or walls, and other items of disrepair present hazards to students.

3. **Lighting adequacy**
Another factor that must be considered is adequate lighting. Report any inadequacies in classroom illumination. Some students may require full-spectrum lighting due to a visual impairment. Should these lights be in a room, reporting their failure as soon as possible will enable that student to have continuity in the learning environment.

4. **Adequate entry/exit access (including handicap accessibility)**
Local fire and safety codes dictate entry and exit standards. In addition, all corridors and classrooms should be wheelchair accessible for students and others who use them. Older schools may not have this accessibility.

5. **Ventilation/climate control**
Another consideration is adequate ventilation and climate control. Some classrooms in some states use air-conditioning extensively. Sometimes it is so cold as to be considered a distraction. Specialty classes (such as science) require specialized hoods for ventilation. Physical education classes have the added responsibility for shower areas and specialized environments that must be heated, such as pool or athletic training rooms.

6. **Coloration**
Classrooms with warmer subdued colors contribute to students' concentration on task items. Neutral hues for coloration of walls, ceiling, and carpet or tile are generally used in classrooms, so distraction due to classroom coloration is minimized.

In the modern classroom, there is a great deal of furniture, equipment, supplies, appliances, and learning aids to help the teacher teach and students learn. The classroom should be provided with furnishings that fit the purpose of the classroom. The kindergarten classroom may have a reading center, a playhouse, a puzzle table, student work desks/tables, a sandbox, and any other relevant learning/interest areas.

Whatever the arrangement of furniture and equipment may be, the teacher must provide for adequate traffic flow. Rows of desks must have adequate space between them for students to move and for the teacher to circulate. All areas must be open to line-of-sight supervision by the teacher.

In all cases, proper care must be taken to ensure student safety. Furniture and equipment should be situated safely at all times. No equipment, materials, boxes, and so on should be placed where there is danger of falling over. Doors must have entry and exit accessibility at all times.

Noise level should also be considered as part of the physical environment. Students vary in the degree of quiet that they need and the amount of background noise or talking that they can tolerate without getting distracted or frustrated. Thus, a teacher must maintain an environment that is conducive to the learning of each child.

Instructional Arrangements

Some students work well in large groups; others prefer small groups or one-to-one instruction with the teacher, aide, or volunteer. Instructional arrangements also involve peer-tutoring situations with the student as tutor or tutee. The teacher also needs to consider how well the student works independently with seatwork.

Skill 9.02   Demonstrates knowledge of strategies for addressing common barriers to accessibility and acceptance faced by students with disabilities.

Please refer to Skill 9.01.

Skill 9.03   Demonstrates knowledge of how to design and adapt physical and learning environments to promote students' active participation, academic success, self advocacy, and independence.

Please refer to Skills 9.01 and 9.02.

Skill 9.04   Demonstrates knowledge of classroom management strategies, including structuring and managing daily routines (e.g., transitions between lessons or classes) to optimize students' time on task and facilitate students' effective use of instructional time.

Classroom management plans should be in place when the school year begins. Developing a management plan takes a proactive approach—that is, deciding on what behaviors will be expected of the class as a whole, anticipating possible problems, and teaching the behaviors early in the school year.

Behavior management techniques should focus on positive procedures that can be used at home as well as at school. Involving the students in the development of the classroom rules lets the students know the rationale for the rules and allows them to assume responsibility for them. Once the rules are established, enforcement and reinforcement for following the rules should begin right away.

Consequences should be introduced at the same time as the rules. They should be clearly stated and understood by all of the students. The severity of the consequence should match the severity of the offense and must be enforceable.

The teacher must apply the consequence consistently and fairly; students should know what to expect when they choose to break a rule.

Like consequences, students should understand what rewards to expect for following the rules. The teacher should never promise a reward that cannot be delivered. The teacher should also follow through with the reward as soon as possible. Consistency and fairness are necessary for rewards to be effective. Students will become frustrated and give up if they see that rewards and consequences are not delivered timely and fairly.

About four to six classroom rules should be posted where students can easily see and read them. These rules should be stated positively and describe specific behaviors so they are easy to understand. Certain rules may also be tailored to meet target goals and IEP requirements of individual students. (For example, a new student who has had problems with leaving the classroom may need an individual behavior contract to assist him or her with adjusting to the class rule about remaining in the assigned area.) As the students demonstrate the behaviors, the teacher should provide reinforcement and corrective feedback. Periodic "refresher" practice can be done as needed, for example, after a long holiday or if students begin to "slack off." A copy of the classroom plan should be readily available for substitute use, and the classroom aide should also be familiar with the plan and procedures.

The teacher should clarify and model the expected behavior for the students. In addition to the classroom management plan, a management plan should be developed for special situations, (e.g., fire drills) and transitions (e.g., going to and from the cafeteria). A periodic review of the rules, as well as modeling and practice, may be conducted as needed (such as after an extended school holiday).

Procedures that use social humiliation, withholding of basic needs, pain, or extreme discomfort should never be used in a behavior management plan.

Emergency intervention procedures used when the student is a danger to him or herself or others are not considered behavior management procedures. Throughout the year, the teacher should periodically review the types of interventions being used, assess the effectiveness of the interventions used in the management plan, and make revisions as needed for the best interests of each child.

Motivation
Before the teacher begins instruction, he or she should choose activities that are meaningful, relevant, and at the appropriate level of student difficulty.

Teacher behaviors that motivate students include the following:

- Maintaining success expectations through teaching, goal setting, establishing connections between effort and outcome, and self-appraisal and reinforcement.
- Having a supply of intrinsic incentives, such as rewards, appropriate competition between students, and the value of the academic activities.
- Focusing on students' intrinsic motivation through adapting the tasks to students' interests, providing opportunities for active response, including a variety of tasks, providing rapid feedback, incorporating games into the lesson, and allowing students the opportunity to make choices, create, and interact with peers.
- Stimulating students' learning by modeling positive expectations and attributions. Project enthusiasm and personalize abstract concepts. Students will be better motivated if they know what they will be learning. The teacher should also model problem solving and task-related thinking so students can see how the process is done.

For adolescents, motivation strategies are usually aimed at getting the student actively involved in the learning process. Since the adolescent has the opportunity to get involved in a wider range of activities outside the classroom (e.g., job, car, being with friends), stimulating motivation may be the focus even more than academics.

Motivation may be achieved through extrinsic reinforcers or intrinsic reinforcers. This is accomplished by allowing the student a degree of choice in what is being taught or how it will be taught. The teacher should, if possible, obtain a commitment either through a verbal or written contract between the student and the teacher. Adolescents also respond to regular feedback, especially when that feedback shows that they are making progress.

Rewards for adolescents often include free time for listening to music, recreation, or games. They may like extra time for a break or exemption from a homework assignment. They may receive rewards at home for satisfactory performance at school. Other rewards include self-charting progress and tangible reinforcers. In summary, motivational activities may be used for goal setting, self-recording of academic progress, self-evaluation, and self-reinforcement.

Classroom Interventions
Classroom interventions anticipate student disruptions and nullify potential discipline problems. Every student is different and each situation is unique; therefore, student behavior cannot be matched to specific interventions. Good classroom management requires the ability to select appropriate interventions strategies from an array of alternatives. The following nonverbal and verbal interventions were explained in Henley, Ramsey, and Algonzzine (1993):

Nonverbal intervention: The use of nonverbal interventions allows classroom activities to proceed without interruption. These interventions also enable teachers to avoid "power struggles" with students.

Body language: Teachers can convey authority and command respect through body language. Posture, eye contact, facial expressions, and gestures are examples of body components that signal leadership to students.

Planned ignoring: Many minor classroom disturbances are best handled through planned ignoring. When teachers ignore attention-seeking behaviors, students often do likewise.

Signal interference: There are numerous nonverbal signals that teachers can use to quiet a class. Some of these are eye contact, snapping fingers, a frown, shaking the head, or making a quieting gesture with the hand. A few teachers present signs like flicking the lights, putting a finger over the lips, or winking at a selective student.

Proximity control: Teachers who move around the room merely need to stand near a student or small group of students, or gently place a hand on a student's shoulder to stop a disturbing behavior. Teachers who stand or sit as if rooted are compelled to issue verbal directions in order to deal with student disruptions.

Removal of seductive objects: Some students become distracted by objects. Removal of those objects may eliminate the need some students have to handle, grab, or touch objects that take the focus of their attention away from instruction. .

Verbal interventions: Because nonverbal interventions are the least intrusive, they are generally preferred. Verbal interventions are useful after it is clear that nonverbal interventions have been unsuccessful in preventing or stopping disruptive behavior.

Humor: Some teachers have been successful in dispelling discipline problems with a quip or an easy comment that produces smiles or gentle laughter from students. This does not include sarcasm, cynicism, or teasing, which increase tension and often create resentment.

Sane messages: Sane messages are descriptive and model appropriate behavior. They help students understand how their behavior affects others. "Karol, when you talk during silent reading, you disturb everyone in your group," is an example of a sane message. Communicating such messages privately to students has proven to have a greater effect than when they are given in front of a class.

Restructuring; When confronted with student disinterest, the teacher may make the decision to change activities. This is an example of an occasion when restructuring could be used by the teacher to regenerate student interest.

Hypodermic affection; Sometimes, students get frustrated, discouraged, and anxious in school. Hypodermic affection lets students know they are valued. Saying a kind word, giving a smile, or just showing interest in a child often gives the encouragement that is needed. This is most effective if you do it daily as your students enter your classroom.

Praise and encouragement; Effective praise should be directed at student behavior rather than at the student personally. "Catching a child being good" is an example of an effective use of praise that reinforces positive classroom behavior. Comments like, "You are really trying hard," encourage student effort.

Alerting; Making abrupt changes from one activity to another can bring on behavior problems. Alerting helps students to make smooth transitions by giving them time to make emotional adjustments to change.

Accepting student feelings; Providing opportunities for students to express their feelings—even those that are distressful—helps them to learn to do so in appropriate ways. Role playing, class meetings or discussions, life-space interviews, journal writings, and other creative modes help students to channel difficult feelings into constructive outlets.

Schedule development depends on the type of class (elementary or secondary) and the setting (regular classroom or resource room). There are, however, general rules of thumb that apply to both types and settings:

1. Allow time for transitions, planning, and setups.
2. Aim for maximum instructional time by pacing the instruction quickly and allotting time for practice of the new skills.
3. Proceed from short assignments to long ones, breaking up long lessons or complex tasks into short sessions or step-by-step instruction.
4. Follow a less preferred academic or activity with a highly preferred academic activity.
5. In settings where students are working on individualized plans, do not schedule all the students at once in activities that require a great deal of teacher assistance. For example, have some students work on math or spelling while the teacher works with the students in reading (as it usually requires more teacher involvement).

6. Break up a longer segment into several smaller segments with a variety of activities.

Special Considerations for Elementary Classrooms

1. Determine the amount of time that is needed for activities such as P.E., lunch, or recess.
2. Allow about 15 to 20 minutes each for opening and closing exercises. Spend this time for "housekeeping" activities, such as collecting lunch money, going over the schedule, cleaning up, reviewing the day's activities, and getting ready to go home.
3. Schedule academics for periods when the students are more alert and motivated—usually in the afternoon.
4. Build in time for slower students to finish their work; others may work at learning centers or other activities of interest. Allowing extra time gives the teacher time to give more attention where it is needed, conduct assessments, or allow students to complete or correct work.

Special Considerations for Secondary Classes

Secondary school days are usually divided into five, six, or seven periods of about 50 minutes each, with time for homeroom and lunch. Students cannot stay behind and finish their work since they have to leave for a different room. Resource room time should be scheduled so that the student does not miss academic instruction in his or her classroom or miss desirable nonacademic activities. In schools where ESE teachers also co-teach or work with students in the regular classroom, the regular teacher will have to coordinate lesson plans with those of the special education teacher. Consultation time will also have to be budgeted into the schedule.

Transfer between Classes and Subjects

Effective teachers use class time efficiently. This results in higher student subject engagement and will likely result in more subject matter retention. One way teachers use class time efficiently is through a smooth transition from one activity to another; this activity is also known as "management transition." Management transition is defined as when the "teacher shifts from one activity to another in a systemic, academically oriented way." One factor that contributes to efficient management transition is the teacher's management of instructional material. Effective teachers gather their materials during the planning stage of instruction. In doing this, a teacher avoids flipping through things looking for the items necessary for the current lesson. Momentum is lost and student concentration is broken when this occurs.

Additionally, teachers who keep students informed of the sequencing of instructional activities maintain systematic transitions because the students are prepared to move on to the next activity. For example, the teacher says, "When we finish with this guided practice together, we will turn to page twenty-three and each student will do the exercises. I will then circulate throughout the classroom helping on an individual basis. Okay, let's begin." Following an example such as this will lead to systematic smooth transitions between activities, because the students will be turning to page twenty-three when the class finishes the practice without a break in concentration.

Another method that leads to smooth transitions is to move students in groups and clusters rather than seat them one-by-one. This is called "group fragmentation." For example, if some students do seat work while other students gather for a reading group, the teacher moves the students in predetermined groups. Instead of calling the individual names of the reading group, which would be time consuming and laborious, the teacher simply says, "Will the blue reading group please assemble at the reading station. The red and yellow groups will quietly do the vocabulary assignment I am now passing out." As a result of this activity, the classroom is ready to move on in a matter of seconds rather than minutes.

Additionally, the teacher may employ academic transition signals, which are defined as any "teacher utterance that indicate[s] movement of the lesson from one topic or activity to another by indicating where the lesson is and where it is going." For example, the teacher may say, "That completes our description of clouds, now we will examine weather fronts." Like the sequencing of instructional materials, this keeps the student informed on what is coming next so he or she will move to the next activity with little or no break in concentration.

Therefore, effective teachers manage transitions from one activity to another in a systematically oriented way by efficiently managing instructional matter, sequencing instructional activities, moving students in groups, and employing academic transition signals. Through an efficient use of class time, achievement is increased because students spend more class time engaged in on-task behavior.

Transition refers to changes in class activities that involve movement. Examples include the following:

1. Breaking up from large group instruction into small groups for learning centers and small-group instructions
2. Moving from the classroom to lunch, to the playground, or to elective classes
3. Finishing reading at the end of one period and getting ready for math the next period
4. Emergency situations such as fire drills

Successful transitions are achieved by using proactive strategies. Early in the year, the teacher pinpoints the transition periods in the day and anticipates possible behavior problems (such as students habitually returning late from lunch). After identifying possible problems with the environment or the schedule, the teacher plans proactive strategies to minimize or eliminate those problems. Proactive planning also gives the teacher the advantage of being prepared, addressing behaviors before they become problems, and incorporating strategies into the classroom management plan right away. Transition plans can be developed for each type of transition and the expected behaviors for each situation taught directly to the students.

Skill 9.05   **Analyzes the ways in which teacher attitudes and behaviors affect individuals with and without disabilities and recognizing effective strategies for establishing and maintaining rapport with all students.**

Influence of Teacher Attitudes
The attitude of the teacher can have both a positive and negative impact on student performance. A teacher's attitude is the expectations that the teacher may have toward the student's potential performance, as well as how the teacher behaves toward the student. This attitude, combined with expectations, can impact the student's self-image as well as his or her academic performance.

Negative teacher attitudes toward students with disabilities are detrimental to the handicapped students mainstreamed in general education classrooms. The phenomenon of a self-fulfilling prophecy is based on the attitude of the teacher. In the context of education, this means that the predictions of a teacher about the ability of a student to achieve or not to achieve educational objectives are often proven to be correct.

This phenomenon also occurs in more subtle ways. Even without realizing it, teachers communicate their expectations of individual students. In turn, the students may adjust their behaviors to match the teacher's expectations. Based on this, the teacher's expectations of what will happen come true.

Researchers in psychology and education have investigated this occurrence and discovered that many people are sensitive to verbal and nonverbal cues from others regarding how they expect to be treated. As a result, they may consciously and subconsciously change their behaviors and attitudes to conform to another person's hopes. Depending on the expectation, this can be either advantageous or detrimental.

The teacher's attitude toward a student can be shaped by a number of variables, including race, ethnicity, disability, behavior, appearance, and social class. All of these variables can impact the teacher's attitude toward the student and how the student will achieve academically.

Teachers have the responsibility to not allow their negative attitudes toward students to impact how they perceive the students interact with them. If the teacher is able to communicate to all of his or her students that they all have great potential and is optimistic regarding this, then the students should excel in some aspect of their educational endeavors. This continues to be true for as long as the teacher is able to make the student believe in him or herself.

It can be hard for teachers to maintain a positive attitude at all times with all students. However, it is important to be encouraging to all students at all times, as every student has the potential to be successful in school. Consistent encouragement can help turn a C student into a B or even an A student. At the same time, negative feedback can lead to failure and loss of self-esteem.

Teachers should utilize their verbal communication skills to ensure that the things they communicate to students are said in the most positive manner possible. For example, instead of saying, "You talk too much," it would be more positive to state, "You have excellent verbal communication skills and are very sociable."

Teachers have a major influence on what happens in their classrooms because they are the primary decision makers. They set the tone for how the information they distribute is absorbed.

In order for teachers to rise above their prejudices and preset attitudes, it is important that teachers are given training and support services to enable them to deal with students who come from challenging backgrounds or present challenging behaviors.

Skill 9.06   Recognizes types and transmission routes of infectious diseases and demonstrating knowledge of universal safety precautions for avoiding transmission of such diseases.

In schools today, as with any workplace, it is important for teachers to avoid exposing themselves or others to infectious diseases. Any body fluid should be considered as having an infectious disease; in this way, the employee can use a standardized set of procedures to ensure no chance of spread occurs. This standardized set of procedures is known as universal safety precautions.

Infectious disease can be spread through contact with spilled body fluids, including blood. Small playground scrapes, a weeping sore, or any other spilled body fluid should be avoided unless using universal precautions. Body fluids that can transmit infectious disease include blood; body fluids with blood visible; cerebrospinal, synovial, pleural, peritoneal, pericardial, and amniotic fluids; semen; and vaginal secretions.

Before attending to or helping someone where there is blood or other spilled body fluid, you should take time to protect yourself. Barrier protection is the first stage. Use of gloves is a must. Be careful with the use of latex gloves, as there are many people with severe latex allergies. Sometimes, it may be necessary to wear protective clothing or eye protection as well.

Hand washing is also important. If any of the blood or body fluids comes in contact with your skin, be sure to wash the area as soon as possible, lathering and washing for 15 or more seconds. It is also imperative to wash hands after removing the gloves. In fact, hand washing is the best germ reducer.

In some cases, the local district may ask/require you to have vaccinations to prevent you from some disease transmissions. An example of this may be the hepatitis B vaccine. Typically, teachers are required to be tested for tuberculosis as well. There are usually procedures for the disposal of hazardous waste or biohazardous waste. The employee should check with the building/school nurse or administrator to understand the specific procedures within each school.

If exposed to blood or other body fluids on the job, it is important to report such an incident to the immediate supervisors as soon as possible. There may be steps in place that need to be followed in order to be best protected.

Skill 9.07   Demonstrates knowledge of strategies for preparing students to live harmoniously and productively in a culturally diverse world, including strategies for creating a learning environment that enables students to retain and appreciate their own and others' linguistic and cultural heritages.

Effective teaching and learning for students begins with teachers who can demonstrate sensitivity for diversity in teaching and in relationships within school communities. Student portfolios should include work that has multicultural perspective and inclusion, enabling students to share cultural and ethnic life experiences in their learning. Effective teachers are responsive to including cultural and diverse resources in their curriculum and instructional practices.

Exposing students to culturally sensitive room decorations and posters that show positive and inclusive messages are a few ways to demonstrate inclusion of multiple cultures. Teachers should also continuously make cultural connections that are relevant and empowering for all students; they should also communicate academic and behavioral expectations. Cultural sensitivity must be communicated beyond the classroom with parents and community members to establish and maintain relationships.

Diversity can be further defined as the following:

- Differences among learners, classroom settings, and academic outcomes
- Biological, sociological, ethnic, socioeconomic, and psychological differences, as well as different learning modalities and styles among learners
- Differences in classroom settings that promote learning opportunities such as collaborative, participatory, and individualized learning groupings
- Expected learning outcomes that are theoretical, affective, and cognitive for students

Teachers should establish a classroom climate that is culturally respectful and engaging for students. In a culturally sensitive classroom, teachers maintain equity and fairness in student interactions and curriculum implementation. Assessments include cultural responses and perspectives that become further learning opportunities for students. Other artifacts that could reflect teacher/student sensitivity to diversity might consist of the following:

- Student portfolios reflecting multicultural/multiethnic perspectives
- Journals and reflections from field trips or guest speakers from diverse cultural backgrounds
- Printed materials and wall displays from multicultural perspectives
- Parent/guardian letters in a variety of languages, reflecting cultural diversity
- Projects that include cultural history and diverse inclusions
- Disaggregated student data reflecting cultural groups
- Classroom climate of professionalism that fosters diversity and cultural inclusion

The target of diversity allows teachers a variety of opportunities to expand their experiences with students, staff, community members, and parents from culturally diverse backgrounds. This allows their experiences to be proactively applied in promoting cultural diversity inclusion in the classroom. Teachers are able to engage and challenge students to develop their own diversity skills in building character and relationships with cultures beyond their own. In changing the thinking patterns of students to become more culturally inclusive in the 21st century, teachers are addressing the globalization of our world.

CULTURAL FACTORS AND PERSPECTIVES THAT AFFECT RELATIONSHIPS

The mobile nature of society today provides a broader mixture of cultures around the country. Students moving from school to school may experience different curriculums and different school cultural factors. As educators expect the students to adapt, they must remember that the schools themselves must also consider the student's individual cultural influences.

Cultural relationships, morals, and values are not unique to students with disabilities. However, it is important to keep in mind that in certain cultures, individual differences may be thought of very differently than that of the current school. Many cultures now accept disabilities and realize the value and capability of students with them; however, there are still some cultures and beliefs that shield and hide those who appear to be different. When discussing a child's disabilities with the parents or guardians, it is important to keep in mind their views on disabilities.

Additionally, acculturation is not something that occurs overnight. It takes years for students to become acculturated. Students who move from a foreign country and do not speak English can take up to seven years to become proficient in English. This is not a disability: it is the natural progression of language acquisition. The timeline can be similar for other aspects of culture. When considering the identification of students who are not succeeding in school, teachers must take into consideration these types of cultural factors. There are a number of acculturation surveys that can be used to help guide the teacher in examining the role of culture in the academic performance of the student.

Community agencies can often help schools bridge these cultural gaps. Reaching out to families by including appropriate translators/translations, encouraging parents to share their heritage and traditions with the school and other students, and respecting that differences of what is acceptable will help all involved parties.

Beyond language, it is important to respect and provide accommodations for other cultural factors. Holidays may be significantly different for certain ethnicities. Another area may even include the food served in the cafeteria; if the culture requires that foods are, for example, Kosher or vegetarian, the school may need to make reasonable modifications.

The general issues that surround multiculturalism within schools are simply exacerbated when dealing with disabilities. Identification of a disability naturally increases the stress level and can damage the relationships; therefore, it is more important to extend any possible method to secure positive interactions. Keeping all of these issues in mind—as well as the issues specific to the culture—will ensure a more productive educational process for all.

Skill 9.08   Demonstrates knowledge of how to use technology for planning and managing the teaching and learning environment.

Part of being a teacher in modern times means being able to perform the simplest and most complicated tasks of the job on a computer. Most schools take attendance electronically; the teacher may need to take a few minutes during class to enter attendance into a computer. Additionally, if a teacher is going to write a letter to all the parents, a standard form (template) may already exist on the database that will allow for individualizing the message to each parent. It may also address envelopes or create mailing labels to the parents.

Grade books can be found in electronic formats. Many school districts use programs like "Easy Grade Pro" and "Grade Quick." Some districts make their teacher's grade books accessible to parents on a daily basis by using Web-based programs such as TeacherEase. This provides teachers with a reason not to fall behind in grading.

Large textbook companies often include electronic lesson planners as part of their packaging. These may come with prepackaged lessons that assist teacher preparation and allow for teachers to individualize their needs. They also train teachers to find the work in PDF (digital format) and attach it directly to the lesson, which allows for easy access to what must be copied for the lesson that day.

Simple programs exist for teachers who choose to use technology for their grade books and/or lesson plans, even if their schools do not use this type of technology. Microsoft offers free templates for teacher grade books, and TeacherEase (http://www.teacherease.com) offers one year free access to the first three teachers in a school who use their program. These are only a few of the programs accessible for free.

Most of these programs stated above require the teacher to spend time learning the system. This most likely means that teachers will have to attend an in-service and/or find a colleague to go to for answers. Remember, these are not shortcuts; they are tools of the trade.

The most important thing a teacher must remember when using this type of technology is that a hardcopy (print out) is his or her salvation when the system goes down. Save information often and plan to print out the work at least weekly.

COMPETENCY 10.0 **UNDERSTAND THE DEVELOPMENT AND IMPLEMENTATION OF EFFECTIVE BEHAVIOR MANAGEMENT AND BEHAVIOR INTERVENTION STRATEGIES FOR STUDENTS WITH DISABILITIES**

Skill 10.01 **Identifies individualized expectations for the personal and social behavior of students with disabilities in given settings and identifying ways to support students' successful integration into various program placements.**

When considering the personal and social behavior of students with disabilities, it is important to be specific and detailed in reporting these expectations in various settings. These expectations can be included in the student's IEP or the Behavior Intervention Plan (BIP).

Students who are struggling with behavior often misread social settings and the nonverbal cues people provide to each other. In this way, their troubles can often increase (this is due to inappropriate understanding on their part, rather than outward defiance). Children with autism also have difficulties in reading social situations and using appropriate behavior.

It is important to clearly develop a plan wherein students are taught the expectations of different settings. In this way, students can begin to make generalizations and become more functional. Understanding in detail that what may be acceptable at home in private may not be acceptable in McDonalds sometimes takes numerous repetitions but is invaluable for certain students.

Students may need to practice or use role playing strategies to begin to make these types of generalizations. Field trips or other practical experiences may be the most beneficial format for ensuring student success.

Developing a plan, which has been individualized for the student, can be helpful as well. Sometimes visual aids can be used to ensure success. A note card with helpful reminders is another tool to help students remember expectations for their personal and social behaviors. A different set of reminders may need to be provided for each setting the student will be integrated into for a placement.

This type of training can begin at very young ages. Students in preschool and elementary school can begin to realize the difference in behavioral expectations, depending upon the setting. Assemblies or other large group activities can provide the public setting for students. Lunch and recess are also good times to work on these types of behavioral skills.

As the child ages, mock interviews, field trips, and frank, honest discussions may be strategies of more use. In any case, students often require direct teaching of these skills; skills most of us take for granted. A teacher may hear a colleague ask why a student doesn't understand why it's inappropriate to do "that" in the classroom. In this situation, the answer may be as simple as no one taught the student it was wrong.

Skill 10.02   Demonstrates knowledge of how to use performance data and information from all stakeholders to modify the learning environment to manage behaviors.

The special education teacher has the additional role of being an advocate for assigned students. It is particularly important when there are students moving from room to room, as they do in a secondary environment, for teachers to listen to the input of all who have interactions with that student. This includes parents, each of the student's teachers, and service providers. As professionals, teachers look for what appears to be causing a problem. What is the antecedent to the behavior? If this can be seen uniformly with those who work with the student, a behavior plan can be easily written. However, student behavior is often influenced by those around them.

For example, Johnny may talk all the way through Algebra with Mrs. Desmond and behave the same with four of his other teachers, but when he is with Mr. Hammond, he may be well behaved. When effective teachers get together and discuss a student's needs, they almost always discover something that works and acknowledge what they know does not work. A discussion about why Johnny does well in Mr. Hammond's class would be the best way to address this issue. Just what does Mr. Hammond do that is different? If Mr. Hammond has assigned Johnny to sit in the front row and in every other class he sits in the back, a possible solution to try would be preferential seating in the front of the room.

Sometimes parents will ask questions about how to address behaviors. Listen to them. They may be asking about something the student needs help with in school. Formulating a plan together with the parents, as well as with other staff and teachers, creates a team approach. It provides a level of consistency that will interfere with a student's ability to successfully manipulate the individual teacher.

Talk to colleagues to find out what is successful. Find out what consistently does not work. If a change in seating works, or if providing opportunities for movement or "planned ignoring" are successful in more than just one classroom, these actions should be given a uniform trial. In this manner, team approaches to behavioral issues often provide a way for students to learn appropriate behaviors in a shorter period of time.

Skill 10.03 **Demonstrates knowledge of ethics, laws, rules, and procedural safeguards related to planning and implementing behavior management and discipline for students with and without disabilities.**

The state of Georgia has its own guidelines for handling behaviors of students with and without disabilities. These guidelines can be found at http://www.gadoe.org.

The specific Georgia law/codes that pertain to the implementation of behavior management of special education students can be found at http://rules.sos.state.ga.us/cgi-bin/page.cgi?d=1.

Positive behavioral interventions and supports (PBS) is IDEA's preferred strategy for handling challenging behaviors of students with disabilities. IDEA requires PBS to be considered in all cases of students whose behavior impedes their learning or the learning of others.

IDEA requires that "in the case of a child whose behavior impedes his or her learning or that of others," a student's IEP team, while developing an IEP (initial development, review, or revision), is required to "consider, when appropriate, strategies, including positive behavioral interventions, strategies, and supports to address that behavior."

PBS involves the use of positive behavioral interventions and systems to attain socially significant behavior change. PBS has four interrelated components: systems change activities, environmental alterations activities, skill instruction activities, and behavioral consequence activities. These come together to form a behaviorally based systems approach to enhance the ability of schools, families, and communities to create effective environments that improve the link between research-validated practices and the environments in which teaching and learning occur.

In most states, a student can be removed from school for disciplinary reasons for a period of time not exceeding 10 consecutive school days. Removals of less than 10 consecutive days may be implemented as long as those removals do not represent an alteration of placement for the student.

The IEP team and additional qualified staff must assess whether the behavior in question is part of the student's disability before a disabled student's placement can be modified as a result of disciplinary action. If the student's behavior is assessed to be part of the student's disability, the student's placement cannot be modified as part of a disciplinary tactic. The IEP team may assess that a modification of placement is required in order to provide a free, appropriate public education (FAPE) in the least restrictive environment.

The district has to give services to a student with a disability who has been taken from his or her current placement for more than 10 school days in the school year as a result of disciplinary action. School staff can place a student in an interim alternative educational setting (IAES) without the consent of the parent for the same time frame that a student without a disability could be placed, but not more than 45 calendar days (e.g., if the student brings a weapon or firearm to school, knowingly possesses or uses illegal drugs, or sells or solicits the sale of a controlled substance while at school).

After the functional behavioral assessment is performed, the IEP team must convene to create a positive behavior intervention plan that addresses the behavior in question and makes sure that the plan is put into place. Information from the FBA is utilized to create meaningful interventions and plan for instruction in replacement behaviors. The IEP team must review the positive behavior intervention plan and how it s implemented to decide if changes are needed to make the plan more effective.

Skill 10.04 **Demonstrates knowledge of the principle of using the least intrusive behavior management strategy consistent with the needs of students with disabilities.**

Please refer to Skill 9.04 for useful classroom interventions.

Below are helpful methods of managing behavior in general; however, Georgia has a system of behavior procedures in a systematic format that can be found at http://public.doe.k12.ga.us/index.aspx.

IDENTIFY WAYS OF FACILITATING POSITIVE STUDENT BEHAVIOR IN AN ACADEMIC SETTING

Social skills training is an essential part of working with students who exhibit academic and social problems. Often, these two problem areas—academic and social deficits—appear together. This issue presents a "chicken-and-egg" situation: Does the learning problem cause the behavior problem, or does the behavior problem cause the learning problem?

Typically social skills are taught within the academic setting in special education. This is accomplished through classroom rules and contingency point systems that focus on both areas at the same time. Rules, few in number, written in a positive direction, and designed jointly with students, help to set standards for acceptable behavior within the classroom. Contingency point systems are established to reinforce the occurrence of these behaviors, as well as other academic and social behaviors that are considered appropriate. Reinforcement contingencies are an important means of encouraging their use.

It is important that the physical environment be arranged so that preventive discipline can occur. By this means, the teacher assumes responsibility for creating and maintaining an environment in which the needs of his or her charges are met. The teacher may modify the physical aspects of the room to create a warm, motivating atmosphere; adapt instructional materials to the respective functioning levels of the students; and deliver specialized services through the use of systematic, reinforcing methods and techniques. When instructional environments, materials, and techniques are implemented that respond to the academic needs of students, the personal needs of the student are often met as well, with a parallel effect of increased learning and appropriate social behaviors.

According to Henley, Ramsey, and Algozzine (1993, 1995), positive student behavior is facilitated by the teacher through techniques such as the following:

1. Provide students with cues about expected behavior. Both verbal and nonverbal signals may become a part of the general classroom routine. The teacher provides cues about acceptable and unacceptable behavior in a consistent manner.
2. Provide appropriate and necessary structure. Based on individual differences and needs, structure should be built into the environment. Children with aggressive and anxious traits may need a high degree of structure, while others with less significant conditions will require lesser, but varied, amounts of structure. In this sense, structure relates to teacher direction, physical arrangement of environment, routines and scheduling, and classroom rules.
3. Involve each student in the learning process. Allow them to manipulate things, to explore surroundings, to experiment with alternative solutions, to compare findings with those of classmates, and to pose questions and seek answers. This helps to instill an internal focus of control while meaningfully involving the child in the learning process.
4. Enable the student to experience success. If the student is not provided tasks or activities in which success can be experienced, the teacher can expect misbehavior or withdrawal. Having successful experiences are vital in developing feelings of self-worth and confidence in attempting new activities (Jones and Jones 1986).
5. Use interest boosting. If signs of disinterest or restlessness occur, the teacher should quickly show interest in the student. Conversing with the student may stimulate renewed interest or enthusiasm.
6. Diffuse tension through humor. A humorous comment may bring forth laughter, thereby lessening the tension in a stressful situation.
7. Help the student hurdle lessons that produce difficulty. The teacher can get a student back on track by assisting in the answering of difficult problems. Thus, the hurdle is removed and the student is back on task.

8. Use signal interference. Cue the student with signals so that a potential problem can be extinguished. Individualized signals may be designed and directed toward specific students.

9. Incorporate antiseptic bouncing when it is obvious that a student needs to be temporarily removed from the classroom situation. This technique is useful in dispelling uncontrollable laughter or hiccups and in helping the student get over feelings of anger or disappointment. This approach involves no punishment; removal may be in the form of delivering a message, getting a drink of water, or other chores that appear routine.

10. Use teacher reinforcing. The teacher "catches the child engaged in appropriate behavior" and reinforces him or her at that time. For example, the teacher praises the student's task-oriented behavior in an effort to keep him or her from getting off task.

11. Employ planned ignoring. Unless the behavior is of a severe, harmful, or self-injurious nature, the teacher purposefully ignores the child. This strategy helps to extinguish inappropriate behavior by removing a viable reinforcer—that of teacher attention. The key is to deliver substantial reinforcement for appropriate behavior.

12. Use teacher commanding. The teacher uses direct verbal commands in an effort to stop the misbehavior. This technique should not be continued, however, if the student does not stop the inappropriate behavior upon the first instance he or she is told to do so. Inappropriate behavior will probably worsen upon repeated verbal commands.

13. Try teacher focusing. The teacher expresses empathy or understanding about the student's feelings, situation, or plight. The teacher uses inquiry to obtain information from the student, and then offers reasons or possible solutions to the problem.

14. Utilize teacher redirecting. The student exhibiting an inappropriate behavior is brought back on task by having him or her perform an action that is compatible to the previous appropriate behavior. For example, the child who stops singing and starts poking a peer might be asked to play a musical instrument.

Skill 10.05   Demonstrates knowledge of strategies for increasing students' self-awareness, self-control, and self-management and identifying strategies for crisis prevention, intervention, and management.

Strategies to address self-awareness, self-control, and self-management require the teacher to address the student's self-concept. Self-concept may be defined as the collective attitudes or feelings that one holds about oneself. Children with disabilities perceive, early in life, that they are deficient in skills that seem easier for their peers without disabilities. They also receive expressions of surprise or even disgust from both adults and children in response to their differing appearance and actions, again resulting in damage to the self-concept. For these reasons, the special education teacher will want to direct special and continuing effort to bettering each child's own perception of him or herself.

1. The poor self-concept of a child with disabilities causes that student, at times, to exhibit aggression or rage over inappropriate things. The teacher can ignore this behavior unless it is dangerous to others or too distracting to the total group, thereby reducing the amount of negative conditioning in the child's life. Further, the teacher can praise this child, quickly and frequently, for the correct responses he or she makes, remembering that these responses may require special effort on the student's part to produce. Further, correction, when needed, can be done tactfully, in private.

2. The child whose poor self-concept manifests itself in withdrawn behavior should be pulled gently into as many social situations as possible by the teacher. This child must be encouraged to share experiences with the class, to serve as teacher helper for projects, and to be part of small groups for tasks. Again, praise for performing these group and public acts is most effective if done immediately.

3. The teacher can plan, in advance, to structure the classroom experiences so that aversive situations will be avoided. Thus, settings that stimulate the aggressive child to act out can be redesigned, and situations that stimulate group participation can be set up in advance for the child who acts in a withdrawn manner.

4. Frequent, positive, and immediate are the best terms to describe the teacher feedback required by children with disabilities. Praise for very small correct acts should be given immediately and repeated when each correct act is repeated. Criticism or outright scolding should be done, whenever possible, in private. The teacher should first check the total day's interactions with students to ensure that the number and qualitative content of verbal stimuli is heavily on the positive side. While this trait is desirable in all good teaching, it is fundamental and utterly necessary to build the fragile self-concept of youngsters with disabilities.

5. The teacher must have a strategy for use with the child who persists in negative behavior outbursts. One system is to intervene immediately and break the situation down into three components. First, the teacher requires the child to identify the worst possible outcome from the situation, the thing that he or she fears. To do this task, the child must be required to state the situation in the most factual way he or she can. Second, he or she is required to state what would really happen if this worst possible outcome happened and to evaluate the likelihood of it happening. Third, he or she is asked to state an action or attitude that can be taken, after examining

the consequences in a new light. This process has been termed **rational emotive therapy**.

Self-Control and Self-Management

Intrinsic rewards are the best method for creating behavioral changes. The difficulty in creating affective intrinsic rewards is that the student needs to understand what the reward is, as well as why he or she should consider the reward. Simple tasks, such as self-monitoring by students filling in their own points on a behavior chart or recording a daily assigned action, provide such a method.

Self-management requires the ability to observe and note one's own behavior. It requires the ability to define what is wrong and what is the desired behavior. It requires the student to have the ability to control his or her behavior at specific times. If a student is able to understand these concepts, self-management programs can and should be developed to address behavioral issues.

Creating and monitoring such a system still requires observation and praise for the desired behaviors, but what should truly be praised is the control the student is exerting over past behaviors. Speaking to the student about these behaviors requires confidentiality—the ability to talk to the student without others listening. The student needs to hear both praise and criticism, but he or she does not need to be embarrassed because the teacher is praising a behavior others may normally exhibit.

Crisis Prevention

According to the Center for Effective Collaboration and Practice, most schools themselves are safe, but violence from surrounding communities has begun to make its way into the schools. Fortunately, there are ways to intervene and prevent crises in our schools.

Administrators, teachers, families, students, support staff, and community leaders must be trained and/or informed on the early warning signs of potentially harmful behavior. However, it should also be emphasized that teachers should not use these warning signs to inappropriately label or stigmatize individual students simply because they may display some of the following warning signs.

Early warning signs
- Social withdraw
- Excessive feelings of isolation and being alone
- Excessive feelings of rejection
- Being a victim of violence
- Feelings of being picked on and persecuted
- Low school interest and poor academic performance
- Expression of violence in writings and drawings
- Uncontrolled anger

- Patterns of impulsive and chronic hitting, intimidating, and bullying behaviors
- History of discipline problems
- Past history of violent and aggressive behavior
- Intolerance for differences and prejudicial attitudes
- Drug use and alcohol use
- Affiliation with gangs
- Inappropriate access to, possession of, and use of firearms
- Serious threats of violence

Early warning signs and imminent warning signs differ; imminent warning signs require an immediate response. Imminent warning signs indicate that a student is very close to behaving in a way that is potentially dangerous to self and/or others.

Imminent warning signs
- Serious physical fighting with peers or family members
- Severe destruction of property
- Severe rage for seemingly minor reasons
- Detailed threats of lethal violence
- Possession and/or use of firearms and other weapons
- Other self-injurious behaviors or threats of suicide

When imminent signs are seen, school staff must follow the school board policies in place. These typically include reporting the behavior to a designated person or persons before handling anything alone.

Intervention and prevention plan
Every school system's plans maybe different, but the plan should be derived from some of the following suggestions:

Share responsibility by establishing a partnership with the child, school, home, and community. Schools should work with community agencies to coordinate their prevention plan (they should also partner to render services to students who may need assistance). The community involvement should include child and family service agencies, law enforcement and juvenile justice systems, mental health agencies, businesses, faith and ethnic leaders, and other community agencies.

Inform parents and listen to them when early warning signs are observed. Effective and safe schools make persistent efforts to involve parents by routinely informing them about school discipline policies, procedures, and rules; informing them about their children's behavior (both good and bad); involving them in making decisions concerning school-wide disciplinary policies and procedures; and encouraging them to participate in prevention.

Maintain confidentiality and parents' rights to privacy. Parental involvement and consent is required before personally identifiable information is shared with other agencies, except in the case of emergencies or suspicion of abuse.

Develop the capacity of staff, students, and families to intervene. Schools should provide the entire school community—teachers, students, parents, and support staff—with training and support in responding to imminent warning signs, preventing violence, and intervening safely and effectively. Interventions must be monitored by professionals who are competent in the approach.

Support students in being responsible for their actions. Schools and members of the community should encourage students to consider themselves to be responsible for their actions and actively engage them in planning, implementing, and evaluating violence prevention initiatives.

Simplify staff requests for urgent assistance. Many school systems and community agencies have complex legalistic referral systems with timelines and waiting lists. This should be a simple process that does not prevent someone from requesting assistance.

Drill and practice. Schools are now required to have drills and provide practice to ensure that everyone is informed of the proper procedure to follow if emergencies occur. In addition to violence caused by a student, the emergency can also be an intruder in the building, a bomb threat, or fire.

Skill 10.06   Demonstrates knowledge of various reinforcement techniques and strategies for planning and implementing individualized reinforcement systems and environmental modifications.

Reinforcement is the procedure in which an event follows a behavior and increases the probability or rate of that behavior. Positive reinforcement refers to the relationship between a behavior and a consequence; a positive reinforcer is the consequence itself. A positive reinforcer increases or maintains the future rate and/or probability of occurrence of a behavior.

In order to be effective, a positive reinforcer must meet the following criteria:

1. Administered contingently upon the production of the desired behavior
2. Administered immediately following the production of the desired behavior
3. Worthwhile in size
4. Administered in such a manner that satiation does not occur

There are two major types of reinforcers that may be used in the school setting: primary reinforcers and secondary reinforcers.

Primary Reinforcers

Primary reinforcers may be referred to as those stimuli that have biological importance to an individual. They may be described as natural, unlearned, unconditioned, and innately motivating. For example, youngsters do not have to be taught that eating tasty foods or drinking refreshing drinks will make them feel good, because they are naturally appealing to most people (Alberto and Troutman 1990; Zirpoli and Melloy 1993).

As a category, primary reinforcers include foods, liquids, sleep, shelter, and love. Two of the most common and appropriate reinforcers for use in the classroom are food and liquids. Edible reinforcers have been found to be strong motivators for students with low functioning abilities, for younger students, and for students who are learning a new behavior.

The necessity for the student to be in a state of deprivation is a major drawback in the use of primary reinforcers. However, a state of hunger is not required in order for treats or special foods to be effective as reinforcers.

The opposite condition of deprivation is satiation. The deprivation state that existed before the instructional session may no longer exist; thus, the stimulus may cease to be an effective motivator.

Some suggestions for preventing satiation include the following:

1. Vary reinforcers with instructional tasks
2. Shorten the instructional sessions, and presentations of reinforcers will decrease
3. Alternate reinforcers (e.g., food, then juice)
4. Decrease the size of edibles presented
5. Have an array of edibles available

Always remember, teachers must be cautious in the administration of edibles.

Medical records may need to be consulted prior to using food reinforcers in the classroom. A student may be on a special diet, have lactose intolerance or allergic reactions to certain foods, or may be susceptible to diabetic reactions. Liquid reinforcers increase the necessity for toileting breaks. Certain cereals or bite-size fruits may be better reinforcers than candy (the sugar content and size are easier to control). Teachers also need to remember that what is reinforcing for one student is not necessarily reinforcing for another.

Secondary Reinforcers

Secondary reinforcers are those that are not necessarily naturally reinforcing to most people. Their value is learned: it is conditioned through an association—or pairing—with activities, praise, body language, and attention. A token economy system is included under secondary reinforcers.

The combined use of primary and secondary reinforcers is known as pairing. By this method, secondary reinforcers become of value to the student. For example, when the teacher pairs verbal praise with the delivery of an edible like cereal or cookies to a child, the verbal praise takes on some of the reinforcement value of the treat. In this case, the teacher is attempting to fade-out, or decrease, the use of a food as a reinforcer, and fade-in, or increase, the value of verbal praise. If the teacher is successful in doing this, verbal praise will become a secondary reinforcer capable of maintaining or increasing the desired behavior (Albern and Troutman 1990; Zirpoli and Melloy 1993).

This conditioning process is important for several reasons:

1. The student may become temporarily satiated with the primary reinforcer.
2. It is not always possible for the teacher to achieve deprivation of the reinforcer.
3. The student may become dependent upon the primary reinforcer.

The effectiveness of primary reinforcers is not based on learning but rather on biological effects produced within the student. Conversely, the effectiveness of secondary reinforcers is based on conditioning or learning.

Other examples of social reinforcers include teacher proximity, physical contact of an appropriate nature between teacher and student, the granting of status privileges, and verbal or nonverbal expressions or words that convey approval of the student's accomplishments or performance. Additional examples of activity reinforcers include activities that students voluntarily participate in when given the chance, selected chores, favored involvement in the classroom (e.g., captain of a team, use of craft center, access to the computer, extra free time), and peer activities (e.g., listening to music, singing, dancing, playing chess). Some limitations to the use of activity reinforcers include the following factors:

1. Access to selected activities may not always be possible
2. Some activities are available regardless of performance, such as the library, art and music classes, physical education, and lunch periods

THE ADVANTAGES AND DISADVANTAGES OF USING VARIOUS TYPES OF REINFORCERS IN THE SCHOOL SETTING

It is a generally accepted fact that teachers need to create positive learning environments that will meet their students' special needs and accommodate individual learning styles. The need to develop appropriate antecedent stimuli (e.g., classroom arrangement, task assignments, instructions preceding performance) is considered to be of much importance; however, emphasis is placed heavily on the consequential events that follow a behavior. This can be seen in the basic rules of behaviorism: (1) behavior that is reinforced tends to occur more frequently; (2) behavior that is no longer reinforced will be extinguished; (3) behavior that is punished will occur less often. Thus, teachers must systematically be able to use reinforcers that are available to all children during the normal course of a school day.

Social Reinforcement

Social reinforcement refers to the behaviors of others that directly influence the increase in a child's behavior. The range of potential social reinforcers includes verbal expressions that convey approval of the students' accomplishments (e.g., praise such as "I like the way you stayed at your desk," or "You did a great job!"), nonverbal expressions (e.g., winking, smiling), teacher proximity to student (e.g., hug, pat on the back), and the granting of privileges that carry status for the student among his or her peers. Social reinforcement can be used as a planned teaching technique, or it can be given spontaneously.

The advantages of using social reinforcement are many. It is easy to use, absorbing little of the teacher's time and effort, and it is available in any setting. The fact that teachers are persons who possess high status in the students' eyes makes it especially appropriate for use. Social reinforcement rarely incurs criticism, is unlikely to satiate, and can be generalized to most situations. The main disadvantage is that it may not be a strong enough reinforcer; thus, teachers may need to pair it with a tangible reinforcer.

Activity Reinforcement

Activity reinforcement refers to the involvement in preferred activities. The systematic use of activity reinforcers is described by the Premack Principle. It states that any activity that a student voluntarily does on a frequent basis (i.e., a high interest activity) can be used as a reinforcer for any activity in which the student seldom participates (e.g., running errands, decorating a bulletin board, leading a group activity, earning free time).

Major advantages in using activity reinforcers include their ready availability and unlimited accessibility, thus preventing satiation. If a student tires of one activity, there are many others that can be used. Special needs children are less likely to be considered "different" when engaged in earned activity time, and activity reinforcers can be combined with social reinforcers. Furthermore, once activity reinforcers are identified with the learning environment, they can be acquired with little effort. Disadvantages in the use of activity reinforcers are few but might include the need for handling delayed gratification and the possibility of interrupting other classroom activities.

Token Reinforcement
A system whereby children are given immediate reinforcement by means of an object that can be exchanged for a reinforcer of value at a future time is called token reinforcement. In using this system, the token is delivered contingent on a desired response. Tokens should be durable, practical, and easily dispensed. They can be in the form of objects (e.g., poker chips, play money, stars, or tickets), or they can be symbols like happy faces, check marks, or points. Used alone, tokens have little or no value or power. Their reinforcing value is attained by virtue of their being exchanged for a variety of reinforcing rewards, known as backup reinforcers. The backup reinforcers must be items desired by all the students using the token reinforcement system. An array of items— tangible objects such as trinkets, school supplies, edibles, and activities—need to be available for selection,.

Use of a token economy system has advantages. They provide a concrete means for immediate reinforcement and an observable record of accomplishments. Tokens can be given without interfering with classroom activities, and their use is generally acceptable by teachers, peers, and parents.

Use of this system necessitates a well-organized management system that does require time and energy to operate successfully. Other considerations include dependency upon receiving concrete, immediate reinforcement, the need to acquire an assortment of desirable backup reinforcers, and the inability to readily generalize this system into another environment. However, many teachers have found the token reinforcement system to be of great benefit in modifying student behavior and report that the advantages far outweigh required efforts on their part.

Tangible Reinforcement
As the name suggests, the use of tangible items as consequential reinforcement for desired behavior is called tangible reinforcement. This system can be used by itself or as a part of another system, such as token reinforcement. Tangible items dispensed in the educational setting are typically those that can be used or consumed in the classroom for academic activities, including pencils, paper, erasers, or items that can be consumed during free activity time, like baseball cards, game items, trinkets, or posters.

Tangible reinforcers are considered desirable by children because they are concrete items. Therefore, their high reinforcing value enhances their effectiveness. This primary advantage, however, must be weighed in relation to possible disadvantages. Tangible reinforcers can be costly and hard to acquire, must be age appropriate, and, if given only to special needs students, may make them appear different from their peers. Children must receive this type of reinforcement less frequently, or else satiation will occur. The less frequent aspect, however, means that immediate reinforcement based on contingent behavior is unlikely to occur.

Many teachers pair tangible reinforcers with activity or social reinforcers, and therefore eventually fade the tangible rewards in lieu of using intangible means of reinforcement.

Schedule Reinforcement

Schedules of reinforcement refer to when the delivery of reinforcement occurs. A continuous schedule of reinforcement is used with new behaviors. Once the new behavior has become established, a more infrequent type of reinforcer is desirable to maintain the behavior and to avoid satiation.

Intermittent schedules are those when reinforcement follows some, but not all, correct or desirable behaviors. Intermittent schedules: (1) require greater numbers of correct responses for reinforcement; (2) require the maintenance of appropriate behavior over longer periods of time; and (3) are more resistant to extinction.

Ratio refers to the number of times a target behavior occurs as the determinant for the timing of the delivery of the reinforcer. Interval refers to the amount of time before a target behavior occurs as the determinant for the timing of the delivery of the reinforcer. A fixed number of behaviors or amount of time may be required; a variable number of behaviors or amount of time may also be established. The four schedules reflecting these components are as follows:

1. **Fixed Ratio.** A fixed ratio schedule requires that a person be reinforced every time he or she completes a fixed number of correct responses. For example, Tom must complete 10 math problems before he receives a point for staying on task.
2. **Variable ratio.** A variable ratio schedule requires that a person be reinforced when he or she completes a variable number of responses. The number of responses required for reinforcement varies every time. For example, as the teacher circulates among students working on math problems, reinforcement may occur upon completion of the second, fifth, or eighth math fact.
3. **Fixed Interval.** In a fixed interval schedule, the person must: (1) wait for a fixed time to pass, during which responses are not reinforced, and (2) make a response after that time that will be reinforced. For example, a

student receives a token or verbal praise following the elapse of a specified number of minutes if he or she is in the correct seat at that instance during reading period.
4. **Variable Interval.** In a variable interval schedule, the person must: (1) wait for a varying length of time to pass during which responses have no effect, and (2) make a response after that time that will be reinforced. For example, a student is reinforced if he or she is in the correct seat following 2, 5, 10, or 20 minutes of working on an assigned task in reading.

Skill 10.07   Demonstrates knowledge of how to integrate academic instruction with behavior management, including knowledge of non-aversive techniques for controlling targeted behavior and maintaining the attention of students with disabilities.

See Skill 9.04 for a breakdown of nonaversive behavior management techniques.

Skill 10.08   Demonstrates knowledge of procedures for reviewing, evaluating, and amending behavior management and intervention strategies.

Please go to http://rules.sos.state.ga.us/cgi-bin/page.cgi?d=1 for specific information for the state of Georgia.

A Functional Behavior Assessment (FBA) is a method of gathering information. The information that is collected is utilized to assess why problem behaviors occur. The data also helps to pinpoint things to do that will help alleviate the behaviors. The data from a functional behavioral assessment is used to create a positive behavioral intervention plan.

The Individuals with Disabilities Education Act (IDEA) specifically calls for a functional behavior assessment when a child with a disability has his or her present placement modified for disciplinary reasons. IDEA does not elaborate on how an FBA should be conducted, as the procedures may vary dependent on the specific child. Even so, there are several specific elements that should be a part of any functional behavior assessment.

The first step is to identify the particular behavior that must be modified. If the child has numerous problem behaviors, it is important to assess which behaviors are the primary ones that should be addressed. This should be narrowed down to one or two primary behaviors. The primary behavior is then described so that everyone is clear as to what the behaviors are. The most typical order of procedures is as follows:

- Identify and come to an agreement about the behaviors that need to be modified.

- Find out where the behaviors are most likely to happen and where they are not likely to happen. Identify what may trigger the behavior to occur.
- The team will ask these types of questions: What is unique about the surroundings where behaviors are not an issue? What is different in the locations where the problem conduct occurs? Could the problems be linked to how the child and teacher get along? Does the number of other students or the work a child is requested to do trigger the difficulty? Could the time of day or a child's frame of mind affect the behaviors? Was there a bus problem or an argument in the hallway? Are the behaviors likely to happen in a precise set of conditions or a specific location? What events seem to encourage the difficult behaviors?
- Assemble data on the child's performance from as many resources as feasible.
- Develop a hypothesis about why difficult behaviors transpire (the function of the behaviors). A hypothesis is an educated deduction based on data. It helps foretell in which location and for what reason problem behaviors are most likely to take place and in which location and for what reason they are least likely to take place. Single out other behaviors that can be taught that will fulfill the same purpose for the child.
- Test the hypothesis. The team develops and utilizes positive behavioral interventions that are written into the child's IEP or behavior intervention plan.
- Assess the success of the interventions. Modify or fine-tune as required.

If children have behaviors that place them or others at risk, they may require a crisis intervention plan. Crisis interventions should be developed before they are required. The team should determine what behaviors are crises, as well as what they (and the child) will do in a crisis. By having a plan that guides actions, teachers can assist children through difficult emotional circumstances.

Essential Elements of Behavior Intervention Plan

A behavior intervention plan is utilized to reinforce or teach positive behavior skills. It is also known as a behavior support plan or a positive intervention plan. The child's team normally develops the behavior intervention plan. The essential elements of a behavior intervention plan are as follows:

- Skills training to increase the likelihood of appropriate behavior
- Modifications that will be made in classrooms or other environments to decrease or remove problem behaviors
- Strategies to take the place of problem behaviors and institute appropriate behaviors that serve the same function for the child
- Support mechanisms for the child to utilize the most appropriate behaviors

The IEP team determines whether the school discipline procedures need to be modified for a child, or whether the penalties need to be different from those written into the policy. This decision should be based on an assessment and a review of the records, including the discipline records or any manifestation determination review(s) that have been concluded by the school.

A child's IEP or behavior intervention plan should concentrate on teaching skills. Sometimes school discipline policies are not successful in rectifying problem behaviors. That is, the child does not learn what the school staff intended through the use of punishments, such as suspension. The child may learn instead that problem behaviors are useful in meeting a need, such as being noticed by peers. When this is true, it is difficult to defend punishment, by itself, as effective in changing problem behaviors.

One of the most useful questions parents can ask when they have concerns about the discipline recommendations for their child is "Where are the data that support the recommendations?" Special education decisions are based on data. If school staff wants to use a specific discipline procedure, they should check for data that support the use of the procedure.

COMPETENCY 11.0 UNDERSTAND PRINCIPLES AND METHODS OF PLANNING AND DELIVERING INSTRUCTION FOR STUDENTS WITH DISABILITIES

Skill 11.01 Demonstrates knowledge of how to adapt or create learning plans for students with disabilities (e.g., sensory, mobility, cognitive, behavioral) in a variety of settings (e.g., classroom, resource room, community).

Please refer to Skill 9.01 about the physical environment.

Just as no two snowflakes are the same, no two children demonstrate exactly the same skills. In this way, school systems need to consider the strengths of all students. Finding the strengths of students is something that all educators need to address.

When we look at the physical abilities of students with special needs, we must take into considerations ways to adapt the instruction and settings to maximize their ability to access the same information as other students with no physical differences.

Keeping in mind that there can be numerous physical conditions that could prevent a student from accessing the regular curriculum, it is important to be flexible in thinking and problem solving. Students may simply need items enlarged or put on tape if they have visual or auditory difficulties. In some cases, in-room audio systems can be utilized to address auditory discrimination issues; these also have a research base for helping students with attention deficit disorder.

Still other times it may be necessary to rearrange the physical layout of the room to allow enough space for walkers or wheelchairs to be maneuvered. Some children may require special pencils, pencil grips, or even regular access to an augmentative communication device to be able to participate. There are special chairs and additive seating devices that can be used to help position the students correctly.

Finding equipment is only half the battle. Sometimes, discussions with nondisabled peers are critical components overlooked by schools. Helping others to understand how to provide what is necessary without enabling is a daunting task, but one well worth undertaking. It is when everyone understands and has the opportunity to ask appropriate questions that they can truly accept others into their world without unnecessary stigma.

Many adaptations are available from a variety of sources. Schools contract with or hire their own speech therapists, occupational therapists, physical therapists, and hearing and vision specialists. Accessing the knowledge these professionals can provide can be the missing critical element to finding the appropriate needs for students to become integral members of the learning community.

Skill 11.02 **Applies knowledge of how to select, adapt, and use research-based instructional methods and materials to address the strengths and needs of students with disabilities.**

Regardless of which instructional approaches are selected as the most appropriate for the learner, the materials in that approach must match the learner's functioning level and style. Texts and workbooks are typically designated for grade-level difficulty. Kits and supplementary materials contain instructions that specify certain progressive levels of difficulty.

Teachers should be familiar with the overall scope and sequence of major subjects (e.g., reading, spelling, math) in the academic areas, from readiness abilities through higher-order learning skills. Since the exceptional students that a teacher instructs will vary in abilities, the sequence in which skills are developmentally approached, and the overall hierarchical range of the curricula from kindergarten through 12th grade, must be known in order to plan for entry-level instruction.

Some authorities assert that grade levels specified for instructional materials, especially those developed for exceptional students, may be inaccurate (Radabaugh and Yukish 1982). In attempting to evaluate the instructional level of teaching materials, several questions should be asked by the teacher. First of all, does the publisher state the readability level of the material, and does the readability level remain consistent throughout? Is there more than one book or story lesson for each level? Is there an attempt to control the use of content-specific vocabulary? Is the interest level appropriate for the content, illustrations, and age of the students who will use the material? The purpose for reading has a great deal to do with whether the material is on a comfortable or difficult level. There are instances when the reader should not encounter many new words or sentences written in a difficult manner. Wiederholt, Hammill, and Brown (1983) list these times as: (1) practicing reading (e.g., pleasure, future discussion); (2) working independently; (3) focusing on one or more aspects of comprehension; and (4) reading orally before an audience.

More difficult material may be appropriate when analyzing how a student attempts to read unknown words or new material. Material in which the student is applying skills that have previously been taught must likewise present sufficient difficulty, otherwise the student's performance may merely reflect recall of the content.

Unfortunately, as students progress into higher grade levels, many special educators become involved in tutoring. This is due to the reading difficulty of the subject content assigned and the lack of time for building foundation skills while assisting with required academic subject content.

One of the major tasks of a special educator is to find an appropriate match between materials and students, particularly in reading, as this skill is necessary in most subject areas. The customary practice is to obtain a measured reading level, either from a diagnostic type of assessment tool or from an individual reading inventory (IRI).

In addition to the instructional level, two other levels are determined when using an IRI: the independent reading level and the student's level of frustration. The IRI consists of a series of grade-level passages and a corresponding list of vocabulary words. Starting with the last level at which all vocabulary words presented are recognized, the student is asked to read the story passage silently and then out loud. Following his or her oral reading, the student is asked to answer predetermined comprehension questions. The student continues in this manner until he or she arrives at a level of frustration. This level of difficulty is considered reached whenever the teacher records 10 errors in a sample of approximately 100 running words, and comprehension questions are answered at the 50 percent level. Instruction should occur on the level where five errors are recorded during the reading sample, and comprehension questions are answered correctly at 75 percent. The student is encouraged to select library books and to pursue other types of comfortable reading at his or her independent reading level, where the student misses only one word while reading the passage, and 90 percent of the answers are considered correct. These criteria (Wiederholt, Hammill, and Brown 1983) appear in the table below.

Reading Levels

LEVEL	WORD RECOGNITION IN CONTEXT (percent)	COMPREHENSION (percent)	OBSERVABLE BEHAVIOR
Independent	99	90	Ease in reading
Instructional	95	75	No signs of frustration
Frustration	90	50	Signs of tension

Some publishing companies include IRIs along with their basal reading series. However, the teacher can easily construct the inventory him or herself. In so doing, it is suggested that passages be taken from the middle of each text in the series, ranging from the preprimer to the fifth- or sixth-grade level. Passages should be chosen that read as complete stories. Suggested approximate length of passages is 50 words at the preprimer level; 100 words at the primer, first, and second levels; and 100 to 150 words at the upper levels. Though one selection at each level to be read orally by the student may be considered by some authorities to be sufficient, an alternative guideline would be to choose two stories, one for oral reading and one for silent reading, at each level.

Word recognition tests serve three major purposes: first, a learner's sight vocabulary can be identified; second, applied word-attack skills can be pinpointed; third, initial reading instruction levels can be attempted.

Teachers can use commercially prepared word recognition lists arranged by grade-level difficulty, or teacher-made lists may be developed. Glossaries included in basal readers, from which 20 to 25 words are selected at random, can also be used. For example, after dividing the total number of words by 20 or 25, every "n^{th}" word is written on the word list.

The predetermined comprehension questions are asked after a student reads a selection from his or her estimated instructional level. It is suggested that five to ten questions be developed, with fewer questions used at the lower reading levels (e.g., preprimer, primer, first), and more questions at the upper grade range (e.g., fifth, sixth). Questions should include vocabulary and higher-level thinking skills (e.g., evaluation, appreciation), as well as those more typically asked to reflect lower-level thinking abilities (e.g., literal recognition or recall).

An informal math inventory is constructed based on grade-level skills delineated on scope and sequence charts. Sample problems are written that represent many different types of skills (e.g., computation, operations, fractions, measurement, time) at many grade levels. Some diagnostic math tests (e.g., Key Math Diagnostic Arithmetic Test-Revised, Brigance Diagnostic Inventory of Basic Skills, Wide Range Achievement Test-Revised) are suitable models from which ideas for developing sample problems can be obtained for use in teacher-made inventories. Math scope and sequence charts present objectives from which items can be selected for sampling skills. Student performance on the math inventory supplies the teacher with a guide for identifying entry level instructional skills.

EVALUATE INSTRUCTIONAL MATERIAL IN TERMS OF ITS RELEVANCE TO VARIOUS TYPES OF SPECIAL NEEDS STUDENTS AND ITS UTILITY IN MEETING THOSE NEEDS

A great amount of time and research has been devoted to developing criteria for selecting instructional materials that meet the needs of special students (Henley, Ramsey, and Algozzine 1996; Morsink 1984). The criteria listed by some authorities in this area (e.g., Brown 1983; Hammill and Bartel 1986; Mercer and Mercer 1993; Smith 1983) can be helpful to teachers as they select materials that are relevant to the needs of their students and will be useful once selected. The effectiveness of materials, of course, can be increased by adapting the way they are used.

Relevance
Materials selected for use with exceptional students should be pertinent to their needs, regardless of their categorical assignment. Hammill and Bartel (1986) recommend an examination of the following factors when evaluating relevance:

1. Are the skills and concepts required of the student present so that success can be realized?
2. Does the student's performance level correspond with the skill sequence?
3. Is there a history of success or failure with use of certain methods? Does the student react positively or negatively to particular modes of instruction (e.g., multimedia versus print only)?
4. Are there characteristics that imply needs (e.g., orthopedic restrictions, family problems, ethnic or cultural diversity)?

Brown (1975) listed 35 factors that should be considered in selecting curriculum materials for disabled learners. Criteria relating more directly to relevance include the following:

1. What range of student difference does the material encompass?
2. Are there readiness behaviors specified that are prerequisites for the student(s)?
3. Has any effort been made to assess or control the complexity of the language, either receptively or expressively?
4. Is the material obviously intended for younger children, or has it been adapted for use with older students (e.g., high interest, low vocabulary)? Does the teacher have to develop or provide background experiences, information, or interests for some students?
5. What processes have been used, and what results are available to determine readability or learner interest?
6. What are the target populations for whom the materials were developed? Are they identified?
7. Is it possible to isolate sensory channels as a major instructional variable?

In summary, the teacher will need to develop ways of determining whether criteria related to the relevancy of the materials for use with his or her special needs students is met. The teacher will need to examine the materials in relation to the academic, behavioral, developmental, and physical needs of students; their learning styles; and the behavioral objectives specified on their IEPs.

Utility

Usefulness or practicality is another criterion essential for evaluating instructional materials to be used with special needs students. When considering the utility, Brown (cited in Smith 1983) suggests that questions similar to the following be asked:

1. What is the comprehensiveness of breadth of the program? Is it useful in meeting the needs of students, or does it supplement existing programs?
2. Is the material sequenced so that mastery can be achieved before progressing to the next step, or are materials spiraled so that areas of difficulty can be left temporarily and then returned to later?
3. Is the presentation of instruction paced for various groups or individuals? Are modifications made within the material so that those who need more or different experiences at various points can receive them?
4. Are the materials useful in their organizational schemata (e.g., units, page arrangements, illustrations)?
5. Is the material teacher directed or student directed? Are materials practical for self-directed use, and if so, how is feedback received (e.g., programmed materials with self-correcting answers) and progress monitored (e.g., self-charting)?

Other questions that might be asked when considering the utility of instructional materials follow:

1. Can the material be used to accomplish a number of objectives? Is the material convenient to use for its intended purposes?
2. Will reasonable demands be made on the teacher's time when using these materials? Does the material allow for flexibility of scheduling?
3. Will additional equipment or supplies be needed to utilize the materials effectively? Does it contain many components? If so, can it be stored or transported easily?
4. Can the material be incorporated into other programs? Can it be adapted to many levels of instruction?

Skill 11.03   Demonstrates knowledge of strategies for helping students with disabilities maintain and generalize skills across learning environments.

Transfer of learning occurs when experience with one task influences performance on another task. Positive transfer occurs when the required responses and stimuli are similar, such as moving from baseball or handball to racquetball, or field hockey to soccer. Negative transfer occurs when the stimuli remain similar, but the required responses change, such as shifting from soccer to football, tennis to racquetball, or boxing to sports karate.

Instructional procedures should stress the similar features between the activities as well as the dimensions that are transferable. Specific information should emphasize when stimuli in the old and new situations are the same or similar, and when responses used in the old situation apply to the new.

To facilitate learning, instructional objectives should be arranged in order of their patterns of similarity. Objectives involving similar responses should be closely sequenced; thus, the possibility for positive transfer is stressed. Likewise, learning objectives that involve different responses should be programmed within instructional procedures in the most appropriate way possible. For example, students should have little difficulty transferring handwriting instruction to writing in other areas; however, there might be some negative transfer when moving from manuscript to cursive writing. By using transitional methods and focusing on the similarities between manuscript and cursive writing, negative transfer can be reduced.

Generalization

Generalization is the occurrence of a learned behavior in the presence of a stimulus other than the one that produced the initial response (novel stimulus). It is the expansion of a student's performance beyond conditions initially anticipated. Students must be able to generalize what is learned in other settings (e.g., reading to word problems in math, resource room to regular classroom).

Generalization training is a procedure in which a behavior is reinforced in each of a series of situations until it generalizes to other members of the same stimulus class. Stimulus generalization occurs when responses, which have been reinforced in the presence of a specific stimulus (the discriminative stimulus, or SD) occur in the presence of related stimuli (e.g., bathrooms labeled women, ladies, dames). In fact, the more similar the stimuli, the more likely it is that stimulus generalization will occur.

This concept applies to intertask similarity in that the more one task resembles another, the greater the probability the student will be able to master it. For example, if Johnny has learned the initial consonant sounds of "b" and "d," and he has been taught to read the word "dad," it is likely that when he is shown the word "bad," he will be able to pronounce this formerly unknown word upon presentation.

Generalization may be enhanced by the following:

1. Using many examples in teaching to deepen application of learned skills
2. Using consistency in initial teaching situations, later introducing variety in format, procedure, and use of examples
3. Having the same information presented by different teachers, in different settings, and under varying conditions
4. Including a continuous reinforcement schedule at first, later changing to delayed and intermittent schedules as instruction progresses
5. Teaching students to record instances of generalization and to reward themselves at that time
6. Associating naturally occurring stimuli when possible

Skill 11.04   Applies knowledge of strategies for teaching students with disabilities how to use self assessment, problem solving, metacognitive skills, and other cognitive strategies to identify and meet their own needs.

A major focus of special education is to prepare students to become working, independent members of society. IDEA 2004 (Individuals with Disabilities Education Act) also includes preparing students for *further education*. Certain skills beyond academics are needed to attain this level of functioning.

Affective and social skills transcend to all areas of life. When an individual is unable to acquire information on expectations and reactions of others, or if the individual misinterprets those cues, he or she is missing an important element needed for success as an adult in the workplace and community. Special education should incorporate a level of instruction in the affective/social area, as many students will not develop these skills without instruction, modeling, practice, and feedback.

Affective and social skills taught throughout the school setting might include social greetings; eye contact with a speaker; interpretation of facial expression, body language, and personal space; the ability to put feelings and questions into words; and use of words to acquire additional information, as needed.

Career/vocational skills of responsibility for actions, a good work ethic, and independence should be incorporated into the academic setting. If students are able to regulate their overall work habits with school tasks, it is likely that the same skills will carry over into the work force. The special education teacher may assess the student's level of career/vocational readiness by using the following list:

- Being prepared by showing responsibility for materials/school tools, such as books, assignments, study packets, pencils, pens, and assignment notebooks
- Knowing expectations by keeping an assignment notebook completed
- Asking questions when unsure of the expectations
- Use of additional checklists, as needed
- Use of needed assistive devices
- Completing assignments on time to the best of his or her ability

An additional responsibility of the special educator when teaching career/vocational skills is recognition that a variety of vocations and skills are present in the community. If academics are not an area in which students excel, other exploratory or training opportunities should be provided. Such opportunities might include art, music, culinary arts, child care, technical, or building instruction. These skills can often be included (although not to the exclusion of additional programs) within the academic setting. For example, a student with strong vocational interest in art may be asked to create a poster to show learned information in a science or social studies unit. While addressing a career/vocational interest and skill this way, the teacher would also be establishing a program of differentiated instruction.

Skill 11.05   Demonstrates knowledge of strategies for modifying classroom tests and for helping students with disabilities learn how to prepare for and take tests (e.g., development of learning strategies, study skills, and test-taking strategies).

Please see Skill 4.04 for student preparation and Skill 6.01 for accommodations in test-taking situations.

Skill 11.06 Applies knowledge of how to modify instruction, adapt materials, and provide feedback based on formative assessment and student feedback (e.g., by modifying pacing, scaffolding instruction, providing organizational cues, integrating student-initiated learning experiences into ongoing instruction, and using multiple approaches to content).

Please refer to Skill 6.01 for adapting materials and Skill 6.03 about modifying instruction.

Skill 11.07 Demonstrates knowledge of specialized materials, curricula, and resources for students with disabilities.

A key federal legislation and resource that helps ensure individuals with disabilities receive services they are entitled to is the Individuals with Disabilities Improvement Education Act of 2004 (IDEA 2004). IDEA states each public agency shall ensure, to the maximum extent appropriate, that students with disabilities are educated along with children who are not disabled. Student participation in the regular education classroom depends largely on the nature and severity of his or her disability. In addition, students with disabilities must be assured access to the general curriculum that applies to all students.

Many students with disabilities require alternate or supplemental educational materials or the use of additional resources in order to reach their fullest potentials. The special educator is responsible for being aware of those options, promoting the acquisition of such materials within their districts and using them to meet the needs of individual students. These may include (but are not limited to) items from the following list.

Books on Tape
Students with visual impairments as well as sighted students who are auditory learners may benefit from books on audiotape/CD. These are available to qualifying students from agencies such as National Library Service for the Blind and Physically Handicapped (NLS). Many titles are also available through textbook companies, libraries, and teacher resource catalogs.

Captioned Videotapes and DVDs
Students who are hearing impaired often use captioned films. Televisions manufactured after 1994 have the caption display capability. Many materials are also available in captioned format through the Captioned Films/Videos (CVF) program. This free material loan program is funded by the U.S. Department of Education.

Braille and Large-Print Materials

Some students with visual impairments benefit from large print material or from material formatted in Braille. Teacher-made worksheets and tests should be typed with a Braille typewriter or enlarged on a copy machine, as needed.

Because of the regulations with IDEA 2004, students are guaranteed access to educational materials at the same time as their general education peers. This means planning ahead to obtain the format needed by the student with a disability in the school setting.

Specially Formatted Print Material

Some students with disabilities learn best from specially formatted print material. For example, a student with a learning disability may be overwhelmed with long lists for matching by drawing lines. He or she may be better able to match short lists by writing a corresponding number or letter.

Although many textbooks highlight or bold key words, there may be times when additional formatting of vocabulary is needed. This may be in the form of a word box with corresponding definitions and example sentences.

Specially Written Curricula

Some curricula are written with a unique approach to introduction of information and skill practice. One example is the Touch Math program (Innovative Learning Concepts, Inc.), in which students learn a pattern by touching the printed numerals to compute math problems.

Certain curricula are available to meet the communication needs of some students with disabilities. The PECS or Picture Exchange Communication System (Pyramid Educational Products, Inc.) is such an example, as are some language development programs like the Apple Tree Curriculum for Developing Written Language (PRO-ED, Inc.).

Technological Resources

With the current emphasis on the use of technology for all students, as well as the general advancements in technology today, many such resources meet the individual needs of students with disabilities. Electronic spell checkers, math calculators, and augmentative communication devices are a few examples of technological resources that may be beneficial in the special education program.

Skill 11.08   Demonstrates knowledge of the impact of students' academic and social abilities, attitudes, interests, and values on instruction and career development.

THE SIGNIFICANCE OF FAMILY LIFE AND THE HOME ENVIRONMENT FOR STUDENT DEVELOPMENT AND LEARNING

The student's capacity and potential for academic success within the overall educational experience are products of her or his total environment: classroom and school system, home and family, and neighborhood and community in general. All of these segments are interrelated and can either be supportive of or divisive against one another. As a matter of course, the teacher will become familiar with all aspects of the system, the school, and the classroom pertinent to the students' educational experiences. This includes not only processes and protocols, but also the availability of resources provided to meet the academic, health, and welfare needs of students. It is incumbent upon the teacher to look beyond the boundaries of the school system to identify additional resources as well as issues and situations that will affect (directly or indirectly) a student's ability to succeed in the classroom.

Examples of Resources

- Libraries, museums, zoos, planetariums, and so on.
- Clubs, societies, and civic organizations; and community outreach programs of private businesses, corporations, and government agencies. These can provide a variety of materials and media, as well as possible speakers and presenters.
- Departments of social services operating within the local community. These can provide background and program information relevant to social issues that may be impacting individual students. These can also be resources for classroom instruction regarding life skills, at-risk behaviors, and so on.

Initial contacts for resources outside of the school system will usually come from within the system itself, including from administration, teacher organizations, department heads, and other colleagues.

Examples of Issues/Situations

1. ***Students from multicultural backgrounds*:**
   Curriculum objectives and instructional strategies may be inappropriate and unsuccessful when presented in a single format that relies on the student's understanding/acceptance of the values and common attributes of a specific culture which is not his or her own.

2. ***Parental/family influences*:**
   Attitude, resources, and encouragement available in the home environment may be attributes for success or failure.

Families with higher incomes are able to provide increased opportunities for students. Students from lower-income families will need to depend on the resources available from the school system and the community. This should be orchestrated by the classroom teacher in cooperation with school administrators and educational advocates in the community.

Family members with higher levels of education often serve as models for students and have high expectations for academic success. Additionally, families with specific aspirations for children (regardless of their own educational backgrounds) often encourage students to achieve academic success and are most active participants in the process.

A family in crisis (caused by economic difficulties, divorce, substance abuse, physical abuse, and so on) creates a negative environment that may profoundly impact all aspects of a student's life and particularly his or her ability to function academically. The situation may require professional intervention. It is often the classroom teacher who will recognize a family in crisis situation and instigate an intervention by reporting on this to school or civil authorities.

Regardless of the positive or negative impacts on the students' education from outside sources, it is the teacher's responsibility to ensure that all students in the classroom have an equal opportunity for academic success. This begins with the teacher's statement of high expectations for every student and develops through planning, delivery, and evaluation of instruction. Such actions provide for inclusion and ensure that all students have equal access to the resources necessary for successful acquisition of the academic skills being taught and measured in the classroom.

EFFECTS OF CULTURAL AND ENVIRONMENTAL INFLUENCES (E.G., CULTURAL AND LINGUISTIC DIVERSITY, SOCIOECONOMIC LEVEL, ABUSE, NEGLECT, SUBSTANCE ABUSE) ON STUDENTS AND THEIR FAMILIES

Hispanic children represent the fastest-growing minority and approximately three-fourths of the children designated as limited English proficiency (LEP). They and other culturally diverse students may speak a dialect of a language (such as Spanish) that has its own system of pronunciation and rules. It should be stressed that speaking a dialect does not in itself mean that the child has a language problem. Certain English sounds and grammar structures may not have equivalents in some languages, and failure to produce these elements may be a function of inexperience with English rather than a language delay.

When minority or culturally diverse children are being screened for language problems, learning disabilities, or other exceptional student programs, the tests and assessment procedures must be nondiscriminatory. Furthermore, testing should be done in the child's native language; however, if school instruction has not been in the native language, there may appear to be a problem because assessments typically measure school language. Even with native English-speaking children, there are differences between the language at home (or in the community) and the language requirements of school.

Normality in child behavior is influenced by society's attitudes and cultural beliefs about what is normal for children (e.g., the motto for the Victorian era was "Children should be seen and not heard"). In addition, cultural and societal attitudes towards gender change over time. While attitudes towards younger boys playing with dolls or girls preferring sports to dolls have relaxed, children eventually are expected, as adults, to conform to the expected behaviors for males and females.

COMPETENCY 12.0 UNDERSTAND STRATEGIES AND TECHNIQUES FOR PROMOTING THE DEVELOPMENT OF COMMUNICATION, SOCIAL, AND LIFE SKILLS OF STUDENTS WITH DISABILITIES

Skill 12.01 Demonstrates knowledge of how to support and enhance communication skills (e.g., developing vocabulary, self-monitoring oral language) of students with disabilities.

Objectives for oral language development are a part of many IEPs. The designated individuals to address such objectives are often speech and language pathologists, teachers, and parents. Although speech and language pathologists work with students one-on-one or in small groups, this is often in a pull-out type of environment. Most often, the student's progress and actual practice with staff and peers is monitored in the classroom by the special education teacher.

Strategies for developing content area vocabulary
- Instruction in how to identify vocabulary in text (highlighted, colored text or bold-faced words)
- Instruction in using context clues and references to synonyms/antonyms in test
- Instruction in how to use a glossary or dictionary
- Practice with study cards (word on one side and definition on the other)
- Practice completing cloze activities in which student must fill in the correct vocabulary word

Strategies for developing general vocabulary
Students will encounter new vocabulary in reading and in conversation. Some school districts use general vocabulary building programs for this purpose. Additional strategies may include:
- Have students keep a notebook or word box of new vocabulary, the word's definition in natural language, and an example sentence.
- Develop a class word wall of new vocabulary. This is sometimes done according to theme. For example, use a barn-shaped poster board to display farm-related words or a flower-shaped board for spring words.
- Reward students for use of their new vocabulary by tracking on a chart for a reward/reinforcer.

Strategies for developing social language vocabulary
- Identification and understanding of social slang
- Identification and understanding of idioms and expressions
- Understanding of personal space
- Understanding the use of eye contact when speaking to others
- Understanding of social oral language skills such as turn taking in conversations

Methods for practicing oral language
- Model the target oral language.
- Practice the target skill in structured situations.
- Expect and reinforce the use of the target oral language in the classroom setting.
- Communicate the student's progress with the target oral language to parents for carry over at home.

Methods of self-monitoring oral language
- ***Note or checklist on desk***
  As a student shows a fair level of proficiency using a target oral language skill, he or she should be expected to use it in the classroom, elsewhere in the school setting, and eventually at home. One way to help the student remember to use the newly learned skills is to attach a note or checklist to his or her desk.
- ***PECS symbols***
  Many students (particularly many autistic students) use the Picture Exchange Communication System (PECS). Some students use these small cards with icons to express wants and needs. However, more verbal students may use the picture cards as a visual prompt to use a certain word, phrase, or sentence structure.

Skill 12.02   Demonstrates knowledge of strategies for providing instruction to students with disabilities in the use of alternative and augmentative communication systems.

Technology allows students to access materials they may otherwise be unable to utilize. For example, students who are unable to speak may use technology devices to communicate. These augmentative communication systems are crucial to the participation and success of these learners. In other incidences, there are programs that will read text to students unable to see or read the text independently. Programs are available that will allow the student to dictate written assignments, after which the program will translate the spoken words into a word processing document to be edited.

Smart boards, which are like wipe boards that are connected to a computer, provide a more interactive nature to oral presentations within the classroom. Students are able to use special markers or their hands to activate the display, allowing them to be more active participants in lectures. Users can write on the board and save the information to a computer for use later.

Digital cameras and digital video recorders can be wonderful enhancements to the instructional process. They allow students to add pictures to their assignments, making them more personal and real. Another use is to provide the students with authenticity to daily routines. For example, a student who is in need of appropriate behavioral reminders could be photographed completing the proper task. This picture reminder can be used within the classroom to provide the student with a visual cue to the behavior he or she should be exhibiting.

Whether the technology is computers, digital cameras, or the more complex smart boards, it is imperative that educators take full advantage of the resources available to them. Technology is a part of our daily lives; in order to prepare students, teachers need to feel comfortable using technology. The flexibility of the inherent nature of technology allows teachers to meet the needs of more students at an individual level than ever before.

Skill 12.03 **Recognizes social skills needed for educational and other environments (e.g., giving and receiving meaningful feedback, engaging in conversations) and demonstrating knowledge of how to design instructional programs that enhance social participation across environments.**

Please refer to Skill 11.03 for information on generalization.

Many children with disabilities have difficulties in developing social behaviors that follow accepted norms. While nondisabled children learn most social behaviors from family and peers, children with disabilities are the product of a wide, complex range of different social experiences. When coupled with one or more disabilities, this experience adds up to a collective deficit in interpersonal relationships.

There is an irreducible philosophical issue underlying the realm of social behavior among children with disabilities. To some extent, the disability itself causes maladaptive behaviors to develop. Regardless of whether social skill deficits are seminal or secondary among youth with disabilities, it is the task of the special education professional to help each child develop as normally as possible in the social-interpersonal realm.

Children with disabilities can be taught social-interpersonal skills through developing sensitivity to other people, through making behavioral choices in social situations, and through developing social maturity.

Sensitivity to Others

Central to the human communication process is the nonverbal domain. Children with disabilities may perceive facial expressions and gestures differently than their nondisabled peers. There are several kinds of activities to use in developing a child's sensitivity to other people. Examples of these activities follow:

1. Offer a selection of pictures with many kinds of faces to the child. Ask the child to identify or classify the faces according to the emotion that appears in the picture. Allow the child to compare his or her reactions to those of other students.

2. Compare common gestures through a mixture of acting and discussion. The teacher can demonstrate shaking his or her head in the negative and then ask the students the meaning of the gesture. Reactions can be compared and a game started in which each student performs a gesture while others tell what it means.

3. Filmstrips, videotapes, and movies are available in which famous people and cartoon characters utilize gestures. Children can be asked what a particular gesture means.

4. Tape recording with playback can be used to present social sounds. Again, a game is possible here: the activity focuses the student's attention on one narrow issue (in this case, the sound and its precise social meaning).

5. Pairs of students can be formed for exercises in reading each other's gestures and nonverbal communications. Friendships of a lasting nature are encouraged by this activity.

Social Situations

Inherent differences in appearances and motions among children with disabilities cause some of them to develop behavior problems in social situations. It is necessary to remediate this situation in order to provide as normal a life and eventual adulthood as possible.

Here are some activities that strengthen a child's social skills in social situations:

- Anticipate the consequence of social actions. Have the students act out roles, tell stories, and discuss the consequences that flow from their actions.

- Gain appropriate independence. Students can be given exercises in going places alone. For the very young, and for those with developmental issues, this might consist of finding a location within the room. Go on a field trip into the city. Allow older students to make purchases on their own. Using play money in the classroom for younger children could also be beneficial.

- Make ethical and/or moral judgments. Tell an unfinished story and require the pupil to finish it at the point where a judgment is required. This calls for an independent critique of the choices made by the characters in the play.

- Plan and execute. Children with disabilities can be allowed to plan an outing, a game, a party, or an exercise.

Having the teacher set an example is always a good way to teach social maturation. If the classroom is orderly, free of an oppressive atmosphere, and full of visibly rational judgments about what is going on, the students absorb the climate of doing things in a mature manner.

In addition to academic skills, the arrangement of peer tutoring can help students work on social skills such as cooperation and self-esteem. Both students may be working on the same material, or the tutee may be working to strengthen areas of weakness. The teacher determines the target goals, selects the material, sets up the guidelines, trains the student tutors in the rules and methods of the sessions, and monitors and evaluates the sessions.

Adaptive life skills refer to the skills that people need to function independently at home, school, and in the community. Adaptive behavior skills include communication and social skills (e.g., intermingling and communicating with other people); independent living skills (e.g., shopping, budgeting, and cleaning); personal care skills (e.g., eating, dressing, and grooming); employment/work skills (e.g., following directions, completing assignments, and being punctual for work); and functional academics (e.g., reading, solving math problems, and telling time).

Measuring Adaptive Behavior Skills

Teaching adaptive behavior skills is part of the special education program for students with disabilities. Parent input is a critical part of the adaptive behavior assessment process, since there are many daily living skills that are observed primarily at home and are not prevalent in the educational setting.

The measurement of adaptive behavior should consist of surveys of the child's behavior and skills in a diverse number of settings. This includes the child's class, school, home, neighborhood, and community. Since it is not possible for one person to observe a child in all of the primary environments, measurement of adaptive behavior depends on the feedback from a number of people. Because parents have many opportunities to observe their children in an assortment of settings, they are normally the best source of information about adaptive behavior.

The most prevalent method for collecting information about a child's adaptive behavior skills in the home environment is to have a school social worker, school psychologist, or guidance counselor interview the parents using a formal adaptive behavior assessment rating scale. These individuals may interview the parents at home or hold a meeting at the school to talk with the parent about their child's behavior. Adaptive behavior information is also procured from school personnel who work with the student, in order to understand how the child functions in the school environment.

Teaching Adaptive Life Skills

There are a variety of strategies for teaching adaptive life skills. One such strategy is incorporating choice, which entails allowing students to select the assignment and the order in which they complete tasks. In addition, priming or pre-practice is an effective classroom intervention for students with disabilities. Priming entails previewing information or activities that a student is likely to have problems with before they begin working on that activity. Partial participation or multilevel instruction is another strategy; it entails allowing a student with a disability to take part in the same projects as the rest of their class, albeit with specific adaptations to the activity so that it suits a student's specific abilities and requirements. Additional instructional practices include self-management, which entails teaching the student to function independently without relying on a teacher or a one-on-one aid. This strategy allows the student to become more involved in the intervention process, and it also improves autonomy.

Cooperative groups are an effective instructional technique for teaching social skills. They have been known to result in increased frequency, duration, and quality of social interactions. Peer tutoring entails two students working together on an activity, where one student gives assistance, instruction, and feedback to the other.

Skill 12.04   Demonstrates knowledge of strategies for enhancing the self-awareness, self management, self-control, self-esteem, self-advocacy, self-determination, and independence of students with disabilities.

Please refer to Skills 3.07 and 10.05 for information on self-concept, self-advocacy, and independence.

Skill 12.05 **Demonstrates knowledge of strategies, methods, and resources for designing and implementing life skills curricula (e.g., independent living, career, vocational, leisure, recreational), including methods for integrating life skills curricula into the general curriculum.**

Please refer to Skill 12.03.

A functional curriculum approach focuses on what students will learn that will be useful to them and prepare them for functioning in society as adults. With this approach, concepts and skills needed for personal-social, daily living, and occupational readiness are taught to students. The specific curriculum contents need to be identified in a student's IEP and be considered appropriate for his or her chronological age and current intellectual, academic, or behavioral performance levels (Clark 1994).

The need for a functional curriculum has been heightened by the current focus on transition—movement from one level to another—until the individual is prepared to live a life in a self-sufficient manner. The simplest form includes movement from school to the world of work. However, like career education, life preparation includes not only occupational readiness, but also personal-social and daily living skills.

Halpern (1992) contends that special education curriculum tends to focus too much on remedial academics and not enough on functional skills. A functional curriculum includes like skills and teaches them in the classroom and in the community. When using this approach, basic academic skills are reinforced in an applied manner. For instance, math skills may be taught in budgeting, balancing checkbooks, and/or computing interest payments for major purchases.

The Adult Performance Level (APL) has been adapted for secondary-level students in special education in a number of school districts across the country. The APL serves as a core curriculum, blending practical academic development with applications to the various demands of community living in adulthood.

Functional competence, as addressed in APL, is conceptualized as two-dimensional. Major skill areas are integrated into general content/knowledge domains. The major skills that have been identified by this curriculum model as requisites for success include reading, writing, speaking, listening, viewing, problem solving, building interpersonal relations, and computation.

Skill 12.06   Demonstrates knowledge of resources, techniques, and procedures for transitioning students with disabilities into and out of school, alternative programs, and post school environments.

Transition procedures are formally included in the IEP by age 14. A statement of transition service needs and related courses of study should be referenced at this time. The student should be invited to the IEP meeting in which transitional goals are discussed. The student's interests and preferences should be considered and given primary consideration. The career goals of the student should be reflected in the transitional program, and the student and parents should be involved in the transition process.

By age 16, a statement of required transition services should be included in every IEP in the areas of instruction, related services, development of employment, community experiences, activities of daily living, and functional vocational evaluation.

The transition process should include a functional vocational evaluation, employment goals and objectives, the availability of age-appropriate instructional environments, independent living goals and objectives, and the circumstances surrounding a referral to an agency.

Because transition is a process, the planning required to help students reach their desired post-school outcomes must become a part of the IEP in time for skills and knowledge to be gained and for goals to be reached to be successful in chosen life endeavors.

Transition Services

Transition services will be different for each student. Transition services must take into account the student's interests and preferences. Evaluation of career interests, aptitudes, skills, and training may be considered.

The transition activities that have to be addressed, unless the IEP team finds it uncalled for, are: (a) instruction; (b) community experiences; (c) the development of objectives related to employment and other post-school areas; and (d) daily living skills.

a) **Instruction**: The instruction part of the transition plan deals with school instruction. The student should have a portfolio completed upon graduation. Each student should research and plan for further education and/or training after high school. Education can be in a college setting, technical school, or vocational center. Goals and objectives created for this transition domain depend on the nature and severity of the student's disability, the student's interests in further education, plans made for accommodations needed in future education and training, and identification of postsecondary institutions that offer the requested training or education.

b) **Community experiences**: This part of the transition plan investigates how the student utilizes community resources. Resources entail places for recreation, transportation services, agencies, and advocacy services. It is essential for students to deal with the following areas:

- Recreation and leisure (examples: movies, YMCA, religious activities)
- Personal and social skills (examples: calling friends, religious groups, going out to eat)
- Mobility and transportation (examples: passing a driver's license test, utilizing Dial-A-Ride)
- Agency access (examples: utilizing a phone book, making calls)
- System advocacy (example: having a list of advocacy groups to contact)
- Citizenship and legal issues (example: registering to vote)

c) ***Development of employment***: This segment of the transition plan investigates becoming employed. Students should complete a career interest inventory. They should have chances to investigate different careers. Many work-skill activities can take place within the classroom, home, and community. Classroom activities may concentrate on employability skills, community skills, mobility, and vocational training. Home and neighborhood activities may concentrate on personal responsibility and daily chores. Community-based activities may focus on part-time work after school and in the summer, cooperative education or work-study, individualized vocational training, and volunteer work.

d) ***Daily living skills***: This segment of the transition plan is also important, although it is not essential to the IEP. Living away from home can be an enormous undertaking for people with disabilities. Numerous skills are needed to live and function as an adult. In order to live as independently as possible, a person should have an income; know how to cook, clean, shop, and pay bills; use transportation; and have a social life. Some living situations may entail independent living, shared living with a roommate, or supported living in group homes. Areas that may need to be looked into include personal and social skills, living options, income and finances, medical needs, community resources, and transportation.

Some students with disabilities cannot be served in the public school program. Reasons for placement in a specialized setting such as a residential placement, hospital, alternate school, or other special education center are varied. Perhaps the student has severe medical or behavioral needs, or perhaps the student has a low-incidence disability such as deafness. These examples can result in a number of students coming from a large geographic area to one place for a particular program. In the case of the Moog Center for Deaf Education in St. Louis, students come from all over the world for instruction in oral communication. Many of the students served in the program are also recipients of cochlear implants, thus requiring advanced medical and audiological follow up.

Staffing Considerations in the Specialized Setting
In some specialized settings, the morale of staff is high and there is a sense of professional pride (such as at the Moog Center). In other specialized settings where the tone is intense (such as a center for autistic children), staff may feel additional stress. A higher turnover rate of teachers and staff can lead to a less stable educational program.

Programming Considerations in the Specialized Setting

In addition to staffing considerations, students in specialized educational settings are somewhat isolated from the general population. While this may offer a better opportunity to focus on the needs of students with a specific disability, effort should be made to include students in the general population. This may be done through field trips and activities in the community, or by bringing the public into the specialized setting for programs, open houses, or as volunteers. In some instances, students from the specialized setting may take classes in the local school.

Staffing Resources in the Specialized Setting

Because of the fact that the specialized setting focuses on a particular area of disability, additional specialized support staff resources may be available. The resources would also be available to a greater level (more time) than in the public school program. In the case of the school for the deaf, an audiologist would be employed full-time onsite. Whereas in the public school setting, a single audiologist may serve a large geographic area.

Ethical and Appropriate Strategies of Education in the Specialized Setting

Although all programs (public or specialized) have policies and procedures to safeguard students, the specialized setting calls for an even higher level of professionalism. Ethical consideration should always be given to student-staff interaction, discipline, and optimum programming.

DOMAIN IV.   WORKING IN A PROFESSIONAL ENVIRONMENT

COMPETENCY 13.0   UNDERSTAND HOW TO COMMUNICATE AND COLLABORATE WITH STUDENTS WITH DISABILITIES AND THEIR FAMILIES TO HELP STUDENTS ACHIEVE DESIRED LEARNING OUTCOMES

Skill 13.01   Demonstrates familiarity with typical concerns of parents/guardians of students with disabilities and recognizing effective strategies for addressing such concerns.

All parents share some basic goals for their children. They want their children to grow up to be healthy, happy members of society who lead independent lives with productive employment. Parents of students with disabilities are no different, although the path that their children take may have additional turns and obstacles along the way.

Health
Many children with disabilities have associated health problems or are at risk for health problems. Many also take medication(s) routinely for health or behavioral conditions.

Parents of students with disabilities are concerned with their children's long-range health, the cost of health care (as children and as adults), and the effects of medication on their child's behavior, health, and school work.

It is not uncommon for special education students to take some medication while at school. Providing the school with the needed medication may be a financial strain for the family. Just the fact that others will be aware of the child's health and medications can also be a parental concern.

Parents are often concerned because their children and teachers may have difficulties identifying changes in health and in communicating possible changes in medication reactions. IEPs often include objectives for the child to communicate changes in his or her health and effects of medication.

Happiness
The quality of life for more severely disabled children is different than that of the general population. Even students with less severe physical conditions (e.g., a learning disability) may have lower self-esteem and feelings of being "stupid" or "different" because they leave the inclusion classroom for some special education services. Students with disabilities often have difficulty making friends, which can also impact happiness.

Parents of students with disabilities (as all parents) feel the emotional impact of the disability on their children. Parents are anxious to help their children feel good about themselves and fit in the general population of their peers.

Social goals may be included on the IEP. Some students (particularly those on the autism spectrum) may have a time (per the IEP minutes) to meet with a speech and language pathologist to work on social language. Other students may meet regularly (again, per IEP minutes) with the social worker to discuss situations from the classroom or general school setting.

Independence
Initially parents of students with disabilities may be somewhat overprotective of their children. Soon after, however, most parents begin to focus on ways to help their children function independently.

Young children with disabilities may be working on self-care types of independence, such as dressing, feeding, and toilet use. Elementary students may be working on asking for assistance, completing work, being prepared for class with materials (e.g., with books or papers). High school students may be working on driving, future job skills, or preparation for postsecondary education.

Job Training
IDEA 2004 addresses the need for students with disabilities to be prepared for jobs or postsecondary education in order to be independent, productive members of society.

Job training goals and objectives for the student with a disability may be vocational (such as food service, mechanical, carpentry, and so on). Job training goals for other students may include appropriate high school coursework to prepare for a college program.

Productivity
Ultimately, the goal of the parents and school is for the student to become a productive member of society who can support him or herself financially and live independently. This type of productivity happens when the student becomes an adult with a measure of good health, positive self-esteem, the ability to interact positively with others, independent personal and work skills, and job training.

Particular Stages of Concern

Parents of students with special needs usually deal with increased concerns when the child reaches a new age or stage of development. Some of these development stages include when the child is first identified as having a disability, entrance into an early childhood special education program, kindergarten (when it is evident that the disability remains despite services received thus far), third grade (when the student is expected to use more skills independently), junior high school, and entrance into high school.

Additional IEP goals and objectives may be warranted at these times, as the student is expected to use a new set of skills or may be entering a new educational setting.

It should be noted that parents are often more concerned when a younger, nondisabled sibling surpasses the child with the disability in some skill (such as feeding or reading). Previously, the parents may not have fully been aware of what most children can do at a particular age.

Skill 13.02   Demonstrates knowledge of strategies for helping students with disabilities and their parents/guardians become active participants on the educational team (e.g., during assessment, during the development and implementation of an individualized program).

Parents can be excellent sources of information and history about a student. As such, an educator must realize the importance of the parents of a child in order to provide adequate services to the student. To ensure the participation of the parent in the educational team, there must be constant contact during all stages of the special education process.

The first contact a teacher has with parents should be before the school year starts. While the teacher may be required to send a letter out stating the required supplies for the class, this does not count as an initial contact.

Parents are used to hearing that their child has done something bad/wrong when they receive a phone call from a teacher. Whenever possible, parents should be contacted to give positive feedback. When you call John's mother and say, "John got an A on the test today," you have just encouraged her to maintain open communication lines with you. Try to give three positive calls for every negative call you must give.

Parent-teacher conferences are scheduled at regular intervals throughout the school year. These provide excellent opportunities to discuss students' progress, what they are learning, and how these accomplishments may relate to future plans for their academic growth. It is not unusual for the parent or teacher to ask for a conference outside of the scheduled parent-teacher conference days. These meetings should be looked at as opportunities to provide momentum to that student's success.

Modern technology has opened two more venues for communicating with parents. School/classroom Web sites are written with the intent of sharing regularly with parents and guardians. Many teachers now post their plans for the marking period and provide extra credit assignments or homework from these Web sites. E-mail is now one of the major modes of communication. Most parents have e-mail accounts and are more than willing to give their e-mail addresses to teachers to be kept appraised of their child's academic progress.

Special events also provide opportunities for parental contact. Poetry readings, science fairs, and ice-cream socials are a few examples of such events.

Role of the Family
Understanding the role of the family will assist a new educator with involving the parents in the educational team. The presence of a child with a disability within the family unit creates changes and possible stresses that will need to be addressed. Many parents feel the demands of the disabled child are greatly in excess of a nondisabled child's requirements. "A child (with a disability) frequently needs more time, energy, attention, patience, and money than the child (without a disability), and frequently returns less success, achievement, parent pride-inducing behavior, privacy, feelings of security and well-being." (Paul 1981, 6).

The family, as a microcosmic unit in a society, plays a vital role in many ways. The family assumes a protective and nurturing function, is the primary unit for social control, and plays a major role in the transmission of cultural values and mores. This role is enacted concurrently with changes in our social system as a whole. Paradoxically, parents who were formerly viewed as the cause of a child's disability are now depended on to enact positive changes in their children's lives.

Siblings play an important role in fostering the social and emotional developments of a brother or sister with a disability. A wide range of feelings and reactions evolve as siblings interact. Some experience guilt over being the normal child and try to overcompensate by being the successful, perfect child for their parents. Others react in a hostile, resentful manner toward the amount of time and care the disabled sibling receives, frequently creating disruption as a way of obtaining parental attention.

The extended family, especially grandparents, can provide support and assistance to the nuclear family unit if they live within a manageable proximity. This support can take the form of childcare services for an evening or a few days, which can provide a means of reprieve for heavily involved parents.

Parents as Advocates

Ironically, establishing the parent-educator partnership, an action that is now sought by educators around the nation, came about largely through the advocacy efforts of parents. The state compulsory education laws began in 1918. They were adopted across the nation with small variances in agricultural regions. However, due to the fact that children with disabilities did not fit in with the general school curriculum, most continued to be turned away at the schoolhouse door, leaving the custodial services at state or private institutions as the primary alternative placement site for parents.

Educational policies reflected the litigation and legislation of the times, which overwhelmingly sided with the educational system and not with the family. After all, the educational policies reflected the prevailing philosophies of the times, including social Darwinism (i.e., survival of the fittest). Thus, persons with disabilities were set apart from the rest of society—literally out of sight, out of mind. Those with severe disabilities were placed in institutions, and those with moderate disabilities were kept at home to do family or farm chores.

Following the two world wars, the realization that disabling conditions could be incurred by a member of any family came to the forefront. Several celebrity families allow stories to be published in national magazines about a family member with an identified disability, thus taking the entire plight of this family syndrome out of the closet. The 1950s brought about the founding of many parent and professional organizations, and the movement continued into the next decade. Learning groups included the National Association of Parents and Friends of Mentally Retarded Children, which was founded in 1950 and later called the National Association for Retarded Children (it is now named the Arc of the United States); the International Parents Organization, founded in 1957; and the parents' branch of the Alexander Graham Bell Association for Parents of the Deaf, founded in 1965. The Epilepsy Foundation of America was founded in 1967. The International Council for Exceptional Children had been established by faculty and students at Columbia University as early as 1922, and the Council for Exceptional Children recognized small parent organizations in the late 1940s.

During the 1950s, Public Law 85-926 brought about support for the preparation of teachers to work with children with disabilities so that these children might receive educational services.

The 1960s was the first period of time during which parents received tangible support from the executive branch of the national government. In 1960, the White House Conference on Children and Youth made the declaration that a child should only be separated from his or her family as a last resort. This gave vital support to parents' efforts toward securing a public education for their children with disabilities.

Parents as Partners
Parent groups are a major component in assuring appropriate services, co-equal with special education and community service agencies, for children with disabilities. Their role is individual and political advocacy, as well as socio-psychological support. Great advances in services for children with disabilities have been made through the efforts of parent advocacy groups. These groups have been formed to represent almost every type of disabling condition.

Skill 13.03 **Demonstrates awareness of culturally responsive strategies for ensuring effective communication and collaboration among families of students with disabilities, school personnel, and representatives of community agencies.**

An educator must be aware of various cultures and be familiar with their different values and traditions. This will ensure no one is mistakenly offended or is misunderstood in any way. Effective communication strategies are required when dealing with families with student's with disabilities. The communication strategies should be flexible and respond to the individual needs of the families.

Teachers traditionally communicate their educational philosophies to families through parent workshops or newsletters. However, these methods have their drawbacks. In many cases, workshops have low attendance when parents have problems with work schedules, transportation, or with getting outside help to take care of a student with disability. Newsletters may be thrown away or not read thoroughly; even when they are taken home, those that are only written in English may present difficulties for parents for whom English is not their first language.

Family-school partnerships are developed when families are encouraged to spend more time in the classroom and are offered more information about their children's education. When families are in the classroom, they have the chance to observe teacher-student interactions, ask the teacher questions, and give feedback on curriculum or development. They also have an opportunity to meet other families.

As the structure of families in today's societies continue to change, teachers may need to try different family outreach strategies that target the new family structure, as what was done in the past may not be effective.

Teachers need to have a range of strategies for contacting parents. This includes using the telephone, e-mail, letters, newsletters, classroom bulletin boards, and parent-teacher conferences.

Teachers also need to be familiar with the student's home culture and have an appreciation for diversity by planning lessons and activities that are inclusive of the multicultural classroom. Through effective communication, teachers can involve parents as leaders and decision makers in the school. As more students with disabilities are included in the general education curriculum, both special and regular educators will need training that focuses on effectively interacting with parents of children with disabilities to involve them as equal partners in the educational planning and decision-making process for their children.

UNDERSTAND WHAT CONSTITUTES EFFECTIVE COMMUNICATION SKILLS BETWEEN THE SENDER AND THE RECEIVER

Communication occurs when one person sends a message and gets a response from another person. In fact, whenever two people can see or hear each other, they are communicating. The receiver changes roles and becomes the sender once the response is given. The communication process may break down if the receiver's interpretation differs from that of the sender.

Effective teaching depends on communication. By using good sending skills, the teacher has more assurance that he or she is getting the correct message across to the students. By being a model of a good listener, a teacher can help his or her students learn to listen and respond appropriately to others.

Attending Skills
The sender is the person who communicates the message; the receiver is the person who ultimately responds to the message.

Attending skills are used to receive a message. Some task-related attending skills that have been identified include the following:

1. Looking at the teacher when information or instructions are being presented
2. Listening to assignment directions
3. Listening for answers to questions
4. Looking at the chalkboard
5. Listening to others speak, when appropriate

For some students, special techniques must be employed to gain and hold attention. For example, the teacher might first call the student by name when asking a question to assure the child is attending, or the teacher may ask the question before calling the name of a student to create greater interest.

Selecting students at random to answer questions helps to keep them alert and listening. Being enthusiastic and keeping lessons short and interactive assists in maintaining the attention of those students who have shorter attention spans. Some students may be better able to focus their attention when environmental distraction are eliminated or at least reduced; nonverbal signals can be used to draw students' attention to the task. Finally, arranging the classroom so that all students can see the teacher helps direct attention to the appropriate location.

Clarity of Expression

Unclear communication between the teacher and special needs students sometimes contributes to problems in academic and behavioral situations. In the learning environment, unclear communication can add to the student's confusion about certain processes or skills he or she is attempting to master.

There are many ways in which the teacher can improve the clarity of communication. Giving clear, precise directions is one. Verbal directions can be simplified by using shorter sentences, familiar words, and relevant explanations. Asking a student to repeat directions or to demonstrate understanding of them by carrying out the instructions is an effective way of monitoring the clarity of expression. In addition, clarification can be achieved by the use of concrete objects, multidimensional teaching aids, and by modeling or demonstrating what should be done in a practice situation.

Finally, a teacher can clarify communication by using a variety of vocal inflections. The use of intonation juncture can help make the message clearer, as can pauses at significant points in the communication. For example, verbal praise should be spoken with inflection that communicates sincerity. Pausing before starting key words, or stressing those that convey meanings, helps students learn the concepts being taught.

Paraphrasing

Paraphrasing—restating what the student says using one's own words—can improve communication between the teacher and students. First, in restating what the student has communicated, the teacher is not judging the content—he or she is simply relating what he or she understands the message to be. If the message has been interpreted differently from the way intended, the student is asked to clarify. Clarification should continue until both parties are satisfied that the message has been understood.

The act of paraphrasing sends the message that the teacher is trying to better understand the student. Restating the student's message as fairly and accurately as possible assists the teacher in seeing things from the student's perspective.

Paraphrasing if often a simple restatement of what has been said. Lead-ins such as "Your position is . . ." or "It seems to you that . . ." are helpful in paraphrasing a student's messages. A student's statement, "I am not going to do my math today" might be paraphrased by the teacher as, "Did I understand you to say that you are not going to do your math today?" By mirroring what the student has just said, the teacher has telegraphed a caring attitude for that student and a desire to respond accurately to the student's message.

To effectively paraphrase a student's message, the teacher should:

1. restate the student's message in his or her own words;
2. preface his or her paraphrasing with such remarks as, "You feel . . ." or "I hear you say that . . "; and
3. avoid indicating any approval or disapproval of the student's statements. Johnson (1978, 139) states the following as a rule to remember when paraphrasing: "Before you can reply to a statement, restate what the sender says, feels, and means correctly and to the sender's satisfaction."

Descriptive feedback is a factual, objective (i.e., unemotional) recounting of a behavioral situation or message sent by a student. Descriptive feedback has the same effect as paraphrasing. When responding to a student's statement, the teacher restates (i.e., paraphrases) what the student has said or factually describes what he or she has seen. It allows the teacher to check his or her perceptions of the student and the student's message. A student may do or say something, but because of the teacher's feelings or state of mind, the student's message or behavior might be totally misunderstood. The teacher's descriptive feedback, which Johnson (1972) refers to as "understanding," indicates that the teacher's intent is to respond only to ask the student whether the statement has been understood, how the student feels about the problem, and how the student perceives the problem. The intent of the teacher is to more clearly "understand" what the student is saying, feeling, or perceiving in relation to a stated message or a behavioral event.

Evaluative feedback is verbalized perception by the teacher that judges, evaluates, approves, or disapproves of the statements made by the student. Evaluative feedback occurs when the student makes a statement and the teacher responds openly with "I think you're wrong," "That was a dumb thing to do," or "I agree with you entirely." The tendency to give evaluative responses is heightened in situations where feelings and emotions are deeply involved. The stronger the feelings, the more likely it is that two persons will each evaluate the other's statements solely from their own point of view.

Since evaluative feedback intones a judgmental approval or disapproval of the student's remark or behavior, it can be a major barrier to mutual understanding and effective communication. However, it is a necessary mechanism for providing feedback of a quantitative (and sometimes qualitative) instructional nature (e.g., test scores, homework results, classroom performance). In order to be effective, evaluative feedback must be offered in a factual, constructive manner. Descriptive feedback tends to reduce defensiveness and feelings of being threatened because it most likely communicates that the teacher is interested in the student as a person, has an accurate understanding of the student and what the student is saying, and encourages the student to elaborate and further discuss his or her problems.

In the learning environment, as in all situations, effective communication depends on good sending and receiving skills. Teaching and managing students involves good communication. By using clear, nonthreatening feedback, the teacher can provide students with information that helps them to understand themselves better, at the same time providing a clearer understanding of each student on the teacher's part.

Skill 13.04 Demonstrates knowledge of family systems and the roles of families in the educational process.

Please refer to Skill 13.02 for information about the role of families in the education process.

The special educator should be knowledgeable of family systems, as well as the impact of the systems on a family's response and contribution to the education of a child with special needs. The family systems theory, as outlined on the Bowen Center for the Study of the Family (http://www.thebowencenter.org/pages/theory.html), has been developed by Murray Bowen over recent decades. The Bowen Theory of Family Systems is outlined as follows.

Triangles refers to the impact on existing relationships between two people in a family when a third individual joins the family.

In the case of a child with a disability, it could refer to the impact of the child's needs and associated physical, emotional, and financial stress on the marriage of the parents.

Differentiation of self refers to the influence of family members to think alike and the individual's ability to think critically and independently while realizing the realistic extent of his or her need for others.

For example, in a family with a deaf child, the parents may be pressured by grandparents not to have the child undergo a cochlear implant, due to the invasive nature of the surgery. While the child's parents realize the importance of family support and relationships, parents with a strong differentiation of self will consider all the information and then make a decision that may go against the thoughts of the grandparents.

Nuclear family emotional system describes four basic relationship patterns that can develop or worsen because of tension. The patterns are marital conflict, dysfunction in one spouse, impairment of one or more children, and emotional distance.

Because of the tension that results from the birth and parenting of a child with a disability, any or all of the relationship patterns may develop.

Family projection process refers to the parental projection of a perception (such as low self-esteem) or problem (learning disability) that results in the treatment of the child as such. With time, the projection may become a self-fulfilling prophecy.

The projection process follows three steps:

1. The parent focuses on a child out of fear that something is wrong with him or her
2. The parent interprets the child's behavior as confirming the fear
3. The parent treats the child as if something is really wrong

Multigenerational transmission process refers to the impact of parenting and the resulting differentiation of self on future generations.

In the case of the parents of a child with a disability, parents who have developed a stronger differentiation of self are more likely to acknowledge their child's disability (regardless of extended family perception of the social stigma it may bring) and to consider all options of treatment and educational programming for their child.

Emotional cutoff occurs when the individual distances him or herself from the family as an adult due to unresolved conflict.

In the case of a child with a disability, a parent may distance him or herself from his or her own parents because of their ongoing opinion that severely disabled children should be institutionalized. By the emotional cutoff between the child's parent and grandparents, ongoing emotional and physical support may be jeopardized or lost completely.

Sibling position is described in Bowen's work and is referenced as "incorporating the work of Walter Toman." According to sibling position, birth order reflects tendencies of children in later interactions. Firstborn children tend to be leaders; younger siblings tend to be followers.

Societal emotional process refers to the carryover of the above systems into all areas of personal interaction in the society (including the workplace and school).

Hypothetical examples of how family systems affect special education students and their families are given above. The special educator should be aware of these systems as he or she interacts with families on a regular basis and communicates with them regarding IEP planning and considerations.

Skill 13.05   Recognizes the potential impact of differences in values, languages, and customs that can exist between the home and school.

Please see Skill 9.07.

COMPETENCY 14.0   UNDERSTAND HOW TO COMMUNICATE AND COLLABORATE WITH COLLEAGUES, ADMINISTRATORS, SERVICE PROVIDERS, AND COMMUNITY AGENCIES TO HELP STUDENTS WITH DISABILITIES ACHIEVE DESIRED LEARNING OUTCOMES

Skill 14.01   Recognizes various roles and responsibilities that school personnel, service providers, and community agencies can take in planning an individualized program.

The special educator is trained to work in a team approach. This starts at the initial identification of students who appear to deviate from what is considered to be normal performance or behavior for particular age- and grade-level students. The special education teacher serves as a consultant (or as a team member, depending on the school district) to the student support team. If the student is referred, the special education teacher may be asked to collect assessment data for the forthcoming comprehensive evaluation. This professional then generally serves on the multidisciplinary eligibility, individualized educational planning, and placement committees. If the student is placed in a special education setting, the special educator continues to coordinate and collaborate with regular classroom teachers and support personnel at the school-based level.

Support professionals are available at both the district- and school-based levels, and they contribute valuable services and expertise in their respective areas. A team approach between district ancillary services and local school-based staff is essential.

1. **School psychologist.** The school psychologist participates in the referral, identification, and program planning processes. He or she contributes to the multidisciplinary team by adding important observations, data, and inferences about the student's performance. As the evaluation is conducted, he or she observes the student in the classroom environment, takes a case history, and administers a battery of formal and informal individual tests. The psychologist is involved as a member of a professional team throughout the stages of referral, assessment, placement, and program planning.

2. **Physical therapist.** This person works with disorders of bones, joints, muscles, and nerves following medical assessment. Under the prescription of a physician, the therapist applies treatment to the students in the form of heat, light, massage, and exercise to prevent further disability or deformity. Physical therapy includes the use of adaptive equipment, as well as prosthetic and orthotic devices to facilitate independent movement. This type of therapy helps individuals with disabilities to develop or recover their physical strength and endurance.

3. **Occupational therapist.** This specialist is trained in helping students develop self-help skills (e.g., self-care, motor, perceptual, and vocational skills). The students are actively involved in the treatment process to quicken recovery and rehabilitation.

4. **Speech and language pathologist.** This specialist assists in the identification and diagnosis of children with speech or language disorders. In addition, he or she makes referrals for medical or habilitation needs, counsels family members and teachers, and works with the prevention of communicative disorders. The speech and language therapist concentrates on rehabilitative service delivery and continuing diagnosis.

5. **Administrators.** Building principals and special education directors (or coordinators) provide logistical and emotional support. Principals implement building policy procedures and control designation of facilities, equipment, and materials. Their support is crucial to the success of the program within the parameters of the base school. Special education directors provide information about federal, state, and local policies, which is vital to the operation of a special education unit. In some districts, the special education director may actually control certain services and materials. Role clarification, preferably in writing, should be accomplished to ensure effectiveness of program services.

6. **Guidance counselors, psychometrists, and diagnosticians.** These persons often lead individual and group counseling sessions and are trained in assessment, diagnostic, and observation skills, as well as personality development and functioning abilities. They can apply knowledge and skills to multidisciplinary teams and assist in the assessment, diagnosis, placement, and program planning process.

7. **Social worker.** The social worker is trained in interviewing and counseling skills. This person possesses knowledge of available community and school services and makes these known to parents. He or she often visits homes of students, conducts intake and assessment interviews, counsels individuals and small groups, and assists in district enforcement policies.

8. **School nurse.** This person offers valuable information about diagnostic and treatment services. He or she is knowledgeable about diets, medications, therapeutic services, health-related services, and care needed for specific medical conditions. Reports of communicable diseases, to which a health professional has access, are filed with the health department. A medical professional can sometimes obtain cooperation with the families of children with disabilities in ways that are difficult for the special education teacher to achieve.

9. **Regular teachers and subject matter specialists.** These professionals are trained in general and specific instructional areas, teaching techniques, and overall child growth and development. They serve as a vital component to the referral process, as well as in the subsequent treatment program if the student is determined eligible. They work with the students with special needs for the majority of the school day and function as a link to the children's special education and medical programs.

10. **Paraprofessional.** This staff member assists the special educator and often works in the classroom with the special needs students. He or she helps prepare specialized materials, tutor individual students, lead small groups, and provide feedback to students about their work.

THE COLLABORATIVE ROLES OF STUDENTS, PARENTS/GUARDIANS, TEACHERS, AND OTHER SCHOOL AND COMMUNITY PERSONNEL IN PLANNING AND IMPLEMENTING AN INDIVIDUALIZED PROGRAM, AND IN APPLYING EFFECTIVE STRATEGIES FOR WORKING COLLABORATIVELY IN VARIOUS CONTEXTS

The roles of the special education teacher and the general education teacher are to work together to ensure that students with disabilities are able to attain their educational objectives in the least restrictive environment. Some students are best served in the general education setting with additional accommodations, while other students may be best served in the special education setting. The educators must work together to decide what educational program is best suited for the student, as well as where the student can best meet his or her goals and objectives.

These decisions should be made during the student's IEP meeting. It is important that the special education teacher, the general education teacher, and other interested professionals (such as the speech teacher) are in attendance at the meeting so they can discuss and collaborate on their roles in helping the student.

Students with disabilities often experience insufficient access to and a lack of success in the general education curriculum. To promote improved access to the general curriculum for all learners, information should be presented in various formats using a variety of media forms; students should be given numerous methods to express and demonstrate what they have learned; and students should be provided with multiple entry points to engage their interest and motivate their learning.

Printed reading materials can be challenging to individuals with disabilities. Technology can help alleviate some of these difficulties by providing a change from printed text to electronic text that can be modified, enhanced, programmed, linked, and searched.

Text styles and font sizes can be changed as required by readers with visual disabilities. Text can be read aloud with computer-based text-to-speech translators and combined with illustrations, videos, and audio soundtracks. Electronic text provides alternative formats for reading materials that can be tailored to match learner needs; it can also be structured in ways that enhance the learning process and expand both physical and cognitive access.

Lesson Plan Collaboration
According to Walther-Thomas, et al. (2000), "Collaboration for Inclusive Education," ongoing professional development that provides teachers with opportunities to create effective instructional practice is vital and necessary. "A comprehensive approach to professional development is perhaps the most critical dimension of sustained support for successful program implementation." The inclusive approach incorporates learning programs that include all stakeholders in defining and developing high-quality programs for students. The figure at the top of the next page shows how an integrated approach of stakeholders can provide the optimal learning opportunity for all students.

Integrated Approach to Learning

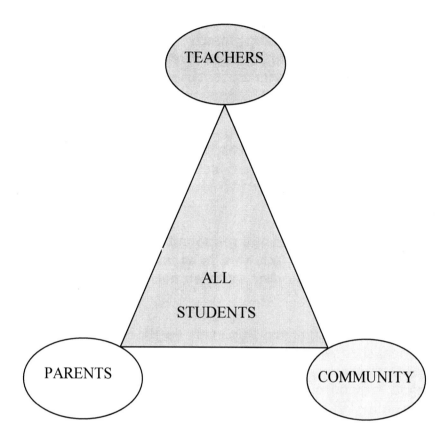

In the integrated approach to learning, teachers, parents, and community support become the integral apexes to student learning. The focus and central core of the school community is triangular as a representation of how effective collaboration can work in creating success for student learners. The goal of student learning and achievement now becomes the heart of the school community. The direction of teacher professional development in constructing effective instruction is clearly articulated in a greater understanding of facilitating learning strategies that develop skills and education equity for students.

Teachers need diversity in their instructional toolkits, which can provide students with clear instruction, mentoring, inquiry, challenge, performance-based assessment, and journal reflections on their learning processes. For teachers, having a collaborative approach to instruction fosters for students a deeper appreciation of learning, subject matter, and knowledge acquisition. Implementing a consistent approach to learning from all stakeholders will create equitable educational opportunities for all learners.

Research has shown that educators who collaborate become more diversified and effective in implementation of curriculum and assessment of effective instructional practices. Collaboration fosters the ability to gain additional insight into how students learn and how modalities of differing learning styles can increase a teacher's capacity to develop proactive instruction methods. Teachers who team teach or have daily networking opportunities can create a portfolio of curriculum articulation and inclusion for students.

People in business are always encouraged to network in order to further their careers. The same can be said for teaching. If English teachers get together and discuss what is going on in their classrooms, those discussions make the "whole" much stronger than the parts. Even if there are not formal opportunities for such networking, it's wise for schools or even individual teachers to develop and seek them.

Skill 14.02 **Recognizes the roles and responsibilities of the Special Education Teacher in regard to seeking assistance from and collaborating with other professionals to support student learning.**

When making eligibility, program, and placement decisions about a student, the special education teacher serves as a member of a multidisciplinary team. Teachers are involved in every aspect regarding the education of individual students; therefore, they need to be knowledgeable not only about teaching and instructional techniques but also about support services. These services will need to be coordinated, and teachers must be able to work in a collaborative manner.

The concept of mainstreaming special needs students—that is, integrating them with their classmates in as many living and learning environments as possible—caught hold about the time that provisions for the Individuals with Disabilities Education Act (IDEA) were formulated in the early- to mid-1970s. Even though mainstreaming is not specifically addressed in this legislation, the education of all children and youth with disabilities in the least restrictive environment is mandated. In addition, this important legislation defines special education, identifies related services that may be required if special education is to be effective, and requires the participation of parents and other persons involved in the education of children and youth with disabilities.

Close contact and communication must be established and maintained between the school district staff, each base school, and the various specialists (or consultants) providing ancillary services. These persons often serve special needs students in auxiliary (i.e., providing help) and supplementary (i.e., in addition to) ways. Thus, the principles and methods of special education must be shared with regular educators, and tenets and practices of regular education must be conveyed to special educators. Job roles and the unique responsibilities and duties of support specialists like speech/language therapists, physical and occupational therapists, social workers, school psychologists and nurses, and others need to be known by all teachers.

Furthermore, the services that can be provided by community resources, and the support that can be given by parents and professional organizations, must be known to all in order for maximum education for exceptional students to occur. Professional services are offered on a local, state, and national level for most areas of disability. Teachers are able to stay abreast of most current practices and changes by reading professional journals, attending professional conferences, and maintaining membership in professional organizations.

IDENTIFYING PRINCIPLES AND ANALYZING FACTORS RELATED TO THE COORDINATION OF EFFORTS

When professionals work together to provide services for students with disabilities, it is important that they work as a cohesive teaching unit that uses information sharing systems and proper scheduling procedures.

A system should be put into place for sharing program materials, tracking student mastery of goals and objectives, and supporting the various requirements of administrative and teaching staff. Because of the variety of learning objectives and the need to make the special education curriculum appropriate for each student, information sharing is critical. It is not uncommon for a teacher in one part of the school to be completely unaware of what another teacher is doing. Two teachers may have similar students with similar intensive needs, and by sharing information, lesson plans, and behavior modification strategies, the workload is shared and students benefit from a more cohesive program.

Professionals also need to work together to ensure that students with disabilities are receiving the services outlined in the IEP. The speech teacher, the occupational therapist, the general education teacher, and the special education teacher may all be providing services to one student. In order to ensure that the proper time is allotted for each service, the professionals involved will have to work together to develop a schedule for the student to ensure that nothing is left out and all areas outlined in the IEP are addressed. This will also help when ensuring that students with disabilities who can be taught in groups are grouped with other students who may have the same requirements. This can only be effectively done when professional share schedules, student information, and student requirements. If they work together, they can accomplish a lot more then when working independently.

DEMONSTRATING AN UNDERSTANDING OF HOW TO WORK EFFECTIVELY WITHIN SCHOOL ADMINISTRATIVE STRUCTURES TO ENSURE THAT STUDENTS WITH DISABILITIES RECEIVE SERVICES AS SPECIFIED IN THEIR IEPS

The student's IEP must state the special education, supplementary aids, and services either to be provided to the student or on behalf of the student. The IEP should also contain a statement of the program modifications and support for school personnel that will allow the student to become involved in and progress through the general curriculum. In the past, students with disabilities were sometimes placed in the regular education classroom for the sake of inclusion without any help or support. IDEA 1997 required that supplementary aids and services, accommodations, modifications, and supports play a more important role in a student's education.

The IEP should specify supports for school personnel. The decisions as to what kind of support is appropriate for a particular student are to be made on an individualized basis by the IEP team. The approach should be to create, from the beginning, a curriculum with built-in supports for diverse learners, rather than to fit supplementary aids and services, accommodations, modifications, or supports after the fact.

The IEP should include ways for the parent and the teacher to objectively measure the student's progress or lack of progress (regression) in the special education program. If the student is not receiving the services specified in his or her IEP, the student may not be able to meet the outlined goals. Careful monitoring and reporting of goals and objectives every quarter should help ensure that students receive the services they are entitled to.

For example, if the student is entitled to additional services from a speech therapist, occupational therapist, or other specialist, the teachers should ensure that the specified services outlined in the IEP are being provided to the students. This can be done by working with the principal or other administrators to discuss how much time has been allotted for the additional services and to ensure that each student receives the time allotted and spelled out in the IEP.

Skill 14.03   Demonstrates knowledge of various models and strategies of consultation and collaboration (e.g., co-teaching, consultant teaching) and their implementation.

INSTRUCTIONAL PLANNING FOR A VARIETY OF INCLUSIVE MODELS (E.G., CO-TEACHING, PUSH-IN, CONSULTANT TEACHING [CT])

According to IDEA 2004, students with disabilities are to participate in the general education program to the extent that it is beneficial for them. As students are included in a variety of general education activities and classes, the need for collaboration among teachers grows.

Co-teaching
One model for general education teachers and special education teachers to use for collaboration is co-teaching. In this model, both teachers actively teach in the general education classroom. Perhaps both teachers will conduct a small science experiment group at the same time, switching groups at some point in the lesson. Perhaps in social studies, one teacher will lecture while the other teacher writes notes on the board or points out information on a map.

In the co-teaching model, the general education teacher and special educator often switch roles back and forth within a class period, or they may do so at the end of a chapter or unit.

Push-in Teaching
In the push-in teaching model, the special educator teaches parallel material in the general education classroom. When the regular education teacher teaches word problems in math, for example, the special educator may work with some students on setting up the initial problems, followed by having them complete the computation. Another example would be in science; when the general education teacher asks review questions for a test, the special educator works with a student who has a review study sheet to find the answer from a group of choices.

In the push-in teaching model, it may appear that two versions of the same lesson are being taught or that two types of student responses/activities are being monitored on the same material. The push-in teaching model is considered one type of differentiated instruction in which two teachers are teaching simultaneously.

Consultant Teaching

In the consultant teaching model, the general education teacher conducts the class after planning with the special educator how to differentiate activities so that the needs of the student with a disability are met.

In a social studies classroom using the consultant teaching model, both teachers may discuss what the expectations will be for a student with a learning disability and fine motor difficulty when the class does reports on states. They may decide that doing a state report is appropriate for the student; however, he or she may use the computer to write the report so that he or she can utilize the spell check feature and so that the work is legible.

Skill 14.04 **Recognizes the roles and responsibilities of paraeducators (e.g., related to instruction, intervention, and direct services) and demonstrating knowledge of strategies and procedures for observing, evaluating, and providing feedback to paraeducators.**

Paraprofessionals and General Education Teachers

Paraprofessionals and general education teachers are important collaborators with teachers of exceptional students. Although they may not have the theoretical experience to assure effective interaction with such students, they do bring valuable perspective to, and opportunities for breadth and variety in, an exceptional child's educational experience.

Paraprofessionals true roles may be different in each school's system. Typically a paraprofessional will provide assistance to students under direct supervision of the general education or special education teacher. Their duties may be, but are not limited to, providing small group or one-on-one instruction, incorporating assistive technology, or providing assistance to students with physical handicaps or minor medical conditions.

General education teachers also offer curriculum and subject matter expertise and a high level of professional support, while paraprofessionals may provide insights born of their particular familiarity with individual students. CEC suggests that teachers can best collaborate with general education teachers and paraprofessionals by the following:

- Offering information about the characteristics and needs of children with exceptional learning needs
- Discussing and brainstorming ways to integrate children with exceptionalities into various settings within the school community
- Modeling best practices, instructional techniques, and accommodations, as well as coaching others in their use
- Keeping communication about children with exceptional learning needs and their families confidential

- Consulting with these colleagues in the assessment of individuals with exceptional learning needs
- Engaging them in group problem solving and in developing, executing, and assessing collaborative activities
- Offering support to paraprofessionals by observing their work with students, as well as offering feedback and suggestions

Skill 14.05 **Recognizes effective strategies for collaborating with school personnel, service providers, and community agencies to integrate students with disabilities into various settings and demonstrating knowledge of strategies for evaluating the effectiveness of collaborative activities.**

Related Service Providers and Administrators

Related service providers and administrators offer specialized skills and abilities that are critical to an exceptional education teacher's ability to advocate for his or her student, to meet a school's legal obligations to the student, and to meet legal obligations to the student's family. Related service providers (e.g., speech, occupational, and language therapists; psychologists; and physicians) offer expertise and resources unparalleled in meeting a child's developmental needs. Administrators are often experts in the resources available at the school and local education agency levels, as well as the culture and politics of a school system. They can be powerful partners in meeting the needs of exceptional education teachers and students.

A teacher's most effective approach to collaborating with these professional includes the following:

- Confirming mutual understanding of the accepted goals and objectives of the student with exceptional learning needs as documented in his or her IEP
- Soliciting input about ways to support related service goals in classroom settings
- Understanding the needs and motivations of each, and acting in support whenever possible
- Facilitating respectful and beneficial relationships between families and professionals
- Regularly and accurately communicating observations and data about the child's progress or challenges

This section will specifically address the working relationship teachers should have with their colleagues in the classroom environment. There are six basic steps to having a rewarding collaborative relationship, whether the others are paraprofessionals, aides, or volunteers.

While it is understood that there are many types of colleagues who may be assisting in a classroom, this section will summarize their titles as "classroom assistant."

1. **Get to know each other.**
    The best way to start a relationship with anyone is to find time alone to get to know each other. Give a new classroom assistant the utmost respect and look at this as an opportunity to share talents and learn those of a coworker. Remember that this is the opportunity to find places of agreement and disagreement, which can help maintain and build a working relationship. Good working relationships require the knowledge of where each other's strengths and weaknesses are. This knowledge may create one of one of the best working relationships possible.

2. **Remember that communication is a two-way street.**
    As a professional educator, it is important to remember that one must actively communicate with others. This is especially important with classroom assistants. Listen to them and let them know that listening is taking place. Pay attention and make sure that the classroom assistant sees an incorporation of his or her thoughts. Encourage them to engage conversations by asking for more information. Asking a classroom assistant for details and insights may help to further meet the needs of students.

    It is also an educator's responsibility to remove and prevent communication barriers in the working relationship. Avoid giving negative criticism or put downs. Do not "read" motivations into the actions of the classroom assistant. Learn about them through open communication.

3. **Establish clear roles and responsibilities.**
   The Access Center for Improving Outcomes of All Students K-8 has defined these roles in the graph below.

	Teacher Role	Classroom Assistant Role	Areas of Communication
nstruction	▪ Plan all instruction, including expected goals/objectives in small groups ▪ Provide instruction in whole-class settings	▪ Work with small groups of students on specific tasks, including review or re-teaching of content ▪ Work with one student at a time to provide intensive instruction or remediation on a concept or skill	▪ Teachers provide specific content and guidance about curriculum, students, and instructional materials ▪ Classroom assistants note student progress and give feedback to teachers
Curriculum & Lesson Plan Development	▪ Develop all lesson plans and instructional materials ▪ Ensure alignment with standards, student needs, and IEPs	▪ Provide assistance in development of classroom activities, retrieval of materials, and coordination of activities	▪ Mutual review of lesson plan components prior to class ▪ Teachers provide guidance about specific instructional methods
Classroom Management	▪ Develop and guide class-wide management plans for behavior and classroom structures ▪ Develop and monitor individual behavior management plans	▪ Assist with the implementation of class-wide and individual behavior management plans ▪ Monitor hallways, study hall, and other activities outside normal class	▪ Teachers provide guidance about specific behavior management strategies and student characteristics ▪ Classroom assistants note student progress and activities and give feedback to teachers

"Working Together: Teacher-Paraeducator Collaboration," The Access Center for Improving Outcomes of All Students K-8, http://www.k8accesscenter.org/documents/RESOURCELIST3-1.doc.

4. Plan together.

Planning together lets the classroom assistant know they are considered valuable. It also provides a timeline of expectations that will aid in the overall classroom delivery to students. This also gives the impression to students that all authority figures are on the same page and know what is going to happen next.

5. Show a united front.

It is essential to let students know that both adults in the room deserve the same amount of respect. Have a plan in place on how to address negative behaviors individually as well as together. *Do not* make a statement in front of the students that the classroom assistant is wrong. Take time to address issues regarding class time privately, not in front of the class.

6. Reevaluate your relationship.

Feedback is wonderful. Stop every now and then and discuss how the team is working. Be willing to listen to suggestions. Taking this time may be the opportunity to improve the working relationship.

Additional Reading:

"Creating a Classroom Team," http://www.aft.org/pubs-reports/psrp/classroom_team.pdf.

"Working Together: Teacher-Paraeducator Collaboration," The Access Center for Improving Outcomes of All Students K-8, http://www.k8accesscenter.org/documents/RESOURCELIST3-1.doc.

Skill 14.06   Demonstrates knowledge of strategies for coaching general education teachers and other service providers in instructional methods, technology, and accommodations for students with disabilities.

A student with a disability may require specialized instructional methods, use of specific technology, and/or other accommodations. These will be outlined in the student's IEP and should be familiar to all educators and staff members working with the student.

In-services and workshops are often used to explain the above needs of a student to a group of professionals. These sessions may be conducted by the special education teacher. In some instances, the special educator may call upon another professional to conduct the in-service, or he or she may work with the other professional to make a joint presentation. This is sometimes the case with hearing impaired students, when the audiologist conducts an in-service on how the loss impacts classroom performance and how to use auditory training equipment. Another example might be an assistive technology consultant explaining the use of an augmentative communication device.

Explanation of disability and student IEP is important so that everyone working with the student is aware of and focusing on the same goals and objectives. Oftentimes, the general education teacher or other school staff will be listed as implementors of some of the IEP goals and objectives. These individuals should not only be aware of the goals but should also be knowledgeable about how to keep record of student progress. The special educator is responsible for making sure that an appropriate type of documentation is being kept. He or she will often need to provide a chart or questionnaire to assist with this. Confidentiality is crucial and should be stressed when explaining the student's IEP, as well as addressing where (in a locked file cabinet) it should be kept.

Observation of the special education teacher is often helpful for those who will be working with the special education student. If the IEP is discussed prior to such an observation, it will help the general education teacher be aware of what to watch for and to better formulate questions for clarification later.

Observation of the general education teacher or other service provider and feedback is helpful once the student is in the general education setting or working with other service providers. The special educator can give feedback on the accommodations and methods being used as well as the student's progress. Observation of the student in these settings provides data needed for future IEP planning, and the feedback of the special educator assists the general education teacher in meeting the needs of the student.

Ongoing evaluation of student progress via the general education teacher can be done in a number of ways besides observation. The special education teacher may provide a questionnaire or checklist for the general education teacher. In addition, conversations and e-mails on student progress should be documented for reference in completing student progress reports and in IEP planning. It is the role of the special educator to communicate the importance of input from the general education teacher for these purposes.

Skill 14.07 Demonstrates knowledge of legal and ethical guidelines in regard to maintaining confidentiality when communicating with school personnel about students with disabilities.

The Family Educational Rights and Privacy Act (1974), also known as the Buckley Amendment, assures confidentiality of student records. Parents are afforded the right to examine, review, and request changes in information deemed inaccurate and stipulate persons who might access their child's records.

"Due process is a set of procedures designed to ensure the fairness of educational decisions and the accountability of both professionals and parents in making these decisions" (Kirk and Gallagher 1986, 24). These procedures serve as a mechanism by which the child and his or her family can voice opinions, concerns, and dissents. Due process safeguards exist in all matters pertaining to identification, evaluation, and educational placement.

Due process occurs in two realms: substantive and procedural. Substantive due process is the content of the law (e.g., appropriate placement for special education students). Procedural due process is the form through which substantive due process is carried out (e.g., parental permission for testing). Public Law 101-476 contains many items of both substantive and procedural due process.

1. A due process hearing may be initiated by parents of the LEA as an impartial forum for challenging decisions about identification, evaluation, or placement. Either party may present evidence, cross-examine witnesses, obtain a record of the hearing, and be advised by counsel or by individuals having expertise in the education of individuals with disabilities. Findings may be appealed to the state education agency (SEA), and, if still dissatisfied, either party may bring civil action in a state of federal district court. Hearing timelines are set by legislation.

2. Parents may obtain an independent evaluation if there is disagreement about the education evaluation performed by the LEA. The results of such an evaluation: (1) must be considered in any decision made with respect to the provision of a free, appropriate public education for the child; and (2) may be presented as evidence at a hearing. Further, the parents may request this evaluation at public expense: (1) if a hearing officer requests an independent educational evaluation; or (2) if the decision from a due process hearing is that the LEA's evaluation was inappropriate. If the final decision holds that the evaluation performed is appropriate, the parent still has the right to an independent educational evaluation but not at public expense.

3. Written notice must be provided to parents prior to a proposal or refusal to initiate or make a change in the child's identification, evaluation, or educational placement. This notice includes the following:

- A listing of parental due process safeguards
- A description and a rationale for the chosen action
- A detailed listing of components (e.g., tests, records, reports) that were the basis for the decision
- Assurance that the language and content of notices were understood by the parents

4. Parental consent must be obtained before evaluation procedures can occur, unless there is a state law specifying otherwise.

5. Sometimes parents or guardians cannot be identified to function in the due process role. When this occurs, a suitable person must be assigned to act as a surrogate. This is done by the LEA in full accordance with legislation.

APPLIES PROCEDURES FOR SAFEGUARDING CONFIDENTIALITY WITH REGARD TO STUDENTS WITH DISABILITIES (E.G., BY MAINTAINING THE CONFIDENTIALITY OF ELECTRONIC CORRESPONDENCE AND RECORDS, OR ENSURING THE CONFIDENTIALITY OF CONVERSATIONS), AND RECOGNIZES THE IMPORTANCE OF RESPECTING STUDENTS' PRIVACY

One of the most important professional practices a teacher must maintain is student confidentiality. This extends far beyond paper records and goes into the realm of oral discussions. Teachers are expected to refrain from mentioning the names of students and often the specifics of their character in conversations with those who are not directly involved with them, both inside and outside of school.

In the school environment, teacher recordkeeping comes in three main formats with specific confidentiality rules. All of the records stated below should be kept in a locked place within the classroom or an office within the school:

1. **A teacher's personal notes on a student**
   When a teacher takes notes on a student's actions, including behaviors and/or grade performances that are not intended to be placed in a school recorded format, the teacher may keep this information private and confidential to his/her own files. Teachers may elect to share this information or not.
2. **Daily recorded grades and attendance of the student**
   A teacher's grade books and attendance records are to be open to the parent/guardian of that child when he or she wishes. Only that child's information may be shared—not that of others.

3. **Teacher notations on records that appear in the student cumulative file**

There are specific rules regarding the sharing of the cumulative records of students.

   a. Cumulative files will follow a student who transfers from school to school within the school district.

   b. All information placed in a cumulative file may be examined by a parent at any time it is requested. If a parent shows up to review his or her child's cumulative file, the file should be shown as it is in its current state (this includes IEPs).

   c. When information from a cumulative file is requested by another person/entity other than the parent/guardian, the information may not be released without the express written consent of the parent/guardian. The parental consent must specify which records may be shared with the other party of interest.

   d. A school in which a student may intend to enroll may receive the student's educational record without parental consent. However, the school sending that information must make a reasonable attempt to notify the parent/guardian of the request. (FERPA)

Today's world is quickly becoming a digital environment. Teachers now communicate with e-mail and are keeping records in digital formats, often within a district-mandated program. Teachers should keep in mind that e-mails and other electronic formats can be forwarded and are as "indelible" as permanent ink. They should maintain a professional decorum just as when they are writing their own records.

COMPETENCY 15.0   UNDERSTAND THE HISTORICAL, SOCIAL, AND LEGAL FOUNDATIONS OF THE FIELD OF SPECIAL EDUCATION

Skill 15.01   Demonstrates knowledge of theories and philosophies that form the foundation for special education practice.

LEGAL MANDATES AND HISTORICAL ASPECTS

Special education is precisely what the term denotes: education of a special nature for students who have special needs. The academic and behavioral techniques that are used today in special education are a culmination of "best practices." They evolved from a number of disciplines (e.g., medicine, psychology, sociology, language, ophthalmology, otology) to include education. Each of these disciplines contributed uniquely to its field so that the needs of special students might be better met in the educational arena.

Unfortunately, during the earlier part of the 1900s and mid-1950s, too many educators placed in positions of responsibility refused to recognize their professional obligation for assuring *all* children a free, appropriate, public education. Today doors can no longer be shut, eyes cannot be closed, and heads cannot be turned; due process rights have established for special needs students and their caregivers. Specific mandates are now stated in national laws, state regulations, and local policies. These mandates are the result of many years of successful litigation and politically advocacy, and they govern the delivery of special education.

What special educators *do* is one thing; *how* services are delivered is yet another. The concept of **inclusion**, which was designed by Evelyn Deno and has been in existence since the early 1970s, stresses the need for educators to rethink the continuum of services. Many school districts developed educational placement sites, which contain options listed on this continuum. These traditional options extend from the least restrictive to the most restrictive special education settings. The least restrictive environment is the regular education classroom. The present trend is to team special education and regular classroom teachers in regular classrooms. This avoids pulling out students for resource room services and provides services by specialists for students who may be showing difficulties similar to those of special education students.

The competencies in this section include the mandates (i.e., laws, regulations, policies) that apply to or have a bearing on the respective states and local districts, as well as the major provisions of federal laws implemented 20 or more years ago, including Public Laws 94-142 (1975), 93-112 (1973), and 101-476 (1990). These laws culminated into the comprehensive statute—IDEA (Individuals with Disabilities Education Act)—which requires the states to offer comprehensive special education service programs to students with disabilities and to plan for their transition into the work world. Most local districts have elaborately articulated delivery systems, which are an extension of national or state Department of Education of Department of Public Instruction. Any inquires should be directed to the unit that administers programs for exceptional children.

MAJOR DEVELOPMENTS IN THE HISTORY OF SPECIAL EDUCATION

Although the origin of special education services for children with disabilities is relatively recent, the history of public attitude toward people with disabling conditions was recorded as early as 1552. The Spartans practiced infanticide, which is the killing or abandonment of malformed or sickly babies. The ancient Greeks and Romans thought people with disabilities were cursed and forced them to beg for food and shelter. Those who could not fend for themselves were allowed to perish. Some with mental disabilities were employed as fools for the entertainment of the Roman royalty.

In the time of Christ, people with disabilities were thought to be suffering the punishment of God. Those with emotional disturbances were considered to be possessed by the devil, and although early Christianity advocated humane treatment of those who were not normal physically or mentally, many remained outcasts of society, sometimes pitied and sometimes scorned.

During the Middle Ages, persons with disabilities were viewed within the aura of the unknown and were treated with a mixture of fear and reverence. Some were wandering beggars, while others were used as jesters in the courts. However, the Reformation brought about a change of attitude. Individuals with disabilities were accused of being possessed by the devil, and exorcism flourished. Many innocent people were put in chains and cast into dungeons.

The early 17th century was marked by a softening of public attitude toward persons with disabilities. Hospitals began to provide treatment for those with emotional disturbances and mental retardation. A manual alphabet for those with deafness was developed, and John Locke became the first person to differentiate between persons who were mentally retarded and those who were emotionally disturbed.

In America, however, the colonists treated people with severe mental disorders as criminals, while those who were harmless were left to beg or were treated as paupers. At one time, it was common practice to sell them to the person who would provide for them at the least cost to the public. When this practice was stopped, persons with mental retardation were put into poorhouses, where conditions were often extremely squalid.

The 19th Century: The Beginning of Training
In 1799, Jean Marc Itard, a French physician, found a 12-year-old boy who had been abandoned in the woods of Averyron, France. His attempts to civilize and educate the boy, Victor, established many of the educational principles presently in use in the field of special education, including developmental and multisensory approaches, sequencing of tasks, individualized instruction, and a curriculum geared toward functional life skills.

Itard's work had an enormous impact on public attitude toward individuals with disabilities. They began to be considered educable. During the late 1700s, rudimentary procedures were devised by which those with sensory impairments (i.e., deaf, blind) could be taught, closely followed in the early 1800s by attempts to teach students with mild intellectual disabilities and emotional disorders (at that time known as the "idiotic" and "insane"). Throughout Europe, schools for students with visual and hearing impairments were erected, paralleled by the founding of similar institutions in the United States. In 1817, Thomas Hopkins Galluder founded the first American school for students who were deaf, known today as Galluder College in Washington, D.C., one of the world's best institutions of higher learning for those with deafness. Galluder's work was followed closely by that of Samuel Gridley Howe, who was instrumental in the founding of the Perkins Institute in 1829 for students who were blind.

The mid-1800s saw the further development of Itard's philosophy of education of students with mental disabilities. Around that time, his student Edward Seguin immigrated to the United States, where he established his philosophy of education for persons with mental retardation in a publication titled *Idiocy and Its Treatment by the Physiological Method* in 1866. Seguin was instrumental in the establishment of the first residential school for individuals with retardation in the United States.

State legislatures began to assume the responsibility for housing people with physical and mental disabilities—the institutional care was largely custodial. Institutions were often referred to as warehouses, due to the deplorable conditions of many. Humanitarians like Dorthea Dix helped to relieve anguish and suffering in institutions for persons with mental illnesses.

1900–1919: Specific Programs

The early 20th century saw the publication of the first standardized test of intelligence by Alfred Binet of France. The test was designed to identify educationally substandard children, but by 1916, the test was revised by an American named Louis Terman. Through Terman, the concept of the intelligence quotient (IQ) was introduced. Since then, the IQ test has come to be used as a predictor of both retarded (delayed) and advanced intellectual development.

At approximately the same time, Italian physician Maria Montessori was concerned with the development of effective techniques for early childhood education. Although she is known primarily for her contributions to this field, her work included methods of education for children with mental retardation, as well, and the approach she developed is used in preschool programs today.

Ironically, it was the advancement of science and the scientific method that led special education to its worst setback in modern times. In 1912, psychologist Henry Goddard published a study based on the Killikak family, in which he traced five generations of the descendants of a man who had one legitimate child and one illegitimate child. Among the descendants of the legitimate child were numerous mental defectives and social deviates. This led Goddard to conclude that mental retardation and social deviation were inherited traits and therefore that mental and social deviates were a threat to society, an observation that he called the Eugenics Theory. Reinforcing the concept of retardation as hereditary deviance was a popular philosophy called positivism, under which these unscientific conclusions were believed to be fixed, mechanical laws that were carrying mankind to inevitable improvement. Falling by the wayside was seen as the natural scientific outcome for the defective person in society. Consequently, during this time, mass institutionalization and sterilization of persons with mental retardation (as well as criminals) were practiced.

Nevertheless, public school programs for persons with retardation gradually increased during this same period. Furthermore, the first college programs for the preparation of special education teachers were established between 1900 and 1920.

1919–1949: Professionalism and Expansion of Services

Awareness of the need for medical and mental health treatments in the community increased during the 1920s. Halfway houses became a means for monitoring the transition from institution to community living; outpatient clinics were established to provide increased medical care. Social workers and other support personnel were dispensed into the community to coordinate services for the needy. The thrust toward humane treatment within the community came to an abrupt halt during the 1930s and 1940s, primarily due to economic depression and widespread dissatisfaction toward the recently enacted social programs.

Two factors related to the world wars helped to improve public opinion toward persons with disabilities. The first was the intensive screening of the population of young men with physical and mental disabilities that were in the United States. The second was patriotism, which caused people to regard the enormous number of young men who returned from the wars with physical and emotional disabilities in a different light than they would have been regarded before that time. People became more sensitive to the problems of the veterans with disabilities, and this acceptance generalized to other groups in the special needs population.

With increased public concern for people with disabilities came new research. John B. Watson introduced behaviorism, which shifted the treatment emphasis from psychoanalysis to learned behavior. He demonstrated in 1920 that maladaptive (or abnormal) behavior was learned by Albert, an 11-month-old boy, through conditioning. B. F. Skinner followed with a book titled the *Behavior of Organisms,* which outlined principles of operant behavior (i.e., voluntary) behavior.

In 1922, the Council for Exceptional Children (first called the International Council for Exceptional Children) was founded. During the 1920s, many comprehensive statewide programs were initiated. The number of special education programs in public schools increased at a rapid rate until the 1930s, when the push for humane and effective treatment of people with disabilities began to diminish once again. This period of the Depression was marked by large-scale institutionalization and an overall lack of treatment. Part of the cause was inadequately planned programs and poorly trained teachers. World War II did much to swing the pendulum back in the other direction, however, and inaugurated the most active period in the history of the development of special education.

1950–1969: The Parents, the Legislators, and the Courts Became Involved
The first two decades of the second half of the century were characterized by increased federal involvement in general education, gradually extending to special education. In 1950 came the establishment of the National Association of Retarded Children, later renamed the National Association of Retarded Citizens (NARC). It was the result of the efforts among concerned parents who felt the need of an appropriated public education. Increased media coverage exposed the miserable conditions in some of the institutions devoted to caring for people with disabilities, especially those with intellectual and emotional disabilities, and treatment consequently became more humane.

It was at about this time that parents of children with disabilities discovered the federal courts as a powerful agent on behalf of their children. The 1954 decision in the *Brown v. the Board of Education of Topeka* case guaranteed equal opportunity rights to a free public education for all citizens, and the parents of children and youth with disabilities insisted that their children be included in that decision. The court cases and public laws enacted as a result of court decisions are too numerous to include in their entirety.[1] Only those few that had the greatest impact on the development of special education as we know it today are listed in Skill 15.02 on the following page. Collectively, they are part of a movement in U.S. Supreme Court history known as the Doctrine of Selective Incorporation, under which the states are compelled to honor various substantive rights under procedural authority of the 14th Amendment.

---

[1] The first cluster of two digits of each public law represents the congressional session during which the law, numbered by the last three digits, was passed. Congressional sessions begin every two years on the odd numbered year. The first biennial session sat in 1787–1788. Bills may be passed and signed into law during either of the two years during which the congressional session is being held. For example, Public Law 94-142 was the 142nd law passed by the 94th Congress, which was in session in 1975–1976 and was passed and signed in 1975.

Skill 15.02 **Demonstrates knowledge of the historical foundations of special education, including classic studies, major contributors, and important legislation (e.g., Individuals with Disabilities Education Improvement Act [IDEA], Section 504 of the Rehabilitation Act, Americans with Disabilities Act [ADA], No Child Left Behind [NCLB] Act).**

Background

The U.S. Constitution does not specify protection for education. However, all states provide education, and thus individuals are guaranteed protection and due process under the 14th Amendment. The basic source of law for special education is the Individuals Disabilities Education Act (IDEA) and its accompanying regulations. IDEA represents the latest phase in the philosophy of educating children with disabilities. Initially, most children with disabilities did not go to school. When they did, they were segregated into special classes in order to avoid disrupting the regular class. Their education usually consisted of simple academics and later training for manual jobs.

By the mid-1900s, advocates for handicapped children argued that segregation was inherently unequal. By the time of Public Law 94-142, about half of the estimated 8 million handicapped children in the United States were either not being appropriately served in school or were excluded from schooling altogether. There were a disproportionate number of minority children placed in special programs. Identification and placement practices and procedures were inconsistent, and parental involvement was generally not encouraged. After segregation on the basis of race was declared unconstitutional in *Brown v. Board of Education of Topeka*, parents and other advocates filed similar lawsuits on behalf of children with handicaps. The culmination of their efforts resulted in Public Law 94-142. This section is a brief summary of that law and other major legislation, which affect the manner in which special education services are delivered to handicapped children.

SIGNIFICANT LEGISLATION AND SUPREME COURT CASES WITH AN IMPACT ON EXCEPTIONAL STUDENT EDUCATION

Brown v. Board of Education of Topeka (1954)

While this case specifically addressed the inequality of "separate but equal" facilities on the basis of race, the concept that segregation was inherently unequal—even if facilities were provided—was later applied to handicapping conditions.

The Cooperative Research Act (1954)

This act passed the first designation of general funds for the use of students with disabilities.

Public Law 85-926 (1958)
This provided grants to intuitions of higher learning and to state education agencies for training professional personnel who would, in turn, train teachers of students with mental retardation.

Elementary and Secondary Education Act (1965)
This provided funds for the education of children who were disadvantaged and disabled (Public Law 89-10).

Educational Consolidation and Improvement Act-State Operated Programs: Public Law 89-313 (1965)
This provided funds for children with disabilities who are or have been in state-operated or state-supported schools.

Public Law 89-750 (1966)
This law authorized the establishment of the Bureau Education for the Handicapped (BEH) and a National Advisory Committee on the Handicapped.

Hanson v. Hobson (1967)
This case ruled that ability grouping (tracking) based on student performance on standardized tests is unconstitutional.

Handicapped Children's Early Education Assistance Act: Public Law 90-538 (1968)
This funded model demonstration programs for preschool students with disabilities.

Public Law 90-247 (1968)
This law included provisions for deaf-blind centers, resource centers, and the expansion of media services for students with disabilities.

Public Law 90-576 (1968)
This law specified that 10 percent of vocational education funds be earmarked for youth with disabilities.

Public Law 91-230 (Amendments to Public Law 89-10) (1969)
Previous enactment relating to children with disabilities was consolidated into one act: Education of the Handicapped.

Pennsylvania Association for Retarded Citizens (PARC) v. Commonwealth of Pennsylvania (1972)
Special education was guaranteed to children with mental retardation. The victory in this case sparked other court cases for children with other disabilities.

Mills v. Board of Education of the District of Columbia (1972)

The right to special education was extended to all children with disabilities, not just mentally retarded children. Judgments in PARC and Mills paved the way for Public Law 94-142.

Section 504, Rehabilitation Act of 1973

Section 504 expands an older law by extending its protection to other areas that receive federal assistance, such as education. Protected individuals must (a) have a physical or mental impairment that substantially limits one or more major life activities (e.g., self-care, walking, seeing, breathing, working, and learning); (b) have a record of such an impairment; or (c) be regarded as having such an impairment. A disability in itself is not sufficient grounds for a complaint of discrimination. The person must be otherwise qualified, or able to meet, the requirements of the program in question.

Goss v. Lopez (1975)

This case ruled that the state could not deny a student education without following due process. While this decision is not based on a special education issue, the process of school suspension and expulsion is obviously critical in assuring an appropriate public education to children with disabilities.

Education for All Handicapped Children Act: Public Law 94-142 (1975)

The philosophy behind these pieces of legislation is that education is to be provided to all children ages 6 to 18 who meet age eligibility requirements. All children are assumed capable of benefiting from education. For children with severe or profound handicaps, "education" may be interpreted to include training in basic self-help skills and vocational training as well as academics.

Gifted and Talented Children's Act: Public Law 95-56 (1978)

This defined the gifted and talented population and focused upon this exceptionally category, which was not included in Public Law 94-142.

Larry P. v. Riles (1979)

This case ordered the re-evaluation of black students enrolled in classes for educable mental retardation (EMR) and enjoined the California State Department of Education from the use of intelligence tests in subsequent EMR placement decisions.

Parents in Action on Special Education (PASE) v. Hannon (1980)

This case ruled that IQ tests are necessarily biased against ethnic and racial subcultures.

Board of Education v. Rowley **(1982)**

Amy Rowley was a deaf elementary school student whose parents rejected their school district's proposal to provide a tutor and speech therapist services to supplement their daughter's instruction in the regular classroom. Her parents insisted on an interpreter, even though Amy was making satisfactory social, academic, and educational progress without one. In deciding in favor of the school district, the Supreme Court ruled that school districts must provide those services that permit a student with disabilities to benefit from instruction. Essentially, the court ruled that the states are obligated to provide a "basic floor of opportunity" that reasonably allows the child to benefit from social education.

Irving Independent School District v. Tatro **(1984)**

IDEA lists health services as one of the "related services" that schools are mandated to provide to exceptional students. Amber Tatro, who had spina bifida, required the insertion of a catheter on a regular schedule in order to empty her bladder. The issue was specifically over the classification of clean, intermittent catheterization (CIC) as a medical service (not covered under IDEA) or a "related health service," which would be covered. In this instance, the catheterization was not declared a medical service but a "related service" necessary for the student to have in order to benefit from special education. The school district was obliged to provide the service. The Tatro case has implications for students with other medical impairments who may need services to allow them to attend classes at the school.

Smith v. Robinson **(1984)**

This case concerned reimbursement of attorney's fees for parents who win litigation under IDEA. At the time of this case, IDEA did not provide for such reimbursement. Following this ruling, Congress passed a law awarding attorney's fees to parents who win their litigation.

Honig v. Doe **(1988***)*

Essentially, students may not be denied education or exclusion from school when their misbehavior is related to their handicap. The "stay put" provision of IDEA allows students to remain in their current educational settings pending the outcome of administrative or judicial hearings. In the case of behavior that is a danger to the student or others, the court allows school districts to apply their normal procedures for dealing with dangerous behavior, such as time-out, loss of privileges, detention, or study carrels. Where the student has presented an immediate threat to others, that student may be temporarily suspended for up to 10 school days to give the school and the parents time to review the IEP and discuss possible alternatives to the current placement.

Public Law 99-457 (1986)

Beginning with the 1991–1992 school year, special education programs were required for children ages 3 to 5, with most states offering outreach programs to identify children with special needs from birth to age 3. In place of, or in addition to, an annual IEP, the entire family's needs are addressed by an Individual Family Service Plan (IFSP), which is reviewed with the family every six months.

Americans with Disabilities Act (ADA) (1990)

This act bars discrimination in employment, transportation, public accommodations, and telecommunications in all aspects of life, not just those receiving federal funding. Title II and Title III are applicable to special education because they cover the private sector (such as private schools) and require access to public accommodations. New and remodeled public buildings, transportation vehicles, and telephone systems now must be accessible to the handicapped. ADA also protects individuals with contagious diseases, such as AIDS, from discrimination.

IDEA : Public Law 101-476 (1990)

The principles of IDEA also incorporate the concept of "normalization." Within this concept, persons with disabilities are allowed access to everyday patterns and conditions of life that are as close as possible or equal to those of their nondisabled peers. There are seven fundamental provisions of IDEA.

1. **Free Appropriate Public Education (FAPE):** Special education services are to be provided at no cost to students or their families. The federal and state governments share any additional costs. FAPE also requires that education be appropriate to the individual needs of the students.
2. **Notification and procedural rights for parents.** These include:
   a. the right to examine records and obtain independent evaluations;
   b. the right to receive a clearly written notice that states the results of the school's evaluation of their child, as well as whether the child meets eligibility requirements for placement or continuation of special services; and
   c. parents who disagree with the school's decision may request a **due process** hearing and a **judicial hearing** if they do not receive satisfaction through due process.
3. **Identification and Services to All Children:** States must conduct public outreach programs to seek out and identify children who may need services.
4. **Necessary Related Services:** Developmental, corrective, and other support services that make it possible for a student to benefit from special education services must be provided. These may include speech, recreation, or physical therapy.
5. **Individualized Assessments:** Evaluations and tests must be nondiscriminatory and individualized.
6. **Individualized Education Plans (IEP):** Each student receiving special

education services must have an individualized education plan developed at a meeting that is attended by a qualified representative of the local education agency (LEA). Others who should attend are the proposed special education teachers, mainstream teachers, parents, and, when appropriate, the student.

7 **Least Restrictive Environment (LRE):** There is no simple definition of LRE. LRE differs with the child's needs. LRE means that the student is placed in an environment that is not dangerous, overly controlling, or intrusive. The student should be given opportunities to experience what other peers of similar mental or chronological age are doing. LRE should be the environment that is the most integrated and normalized for the student's strengths and weaknesses. LRE for one child may be a regular classroom with support services, while LRE for another may be a self-contained classroom in a special school.

Florence County School District Four v. Shannon Carter (1993)

This case established that when a school district does not provide FAPE for a student with disability, the parents may seek reimbursement for private schooling. This decision has encouraged districts to be more inclusive of students with autism who receive ABA/Lovaas therapy.

Reauthorization of IDEA: Public Law 105-17 (1997)

This required involvement of a regular education teacher as part of the IEP team. It provides additional strength to school administrators for the discipline of students with special needs.

In 1997, IDEA was revised and reauthorized as Public Law 105-17 as progressive legislation for the benefit of school-age children with special needs, their parents, and those who work with these children. The 1997 reauthorization of IDEA made major changes in the areas of the evaluation procedures, parent rights, transition, and discipline.

The evaluation process was amended to require members of the evaluation team to look at previously collected data, tests, and information and to use it when deemed appropriate. Previous to IDEA 1997, an entire re-evaluation had to be conducted every three years to determine if the child continued to be a "child with a disability." This was changed to allow existing information/evaluations to be considered to prevent unnecessary assessment of students and reduce the cost of evaluations.

Parent participation was not a requirement under the previous IDEA for an evaluation team to make decisions regarding a student's eligibility for special education and related services. Under IDEA 1997, parents were specifically included as members of the group making the eligibility decision.

The IEP was modified under IDEA 1997 to emphasize the involvement of students with special needs in a general education classroom setting, with the services and modifications deemed necessary by the evaluation team.

The "Present Levels of Educational Performance" (PLEP) was changed to require a statement of how the child's disability affects his or her involvement and progress in the general curriculum. IDEA 1997 established that there must be a connection between the special education and general education curriculum. For this reason, the PLEP was required to include an explanation of the extent to which the student will *not* be participating with nondisabled children in the general education class, as well as in extracurricular and nonacademic activities.

After this Public Law, the IEP now had an established connection to the general education setting. The IEP had to provide the needed test accommodations that would be provided on all state and district-wide assessments of the student with special needs. IDEA 1997's emphasis on raising the standards of those in special education placed an additional requirement of definitive reasons why a standard general education assessment would not be deemed appropriate for a child, as well as how the child should then be assessed.

IDEA 1997 looked at how parents were receiving annual evaluations on their children's IEP goals and determined that this was not sufficient feedback for parents. It required schools to make reports to parents on the progress of their child at least as frequently as progress of their nondisabled peers.

The IEP was also modified to include a review of the student's transitional needs and services, specifically:

- beginning when a student is 14, and annually thereafter, the student's IEP must contain a statement of his or her transition service needs under the various components of that IEP that focus on the student's courses of study (e.g., vocational education or advanced placement); and
- beginning at least one year before the student reaches the age of majority under state law, the IEP must contain a statement that the student has been informed of the rights under the law that will transfer to him or her upon reaching the age of majority.

IDEA 1997 also broadened a school's right to take disciplinary action with children who have been classified as needing special education services when those students knowingly possess or use illegal drugs, or sell or solicit the sale of a controlled substance while at school or school functions.

Under IDEA 1997, suspensions and disciplinary consequences could result in an alternative educational placement. This possibility was to be weighed by a Manifest Determination Review, which is held by an IEP team. Manifest Determination Reviews must occur no more than 10 days after the disciplinary action. This review team has the sole responsibility of determining the following:

1. Does the child's disability impair his or her understanding of the impact and consequences of the behavior under disciplinary action?
2. Did the child's disability impair the ability of the child to control the behavior subject to discipline?

Determination of a relationship of the student's disability and an inappropriate behavior could allow current placement to occur.

When no relationship between the "inappropriate" behavior is established, IDEA 1997 utilized FAPE to allow the relevant disciplinary procedures applicable to children without disabilities to be applied to the child in the same manner in which they would be applied to children with disabilities. Functional Behavioral Assessments (FBAs) and Behavior Intervention Plans (BIPs) became a requirement in many situations for schools to both modify and provide disciplinary consequences.

No Child Left Behind Act (NCLB) (2002)
No Child Left Behind, Public Law 107-110, was signed on January 8, 2002. It addresses accountability of school personnel for student achievement with the expectation that every child will demonstrate proficiency in reading, math, and science. The first full wave of accountability will be in 12 years, when children who first started to attend school under NCLB graduate; however, the process to meet that accountability began in 2002. In fact, as students progress through the school system, testing shows if an individual teacher has effectively met the needs of his or her students. Through testing, each student's adequate yearly progress or lack thereof is tracked.

NCLB affects regular and special education students, gifted students, slow learners, and children of every ethnicity, culture, and environment. NCLB is a document that encompasses every American educator and student.

Educators are affected in many ways. Elementary teachers (K-3) are responsible for teaching reading and using different, scientific-based approaches, as needed. Elementary teachers of upper grades teach reading, math, and science. Middle and high school teachers teach to new, higher standards. Sometimes, they have the task of playing catch up with students who did not have adequate education in earlier grades.

Special educators are responsible for teaching students to a level of comparable proficiency as their nondisabled peers. This will raise the bar of academic expectations throughout the grades. For some students with disabilities, the criteria for getting a diploma becomes more difficult. Although a small percentage of students with disabilities need alternate assessments, they still need to meet grade-appropriate goals.

In order for special education teachers to meet the professional criteria of this act, they must be *highly qualified*—that is, certified or licensed in their area of special education—and show proof of a specific level of professional development in the core subjects that they teach. As special education teachers receive specific education in the core subjects they teach, they become better prepared to teach to the same level of learning standards as the general education teacher.

M.L. v. Federal Way School District, State of Washington (2004)
The Ninth Circuit Court of Appeals ruled that absence of a regular education teacher on an IEP team was a serious procedural error.

Reauthorization of IDEA (2004)
This required all special education teachers on a secondary level to be no less qualified than other teachers of the subject areas.

This second revision of IDEA occurred in 2004. IDEA was reauthorized as the Individuals with Disabilities Education Improvement Act of 2004 (IDEIA 2004) and is commonly referred to as IDEA 2004. IDEA 2004 was effective as of July 1, 2005.

It was the intention to improve IDEA by adding the philosophy/understanding that special education students need preparation for further study beyond the high school setting by teaching compensatory methods. Accordingly, IDEA 2004 provided a close tie to Public Law 89-10, the Elementary and Special Education Act of 1965, and stated that students with special needs should have maximum access to the general curriculum. This was defined as the amount of education necessary for an individual student to reach his or her fullest potential. Full inclusion was stated as not the only option by which to achieve this; it was specified that skills should be taught to compensate students later in life in cases where inclusion was not the best setting.

IDEA 2004 added a new requirement for special education teachers on the secondary level, enforcing NCLB's "highly qualified" requirements in the subject area of their curriculum. The rewording in this part of IDEA states that they shall be "no less qualified" than teachers in the core areas.

FAPE was revised by mandating that students have maximum access to appropriate general education. Additionally, LRE placement for those students with disabilities must have the same school placement rights as those students who are not disabled. IDEA 2004 recognizes that due to the nature of some disabilities, appropriate education may vary in the amount of participation/placement in the general education setting. For some students, FAPE means a choice as to the type of educational institution they attend (e.g., public vs. private school), any of which must provide the special education services deemed necessary for the student through the IEP.

Skill 15.03   Demonstrates knowledge of current issues and trends in the field of special education (e.g., full inclusion, standards-based reforms, access to new technologies, person centered planning).

Present and Future Perspectives
What is the state of special education today? What can we anticipate as far as changes that might occur in the near future? It has been two decades since the passage of the initial Individuals with Disabilities Education Act as Public Law 93-142 in 1975. So far, mandates stand with funding intact. The clients are still here, and in greater numbers (thanks to improved identification procedures and to medical advances that have left many who might have died in the past with conditions considered disabling). Among the disabling conditions afflicting the population with recently discovered lifesaving techniques are blindness, deafness, amputation, central nervous system or neurological impairments, brain dysfunction, and mental retardation from environmental, genetic, traumatic, infectious, and unknown etiologies.

Despite challenges to the principles underlying Public Law 94-142 in the early 1980s, total federal funding for the concept increased as new amendments were passed. These amendments expanded services to infants, preschoolers, and secondary students (Rothstein 1995).

Following public hearings, Congress voted in 1990 not to include ADD as a new exceptionality area. Determining factors included the alleged ambiguity of the definition and eligibility criteria for students with ADD, the large number of students who might be identified if it became a service delivery area, the subsequent cost of serving such a large population, and the fact that many of these students are already served in the exceptionality areas of learning disabilities and behavior disorders.

The revision of the original law, which we now call IDEA, included some other changes. These changes were primarily in language (terminology), procedures (especially transition), and the addition of new categories (autism and traumatic brain injury).

Thus, we can see that despite challenges to federal services and mandates in special education as an extension of the 14th Amendment since 1980, there has actually been growth in mandated categories and net funding. The Doctrine of Selective Incorporation is the name for one major set of challenges to this process. While the 1994 conservative turnover in Congress might seem to undercut the force of Public Law 94-132, two decades of recent history show strong bipartisan support for special education; consequently, IDEA, or a joint federal-state replacement, will most likely remain strong. Lobbyists and activists representing coalition and advocacy groups for those with disabilities combined with bipartisan congressional support to avert the proposed changes, which would have meant drastic setbacks in services for persons with disabilities.

Nevertheless, there remain several philosophical controversies in special education. The need for labels for categories continues to be questioned. Many states are serving special needs students by severity level rather than by the exceptionality category.

Special educators are faced with possible changes in what is considered to be the least restrictive environment for educating students with special needs. Following upon the heels of the Regular Education Initiative, the concept of inclusion has come to the forefront. Both of these movements were, and are, an attempt to educate special needs students in the mainstream of the regular classroom. Both would eliminate pulling out students from regular classroom instructional activities, and both would incorporate the services of special education teachers in the regular classroom in collaboration with general classroom teachers.

Special education has changed significantly in recent decades. From separated, specialized classrooms for virtually every area of disability, special education has moved into the world of inclusion and undergone stricter accountability for general education learning standards.

According to IDEA 2004, special education students are to participate in general education programs to the fullest extent from which they can receive benefit. This often means accommodations and modifications in class work, employment of classroom assistants, and, in some cases, individual care aides. It also means there needs to be a closer working relationship between the special educator and general education teacher. Special education services are likely to be in the form of push-in services in the general education classroom, including team teaching or through consultation with the special educator. Fewer students are served in special education classrooms for the entire day, and resource services are used only as deemed absolutely necessary by the IEP team.

Special educators are accountable for meeting the same learning standards as general educators. NCLB stipulates that students are expected to read by grade 3, requiring the use of a variety of reading methods (including phonics) to that end. In addition, all students are expected to show adequate yearly progress (AYP) as measured by the same standardized tests used in general education. In very few cases, when the disability is severe, the student may be given alternate assessment.

New and ever-advancing technology has been beneficial to special education students, particularly those in the inclusion setting. Among commonly used technology are calculators, spell checking technology, augmentative communication devices, and computers (which are often effective for students to use for writing and revisions). In the area of education of the hearing impaired, fm auditory trainers allow students to focus on the teacher's voice while the environmental noise input from the classroom is minimized. Additionally, some deaf students have cochlear implants that allow them to hear speech and develop optimum speaking skills.

In some instances, person-centered planning is utilized to establish an educational program with the long-range personal goals of the individual with disabilities in mind. Like the traditional IEP team, the person-centered planning team includes family and school personnel. Additionally, friends may be included in the team. In contrast to traditional IEPs, which seek to find a placement within the existing system, the person-centered approach develops a program based on the student's strengths, weaknesses, and personal goals.

Skill 15.04   Demonstrates knowledge of definitions and issues in the identification of individuals with disabilities, including factors influencing the overrepresentation of students from culturally/linguistically diverse backgrounds in programs for students with disabilities.

Please refer to http://rules.sos.state.ga.us/cgi-bin/page.cgi?d=1 for Georgia-specific information.

IDEA 2004 Section 300.8 defines a child with a disability as "having mental retardation, a hearing impairment (including deafness), a speech or language impairment, a visual impairment (including blindness), a serious emotional disturbance (referred to in this part as emotional disturbance), an orthopedic impairment, autism, traumatic brain injury, another health impairment, a specific learning disability, deaf-blindness, or multiple disabilities, and who, by reason thereof, needs special education and related services."

Eligibility for special education services is based on a student having one of the above disabilities (or a combination thereof) and a demonstration of educational need through professional evaluation.

Seldom does a student with a disability fall into only one of the characteristics listed in IDEA 2004. For example, a student with a hearing impairment may also have a specific learning disability, or a student on the autism spectrum may also demonstrate a language impairment. In fact, language impairment is inherent in autism. Sometimes, the eligibility is defined as multiple disabilities (with one listed as a primary eligibility on the IEP, and the others listed as secondary). Sometimes there are overlapping needs that are not necessarily listed as a secondary disability.

The table below shows disability prevalence among children in the United States according to the 1988 National Educational Longitudinal Study (NELS).

Disability	Prevalence/Incidence
Mental retardation	0.1
Specific learning problem	6.1
Emotional problem	2.8
Speech problem	1.6
Hearing problem	2.2
Deafness	0.4
Visual handicap (not correctable with glasses)	1.6
Orthopedic problem	0.9
Other physical disability	1.1
Any other health problem	3.7

ANALYZES ISSUES RELATING TO DEFINITION AND IDENTIFICATION PROCEDURES FOR INDIVIDUALS WITH DISABILITIES, INCLUDING INDIVIDUALS FROM CULTURALLY AND/OR LINGUISTICALLY DIVERSE BACKGROUNDS

People with disabilities from diverse cultures are considerably disadvantaged in attaining complete participation in all areas of society. This is based on a wide range of barriers to the full benefits of civil and human rights. The obstacles that people from diverse cultures have to withstand include a lack of culturally appropriate outreach, language and communication barriers, attitudinal barriers, and the lack of individuals from diverse cultures in the disability services profession.

People with disabilities from diverse cultures have a harder time receiving services. IDEA is a legislative act guaranteeing rights to individuals with disabilities to a full inclusive education, but IDEA has not fully reached people with disabilities from underserved populations.

Individuals from diverse backgrounds are at a disadvantage when it comes to receiving services related to their disability and even being diagnosed with a disability. This is compounded by not having a significant number of teachers and other professional from diverse cultures, meaning that the communication barriers continue to exist.

Skill 15.05   Demonstrates knowledge of the rights and responsibilities of all stakeholders related to the education of students with disabilities (e.g., students, parents/guardians, teachers, other professionals, schools).

Please refer to Skill 14.01.

Skill 15.06   Demonstrates knowledge of laws, litigation, policies, and ethical principles related to referral, assessment, eligibility, and placement within a continuum of services for students with disabilities, including issues, assurances, and due process rights.

Please see Skill 5.01 for legal issues on assessments.
Please see IDEA: Public Law 101-476 (1990) in Skill 15.02 for laws related to IDEA.

COMPETENCY 16.0 UNDERSTAND THE PROFESSIONAL, ETHICAL, AND LEGAL ROLES AND RESPONSIBILITIES OF THE SPECIAL EDUCATOR

Skill 16.01 Applies knowledge of how to uphold high standards for professional practice, including participating in professional activities and organizations that benefit students with disabilities, their families, and colleagues.

Please refer to Skill 16.03 for more information about professional organizations.

The special education teacher comes to the job with past experiences, as well as personal opinions and beliefs. It is vital that he or she not let those personal persuasions guide any area of professional conduct. Objective professional judgment is important in all areas of the teacher's role.

Objective professional judgment should be exercised when considering the cultural, religious, and sexual orientations of the special educator's students and their respective families. An unbiased approach to communication maintains positive interaction and increased cooperation between home and school. The result is a better educational program that will meet the individual student's needs.

Objectivity should also be exercised when considering assessment of possible disability. Educator preference for a particular assessment should be secondary to matching the needs of the child with a specific instrument. Assessment tools should be researched based and determined to be appropriate for the needs of the specific student.

When establishing the special education program, the specific student's IEP must be followed. If the special educator determines that the goals and objectives of the IEP no longer fit the child's needs, an IEP meeting should be called to review and possibly revise the document. Again, the revision of the IEP should be based on the needs of the child as determined objectively, not the personal preference of the teacher for a particular type of program or schedule. This objectivity should include materials, scheduling, activities, and evaluation.

The student's IEP should also be focused on the learning standards established by the state. In particular, learning activities that provide measurable outcomes should be employed. Such data provide objective evaluations of student progress as well as the student's possible mastery of the targeted standards.

Professional objectivity is crucial in communication with administration for the representation of students' needs for placement, programming, materials, scheduling, and staffing. When documented, data-driven information is presented, optimum decisions are made for students with disabilities and for the school community in general.

Skill 16.02 **Demonstrates knowledge of how to use resources (e.g., professional organizations and journals, online resources, conferences, workshops, mentors) to enhance one's own professional knowledge (e.g., current research-validated practices, information about the characteristics and needs of students with disabilities) and engage in lifelong professional growth and development.**

The professional associations representing the spectrum of services for individuals with disabilities are listed in the table below. Some of these organizations date from the pioneer times of special education and are still in active service.

Organization	Members	Mission
Alexander Graham Bell Association for the Deaf and Hard of Hearing 3417 Volta Place, N.W. Washington, DC 20007 http://www.agbell.org	Teachers of the deaf, speech-language pathologists, audiologists, physicians, hearing aid dealers	To promote the teaching of speech, lip reading, and use of residual hearing to persons who are deaf; encourage research; and work to further better education of persons who are deaf.
Alliance for Technology Access 1304 Southpoint Blvd., Suite 240, Petaluma, CA 94954 Phone (707) 778-3011 Fax (707) 765-2080 TTY (707) 778-3015 E-mail: ATAinfo@ATAccess.org http://www.Ataccess.org	People with disabilities, family members, and professionals in related fields, and organizations with work in their own communities and ways to support our mission.	To increase the use of technology by children and adults with disabilities and functional limitations.

Organization	Members	Mission
American Council of the Blind 1155 15th Street, NW, Suite 1004, Washington, DC 20005 Phone: (202) 467-5081 (800) 424-8666 FAX: (202) 467-5085 http://Acb.org		To improve the well-being of all blind and visually impaired people by serving as a representative national organization of blind people and conducting a public education program to promote greater understanding of blindness and the capabilities of blind people.
American Council on Rural Special Education (ACRES) Utah State University 2865 Old Main Hill Logan, Utah 84322 Phone: (435) 797-3728 E-mail: inquiries@acres-sped.org	Open to anyone interested in supporting their mission	To provide leadership and support that will enhance services for individuals with exceptional needs, their families, and the professionals who work with them, and for the rural communities in which they live.
American Society for Deaf Children 3820 Hartzdale Drive, Camp Hill, PA 17011 Phone: (717) 703-0073 (866) 895-4206 FAX: (717) 909-5599 E-mail: asdc@deafchildren.org http://www.deafchildren.org	Open to all who support the mission of the association	To provide support, encouragement and information to families raising children who are deaf or hard of hearing.
American Speech-Language-Hearing Association 10801 Rockville Pike Rockville, MD 20852	Specialists in speech-language pathology and audiology	To advocate for the provision of speech-language and hearing services in school and clinic settings; advocate for legislation relative to the profession; and work to promote effective services and development of the profession.
Asperger Syndrome Education Network (ASPEN) 9 Aspen Circle Edison, NJ 08820 Phone: (732) 321-0880 E-mail: info@AspenNJ.org http://www.aspennj.org		Provides families and individuals whose lives are affected by autism spectrum disorders and nonverbal learning disabilities with education, support, and advocacy.

Organization	Members	Mission
Attention Deficit Disorder Association 15000 Commerce Pkwy, Suite C Mount Laurel, NJ 08054 Phone: (856) 439-9099 FAX: (856) 439-0525 http://www.add.org/	Open to all who support the mission of ADDA	Provides information, resources and networking to adults with AD/HD and to the professionals who work with them.
Autism Society of America 7910 Woodmont Avenue, Suite 300 Bethesda, MD 20814 Phone: (800) 328-8476 http://www.autism-society.org	Open to all who support the mission of ASA	To increase public awareness about autism and the day-to-day issues faced by individuals with autism, their families, and the professionals with whom they interact. The society and its chapters share a common mission of providing information and education and supporting research and advocating for programs and services for the autism community.
Brain Injury Association of America 8201 Greensboro Drive Suite 611 McLean, VA 22102 Phone: (703) 761-0750 http://www.biausa.org	Open to all	Provides information, education, and support to assist the 5.3 million Americans currently living with traumatic brain injury and their families.
Child and Adolescent Bipolar Association (CABF) 1187 Wilmette Ave. P.M.B. #331 Wilmette, IL 60091 http://www.bpkids.org	Physicians, scientific researchers, and allied professionals (therapists, social workers, educators, attorneys, and others) who provide services to children and adolescents with bipolar disorder or do research on the topic	Educates families, professionals, and the public about pediatric bipolar disorder; connects families with resources and support; advocates for and empowers affected families; and supports research on pediatric bipolar disorder and its cure.

Organization	Members	Mission
Children and Adults with Attention Deficit/ Hyperactive Disorder (CHADD) 8181 Professional Place - Suite 150 Landover, MD 20785 Phone: (301) 306-7070 Fax: (301) 306-7090 E-mail: national@chadd.org http://www.chadd.org	Open to all	Providing resources and encouragement to parents, educators and professionals on a grassroots level through CHADD chapters.
Council for Exceptional Children (CEC) 1110 N. Glebe Road Suite 300 Arlington, VA 22201 Phone: (888) 232-7733 TTY: (866) 915-5000 FAX: (703) 264-9494 http://www.cec.sped.org	Teachers, administrators, teacher educators, and related service personnel	Advocates for services for disabled and gifted individuals. It is a professional organization that addresses service, training, and research relative to exceptional persons.
Epilepsy Foundation of America (EFA) 8301 Professional Place Landover, MD 20785 Phone: (800) 332-1000 http://www.epilepsyfoundation.org	A nonmembership organization	Works to ensure that people with seizures are able to participate in all life experiences; and to prevent, control and cure epilepsy through research, education, advocacy and services
Family Center on Technology and Disability (FCTD) 1825 Connecticut Ave., NW 7th Floor Washington, DC 20009 Phone: (202) 884-8068 fax: (202) 884-8441 E-mail: fctd@aed.org http://www.fctd.info/	Nonmember association	A resource designed to support organizations and programs that work with families of children and youth with disabilities.

Organization	Members	Mission
Hands and Voices P.O. Box 371926 Denver, CO 80237 Phone: (866) 422-0422 E-mail: parentadvocate@handsand voices.org http://www.handsandvoices. org	Families, professionals, other organizations, pre-service students, and deaf and hard of hearing adults who are all working towards ensuring successful outcomes for children who are deaf and hard of hearing	To support families and their children who are deaf or hard of hearing, as well as the professionals who serve them.
The International Dyslexia Association Chester Building, Suite 382 8600 LaSalle Road Baltimore, Maryland 21286 Phone: (410) 296-0232 Fax: (410) 321-5069 http://www.interdys.org	Anyone interested in IDA and its mission can become a member	Provides information and referral services, research, advocacy, and direct services to professionals in the field of learning disabilities.
Learning Disabilities Association of America (LDA) 4156 Library Road Pittsburgh, PA 15234 Phone: (412) 341-1515 Fax: (412) 344-0224 http://www.ldanatl.org/	Anyone interested in LDA and its mission can become a member	Provides cutting edge information on learning disabilities, practical solutions, and a comprehensive network of resources.
National Association of the Deaf (NAD) 8630 Fenton Street Suite 820 Silver Spring, MD 20910 Phone: (209) 210-3819 TTY: (301) 587-1789 FAX: (301) 587-1791 E-mail: NADinfo@nad.org http://nad.org	Anyone interested in NAD and its mission can become a member	To promote, protect, and preserve the rights and quality of life of deaf and hard of hearing individuals in the United States of America.

Organization	Members	Mission
National Mental Health Information Center P.O. Box 42557 Washington, DC 20015 Phone: (800) 789-2647 http://www.mentalhealth.samhsa.gov	Government agency	Developed for users of mental health services and their families, the general public, policy makers, providers, and the media.
National Dissemination Center for Children with Disabilities (NICHCY) P.O. Box 1492 Washington, DC 20013 Phone: (800) 695-0285 · Fax: (202) 884-8441 E-mail: nichcy@aed.org http://www.nichcy.org/Pages/Home.aspx	Nonmembership association	A central source of information on: • disabilities in infants, toddlers, children, and youth; • IDEA, which is the law authorizing special education; • No Child Left Behind (as it relates to children with disabilities); and research-based information on effective educational practices.
US Department of Education **Office of Special Education and Rehabilitative Services** http://www.ed.gov/about/offices/list/osers/index.html	Government resource	Committed to improving results and outcomes for people with disabilities of all ages.
Wrights Law E-mail: webmaster@wrightslaw.com http://wrightslaw.com	Nonmembership organization	Parents, educators, advocates, and attorneys come to Wrightslaw.com for accurate, reliable information about special education law, education law, and advocacy for children with disabilities. Provides parent advocacy training and updates on the law throughout the country.

Organization	Members	Mission
TASH (Formerly the Association for Persons with Severe Handicaps) 29 W. Susquehanna Ave., Suite 210 Baltimore, MD 21204 Phone: (410) 828-8274 Fax: (410) 828-6706 http:// www.tash.org	Anyone interested in TASH and its mission can become a member	To create change and build capacity so that all people, no matter their perceived level of disability, are included in all aspects of society.
American Psychological Association 750 First Street, NE, Washington, DC 20002-4242 Phone: (800) 374-2721 FAX: (202) 336-5500 TTY: (202) 336-6123 http://www.apa.org	Psychologists and professors of psychology	Scientific and professional society working to improve mental health services and to advocate for legislation and programs that will promote mental health; facilitates research and professional development.
Association for Children and Adults with Learning Disabilities 4156 Library Road Pittsburgh, PA 15234 http://www.acldonline.org/	Parents of children with learning disabilities and interested professionals	Advance the education and general well-being of children with adequate intelligence who have learning disabilities arising from perceptual, conceptual, or subtle coordinative problems, sometimes accompanied by behavior difficulties.
National Association for Gifted Children 1707 L Street, NW Suite 550 Washington, DC 20036 Phone: (202) 785-4368 FAX: (202) 785-4248 E-mail: nagc@nagc.org http://www.nagc.org		
Council for Children with Behavioral Disorders Two Ballston Plaza 1110 N. Glebe Road Arlington, VA 22201 Phone: (800) 224-6830 FAX: (703) 264-9494	Parents, educators, community leaders, and other professionals who work with gifted children.	To address the unique needs of children and youth with demonstrated gifts and talents.

Organization	Members	Mission
Council for Educational Diagnostic Services Two Ballston Plaza 1110 N. Glebe Road Arlington, VA 22201	Members of the Council for Exceptional Children who teach children with behavior disorders or who train teachers to work with those children	Promote education and general welfare of children and youth with behavior disorders or serious emotional disturbances; promote professional growth and research on students with behavior disorders and severe emotional disturbances.
Council of Administrators of Special Education Two Ballston Plaza 1110 N. Glebe Road Arlington, VA 22201	Members of the Council for Exceptional Children who are school psychologists, educational diagnosticians, and social workers who are involved in diagnosing educational difficulties	Promote the most appropriate education of children and youth through appraisal, diagnosis, educational intervention, implementation, and evaluation of a prescribed educational program. Work to facilitate the professional development of those who assess students. Work to further development of better diagnostic techniques and procedures.
Division for Children with Communication Disorders Two Ballston Plaza 1110 N. Glebe Road Arlington, VA 22201	Members of the Council for Exceptional Children who are administrators, directors, coordinators, or supervisors of programs, schools, or classes for exceptional children; college faculty who train administrators	Promote professional leadership; provide opportunities for the study of problems common to its members; communicate through discussion and publications information that will facilitate improved services for children with exceptional needs.

Organization	Members	Mission
Division for Early Childhood Two Ballston Plaza 1110 N. Glebe Road Arlington, VA 22201	Members of the Council for Exceptional Children who are speech-language pathologists, audiologists, teachers of children with communication disorders, or educators of professionals who plan to work with children who have communication disorders	Promote the education of children with communication disorders. Promote professional growth and research.
Division for the Physically Handicapped Two Ballston Plaza 1110 N. Glebe Road Arlington, VA 22201	Members of the Council for Exceptional Children who teach preschool children and infants or educate teachers to work with young children	Promote effective education for young children and infants. Promote professional development of those who work with young children and infants. Promote legislation and research.
Division for the Visually Handicapped Two Ballston Plaza 1110 N. Glebe Road Arlington, VA 22201	Members of the Council for Exceptional Children who work with individuals who have physical disabilities or educate professionals to work with those individuals	Promote closer relationships among educators of students who have physical impairments or are homebound. Facilitate research and encourage development of new ideas, practices, and techniques through professional meetings, workshops, and publications.
Division on Career Development Two Ballston Plaza 1110 N. Glebe Road Arlington, VA 22201	Members of the Council for Exceptional Children who work with individuals who have visual disabilities or educate professionals to work with those individuals	Work to advance the education and training of individuals with visual impairments. Work to bring about better understanding of educational, emotional, or other problems associated with visual impairment. Facilitate research and development of new techniques or ideas in education and training of individuals with visual problems.

Organization	Members	Mission
Division on Mental Retardation Two Ballston Plaza 1110 N. Glebe Road Arlington, VA 22201	Members of the Council for Exceptional Children who teach or in other ways work toward career development and vocational education of exceptional children	Promote and encourage professional growth of all those concerned with career development and vocational education. Promote research, legislation, information dissemination, and technical assistance relevant to career development and vocational education.
Gifted Child Society P.O. Box 120 Oakland, NJ 07436	Members of the Council for Exceptional Children who work with students with mental retardation or educate professionals to work with those students	Work to advance the education of individuals with mental retardation, research mental retardation, and the training of professionals to work with individuals with mental retardation. Promote public understanding of mental retardation and professional development of those who work with persons with mental retardation.
National Association for the Education of Young Children 1313 L St. NW Suite 500 Washington, DC 20005 Phone: (800) 424-2460 E-mail: webmaster@naeyc.org http://www.naeyc.org	Parents and educators of children who are gifted	Train educators to meet the needs of students with gifted abilities, offer assistance to parents facing special problems in raising children who are gifted, and seek public recognition of the needs of these children.
The Arc of the United States 1660 L Street, NW, Suite 301 Washington, DC 20036 Phone: (202) 534-3700 / (800) 433-5255 E-mail: administration@thearc.org http://www.thearc.org	Parents, professionals, and others interested in individuals with mental retardation	Work on local, state, and national levels to promote treatment, research, public understanding, and legislation for persons with mental retardation; provide counseling for parents of students with mental retardation.

Organization	Members	Mission
National Easter Seal Society 230 West Monroe Street, Suite 1800 Chicago, IL 60606 Phone: (800) 221-6827 TTY: (312) 726-1494 http://www.easterseals.com		Promotes and protects the human rights of people with intellectual and developmental disabilities and actively supports their full inclusion and participation in the community throughout their lifetimes
The National Association of Special Education Teachers 1201 Pennsylvania Ave. NW Suite 300 Washington D.C. 20004 Phone: (800) 754-4421 FAX: (800) 424-0371 E-mail: contactus@naset.org	State units (49) and local societies (951); no individual members	Establish and run programs for individuals with physical impairments, usually including diagnostic services, speech therapy, preschool services, physical therapy, and occupational therapy.
	Special education teachers	To render all possible support and assistance to professionals who teach children with special needs; to promote standards of excellence and innovation in special education research, practice, and policy in order to foster exceptional teaching for exceptional children

Skill 16.3 **Applies knowledge of the Council for Exceptional Children (CEC) Code of Ethics and the Georgia Professional Standards Commission Code of Ethics for Educators.**

In 1922, the Council for Exceptional Children (first called the International Council for Exceptional Children) was founded. During the 1920s, many comprehensive statewide programs were initiated.

Various divisional organizations of the Council for Exceptional Children publish professional journals in their areas of exceptionality. These journals and their corresponding organizations are listed, along with addresses from which journals may be ordered. Other journals are published by related fields such as rehabilitation, mental health, and occupational guidance.

1. Behavioral Disorders
   Council for Children with Behavioral Disorders (CCBD)
   1920 Association Drive
   Reston, VA 22091-1589

2. Career Development for Exceptional Individuals
   Division on Career Development (DCD)
   1920 Association Drive
   Reston, VA 22091-1589

3. Diagnostique
   Council for Educational Diagnostic Services (CEDS)
   1920 Association Drive
   Reston, VA 22091-1589

4. Education and Training of the Mentally Retarded
   Division on Mental Retardation (CEC-MR)
   1920 Association Drive
   Reston, VA 22091-1589

5. Journal of Childhood Communication Disorders
   Division for Children with Communication Disorders (DCCD)
   1920 Association Drive
   Reston, VA 22091-1589

6. Journal of the Division for Early Childhood
   Division for Early Childhood (DEC)
   1920 Association Drive
   Reston, VA 22091-1589

7. Journal for the Education of the Gifted
    The Association for the Gifted (TAG)
    JEG, Wayne State University Press
    5959 Woodward Avenue
    Detroit, MI 48202

8. Journal of Special Education Technology
    Technology and Media Division (TAM)
    JSET, UMC 68
    Utah State University
    Logan, UT 84322

9. Learning Disabilities Focus
    Learning Disabilities Research
    Division for Learning Disabilities
    1920 Association Drive
    Reston, VA 22091-1589

10. Teacher Education and Special Education
    Teacher Education Division (TED)
    Special Press
    P.O. Box 2524, Dept. CEC
    Columbus, OH 43216

11. Exceptional Children
    1920 Association Drive
    Reston, VA 22091-1589

12. Teaching Exceptional Children
    1920 Association Drive
    Reston, VA 22091-1589

13. Exceptional Child Education Resources
    1920 Association Drive
    Reston, VA 22091-1589

14. Canadian Journal for Exceptional Children
    Publication Services
    4-116 Education North
    The University of Alberta
    Edmonton, Alberta, Canada T6G 2G5

Originally adopted by the Delegate Assembly of the Council for Exceptional Children in April 1983

The Georgia Professional Standards Commissions (GA PSC) Code of Ethics defines the professional behavior of educators in the state of Georgia and acts as a reference point for ethical conduct. The Professional Standards Commission has adopted standards that represent the conduct generally accepted by the education profession. The code protects the health, safety, and general welfare of students and educators, guarantees the citizens of Georgia a degree of accountability within the education profession, and defines unethical conduct warranting disciplinary sanction.

There are 10 standards outlined in the GA PSC Code of Ethics. The standards are outlined below.

Standard 1: Criminal Acts - An educator should follow federal, state, and local laws and regulations. Unethical conduct includes but is not limited to the commission or conviction of a felony or of any crime involving moral turpitude.

Standard 2: Abuse of Students - An educator should uphold a professional relationship with all students, both in school and outside the school setting.

Standard 3: Alcohol or Drugs - An educator should abstain from the utilization of alcohol or illegal or unauthorized drugs during the course of professional practice.

Standard 4: Misrepresentation or Falsification - An educator should embody truthfulness and uprightness in the course of his or her professional duties.

Standard 5: Public Funds and Property - An educator entrusted with public funds and property should respect that trust with a high degree of truthfulness, correctness, and accountability.

Standard 6: Improper Remunerative Conduct - An educator should preserve his or her integrity with students, colleagues, parents, patrons, or businesses when accepting donations, gifts, favors, and additional compensation.

Standard 7: Confidential Information - An educator should follow state and federal laws and local school board/governing board policies involving the confidentiality of student and personnel records, standardized test documents, and other information covered by confidentiality agreements.

Standard 8: Abandonment of Contract - An educator should satisfy all of the terms and obligations detailed in the contract with the local board of education or education agency for the length of the contract.

Standard 9: Failure to Make a Required Report – An educator should submit reports describing a violation of any of the standards in the code of ethics, child abuse, or any other required report.

Standard 10: Professional Conduct – An educator should exemplify the highest standards of professional conduct.

For additional information on the standards, please visit the GA PSC Web site at http://www.gapsc.com

Their mailing address is:

Georgia Professional Standards Commission
Two Peachtree Street
Suite 6000
Atlanta, GA 30303
(404) 232-2500
ethics@gapsc.com
FAX: 404-232-2720

Skill 16.04   Demonstrates knowledge of laws, policies, and ethical principles related to behavior management, the provision of specialized health care in the educational setting, and mandated reporting.

Please refer to http://rules.sos.state.ga.us/cgi-bin/page.cgi?d=1 for Georgia-specific information.

Skill 16.05   Applies knowledge of how to uphold high standards of competence, good judgment, and integrity when conducting instructional and other professional activities, including complying with all applicable laws, policies, and procedures (e.g., local, state, and federal monitoring and evaluation requirements).

Please refer to Skill 16.01 and http://rules.sos.state.ga.us/cgi-bin/page.cgi?d=1.

Skill 16.06   Recognizes effective strategies for engaging in reflection and self-assessment activities for the purposes of identifying one's own personal cultural biases, improving instruction, and guiding professional growth.

The role of the special education teacher is to advocate for the most appropriate education for students and to guide them in discovering new knowledge and developing new skills to the best of their potential. According to IDEA 2004, teachers are to prepare students for future, purposeful work in society with the possibility of postsecondary education or training.

Although each special educator is also a person with a set of experiences, opinions, and beliefs, it is important to remain unbiased and positive in the professional role with students, parents, administration, and the community. Differences in culture, religion, gender, or sexual orientation should not influence the teacher's approach to instruction, student goals, student expectations, or advocacy.

In order to remain unbiased, the special educator should avail him or herself of opportunities to learn about various cultures, religions, genders, and sexual orientations. This can be accomplished through reading, appropriate classroom awareness activities, and teacher in-service.

Reading to increase awareness and acceptance of cultural differences may be done through professional, adult literature as well as through books to be read with the class.

Cultural activities in the classroom are especially well received; foods, dress, and games are easily added to curriculum and often address learning standards.

The special educator is charged with academic, social, communicative, and independent skills instruction. Education or influence in other areas is not appropriate.

When the special educator remains unbiased, he or she is better able to meet the needs of students and to not react to additional factors. The students and their families are also more open to school-related suggestions.

The teacher's reaction to differences with students and their families models the commonly taught character education trait of respect. When the teacher demonstrates respect for all individuals in his or her program, it is likely that respect will also be practiced by students, parents, and administration.

Skill 16.07 Demonstrates knowledge of how to advocate effectively for individual students with disabilities, their families, and the special education program in general.

Because of the unique needs of each student with disabilities, special education teachers are frequently advocates for their students and the special education program in general.

In order to be an effective advocate, the teacher must be knowledgeable in a number of areas. First, the special educator must understand the general education program that is the counterpart of his or her program. Factors such as student expectations (learning standards), materials used, and teacher training and in-service provide a starting point. If the special educator is familiar with the goals and overall programs for all students at his or her grade level, the educator will have a clear picture of the direction he or she should be moving with students with disabilities.

The special educator should also have a clear understanding of each student's strengths and needs. He or she must consider how each student can participate in the general education curriculum to the extent that it is beneficial for that student (IDEA 2004). For example, when should services and instruction take place outside of the general education classroom?

In addition, special educators should have an understanding of alternate materials that would be useful or necessary for the students, as well as what resources for materials are available.

Knowledge of IDEA 2004 and NCLB provides an outline of legislative mandates for special education.

A clear understanding of the above points will allow the special educator to most effectively advocate for the most appropriate placement, programming, and materials for each student. He or she will be able to advocate for research-based methods with measurable outcomes.

Advocacy often happens between general and special education teachers. A special educator may see modification or accommodation possibilities that could take place in the general education classroom. It is his or her responsibility to advocate those practices. The special education teacher may also offer to make supplementary materials or to work with a group of students in the general education setting to achieve that goal. When students with disabilities are in an inclusion classroom, give and take on the part of both teachers as a team is crucial.

The special education teacher may also need to be an advocate for his or her program (or the needs of an individual student) with the administration. Although success for all students is important to administration, it is often up to the teacher to explain the need for comparable materials written at the different reading level, the need for assistance in the classroom, or the need for offering specific classes or therapies.

Occasionally, the local school district cannot provide an appropriate educational setting. The special educator must advocate with the school district for appropriate placement of the child in another, more suitable environment.

Skill 16.08 Recognizes appropriate procedures for creating and maintaining records regarding students with disabilities, including following legal and ethical guidelines for maintaining confidentiality

Please refer to Skill 14.07.

Post-Test

1. Skilled readers use all but which one of these knowledge sources to construct meanings beyond the literal text:
   (Rigorous) (Skill 1.01)

   a. Text knowledge
   b. Syntactic knowledge
   c. Morphological knowledge
   d. Semantic knowledge

2. Which of these characteristics is *not* included in the Pubic Law 94-142 definition of emotional disturbance:
   (Rigorous) (Skill 1.01)

   a. General pervasive mood of unhappiness or depression
   b. Social maladjustment manifested in a number of settings
   c. Tendency to develop physical symptoms, pains, or fear associated with school or personal problems
   d. An inability to learn that is not attributed to intellectual, sensory, or health factors

3. Poor moral development, lack of empathy, and behavioral excesses (such as aggression) are the most obvious characteristics of which behavioral disorder?
   (Rigorous) (Skill 1.01)

   a. Autism
   b. ADD-H
   c. Conduct disorder
   d. Pervasive development disorder

4. Signs of depression typically do not include:
   (Easy) (Skill 1.01)

   a. Hyperactivity
   b. Changes in sleep patterns
   c. Recurring thoughts of death or suicide
   d. Significant changes in weight or appetite

5. Which of these is listed as only a minor scale on the Behavior Problem Checklist?
   (Average Rigor) (Skill 1.01)

   a. Motor excess
   b. Conduct disorder
   c. Socialized aggression
   d. Anxiety/withdrawal

6. Indirect requests and attempts to influence or control others through one's use of language is an example of:
   (Rigorous) (Skill 1.01)

   a. Morphology
   b. Syntax
   c. Pragmatics
   d. Semantics

7. Kenny, a fourth grader, has trouble comprehending analogies; using comparative, spatial, and temporal words; and understanding multiple meanings. Language interventions for Kenny would focus on:
    (Rigorous) (Skill 1.01)

    a. Morphology
    b. Syntax
    c. Pragmatics
    d. Semantics

8. Celia, who is in first grade, asked, "Where are my ball?" She also has trouble with passive sentences. Language interventions for Celia would target:
    (Rigorous) (Skill 1.01)

    a. Morphology
    b. Syntax
    c. Pragmatics
    d. Semantics

9. Scott is in middle school but still says statements like "I gotted new high-tops yesterday," and, "I saw three mans in the front office." Language interventions for Scott would target:
    (Average Rigor) (Skill 1.01)

    a. Morphology
    b. Syntax
    c. Pragmatics
    d. Semantics

10. Mr. Mendez is assessing his students' written expressions. Which of these is not a component of written expression?
    (Rigorous) (Skill 1.01)

    a. Vocabulary
    b. Morphology
    c. Content
    d. Sentence structure

11. Which of these explanations would *not* likely account for the lack of a clear definition of behavior disorders?
    (Rigorous) (Skill 1.01)

    a. Problems with measurement
    b. Cultural and/or social influences and views of what is acceptable
    c. The numerous types of manifestations of behavior disorders
    d. Differing theories that use their own terminology and definitions

12. Social withdrawal, anxiety, depression, shyness, and guilt are indicative of:
    (Rigorous) (Skill 1.01)

    a. Conduct disorder
    b. Personality disorders
    c. Immaturity
    d. Socialized aggression

13. Short attention span, daydreaming, clumsiness, and preference for younger playmates are associated with: *(Rigorous) (Skill 1.01)*

   a. Conduct disorder
   b. Personality disorders
   c. Immaturity
   d. Socialized aggression

14. Truancy, gang membership, and feelings of pride in belonging to a delinquent subculture are indicative of: *(Average Rigor) (Skill 1.01)*

   a. Conduct disorder
   b. Personality disorders
   c. Immaturity
   d. Socialized aggression

15. Temper tantrums, disruption of class, disobedience, and bossiness are associated with: *(Rigorous) (Skill 1.01)*

   a. Conduct disorder
   b. Personality disorders
   c. Immaturity
   d. Socialized aggression

16. Which of these is *not* true for most children with behavior disorders? *(Average Rigor) (Skill 1.01)*

   a. Many score in the "slow learner" or "mildly retarded" range on IQ tests.
   b. They are frequently behind their classmates in terms of academic achievement.
   c. They are bright but bored with their surroundings.
   d. A large amount of time is spent on nonproductive, nonacademic behaviors.

17. Which behavioral disorder is easier to diagnose in children because the symptoms are manifested quite differently than in adults? *(Rigorous) (Skill 1.01)*

   a. Anorexia
   b. Schizophrenia
   c. Paranoia
   d. Depression

18. Parents are more likely to have a child with a learning disability if: *(Average Rigor) (Skill 1.01)*

   a. They smoke tobacco
   b. The child is less than five pounds at birth
   c. The mother drank alcohol on a regular basis until she planned for a baby
   d. The father was known to consume large quantities of alcohol during the pregnancy

19. A developmental delay may be indicated by a:
(Rigorous) (Skill 1.01)

   a. Second grader having difficulty buttoning clothing
   b. Stuttered response
   c. Kindergartner not having complete bladder control
   d. Withdrawn behavior

20. According to IDEA, a child whose disability is related to being deaf and blind may *not* be classified as:
(Rigorous) (Skill 1.01)

   a. Multiple disabilities
   b. Other health impaired
   c. Mentally retarded
   d. Visually impaired

21. Mark is a sixth grader. The teacher has noticed that he doesn't respond to simple requests like the other students in the class. If asked to erase the board, he may look, shake his head, and say no, but then he will clean the board. When the children gather together for recess, he joins them. Yet, the teacher observes that it takes him much longer to understand the rules to a game. Mark retains what he reads. Mark most likely has:
(Rigorous) (Skill 1.01)

   a. Autism
   b. Tourette's syndrome
   c. Mental retardation
   d. A pragmatic language disability

22. A child may be classified under the special education "umbrella" as having Traumatic Brain Injury (TBI) if he or she does *not* have which of the following causes?
(Rigorous) (Skill 1.01)

   a. Stroke
   b. Anoxia
   c. Encephalitis
   d. Birth trauma

23. Which body language would not likely be interpreted as a sign of defensiveness, aggression, or hostility?
(Easy) (Skill 2.01)

   a. Pointing
   b. Direct eye contact
   c. Hands on hips
   d. Arms crossed

24. Of the various factors that contribute to delinquency and antisocial behavior, which has been found to be the weakest?
(Rigorous) (Skill 2.01)

   a. Criminal behavior and/or alcoholism in the father
   b. Lax mother and punishing father
   c. Socioeconomic disadvantage
   d. Long history of broken home or marital discord among parents

25. Children who are characterized by impulsivity generally:
(Average Rigor) (Skill 2.01)

    a. Do not feel sorry for their actions
    b. Blame others for their actions
    c. Do not weigh alternatives before acting
    d. Do not outgrow their problem

26. Echolalia, repetitive stereotype actions, and a severe disorder of thinking and communication are indicative of:
(Average Rigor) (Skill 2.01)

    a. Psychosis
    b. Schizophrenia
    c. Autism
    d. Paranoia

27. Across America, there is one toxic substance that is contributing to the creation of disabilities in our children. What is it?
(Average Rigor) (Skill 2.01)

    a. Children's aspirin
    b. Fluoride water
    c. Chlorine gas
    d. Lead

28. Janice is a new student in a self-contained class. She is extremely quiet and makes little, if any, eye contact. Yesterday, she started to "parrot" what another student said. Today the teacher became concerned when she did not follow directions and seemed not to even recognize his presence. Her cumulative file arrived today; when the teacher reviews the health section, it most likely will state that she is diagnosed with:
(Average Rigor) (Skill 2.01)

    a. Autism
    b. Central processing disorder
    c. Traumatic brain injury
    d. Mental retardation

29. Justin is diagnosed with autism and is in an inclusive setting. You were called down to "Stop him from turning the lights off and remove him." When you arrive, you learn that today a movie was supposed to be finished, but the VCR broke, so the teacher planned another activity. What is the best way to explain to the teacher why Justin was turning off the lights?
(Easy) (Skill 2.01)

a. He is perseverating and will stop shortly.
b. He is telling you the lights bother him.
c. He needs forewarning before a transition. Next time you have an unexpected change in classroom schedule, please let him know.
d. Please understand, this is part of who Justin is. He will leave the lights alone after I talk to him.

30. Of the following, which does not describe the term delinquency?
(Average Rigor) (Skill 2.01)

a. Behavior that would be considered criminal if exhibited by an adult
b. Socialized aggression
c. Academic truancy
d. Inciting fights with verbal abuse

31. A student on medication may have his or her dosage adjusted as his or her body grows. Parents may call and ask questions about their child's adjustment to the medication during the school day. During this time, you should:
(Average Rigor) (Skill 2.02)

a. Observe the student for changes in behavior.
b. Watch for a progression of changed behavior.
c. Communicate with the parent concerns about sleepiness.
d. All of the above

32. School refusal, obsessive-compulsive disorders, psychosis, and separation anxiety are also frequently accompanied by:
(Rigorous) (Skill 3.01)

a. Conduct disorder
b. ADD-H
c. Depression
d. Autism

33. What is the highest goal a teacher should aim for while preparing a student for success?
(Average Rigor) (Skill 3.07)

a. Reading
b. Budgeting
c. Cooking
d. Self-Advocacy

34. Examples of behaviors that are appropriate to be measured for their duration include all *except*:
(Easy) (Skill 4.01)

   a. Thumb-sucking
   b. Hitting
   c. Temper tantrums
   d. Maintaining eye contact

35. Examples of behaviors that are appropriate to be monitored by measuring frequency include all *except*:
(Average Rigor) (Skill 4.01)

   a. Teasing
   b. Talking out
   c. Being on time for class
   d. Daydreaming

36. Criteria for choosing behaviors to measure by frequency include all *except* those that:
(Easy) (Skill 4.01)

   a. Have an observable beginning
   b. Last a long time
   c. Last a short time
   d. Occur often

37. Criteria for choosing behaviors to measure by duration include all *except* those that:
(Easy) (Skill 4.01)

   a. Last a short time
   b. Last a long time
   c. Have no readily observable beginning or end
   d. Do not happen often

38. Ms. Beekman has a class of students who frequently talk out. She wishes to begin interventions with the students who are talking out the most. She monitors the talking behavior of the entire class for one-minute samples every half hour. This is an example of collecting data on:
(Average Rigor) (Skill 4.01)

   a. Multiple behaviors for single subjects
   b. Reciprocal behaviors
   c. Single behaviors for multiple subjects
   d. Continuous behaviors for fixed intervals

39. Which is *not* an example of a standard score?
(Average Rigor) (Skill 4.01)

   a. T Score
   b. Z Score
   c. Standard deviation
   d. Stanine

40. The most direct method of obtaining assessment data (and perhaps the most objective) is:
(Easy) (Skill 4.01)

   a. Testing
   b. Self-recording
   c. Observation
   d. Experimenting

41. The extent that a test measures what it claims to measure is called:
(Average Rigor) (Skill 4.01)

   a. Reliability
   b. Validity
   c. Factor Analysis
   d. Chi Square

42. Ms. Wright is planning an analysis of Audrey's out-of-seat behavior. Her initial data would be called:
(Rigorous) (Skill 4.01)

   a. Pre-referral phase
   b. Intervention phase
   c. Baseline phase
   d. Observation phase

43. To reinforce Audrey each time she is on-task and in her seat, Ms. Wright decides to deliver specific praise and stickers, which Audrey may collect and redeem for a reward. The data collected during the time Ms. Wright is using this intervention is called:
(Average Rigor) (Skill 4.01)

   a. Referral phase
   b. Intervention phase
   c. Baseline phase
   d. Observation phase

44. Ryan is 3, and her temper tantrums last for an hour. Bryan is 8, and he does not stay on task for more than 10 minutes without teacher prompts. These behaviors differ from normal children in terms of their:
(Average Rigor) (Skill 4.01)

   a. Rate
   b. Topography
   c. Duration
   d. Magnitude

45. All children cry, hit, fight, and play alone at different times. Children with behavior disorders will perform these behaviors at a higher than normal:
(Average Rigor) (Skill 4.01)

   a. Rate
   b. Topography
   c. Duration
   d. Magnitude

46. The purpose of an error analysis of a test is to:
(Easy) (Skill 4.01)

   a. Determine what events were labeled in error
   b. Determine if the test length was the cause of error
   c. Evaluate the types of errors made by categorizing incorrect answers
   d. Establish a baseline

47. Marcie is often not in her seat when the bell rings. She may be found at the pencil sharpener, throwing paper away, or fumbling through her notebook. Which of these descriptions of her behavior can be described as a pinpoint?
(Average Rigor) (Skill 4.01)

a. Is tardy a lot
b. Is out of seat
c. Is not in seat when late bell rings
d. Is disorganized

48. Statements like, "Darren is lazy," are not helpful in describing his behavior for all *except* which of these reasons?
(Rigorous) (Skill 4.02)

a. There is no way to determine if any change occurs from the information given
b. The student—not the behavior—becomes labeled
c. Darren's behavior will manifest itself clearly enough without any written description
d. Constructs are open to various interpretations among the people who are asked to define them

49. Which of the following is *not* one of the three aspects of the issue of fair assessment for individuals from minority groups that Slavia and Ysseldyke (1995) point out as particularly relevant to the assessment of students?
(Rigorous) (Skill 5.02)

a. Representation
b. Diversity
c. Acculturation
d. Language

50. Marisol has been mainstreamed into a ninth-grade language arts class. Although her behavior is satisfactory and she likes the class, Marisol's reading level is about two years below grade level. The class has been assigned to read *Great Expectations* and write a report. What intervention would be *least* successful in helping Marisol complete this assignment?
(Average Rigor) (Skill 6.01)

a. Having Marisol listen to a taped recording while following the story in the regular text
b. Giving her a modified version of the story
c. Telling her to choose a different book that she can read
d. Showing a film to the entire class and comparing and contrasting it to the book

51. Which would *not* be an advantage of using a criterion-referenced test?
(Average Rigor) (Skill 6.01)

   a. Information about an individual's ability level is too specific for the purposes of the assessment
   b. It can pinpoint exact areas of weaknesses and strengths
   c. You can design them yourself
   d. You do not get comparative information

52. Lack of regular follow-up, difficulty in transporting materials, and lack of consistent support for students who need more assistance are disadvantages of which type of service model?
(Rigorous) (Skill 6.01)

   a. Regular classroom
   b. Consultant with regular teacher
   c. Itinerant
   d. Resource room

53. An emphasis on instructional remediation and individualized instruction in problem areas, as well as a focus on mainstreaming students, are characteristics of which model of service delivery?
(Average Rigor) (Skill 6.01)

   a. Regular classroom
   b. Consultant teacher
   c. Itinerant teacher
   d. Resource room

54. A best practice for evaluating student performance and progress on IEPs is:
(Rigorous) (Skill 6.01)

   a. Formal assessment
   b. Curriculum-based assessment
   c. Criterion-based assessment
   d. Norm-referenced evaluation

55. In exceptional student education, assessment is used to make decisions about all of the following *except*:
(Average Rigor) (Skill 6.01)

   a. Screening and initial identification of children who may need services
   b. Selection and evaluation of teaching strategies and programs
   c. Determining the desired attendance rate of a student
   d. Development of goals, objectives, and evaluation for the IEP

56. Which of the following is *not* an appropriate assessment modification or accommodation for a student with a learning disability?
(Average Rigor) (Skill 6.01)

   a. Having the test read orally to the student
   b. Writing down the student's dictated answers
   c. Allowing the student to take the assessment home to complete
   d. Extending the time for the student to take the assessment

57. The basic tools necessary to observe and record behavior include all *but*:
(Average Rigor) (Skill 6.03)

a. Cameras
b. Timers
c. Counters
d. Graphs or charts

58. Shyquan is in your inclusive class, and she exhibits a slower comprehension of assigned tasks and concepts. Her first two grades were Bs, but she is now receiving failing marks. She has seen the resource teacher. You should:
(Average Rigor) (Skill 6.04)

a. Ask for a review of current placement
b. Tell Shyquan to seek extra help
c. Ask Shyquan if she is frustrated
d. Ask the regular education teacher to slow instruction

59. Teachers in grades K-3 are mandated to teach what to all students using scientifically based methods with measurable outcomes?
(Average Rigor) (Skill 7.04)

a. Math
b. Reading
c. Citizenship
d. Writing

60. In a positive classroom environment, errors are viewed as:
(Easy) (Skill 7.07)

a. Symptoms of deficiencies
b. Lack of attention or ability
c. A natural part of the learning process
d. The result of going too fast

61. Which of these would be the least effective measure of behavioral disorders?
(Easy) (Skill 7.07)

a. Projective test
b. Ecological assessment
c. Standardized test
d. Psychodynamic analysis

62. Cooperative learning does *not* utilize:
(Easy) (Skill 7.07)

a. Shared ideas
b. Small groups
c. Independent practice
d. Student expertise

63. When a student begins to use assistive technology, it is important for the teacher to have a clear outline as to when and how the equipment should be used. Why?
(Rigorous) (Skill 8.02)

   a. To establish a level of accountability with the student
   b. To establish that the teacher has responsibility of the equipment that is in use in his or her room
   c. To establish that the teacher is responsible for the usage of the assistive technology
   d. To establish a guideline for evaluation

64. Organizing ideas by use of a web or outline is an example of which writing activity?
(Easy) (Skill 8.04)

   a. Revision
   b. Drafting
   c. Prewriting
   d. Final draft

65. Ryan is working on a report about dogs. He uses scissors and tape to cut and rearrange sections and paragraphs and then photocopies the paper so he can continue writing. Ryan is in which stage of the writing process?
(Average Rigor) (Skill 8.04)

   a. Final draft
   b. Prewriting
   c. Revision
   d. Drafting

66. Talking into a tape recorder is an example of which writing activity?
(Average Rigor) (Skill 8.04)

   a. Prewriting
   b. Drafting
   c. Final draft
   d. Revision

67. All of these are effective in teaching written expression *except*:
(Average Rigor) (Skill 8.04)

   a. Exposure to various styles and direct instruction in those styles
   b. Immediate feedback from the teacher with all mistakes clearly marked
   c. Goal setting and peer evaluation of written products according to a set criteria
   d. Incorporating writing with other academic subjects

68. Which of the follow is does *not* have an important effect on the spatial arrangement (physical setting) of your classroom?
(Average Rigor) (Skill 9.01)

   a. Adequate physical space
   b. Ventilation
   c. Window placement
   d. Lighting adequacy

69. Mr. Brown finds that his chosen consequence does not seem to be having the desired effect of reducing the target misbehavior. Which of these would *least likely* account for Mr. Brown's lack of success with the consequence?
(*Easy*) (*Skill 9.04*)

    a. The consequence was aversive in Mr. Brown's opinion, but not the students'
    b. The students were not developmentally ready to understand the connection between the behavior and the consequence
    c. Mr. Brown was inconsistent in applying the consequence
    d. The intervention had not previously been shown to be effective in studies

70. Which of the following is *not* a feature of effective classroom rules?
(*Easy*) (*Skill 9.04*)

    a. They are about four to six in number
    b. They are negatively stated
    c. Consequences for infractions are consistent and immediate
    d. They can be tailored to individual classroom goals and teaching styles

71. An effective classroom behavior management plan includes all but which of the following?
(*Easy*) (*Skill 9.04*)

    a. Transition procedures for changing activities
    b. Clear consequences for rule infractions
    c. Concise teacher expectations for student behavior
    d. Copies of lesson plans

72. Effective management transition involves all of the following *except*:
(*Rigorous*) (*Skill 9.04*)

    a. Keeping students informed of the sequencing of instructional activities
    b. Using group fragmentation
    c. Changing the schedule frequently to maintain student interest
    d. Using academic transition signals

73. Otumba is a 16 year old in your class who recently came from Nigeria. The girls in your class have come to you to complain about the way he treats them in a sexist manner. When they complain, you reflect that this is also the way he treats adult females. You have talked to Otumba before about appropriate behavior. What should you do first?
(Average Rigor) (Skill 9.07)

a. Complain to the principal
b. Ask for a parent-teacher conference
c. Check to see if this is a cultural norm in his country
d. Create a behavior contract for him to follow

74. Which of the following should be avoided when writing objectives for social behavior?
(Easy) (Skill 10.01)

a. Nonspecific adverbs
b. Behaviors stated as verbs
c. Criteria for acceptable performance
d. Conditions where the behavior is expected to be performed

75. Criteria for choosing behaviors that are in the most need of change involve all *except* the following:
(Average Rigor) (Skill 10.03)

a. Observations across settings to rule out certain interventions
b. Pinpointing the behavior that is the poorest fit in the child's environment
c. The teacher's concern about what is the most important behavior to target
d. Analysis of the environmental reinforcers

76. Which of the following is *not* one of the four interrelated components of Positive Behavioral Interventions and Supports (PBS)?
(Rigorous) (Skill 10.03)

a. Systems change activities
b. Environmental alterations activities
c. Behavioral consequences activities
d. Support provision activities

77. Sam is working to earn half an hour of basketball time with his favorite P.E. teacher. At the end of each half hour, Sam marks his point sheet with an X if he reached his goal of no call-outs. When he has received 25 marks, he will receive his basketball free time. This behavior management strategy is an example of:
(Average Rigor) (Skill 10.05)

a. Self-recording
b. Self-evaluation
c. Self-reinforcement
d. Self-regulation

78. Mark has been working on his target goal of completing his mathematics class work. Each day he records, on a scale of 0 to 3, how well he has done his work, and his teacher provides feedback. This self-management technique is an example of:
(Average Rigor) (Skill 10.05)

a. Self-recording
b. Self-reinforcement
c. Self-regulation
d. Self-evaluation

79. When Barbara reached her target goal, she chose her reinforcer and softly said to herself, "I worked hard, and I deserve this reward." This self-management technique is an example of:
(Average Rigor) (Skill 10.05)

a. Self-reinforcement
b. Self-recording
c. Self-regulation
d. Self-evaluation

80. A student with a poor self-concept may manifest in all of the ways listed below except:
(Easy) (Skill 10.05)

a. Withdrawn actions
b. Aggression
c. Consistently announcing his or her achievements
d. Shyness

81. If the arrangement in a fixed-ratio schedule of reinforcement is three, when will the student receive the reinforcer?
(Rigorous) (Skill 10.06)

a. After every third correct response
b. After every third correct response in a row
c. After the third correct response in the time interval of the behavior sample
d. After the third correct response even if the undesired behavior occurs in between correct responses

82. Laura is beginning to raise her hand first instead of talking out. An effective schedule of reinforcement would be: *(Rigorous) (Skill 10.06)*

   a. Continuous
   b. Variable
   c. Intermittent
   d. Fixed

83. As Laura continues to raise her hand to speak, the teacher would want to change this schedule of reinforcement in order to wean her from reinforcement: *(Rigorous) (Skill 10.06)*

   a. Continuous
   b. Variable
   c. Intermittent
   d. Fixed

84. Laura has demonstrated that she has mastered the goal of raising her hand to speak; reinforcement during the maintenance phase should be: *(Average Rigor) (Skill 10.06)*

   a. Continuous
   b. Variable
   c. Intermittent
   d. Fixed

85. Data on quiet behaviors (e.g., nail biting or daydreaming) are best measured using a/n: *(Rigorous) (Skill 10.06)*

   a. Interval or time sample
   b. Continuous sample
   c. Variable sample
   d. Fixed-ratio sample

86. Which is the least effective of reinforcers in programs for mildly to moderately handicapped learners? *(Average Rigor) (Skill 10.06)*

   a. Tokens
   b. Social
   c. Food
   d. Activity

87. The Premack principle of increasing the performance of a less-preferred activity by immediately following it with a highly preferred activity is the basis of: *(Rigorous) (Skill 10.06)*

   a. Response cost
   b. Token systems
   c. Contingency contracting
   d. Self-recording management

88. Justin, a second grader, is reinforced if he is on task at the end of each 10-minute block of time that the teacher observes him. This is an example of what type of reinforcement schedule? *(Average Rigor) (Skill 10.06)*

   a. Continuous
   b. Fixed interval
   c. Fixed ratio
   d. Variable ratio

89. At the beginning of the school year, Annette had a problem with being late to class. Her teacher reinforced her each time she was in her seat when the bell rang. In October, her teacher decided to reward her every other day when she was not tardy to class. The reinforcement schedule appropriate for making the transition to the maintenance phase would be:
(Rigorous) (Skill 10.06)

   a. Continuous
   b. Fixed interval
   c. Variable ratio
   d. Fixed ratio

90. By November, Annette's teacher is satisfied with her record of being on time and decides to change the schedule of reinforcement. The best type of reinforcement schedule for maintenance of behavior is:
(Rigorous) (Skill 10.06)

   a Continuous
   b. Fixed interval
   c. Variable ratio
   d. Fixed ratio

91. Teacher feedback, task completion, and a sense of pride over mastery or accomplishment of a skill are examples of:
(Average Rigor) (Skill 10.06)

   a. Extrinsic reinforcers
   b. Behavior modifiers
   c. Intrinsic reinforcers
   d. Positive feedback

92. Social approval, token reinforcers, and rewards (such as pencils or stickers) are examples of:
(Average Rigor) (Skill 10.06)

   a. Extrinsic reinforcers
   b. Behavior modifiers
   c. Intrinsic reinforcers
   d. Positive feedback

93. Token systems are popular for all of these advantages *except*:
(Rigorous) (Skill 10.06)

   a. The number needed for rewards may be adjusted as needed
   b. Rewards are easy to maintain
   c. They are effective for students who generally do not respond to social reinforcers
   d. Tokens reinforce the relationship of desirable behavior and reinforcement

94. Free time, shopping at the school store, and candy are examples of:
(Easy) (Skill 10.06)

   a. Privileges
   b. Allowances
   c. Rights
   d. Entitlements

95. When would proximity control not be a good behavioral intervention?
(Easy) (Skill 10.07)

a. Two students are arguing
b. A student is distracting others
c. One student threatens another
d. A situation involving fading and shaping

96. A BIP (Behavior Intervention Plan) is written to teach positive behavior. Which element listed below is *not* a standard feature of the plan?
(Rigorous) (Skill 10.08)

a. Identification of behavior to be modified
b. Strategies to implement the replacement behavior
c. Statement of distribution
d. Team creation of BIP

97. Crisis intervention methods are above all concerned with:
(Easy) (Skill 10.08)

a. Safety and well-being of the staff and students
b. Stopping the inappropriate behavior
c. Preventing the behavior from occurring again
d. The student learning that outbursts are inappropriate

98. Ricky, a third-grade student, runs out of the classroom and onto the roof of the school. He paces around the roof, looks around to see who is watching, and laughs at the people on the ground. He appears to be in control of his behavior. What should the teacher do?
(Rigorous) (Skill 10.08)

a. Go back inside and leave him up there until he decides he is ready to come down
b. Climb up to get Ricky so he doesn't fall off and get hurt
c. Notify the crisis teacher and arrange to have someone monitor Ricky
d. Call the police

99. Mr. Smith is on a field trip with a group of high school EH students. On the way, they stop at a fast-food restaurant for lunch, and Warren and Raul get into a disagreement. After some heated words, Warren stalks out of the restaurant and refuses to return to the group. He leaves the parking lot, continues walking away from the group, and ignores Mr. Smith's directions to come back. What would be the best course of action for Mr. Smith? (Rigorous) (Skill 10.08)

a. Leave the group with the class aide and follow Warren to try to talk him into coming back
b. Wait a little while and see if Warren cools off and returns
c. Telephone the school and let the crisis teacher notify the police in accordance with school policy
d. Call the police himself

100. Which of the following sentences will *not* test recall? (Average Rigor) (Skill 11.02)

a. What words in the story describe Goldilocks?
b. Why did Goldilocks go into the three bears' house?
c. Name in order the things that belonged to the three bears that Goldilocks tried.
d. What did the three bears learn about leaving their house unlocked?

101. Transfer of learning occurs when: (Rigorous) (Skill 11.03)

a. Experience with one task influences performance on another task
b. Content can be explained orally
c. Student experiences the "I got it!" syndrome
d. Curricular objective is exceeded

102. To facilitate learning instructional objectives: (Rigorous) (Skill 11.03)

a. They should be taken from a grade-level spelling list
b. They should be written and shared
c. They should be arranged in order of similarity
d. They should be taken from a scope and sequence

103. Measurement of adaptive behavior should include all *except*: (Rigorous) (Skill 12.03)

a. Student behavior in a variety of settings
b. Student skills displayed in a variety of settings
c. Comparative analysis to other students in a class
d. Analysis of the student's social skills

104. Teaching children functional skills that will be useful in their home life and neighborhoods is the basis of:
(Rigorous) (Skill 12.05)

a. Curriculum-based instruction
b. Community-based instruction
c. Transition planning
d. Functional curriculum

105. The transition activities that have to be addressed, unless the IEP team finds it uncalled for, include all of the following *except*:
(Rigorous) (Skill 12.06)

a. Instruction
b. Volunteer opportunities
c. Community experiences
d. Development of objectives related to employment and other post-school areas

106. Parent contact should first begin when:
(Average Rigor) (Skill 13.02)

a. You are informed the child will be your student
b. The student fails a test
c. The student exceeds others on a task
d. A CSE is coming and you have had no previous replies to letters

107. Which of the following is an effective method of gaining and holding students' attention if they are deficient in attending skills?
(Easy) (Skill 13.03)

a. Eliminating or reducing environmental distractions
b. Asking the question before calling the name of a student to create greater interest
c. Being enthusiastic and keeping lessons short and interactive
d. All of the above

108. Task-related attending skills include:
(Rigorous) (Skill 13.03)

a. Compliance to requests
b. Writing the correct answer on the chalkboard
c. Listening to the assignment
d. Repeating instructions

109. Which is *not* **a goal of collaborative consultation?**
(Easy) (Skill 14.01)

a. Prevent learning and behavior problems with mainstreamed students
b. Coordinate the instructional programs between mainstream and ESE classes
c. Facilitate solutions to learning and behavior problems
d. Function as an ESE service model

110. An important goal of collaborative consultation is:
(Easy) (Skill 14.01)

   a. Mainstream as many ESE students as possible
   b. Provide guidance on how to handle ESE students from the ESE teacher
   c. Mutual empowerment of both the mainstream and the ESE teacher
   d. Document progress of mainstreamed students.

111. Knowledge of evaluation strategies, program interventions, and types of data are examples of which variable for a successful consultation program?
(Average Rigor) (Skill 14.01)

   a. People
   b. Process
   c. Procedural implementation
   d. Academic preparation

112. Skills as an administrator and a background in client consultation skills are examples of which variable in a successful consultation program?
(Average Rigor) (Skill 14.01)

   a. People
   b. Process
   c. Procedural implementation
   d. Academic preparation

113. The ability to identify problems, the generation of solutions, and knowledge of theoretical perspectives of consultation are examples of which variable in a successful consultation program?
(Average Rigor) (Skill 14.01)

   a. People
   b. Process
   c. Procedural implementation
   d. Academic preparation

114. The key to success for the exceptional student placed in a regular classroom is:
(Easy) (Skill 14.01)

   a. Access to the special aids and materials
   b. Support from the ESE teacher
   c. Modifications in the curriculum
   d. The mainstream teacher's belief that the student will profit from the placement

115. Ms. Taylor takes her students to a special gymnastics presentation that the P.E. coach has arranged in the gym. She has a rule against talk-outs and reminds the students that they will lose five points on their daily point sheet for talking out. The students get a chance to perform some of the simple stunts. They all easily go through the movements except for Sam, who is known as the class klutz. Sam does not give up, and he finally completes the stunts. His classmates cheer him on with comments such as, "Way to go!" Their teacher, however, reminds them that they broke the no-talking rule and will lose the points. What mistake was made here?
(Average Rigor) (Skill 14.01)

a. The students forgot the no-talking rule
b. The teacher considered talk-outs to be maladaptive in all school settings
c. The other students could have distracted Sam with talk-outs and caused him to get hurt
d. The teacher should have let the P.E. coach handle the discipline in the gym

116. The integrated approach to learning utilizes all resources available to address student needs. What are the resources?
(Rigorous) (Skill 14.01)

a. The student, his or her parents, and the teacher.
b. The teacher, the parents, and the special education team.
c. The teacher, the student, and an administrator to perform needed interventions
d. The student, his or her parents, the teacher, and community resources.

117. The following words describe an IEP objective *except*:
(Average Rigor) (Skill 14.02)

a. Specific
b. Observable
c. Measurable
d. Criterion-referenced

118. A serious hindrance to successful mainstreaming is:
(Average Rigor) (Skill 14.02)

a. Lack of adapted materials
b. Lack of funding
c. Lack of communication among teachers
d. Lack of support from administration

119. Which one of the following is *not* a primary purpose of an IEP?
(Rigorous) (Skill 14.02)

a. To outline instructional programs
b. To develop self-advocacy skills
c. To function as the basis for evaluation
d. To facilitate communication among staff members, teachers, parents, and students

120. Teachers have a professional obligation to do all of the following *except*:
(Average Rigor) (Skill 14.02)

a. Join a professional organization such as CEC, or LDA
b. Attend in-services or seminars related to your position
c. Stay after school to help students
d. Run school clubs

121. The ability to supply specific instructional materials, programs, and methods, as well as the ability to influence environmental learning variables, are advantages of which service model for exceptional students?
(Average Rigor) (Skill 14.03)

a. Regular classroom
b. Consultant teacher
c. Itinerant teacher
d. Resource room

122. Which is not a goal of collaboration for a consult teacher?
(Average Rigor) (Skill 14.03)

a. To have the regular education teacher understand the student's disability
b. Review content for accuracy
c. Review lessons for possible necessary modifications
d. Understanding the reasons for the current grade

123. A consultant teacher should be meeting the needs of his or her students by:
(Easy) (Skill 14.03)

a. Pushing in to do small group instruction with regular education students
b. Asking the student to show his or her reasoning for failing
c. Meeting with the teacher before class to discuss adaptations and expectations
d. Accompanying the student to class

124. You are having continual difficulty with your classroom assistant. A good strategy to address this problem would be:
(Rigorous) (Skill 14.05)

a. To address the issue immediately
b. To take away responsibilities
c. To write a clearly established role plan to discuss
d. To speak to your supervisor

125. Related service providers include all of the following except:
(Average Rigor) (Skill 14.05)

a. General education teachers
b. Speech and language therapists
c. Occupational therapists
d. Physicians

126. Kareem's father sounds upset and is in the office demanding to see his son's cumulative record. You should:
(Rigorous) (Skill 14.07)

a. Tell him that he will have to make an appointment
b. Bring the record to a private room for him to review with either an administrator or yourself
c. Take the record to the principal's office for review
d. Give the record to the parent

127. Educators who advocate educating all children in their neighborhood classrooms and schools, propose the end of labeling and segregation of special needs students in special classes, and call for the delivery of special supports and services directly in the classroom may be said to support the:
(Rigorous) (Skill 15.01)

a. Full-service model
b. Regular education initiative
c. Full-inclusion model
d. Mainstream model

128. The movement towards serving as many children with disabilities as possible in the regular classroom with supports and services is known as:
(Average Rigor) (Skill 15.01)

a. Full-service model
b. Regular education initiative
c. Full-inclusion model
d. Mainstream model

129. Which of the following statements was not offered as a rationale for the REI?
(Rigorous) (Skill 15.02)

a. Special education students are not usually identified until their learning problems have become severe
b. Lack of funding will mean that support for the special needs children will not be available in the regular classroom
c. Putting children in segregated special education placements is stigmatizing
d. There are students with learning or behavior problems who do not meet special education requirements but who still need special services

130. Which of these would not be considered a valid attempt to contact a parent for an IEP meeting?
(Average Rigor) (Skill 15.02)

a. Telephone call
b. Copy of correspondence
c. Message left on an answering machine
d. Record of home visits

131. Guidelines for an Individualized Family Service Plan (IFSP) would be described in which legislation?
(Rigorous) (Skill 15.02)

    a. Public Law 94-142
    b. Public Law 99-457
    c. Public Law 101-476
    d. ADA

132. Cheryl is a 15-year-old student receiving educational services in a full-time EH classroom. The date for her IEP review will take place two months before her 16th birthday. According to the requirements of IDEA, what must *additionally* be included in this review?
(Rigorous) (Skill 15.02)

    a. Graduation plan
    b. Individualized transition plan
    c. Individualized Family Service Plan
    d. Transportation planning

133. Hector is a 10th grader in a program for the severely emotionally handicapped. After a classmate taunted him about his mother, Hector threw a desk at the other boy and attacked him. As a crisis intervention team attempted to break up the fight, one teacher hurt his knee. The other boy received a concussion. Hector now faces disciplinary measures. How long can he be suspended without the suspension constituting a change of placement?
(Rigorous) (Skill 15.02)

    a. 5 days
    b. 10 days
    c. 10 + 30 days
    d. 60 days

134. The concept that a handicapped student cannot be expelled for misconduct that is a manifestation of the handicap itself is not limited to students labeled "seriously emotionally disturbed." Which reason does *not* explain this concept?
(Easy) (Skill 15.02)

    a. Emphasis on individualized evaluation
    b. Consideration of the problems and needs of handicapped students
    c. Right to a free and appropriate public education
    d. Putting these students out of school will just leave them on the streets to commit crimes

135. The minimum number of IEP meetings required per year is:
(Rigorous) (Skill 15.02)

a. As many as necessary
b. One
c. Two
d. Three

136. Satisfaction of the LRE requirement means that:
(Rigorous) (Skill 15.02)

a. A school is providing the best services it can offer there
b. The school is providing the best services the district has to offer
c. The student is being educated with the fewest special education services necessary
d. The student is being educated in the least restrictive setting that meets his or her needs

137. A review of a student's eligibility for an exceptional student program must be done:
(Rigorous) (Skill 15.02)

a. At least once every three years
b. At least once a year
c. Only if a major change occurs in academic or behavioral performance
d. When a student transfers to a new school

138. Section 504 differs from the scope of IDEA because its main focus is on:
(Rigorous) (Skill 15.02)

a. Prohibition of discrimination on the basis of disability
b. A basis for additional support services and accommodations in a special education setting
c. Procedural rights and safeguards for the individual
d. Federal funding for educational services

139. Public Law 99-457 amended the EHA to make provisions for:
(Easy) (Skill 15.02)

a. Education services for "uneducable" children
b. Educational services for children in jail settings
c. Special education benefits for children birth to five years
d. Education services for medically fragile children

140. Under the provisions of IDEA, the student is entitled to all of these *except*:
(Average Rigor) (Skill 15.02)

a. Placement in the best environment
b. Placement in the least restrictive environment
c. Provision of educational needs at no cost
d. Provision of individualized, appropriate educational programs

141. What legislation started FAPE?
(Rigorous) (Skill 15.02)

a. Section 504
b. EHCA
c. IDEA
d. Education Amendment 1974

142. Taiquan's parents are divorced and have joint custody. They both have requested to be present at the CSE. You call to make sure that they received the letter informing them of the coming CSE. Taiquan's father did not receive the notification and is upset. You should:
(Average Rigor) (Skill 15.02)

a. Tell him that you could review the meeting with him later
b. Ask him if he can adjust his schedule
c. Tell him you can reschedule the meeting
d. Ask him to coordinate a time for the CSE to meet with his ex-wife

143. NCLB (No Child Left Behind Act), was signed on January 8, 2002. It addresses what?
(Rigorous) (Skill 15.02)

a. Accessibility of curriculum to the student
b. Administrative incentives for school improvements
c. The funding to provide services required
d. Accountability of school personnel for student achievement

144. NCLB changed:
(Rigorous) (Skill 15.02)

a. Special education teacher placement
b. Classroom guidelines
c. Stricter behavioral regulations
d. Academic content

145. Which law specifically states that "Full Inclusion is not the only way for a student to reach his/her highest potential?"
(Rigorous) (Skill 15.02)

a. IDEA
b. IDEA 97
c. IDEA 2004
d. Part 200

146. If a child does not qualify for classification under special education, the committee shall:
(Average Rigor) (Skill 15.02)

a. Refer the parental interventions to the 504 Plan
b. Provide temporary remedial services for the student
c. Recommend to the parent possible resources outside of the committee for which the child may qualify
d. Give the parents the information about possible reviews by an exterior source

147. According to IDEA 2004, students with disabilities are to do what?
(Average Rigor) (Skill 15.02)

a. Participate in the general education program to the fullest extent that it is beneficial for them
b. Participate in a vocational training within the general education setting
c. Participate in a general education setting for physical education
d. Participate in a modified program that meets his or her needs

148. John has attention deficit hyperactivity disorder (ADHD). He is in a regular classroom and appears to be doing okay. However, his teacher does not want John in her class because he will not obey her when she asks him to stop doing a repetitive action such as tapping his foot. The teacher sees this as distractive during tests. John needs:
(Easy) (Skill 15.04)

a. An IEP
b. A 504 Plan
c. A VESID evaluation
d. A more restrictive environment

149. Kara's mother has requested a computer for her child to do class work and homework, but the CSE does not agree. Kara complains to you. You should:
(Easy) (Skill 15.06)

a. Tell her you agree with her
b. Recommend an outside source that may provide a free laptop computer
c. Tell Kara's mother she can still fight the CSE's decision by requesting a due process hearing
d. Tell the parent to call a lawyer

150. What is required of a special education teacher when approaching an administrator regarding a request to change placement of a student?
(Rigorous) (Skill 16.01)

a. Observation
b. Objectivity
c. Assessments
d. Parent permission

1. c	44. c	87. c	130. c
2. b	45. a	88. b	131. b
3. c	46. c	89. b	132. b
4. a	47. c	90. c	133. b
5. a	48. c	91. c	134. d
6. c	49. b	92. a	135. b
7. d	50. c	93. b	136. d
8. b	51. d	94. a	137. a
9. a	52. c	95. c	138. a
10. b	53. d	96. c	139. c
11. c	54. b	97. a	140. a
12. b	55. c	98. c	141. a
13. c	56. c	99. c	142. c
14. d	57. a	100. d	143. d
15. a	58. a	101. a	144. a
16. c	59. b	102. c	145. c
17. d	60. c	103. c	146. c
18. b	61. c	104. b	147. a
19. a	62. c	105. b	148. b
20. a	63. a	106. a	149. c
21. d	64. c	107. d	150. b
22. d	65. c	108. c	
23. b	66. c	109. d	
24. c	67. b	110. c	
25. c	68. c	111. b	
26. c	69. d	112. a	
27. d	70. b	113. c	
28. a	71. d	114. d	
29. c	72. c	115. d	
30. d	73. c	116. d	
31. d	74. a	117. d	
32. c	75. c	118. c	
33. d	76. d	119. b	
34. b	77. a	120. d	
35. d	78. d	121. b	
36. b	79. a	122. b	
37. a	80. c	123. a	
38. c	81. b	124. c	
39. c	82. a	125. a	
40. c	83. d	126. b	
41. b	84. c	127. c	
42. c	85. a	128. c	
43. b	86. c	129. b	

Rigor Table

	Easy 20%	Average Rigor 40%	Rigorous 40%
Question #	4, 23, 29, 34, 36, 37, 40, 46, 60, 61, 62, 64, 69, 70, 71, 74, 80, 94, 95, 97, 107, 109, 110, 114, 123, 134, 139, 148, 149	5, 9, 14, 16, 18, 25, 26, 27, 28, 30, 31, 33, 35, 38, 39, 41, 43, 44, 45, 47, 50, 51, 53, 55, 56, 57, 58, 59, 65, 66, 67, 68, 73, 75, 77, 78, 79, 84, 86, 88, 91, 92, 100, 106, 111, 112, 113, 115, 117, 118, 120, 121, 122, 125, 128, 130, 140, 142, 146, 147	1, 2, 3, 6, 7, 8, 10, 11, 12, 13, 15, 17, 19, 20, 21, 22, 24, 32, 42, 48, 49, 52, 54, 63, 72, 76, 81, 82, 83, 85, 87, 89, 90, 93, 96, 98, 99, 101, 102, 103, 104, 105, 108, 116, 119, 124, 126, 127, 129, 131, 132, 133, 135, 136, 137, 138, 141, 143, 144, 145, 150

Rationales for Sample Questions

1. **Skilled readers use all but which one of these knowledge sources to construct meanings beyond the literal text:**
    (Rigorous) (Skill 1.01)

    a. Text knowledge
    b. Syntactic knowledge
    c. Morphological knowledge
    d. Semantic knowledge

Correct answer is "c."
Rationale: The student is already skilled, so morphological knowledge is already in place.

2. **Which of these characteristics is *not* included in the Public Law 94-142 definition of emotional disturbance?**
    (Rigorous) (Skill 1.01)

    a. General pervasive mood of unhappiness or depression
    b. Social maladjustment manifested in a number of settings
    c. Tendency to develop physical symptoms, pains, or fear associated with school or personal problems
    d. An inability to learn that is not attributed to intellectual, sensory, or health factors

Correct answer is "b."
Rationale: Social maladjustment is not considered a disability.

3. **Poor moral development, lack of empathy, and behavioral excesses (such as aggression) are the most obvious characteristics of which behavioral disorder?**
    (Rigorous) (Skill 1.01)

    a. Autism
    b. ADD-H
    c. Conduct disorder
    d. Pervasive developmental disorder

Correct answer is "c."
Rationale: A student with conduct disorder or social maladjustment displays behaviors and/or values that are in conflict with the school, home, or community. The characteristics listed are all behavioral/social.

4. **Signs of depression typically do not include:**
    (Easy) (Skill 1.01)

    a. Hyperactivity
    b. Changes in sleep patterns
    c. Recurring thoughts of death or suicide
    d. Significant changes in weight or appetite

Correct answer is "a."
Rationale: Depression is usually characterized by listlessness, brooding, low anxiety, and little activity. Conversely, hyperactivity is over activity.

5. **Which of these is listed as only a minor scale on the Behavior Problem Checklist?**
    (Average Rigor) (Skill 1.01)

    a. Motor excess
    b. Conduct disorder
    c. Socialized aggression
    d. Anxiety/withdrawal

Correct answer is "a."
Rationale: Motor excess has to do with over activity, or hyperactivity, in physical movement. The other three items are disorders, all of which may be characterized by excessive activity.

6. **Indirect requests and attempts to influence or control others through one's use of language is an example of:**
    (Rigorous) (Skill 1.01)

    a. Morphology
    b. Syntax
    c. Pragmatics
    d. Semantics

Correct answer is "c."
Rationale: Pragmatics involves the way that language is used to communicate and interact with others. It is often used to control the actions and attitudes of people.

7. Kenny, a fourth grader, has trouble comprehending analogies; using comparative, spatial, and temporal words; and understanding multiple meanings. Language interventions for Kenny would focus on:
(Rigorous) (Skill 1.01)

    a. Morphology
    b. Syntax
    c. Pragmatics
    d. Semantics

Correct answer is "d."
Rationale: Semantics has to do with word meanings. Semantic tests measure receptive and expressive vocabulary skills.

8. Celia, who is in first grade, asked, "Where are my ball?" She also has trouble with passive sentences. Language interventions for Celia would target:
(Rigorous) (Skill 1.01)

    a. Morphology
    b. Syntax
    c. Pragmatics
    d. Semantics

Correct answer is "b."
Rationale: Syntax refers to the rules for arranging words to make sentences.

9. Scott is in middle school but still makes statements like, "I gotted new high-tops yesterday," and "I saw three mans in the front office." Language interventions for Scott would target:
(Average Rigor) (Skill 1.01)

    a. Morphology
    b. Syntax
    c. Pragmatics
    d. Semantics

Correct answer is "a."
Rationale: Morphology is the process of combining phonemes into meaningful words.

10. **Mr. Mendez is assessing his students' written expressions. Which of these is not a component of written expression?**
    (Rigorous) (Skill 1.01)

    a. Vocabulary
    b. Morphology
    c. Content
    d. Sentence structure

Correct answer is "b."
Rationale: Morphology is the correct answer. Vocabulary consists of words, content is made up of ideas (which are expressed in words), and sentences are constructed from words. Morphemes, however, are not always words. They may be prefixes or suffixes.

11. **Which of these explanations would *not* likely account for the lack of a clear definition of behavior disorders?**
    (Rigorous) (Skill 1.01)

    a. Problems with measurement
    b. Cultural and/or social influences and views of what is acceptable
    c. The numerous types of manifestations of behavior disorders
    d. Differing theories that use their own terminology and definitions

Correct answer is "c."
Rationale: A, B, and D are factors that account for the lack of a clear definition of some behavioral disorders. C is not a factor.

12. **Social withdrawal, anxiety, depression, shyness, and guilt are indicative of:**
    (Rigorous) (Skill 1.01)

    a. Conduct disorder
    b. Personality disorders
    c. Immaturity
    d. Socialized aggression

Correct answer is "b."
Rationale: These are all personality disorders.

13. **Short attention span, daydreaming, clumsiness, and preference for younger playmates are associated with:**
    (Rigorous) (Skill 1.01)

    a. Conduct disorder
    b. Personality disorders
    c. Immaturity
    d. Socialized aggression

Correct answer is "c."
Rationale: These disorders show immaturity. The student is not acting age appropriately.

14. **Truancy, gang membership, and feelings of pride in belonging to a delinquent subculture are indicative of:**
    (Average Rigor) (Skill 1.01)

    a. Conduct disorder
    b. Personality disorders
    c. Immaturity
    d. Socialized aggression

Correct answer is "d."
Rationale: The student is acting out by using aggression. This gives him or her a sense of belonging.

15. **Temper tantrums, disruption of class, disobedience, and bossiness are associated with:**
    (Rigorous) (Skill 1.01)

    a. Conduct disorder
    b. Personality disorders
    c. Immaturity
    d. Socialized aggression

Correct answer is "a."
Rationale: These behaviors are designed to attract attention. They are conduct disorders.

16. **Which of these is *not* true for most children with behavior disorders? (Average Rigor) (Skill 1.01)**

    a. Many score in the "slow learner" or "mildly retarded" range on IQ tests
    b. They are frequently behind their classmates in academic achievement
    c. They are bright but bored with their surroundings
    d. A large amount of time is spent in nonproductive, nonacademic behaviors

Correct answer is "c."
Rationale: Most children with conduct disorders display the traits found in A, B, and D.

17. **Which behavioral disorder is easier to diagnose in children because the symptoms are manifested quite differently than in adults? (Rigorous) (Skill 1.01)**

    a. Anorexia
    b. Schizophrenia
    c. Paranoia
    d. Depression

Correct answer is "d."
Rationale: In an adult, depression may be displayed as age-appropriate behavior and therefore go undiagnosed. In a child, it may be displayed as not age appropriate, so it is easier to recognize.

18. **Parents are more likely to have a child with a learning disability if: (Average Rigor) (Skill 1.01)**

    a. They smoke tobacco.
    b. The child is less than five pounds at birth
    c. The mother drank alcohol on a regular basis until she planned for a baby
    d. The father was known to consume large quantities of alcohol during the pregnancy

Correct answer is "b."
Babies that are born weighing less than five pounds at birth are more likely to have a form of learning disability. The reasoning is that the babies may not have fully developed before birth.

19.   A developmental delay may be indicated by a:
      (Rigorous) (Skill 1.01)

      a. Second grader having difficulty buttoning clothing
      b. Stuttered response
      c. Kindergartner not having complete bladder control
      d. Withdrawn behavior

Correct answer is "a."
Buttoning clothing is generally mastered by the age of four. While many children have full bladder control by age four, it is not unusual for "embarrassing accidents" to occur.

20.   According to IDEA, a child whose disability is related to being deaf and blind may *not* be classified as:
      (Rigorous) (Skill 1.01)

      a. Multiple disabilities
      b. Other health impaired
      c. Mentally retarded
      d. Visually impaired

Correct answer is "a."
The only stated area where deaf-blindness is not accepted is in multiple disabilities.

21.   Mark is a sixth grader. The teacher has noticed that he doesn't respond to simple requests like the other students in the class. If asked to erase the board, he may look, shake his head, and say no, but then he will clean the board. When the children gather together for recess, he joins them. Yet, the teacher observes that it takes him much longer to understand the rules to a game. Mark retains what he reads. Mark most likely has:
      (Rigorous) (Skill 1.01)

      a. Autism
      b. Tourette's syndrome
      c. Mental retardation
      d. A pragmatic language disability

Correct answer is "d."
Pragmatics is the basic understanding of a communicator's intent. The issue here is Mark's ability to respond correctly to another person.

22. **A child may be classified under the special education "umbrella" as having Traumatic Brain Injury (TBI) if he or she does *not* have which of the following causes?**
(Rigorous) (Skill 1.01)

   a. Stroke
   b. Anoxia
   c. Encephalitis
   d. Birth trauma

Correct answer is "d."
According to IDEA and Part 200, a child may not be labeled as having traumatic brain injury if the injury is related to birth.

23. **Which body language would not likely be interpreted as a sign of defensiveness, aggression, or hostility?**
(Easy) (Skill 2.01)

   a. Pointing
   b. Direct eye contact
   c. Hands on hips
   d. Arms crossed

Correct answer is "b."
Rationale: In our culture, A, C, and D are considered nonverbal acts of defiance. Direct eye contact is not considered an act of defiance.

24. **Of the various factors that contribute to delinquency and antisocial behavior, which has been found to be the weakest?**
(Rigorous) (Skill 2.01)

   a. Criminal behavior and/or alcoholism in the father
   b. Lax mother and punishing father
   c. Socioeconomic disadvantage
   d. Long history of broken home and marital discord among parents

Correct answer is "c."
Rationale: There are many examples of A, B, and D where there is socioeconomic advantage.

25. Children who are characterized by impulsivity generally:
     (Average Rigor) (Skill 2.01)

     a. Do not feel sorry for their actions
     b. Blame others for their actions
     c. Do not weigh alternatives before acting
     d. Do not outgrow their problem

Correct answer is "c."
Rationale: They act without thinking, so they either cannot think or do not think before they act.

26. Echolalia, repetitive stereotyped actions, and a severe disorder of thinking and communication are indicative of:
     (Average Rigor) (Skill 2.01)

     a. Psychosis
     b. Schizophrenia
     c. Autism
     d. Paranoia

Correct answer is "c."
Rationale: The behaviors listed are indicative of autism.

27. Across America, there is one toxic substance that is contributing to the creation of disabilities in our children. What is it?
     (Average Rigor) (Skill 2.01)

     a. Children's aspirin
     b. Fluoride water
     c. Chlorine gas
     d. Lead

Correct answer is "d."
Lead poisoning is still a major factor influencing and causing disabilities. Today many homes in urban, suburban, and rural neighborhoods are still being worked on to remove the lead paint.

28. **Janice is a new student in your self-contained class. She is extremely quiet and makes little, if any, eye contact. Yesterday, she started to "parrot" what another student said. Today the teacher became concerned when she did not follow directions and seemed not to even recognize his presence. Her cumulative file arrived today; when the teacher reviews the health section, it most likely will state that she is diagnosed with:**
(Average Rigor) (Skill 2.01)

    a. Autism
    b. Central processing disorder
    c. Traumatic brain injury
    d. Mental retardation

Correct answer is "a."
Janice is exhibiting three symptoms of autism. While a child may demonstrate some of these behaviors if he or she is diagnosed with traumatic brain injury or mental retardation, the combination of these symptoms are more likely to indicate autism.

29. **Justin is diagnosed with autism and is in an inclusive setting. You were called down to "Stop him from turning the lights off and remove him." When you arrive, you learn that today a movie was supposed to be finished, but the VCR broke, so the teacher planned another activity. What is the best way to explain to the teacher why Justin was turning off the lights?**
(Easy) (Skill 2.01)

    a. He is perseverating and will stop shortly.
    b. He is telling you the lights bother him.
    c. He needs forewarning before a transition. Next time you have an unexpected change in classroom schedule, please let him know.
    d. Please understand, this is part of who Justin is. He will leave the lights alone after I talk to him.

Correct answer is "c."
The teacher already knows that Justin will stop after you talk to him. That is why she called you. She needs to know what to do if this happens again. Explaining the problem with transition may enable the teacher to see a problem before it occurs or to prevent future problems.

30. Of the following, which does not describe the term delinquency?
    (Average Rigor) (Skill 2.01)

    a. Behavior that would be considered criminal if exhibited by an adult
    b. Socialized aggression
    c. Academic truancy
    d. Inciting fights with verbal abuse

Correct answer is "d."
Socialized aggression and criminal behavior are characteristics of gang membership and delinquency. Truancy is also characteristic of this behavior. Verbal abuse, however, is not descriptive of this, as it is not seen as criminal behavior.

31. A student on medication may have his or her dosage adjusted as his or her body grows. Parents may call and ask questions about their child's adjustment to the medication during the school day. During this time, you should:
    (Average Rigor) (Skill 2.02)

    a. Observe the student for changes in behavior.
    b. Watch for a progression of changed behavior.
    c. Communicate with the parent concerns about sleepiness.
    d. All of the above

Correct answer is "d."
If you have students on medication, it is important to communicate with the parents any changes in behavior, as the students' bodies are constantly growing. Being informed about the medication(s) your students are on allows you to assist the students and the parents as an objective observer.

32. School refusal, obsessive-compulsive disorders, psychosis, and separation anxiety are also frequently accompanied by:
    (Rigorous) (Skill 3.01)

    a. Conduct disorder
    b. ADD-H
    c. Depression
    d. Autism

Correct answer is "c."
Rationale: These behaviors are usually accompanied by depression in ADD-H.

33. **What is the highest goal a teacher should aim for while preparing a student for success?**
(Average Rigor) (Skill 3.07)

   a. Reading
   b. Budgeting
   c. Cooking
   d. Self-advocacy

Correct answer is "d."
When a student is able to self-advocate well, he or she is on the road to independence, with an understanding of his or her limits and specific needs to find success.

34. **Examples of behaviors that are appropriate to be monitored by measuring frequency include all *except*:**
(Easy) (Skill 4.01)

   a. Thumb sucking
   b. Hitting
   c. Temper tantrums
   d. Maintaining eye contact

Correct answer is "b."
Rationale: Hitting takes place in an instant. This should be measured by frequency.

35. **Examples of behaviors that are appropriate to be monitored by measuring frequency include all *except*:**
(Average Rigor) (Skill 4.01)

   a. Teasing
   b. Talking out
   c. Being on time for class
   d. Daydreaming

Correct answer is "d."
Rationale: Daydreaming cannot be measured by frequency. It should be measured by duration.

36. **Criteria for choosing behaviors to measure by frequency include all *except* those that:**
    (Easy) (Skill 4.01)

    a. Have an observable beginning
    b. Last a long time
    c. Last a short time
    d. Occur often

Correct answer is "b."
Rationale: We use frequency to measure behaviors that do not last a long time.

37. **Criteria for choosing behaviors to measure by duration include all *except* those that:**
    (Easy) (Skill 4.01)

    a. Last a short time
    b. Last a long time
    c. Have no readily observable beginning or end
    d. Do not happen often

Correct answer is "a."
Rationale: We use duration to measure behaviors that do not last a short time.

38. **Ms. Beekman has a class of students who frequently talk out. She wishes to begin interventions with the students who are talking out the most. She monitors the talking behavior of the entire class for one-minute samples every half hour. This is an example of collecting data on:**
    (Average Rigor) (Skill 4.01)

    a. Multiple behavior for single subjects
    b. Reciprocal behaviors
    c. Single behaviors for multiple subjects
    d. Continuous behaviors for fixed intervals

Correct answer is "c."
Rationale: Talking out is the only behavior being observed.

39. **Which is *not* an example of a standard score?**
    (Average Rigor) (Skill 4.01)

    a. T score
    b. Z score
    c. Standard deviation
    d. Stanine

Correct answer i

Rationale: A, B, a ~~Stanine :~~ scores. Stanines are whole number scores from one t ~~@. (1-9)~~ wide range of raw scores. Standard deviation is *not a* ~~lely~~ scores vary from the mean.

[handwritten: Stanine: @. (1-9)]

[handwritten: Standard Deviation · represent raw score]

40. **The most** g assessment data (and perhaps the most o ~~Standard~~ *(Easy) (Sk* ~~Deviation~~

    a. Testing
    b. Self-rec
    c. Observa
    d. Experim

Correct answer is
Rationale: Observation is often better than testing, due to language, culture, or other factors.

41. **The extent that a test measures what it claims to measure is called:**
    (Average Rigor) (Skill 4.01)

    a. Reliability
    b. Validity
    c. Factor analysis
    d. Chi square

Correct answer is "b."
Rationale: The definition of validity is the degree to which a test measures what it claims to measure.

42. **Ms. Wright is planning an analysis of Audrey's out-of-seat behavior. Her initial data would be called:**
(Rigorous) (Skill 4.01)

   a. Pre-referral phase
   b. Intervention phase
   c. Baseline phase
   d. Observation phase

Correct answer is "c."
Rationale: Ms. Wright is a teacher. She should begin at the baseline phase.

43. **To reinforce Audrey each time she is on task and in her seat, Ms. Wright delivers specific praise and stickers, which Audrey may collect and redeem for a reward. The data collected during the time Ms. Wright is using this intervention is called:**
(Average Rigor) (Skill 4.01)

   a. Referral phase
   b. Intervention phase
   c. Baseline phase
   d. Observation phase

Correct answer is "b."
Rationale: Ms. Wright is involved in behavior modification. This is the intervention phase.

44. **Ryan is 3, and her temper tantrums last for an hour. Bryan is 8, and he does not stay on task for more than 10 minutes without teacher prompts. These behaviors differ from normal children in terms of their:**
(Average Rigor) (Skill 4.01)

   a. Rate
   b. Topography
   c. Duration
   d. Magnitude

Correct answer is "c."
Rationale: It is not normal for temper tantrums to last an hour. At age eight, a normal student stays on task much longer than 10 minutes without teacher prompts.

45. **All children cry, hit, fight, and play alone at different times. Children with behavior disorders will perform these behaviors at a higher than normal:**
(Average Rigor) (Skill 4.01)

   a. Rate
   b. Topography
   c. Duration
   d. Magnitude

Correct answer is "a."
Rationale: Children with behavior disorders display them at a much higher rate than normal children.

46. **The purpose of an error analysis of a test is to:**
(Easy) (Skill 4.01)

   a. Determine what events were labeled in error
   b. Determine if the test length was the cause of error
   c. Evaluate the types of errors made by categorizing incorrect answers
   d. Establish a baseline

Correct answer is "c."
Error analyses examine how and why a person makes a mistake. In an informal reading inventory, like Burns and Roe, questions are given to specifically address possible errors. Other tests that utilize error analysis provide specific possible answers to denote which error was made. The purpose of both is to see where problems lie and to provide clues to assist the learning process.

47. **Marcie is often not in her seat when the bell rings. She may be found at the pencil sharpener, throwing paper away, or fumbling through her notebook. Which of these descriptions of her behavior can be described as a pinpoint?**
(Average Rigor) (Skill 4.01)

   a. Is tardy a lot
   b. Is out of seat
   c. Is not in seat when late bell rings
   d. Is disorganized

Correct answer is "c."
Rationale: Even though A, B, and D describe the behavior, C is most precise.

48. **Statements like, "Darren is lazy," are not helpful in describing his behavior for all *except* which of these reasons?**
(Rigorous) (Skill 4.02)

   a. There is no way to determine if any change occurs from the information given
   b. The student—not the behavior—becomes labeled
   c. Darren's behavior will manifest itself clearly enough without any written description
   d. Constructs are open to various interpretations among the people who are asked to define them

Correct answer is "c."
Rationale: "Darren is lazy" is a label. It can be interpreted in a variety of ways, and there is no way to measure this description for change. A description should be measurable.

49. **Which of the following is *not* one of the three aspects of the issue of fair assessment for individuals from minority groups that Slavia and Ysseldyke (1995) point out as particularly relevant to the assessment of students?**
(Rigorous) (Skill 5.02)

   a. Representation
   b. Diversity
   c. Acculturation
   d. Language

Correct answer is "b."
The issue of fair assessment for individuals from minority groups has a long history in the law, philosophy, and education. Individuals from diverse backgrounds need to be represented in assessment materials. It is also important that individuals from different backgrounds receive opportunities to acquire the tested skills, information, and values. The language and concepts that comprise test items should be unbiased, and students should be familiar with terminology and references to which the language is being made when they are administered tests, especially when the results of the tests are going to be used for decision-making purposes.

50. **Marisol has been mainstreamed into a ninth-grade language arts class. Although her behavior is satisfactory, and she likes the class, Marisol's reading level is about two years below grade level. The class has been assigned to read *Great Expectations* and write a report. What intervention would be *least* successful in helping Marisol complete this assignment?**
(Average Rigor) (Skill 6.01)

    a. Having Marisol listen to a taped recording while following the story in the regular text
    b. Giving her a modified version of the story
    c. Telling her to choose a different book that she can read
    d. Showing a film to the entire class and comparing and contrasting it with the book

Correct answer is "c."
Rationale: A, B, and D are positive interventions. C is not an intervention.

51. **Which would *not* be an advantage of using a criterion-referenced test?**
(Average Rigor) (Skill 6.01)

    a. Information about an individual's ability level is too specific for the purposes of the assessment
    b. It can pinpoint exact areas of weaknesses and strengths
    c. You can design them yourself
    d. You do not get comparative information

Correct answer is "d."
Rationale: Criterion-referenced tests measure mastery of content rather than performance compared to others. Test items are usually prepared from specific educational objectives and may be teacher made or commercially prepared. Scores are measured by the percentage of correct items for a skill (e.g., adding and subtracting fractions with like denominators).

52. **Lack of regular follow-up, difficulty in transporting materials, and lack of consistent support for students who need more assistance are disadvantages of which type of service model?**
(Rigorous) (Skill 6.01)

   a. Regular classroom
   b. Consultant with regular teacher
   c. Itinerant
   d. Resource room

Correct answer is "c."
Rationale: The itinerant model, as the name implies, is not regular.

53. **An emphasis on instructional remediation and individualized instruction in problem areas, as well as a focus on mainstreaming, are characteristics of which model of service delivery?**
(Average Rigor) (Skill 6.01)

   a. Regular classroom
   b. Consultant teacher
   c. Itinerant teacher
   d. Resource room

Correct answer is "d."
Rationale: The resource room is usually a bridge to mainstreaming.

54. **A best practice for evaluating student performance and progress on IEPs is:**
(Rigorous) (Skill 6.01)

   a. Formal assessment
   b. Curriculum-based assessment
   c. Criterion-based assessment
   d. Norm-referenced evaluation

Correct answer is "b."
Rationale: This is a teacher-prepared test that measures the student's progress but at the same time shows the teacher whether or not the accommodations are effective.

55. In exceptional student education, assessment is used to make decisions about all of the following *except:*
(Average Rigor) (Skill 6.01)

    a. Screening and initial identification of children who may need services
    b. Selection and evaluation of teaching strategies and programs
    c. Determining the desired attendance rate of a student
    d. Development of goals, objectives, and evaluation for the IEP

Correct answer is "c."
School attendance is required, and assessment is not necessary to measure a child's attendance rate.

56. Which of the following is *not* an appropriate assessment modification or accommodation for a student with a learning disability?
(Average Rigor) (Skill 6.01)

    a. Having the test read orally to the student
    b. Writing down the student's dictated answers
    c. Allowing the student to take the assessment home to complete
    d. Extending the time for the student to take the assessment

Correct answer is "c."
Unless a student is homebound, the student should take assessments in class or in another classroom setting. All the other items listed are appropriate accommodations.

57. The basic tools necessary to observe and record behavior include all but:
(Average Rigor) (Skill 6.03)

    a. Cameras
    b. Timers
    c. Counters
    d. Graphs or charts

Correct answer is "a."
Rationale: The camera gives a snapshot. It does not record behavior.

58. Shyquan is in your inclusive class, and she exhibits a slower comprehension of assigned tasks and concepts. Her first two grades were Bs, but she is now receiving failing marks. She has seen the resource teacher. You should:
(Average Rigor) (Skill 6.04)

a. Ask for a review of current placement.
b. Tell Shyquan to seek extra help.
c. Ask Shyquan if she is frustrated.
d. Ask the regular education teacher to slow instruction.

Correct answer is "a."
All of the responses listed above can be deemed correct, but you are responsible for reviewing her ability to function in the inclusive environment. Shyquan may or may not know she is not grasping the work, and she has sought extra help with the resource teacher. Also, if the regular education class students are successful, the class should not be slowed to adjust to Shyquan's learning rate. It is more likely that she may require a more modified curriculum to stay on task and to succeed academically. This would require a more restrictive environment.

59. Teachers in grades K-3 are mandated to teach what to all students using scientifically based methods with measurable outcomes?
(Average Rigor) (Skill 7.04)

a. Math
b. Reading
c. Citizenship
d. Writing

Correct answer is "b."
Reading is the mandated subject, as it is looked at as the fountain from which all learning can be secured.

60. In a positive classroom environment, errors are viewed as:
(Easy) (Skill 7.07)

a. Symptoms of deficiencies
b. Lack of attention or ability
c. A natural part of the learning process
d. The result of going too fast

Correct answer is "c."
Rationale: We often learn a great deal from our mistakes and shortcomings. It is normal. Where it is not normal, fear develops. This fear of failure inhibits children from working and achieving. Copying and other types of cheating result from this fear of failure.

61.   **Which of these would be the least effective measure of behavioral disorders?**
(Easy) (Skill 7.07)

    a. Projective test
    b. Ecological assessment
    c. Standardized test
    d. Psychodynamic analysis

Correct answer is "c."
Rationale: These tests make comparisons rather than measure skills.

62.   **Cooperative learning does *not* utilize:**
(Easy) (Skill 7.07)

    a. Shared ideas
    b. Small groups
    c. Independent practice
    d. Student expertise

Correct answer is "c."
Cooperative learning focuses on group cooperation. It allows for the sharing of student expertise and provides some flexibility for creative presentation of the students as they share with others.

63.   **When a student begins to use assistive technology, it is important for the teacher to have a clear outline as to when and how the equipment should be used. Why?**
(Rigorous) (Skill 8.02)

    a. To establish a level of accountability with the student
    b. To establish that the teacher has responsibility of the equipment that is in use in his or her room
    c. To establish that the teacher is responsible for the usage of the assistive technology
    d. To establish a guideline for evaluation

Correct answer is "a."
Clear parameters as to the usage of assistive technology in a classroom creates a level of accountability in the student, as he or she will know that the teacher understands the intended purpose and appropriate manner of use of the device.

64. Organizing ideas by us⬚ ⬚⬚⬚⬚ ⬚⬚⬚⬚ ⬚ample of which
writing activity?
(Easy) (Skill 8.04)

① organiti
② Draftin
③ Final D
④ revision

8.04

 a. Revision
 b. Drafting
 c. Prewriting
 d. Final draft

Correct answer is "c."
Rationale: Organizing ideas come before drafting, final draft, and revision.

65. Ryan is working on a report about dogs. He uses scissors and tape
to cut and rearrange sections and paragraphs and then photocopies
the paper so he can continue writing. Ryan is in which stage of the
writing process?
(Average Rigor) (Skill 8.04)

 a. Final draft
 b. Prewriting
 c. Revision
 d. Drafting

Correct answer is "c."
Rationale: Ryan is revising and reordering before final editing.

66. Talking into a tape recorder is an example of which writing activity?
(Average Rigor) (Skill 8.04)

 a. Prewriting
 b. Drafting
 c. Final draft
 d. Revision

Correct answer is "c."
Rationale: Talking into a tape recorder is part of preparing the final draft.

67.	All of these are effective in teaching written expression *except*:
	(Average Rigor) (Skill 8.04)

	a.	Exposure to various styles and direct instruction in those styles
	b.	Immediate feedback from the teacher with all mistakes clearly marked
	c.	Goal setting and peer evaluation of written products according to set criteria
	d.	Incorporating writing with other academic subjects

Correct answer is "b."
Rationale: Teacher feedback is not always necessary. The student can have feedback from his or her peers or emotional responses, or the student can apply skills learned to other subjects.

68.	Which of the follow is does *not* have an important effect on the spatial arrangement (physical setting) of your classroom?
	(Average Rigor) (Skill 9.01)

	a.	Adequate physical space
	b.	Ventilation
	c.	Window placement
	d.	Lighting adequacy

Correct answer is "c."
Many classrooms today do not have windows, as they may be placed in the middle of a building. Choice C is also the only factor listed that cannot be controlled or adjusted by the teacher or the administration.

69.	Mr. Brown finds that his chosen consequence does not seem to be having the desired effect of reducing the target misbehavior. Which of these would *least likely* account for Mr. Brown's lack of success with the consequence?
	(Easy) (Skill 9.04)

	a.	The consequence was aversive in Mr. Brown's opinion but not the students'
	b.	The students were not developmentally ready to understand the connection between the behavior and the consequence
	c.	Mr. Brown was inconsistent in applying the consequence
	d.	The intervention had not previously been shown to be effective in studies

Correct answer is "d."
Rationale: A, B, and C might work if applied in the classroom, but research is the least of Mr. Brown's options.

70. **Which of the following is *not* a feature of effective classroom rules?**
(Easy) (Skill 9.04)

   a. They are about four to six in number
   b. They are negatively stated
   c. Consequences are consistent and immediate
   d. They can be tailored to individual teaching goals and teaching styles

Correct answer is "b."
Rationale: Rules should be positively stated, and they should follow the other three features listed.

71. **An effective classroom behavior management plan includes all but which of the following?**
(Easy) (Skill 9.04)

   a. Transition procedures for changing activities
   b. Clear consequences for rule infractions
   c. Concise teacher expectations for student behavior
   d. Copies of lesson plans

Correct answer is "d."
Rationale: D is not a part of any behavior management plan. A, B, and C are.

72. **Effective management transition involves all of the following *except*:**
(Rigorous) (Skill 9.04)

   a. Keeping students informed of the sequencing of instructional activities
   b. Using group fragmentation
   c. Changing the schedule frequently to maintain student interest
   d. Using academic transition signals

Correct answer is "c."
While you do want to use a variety of activities to maintain student interest, changing the schedule too frequently will result in loss of instructional time due to unorganized transitions. Effective teachers manage transitions from one activity to another in a systematically oriented way through efficient management of instructional matter, sequencing of instructional activities, movement of students in groups, and employment of academic transition signals. Through an efficient use of class time, achievement is increased, as students spend more class time engaged in on-task behavior.

73. **Otumba is a 16 year old in your class who recently came from Nigeria. The girls in your class have come to you to complain about the way he treats them in a sexist manner. When they complain, you reflect that this is also the way he treats adult females. You have talked to Otumba before about appropriate behavior. What should you do first?**
(Average Rigor) (Skill 9.07)

   a. Complain to the principal
   b. Ask for a parent-teacher conference
   c. Check to see if this is a cultural norm in his country
   d. Create a behavior contract for him to follow

Correct answer is "c."
While A, B, and D are good actions, it is important to remember that Otumba comes from a culture where women are treated differently than they are in America. Learning this information will enable the school as a whole to address this behavior.

74. **Which of the following should be avoided when writing objectives for social behavior?**
(Easy) (Skill 10.01)

   a. Nonspecific adverbs
   b. Behaviors stated as verbs
   c. Criteria for acceptable performance
   d. Conditions where the behavior is expected to be performed

Correct answer is "a."
Rationale: Behaviors should be specific. The more clearly the behavior is described, the less the chance for error.

75. **Criteria for choosing behaviors that are in the most need of change involve all *except* the following:**
(Average Rigor) (Skill 10.03)

   a. Observations across settings to rule out certain interventions
   b. Pinpointing the behavior that is the poorest fit in the child's environment
   c. The teacher's concern about what is the most important behavior to target
   d. Analysis of the environmental reinforcers

Correct answer is "c."
Rationale: The teacher must take care of the criteria in A, B, and D. His or her concerns are of the least importance.

76. **Which of the following is *not* one of the four interrelated components of Positive Behavioral Interventions and Supports (PBS)?**
    (Rigorous) (Skill 10.03)

    a. Systems change activities
    b. Environmental alterations activities
    c. Behavioral consequences activities
    d. Support provision activities

Correct answer is "d."
The use of Positive Behavioral Interventions and Supports (PBS) is IDEA's preferred strategy for handling challenging behaviors of students with disabilities. IDEA requires PBS to be considered in all cases of students whose behavior impedes their learning or the learning of others. PBS involves the use of positive behavioral interventions and systems to attain socially significant behavior changes. PBS has four interrelated components: systems change activities, environmental alterations activities, skill instruction activities, and behavioral consequence activities.

77. **Sam is working to earn half an hour of basketball time with his favorite P.E. teacher. At the end of each half hour, Sam marks his point sheet with an X if he reached his goal of no call-outs. When he has received 25 marks, he will receive his basketball free time. This behavior management strategy is an example of:**
    (Average Rigor) (Skill 10.05)

    a. Self-recording
    b. Self-evaluation
    c. Self-reinforcement
    d. Self-regulation

Correct answer is "a."
Rationale: Sam is recording his behavior. Self-management is an important part of social skills training, especially for older students preparing for employment. Components for self-management include the following:

- Self-monitoring: choosing behaviors and alternatives, and monitoring those actions
- Self-evaluation: deciding the effectiveness of the behavior in solving the problem
- Self-reinforcement: telling oneself that one is capable of achieving success

78. Mark has been working on his target goal of completing his mathematics class work. Each day he records, on a scale of 0 to 3, how well he has done his work, and his teacher provides feedback. This self-management technique is an example of:
(Average Rigor) (Skill 10.05)

    a. Self-recording
    b. Self reinforcement
    c. Self-regulation
    d. Self-evaluation

Correct answer is "d."
Rationale: Mark is evaluating his behavior, not merely recording it.

79. When Barbara reached her target goal, she chose her reinforcer and softly said to herself, "I worked hard, and I deserve this reward." This self-management technique is an example of:
(Average Rigor) (Skill 10.05)

    a. Self-reinforcement
    b. Self-recording
    c. Self-regulation
    d. Self-evaluation

Correct answer is "a."
Rationale: Barbara is reinforcing her behavior.

80. A student with a poor self-concept may manifest in all of the ways listed below *except*:
(Easy) (Skill 10.05)

    a. Withdrawn actions
    b. Aggression
    c. Consistently announcing his or her achievements
    d. Shyness

Correct answer is "c."
A poor self-concept is not evident in someone who boasts of his or her achievements.

81.   **If the arrangement in a fixed-ratio schedule of reinforcement is three, when will the student receive the reinforcer?**
       (Rigorous) (Skill 10.06)

       a. After every third correct response
       b. After every third correct response in a row
       c. After the third correct response in the time interval of the behavior sample
       d. After the third correct response even if the undesired behavior occurs in between correct responses

Correct answer is "b."
Rationale: This is the only one that follows a pattern. A fixed ratio is a pattern.

82.   **Laura is beginning to raise her hand first instead of talking out. An effective schedule of reinforcement would be:**
       (Rigorous) (Skill 10.06)

       a. Continuous
       b. Variable
       c. Intermittent
       d. Fixed

Correct answer is "a."
Rationale: The pattern of reinforcement should not be variable, intermittent, or fixed. It should be continuous.

83.   **As Laura continues to raise her hand to speak, the teacher would want to change to this schedule of reinforcement in order to wean her from the reinforcement:**
       (Rigorous) (Skill 10.06)

       a. Continuous
       b. Variable
       c. Intermittent
       d. Fixed

Correct answer is "d."
Rationale: The pattern should be in a fixed ratio.

84. **Laura has demonstrated that she has mastered the goal of raising her hand to speak; reinforcement during the maintenance phase should be:**
(Average Rigor) (Skill 10.06)

    a. Continuous
    b. Variable
    c. Intermittent
    d. Fixed

Correct answer is "c."
Rationale: Reinforcement should be intermittent, as the behavior should occur infrequently.

85. **Data on quiet behaviors (e.g., nail biting or daydreaming, are best measured using a/n:**
(Rigorous) (Skill 10.06)

    a. Interval or time sample
    b. Continuous sample
    c. Variable sample
    d. Fixed ratio sample

Correct answer is "a."
Rationale: An interval or time sample is best to measure the duration of the behavior.

86. **Which is the least effective of reinforcers in programs for mildly to moderately handicapped learners?**
(Average Rigor) (Skill 10.06)

    a. Tokens
    b. Social
    c. Food
    d. Activity

Correct answer is "c."
Rationale: Food is the least effective reinforcer for most handicapped children. Tokens, social interaction, or activity are more desirable. The use of too much food may cause the student to reach satiation.

87.   The Premack principle of increasing the performance of a less-preferred activity by immediately following it with a highly preferred activity is the basis of:
       (Rigorous) (Skill 10.06)

       a. Response cost
       b. Token systems
       c. Contingency contracting
       d. Self-recording management

Correct answer is "c."
Rationale: In a contingency contract, the student eagerly completes the less desirable activity to obtain the reward of the more desirable activity.

88.   Justin, a second grader, is reinforced if he is on task at the end of each 10-minute block of time that the teacher observes him. This is an example of what type of schedule?
       (Average Rigor) (Skill 10.06)

       a. Continuous
       b. Fixed interval
       c. Fixed ratio
       d. Variable ratio

Correct answer is "b."
Rationale: Ten minutes is a fixed interval of time.

89.   At the beginning of the school year, Annette had a problem with being late for class. Her teacher reinforced her each time she was in her seat when the bell rang. In October, her teacher decided to reward her every other day when she was not tardy to class. The reinforcement schedule appropriate for making the transition to maintenance phase would be:
       (Rigorous) (Skill 10.06)

       a. Continuous
       b. Fixed interval
       c. Variable ratio
       d. Fixed ratio

Correct answer is "b."
Rationale: Every other day is a fixed interval of time.

90. By November, Annette's teacher is satisfied with her record of being on time and decides to change the schedule of reinforcement. The best type of reinforcement schedule for maintenance of behavior is: *(Rigorous) (Skill 10.06)*

   a. Continuous
   b. Fixed interval
   c. Variable ratio
   d. Fixed ratio

Correct answer is "c."
Rationale: The behavior will occur infrequently. A variable ratio provides the best schedule.

91. Teacher feedback, task completion, and a sense of pride over mastery or accomplishment of a skill are examples of: *(Average Rigor) (Skill 10.06)*

   a. Extrinsic reinforcers
   b. Behavior modifiers
   c. Intrinsic reinforcers
   d. Positive feedback

Correct answer is "c."
Rationale: These are intangibles. Motivation may be achieved through intrinsic reinforcers or extrinsic reinforcers. Intrinsic reinforcers are usually intangible, and extrinsic reinforcers are usually tangible rewards from an external source.

92. Social approval, token reinforcers, and rewards (such as pencils or stickers) are examples of: *(Average Rigor) (Skill 10.06)*

   a. Extrinsic reinforcers
   b. Behavior modifiers
   c. Intrinsic reinforcers
   d. Positive feedback

Correct answer is "a."
Rationale: These are rewards from external sources.

93.   Token systems are popular for all of these advantages *except*:
        (Rigorous) (Skill 10.06)

        a. The number needed for rewards may be adjusted as needed
        b. Rewards are easy to maintain
        c. They are effective for students who generally do not respond to social reinforcers
        d. Tokens reinforce the relationship between desirable behavior and reinforcement

Correct answer is "b."
Rationale: The ease of maintenance is not a valid reason for developing a token system.

94.   Free time, shopping at the school store, and candy are examples of:
        (Easy) (Skill 10.06)

        a. Privileges
        b. Allowances
        c. Rights
        d. Entitlements

Correct answer is "a."
Rationale: These are privileges, or positive consequences.

95.   When would proximity control not be a good behavioral intervention?
        (Easy) (Skill 10.07)

        a. Two students are arguing.
        b. A student is distracting others.
        c. One student threatens another.
        d. A situation involving fading and shaping

Correct answer is "c."
Threats can break into fights. Standing in the middle of a fight can be threatening to your ability to supervise the class as a whole or to get the help needed to stop the fight.

96.   A BIP (Behavior Intervention Plan) is written to teach positive behavior. Which element listed below is *not* a standard feature of the plan?
(*Rigorous*) (*Skill 10.08*)

    a. Identification of behavior to be modified
    b. Strategies to implement the replacement behavior
    c. Statement of distribution
    d. Team creation of BIP

Correct answer is "c."
There is no statement on how or who shall receive the BIP on the student.

97.   Crisis intervention methods are above all concerned with:
(*Easy*) (*Skill 10.08*)

    a. Safety and well-being of the staff and students
    b. Stopping the inappropriate behavior
    c. Preventing the behavior from occurring again
    d. The student learning that outbursts are inappropriate

Correct answer is "a."
Rationale: This answer encompasses B, C, and D.

98.   Ricky, a third-grade student, runs out of the classroom and onto the roof of the school. He paces around the roof, looks around to see who is watching, and laughs at the person standing on the ground. He appears to be in control of his behavior. What should the teacher do?
(*Rigorous*) (*Skill 10.08*)

    a. Go back inside and leave him up there until he decides he is ready to come down
    b. Climb up to get Ricky so he doesn't fall off and get hurt
    c. Notify the crisis teacher and arrange to have someone monitor Ricky
    d. Call the police

Correct answer is "c."
Rationale: The teacher cannot be responsible for both Ricky and the class. He must pass the responsibility to the appropriate person.

99. Mr. Smith is on a field trip with a group of high school EH students. On the way, they stop at a fast-food restaurant for lunch, and Warren and Raul get into an argument. After some heated words, Warren stalks out of the restaurant and refuses to return to the group. He leaves the parking lot, continues walking away from the group, and ignores Mr. Smith's directions to come back. What would be the best course of action for Mr. Smith?
(Rigorous) (Skill 10.08)

   a. Leave the group with the class aide and follow Warren to try to talk him into coming back
   b. Wait a little while and see if Warren cools off and returns
   c. Telephone the school and let the crisis teacher notify the police in accordance with school policy
   d. Call the police himself

Correct answer is "c."
Rationale: Mr. Smith is still responsible for his class. This is his only option.

100. Which of the following sentences will *not* test recall?
(Average Rigor) (Skill 11.02)

   a. What words in the story describe Goldilocks?
   b. Why did Goldilocks go into the three bears' house?
   c. Name in order the things that belonged to the three bears that Goldilocks tried.
   d. What did the three bears learn about leaving their house unlocked?

Correct answer is "d."
Recall requires the student to produce from memory ideas and information explicitly stated in the story. Answer D requires an inference.

101. **Transfer of learning occurs when:**
(Rigorous) (Skill 11.03)

    a. Experience with one task influences performance on another task
    b. Content can be explained orally
    c. Student experiences the "I got it!" syndrome
    d. Curricular objective is exceeded

Correct answer is "a."
Transfer of learning occurs when experience with one task influences performance on another task. Positive transfer occurs when the required responses and the stimuli are similar, such as moving from baseball to handball to racquetball or from field hockey to soccer. Negative transfer occurs when the stimuli remain similar, but the required responses change, such as shifting from soccer to football, tennis to racquetball, or boxing to sports karate.

102. **To facilitate learning instructional objectives:**
(Rigorous) (Skill 11.03)

    a. They should be taken from a grade-level spelling list.
    b. They should be written and shared.
    c. They should be arranged in order of similarity.
    d. They should be taken from a scope and sequence.

Correct answer is "c."
To facilitate learning, instructional objectives should be arranged in order according to their patterns of similarity. Objectives involving similar responses should be closely sequenced; thus, the possibility for positive transfer is stressed. Likewise, learning objectives that involve different responses should be programmed within instructional procedures in the most appropriate way possible.

103. **Measurement of adaptive behavior should include all *except*:**
(Rigorous) (Skill 12.03)

    a. Student behavior in a variety of settings
    b. Student skills displayed in a variety of settings
    c. Comparative analysis to other students in a class
    d. Analysis of the student's social skills

Correct answer is "c."
Evaluating a student's adaptability requires analysis only of that person and does not allow for comparative analysis. Comparing how students interact with others or comparing skill levels is not a good measure of adaptability.

104. **Teaching children functional skills that will be useful in their home life and neighborhoods is the basis of:**
    (Rigorous) (Skill 12.05)

    a. Curriculum-based instruction
    b. Community-based instruction
    c. Transition planning
    d. Functional curriculum

Correct answer is "b."
Rationale: Teaching functional skills in the wider curriculum is considered community-based instruction.

105. **The transition activities that have to be addressed, unless the IEP team finds it uncalled for, include all of the following *except*:**
    (Rigorous) (Skill 12.06)

    a. Instruction
    b. Volunteer opportunities
    c. Community experiences
    d. Development of objectives related to employment and other post-school areas

Correct answer is "b."
Volunteer opportunities, although worthwhile, are not listed as one of the three transition activities that have to be addressed on a student's IEP.

106. **Parent contact should first begin when:**
    (Average Rigor) (Skill 13.02)

    a. You are informed the child will be your student
    b. The student fails a test
    c. The student exceeds others on a task
    d. A CSE is coming and you have had no previous replies to letters

Correct answer is "a."
Student contact should begin as a getting-to-know-you piece, which allows the teacher to begin on a nonjudgmental platform. It also allows the parent to receive a view that you are a professional who is willing to work with them.

107. **Which of the following is an effective method of gaining and holding students' attention if they are deficient in attending skills?**
(Easy) (Skill 13.03)

    a. Eliminating or reducing environmental distractions
    b. Asking the question before calling the name of a student to create greater interest
    c. Being enthusiastic and keeping lessons short and interactive
    d. All of the above

Correct answer is "d."
For some students, special techniques must be employed to gain and hold attention. All of the methods listed above are effective.

108. **Task-related attending skills include:**
(Rigorous) (Skill 13.03)

    a. Compliance to requests
    b. Writing the correct answer on the chalkboard
    c. Listening to the assignment
    d. Repeating instructions

Correct answer is "c."
Attending skills are used to receive a message. Compliance may have nothing to do with what was said at the moment. Repetition of instructions may be a compensatory strategy.

109. **Which is *not* a goal of collaborative consultation?**
(Easy) (Skill 14.01)

    a. Prevent learning and behavior problems with mainstreamed students
    b. Coordinate the instructional programs between mainstream and ESE classes
    c. Facilitate solutions to learning and behavior problems
    d. Function as an ESE service model

Correct answer is "d."
Rationale: A, B, and C are goals. Functioning as an ESE model is not a goal. Collaborative consultation is necessary for the classification of students with disabilities and the provision of services to satisfy their needs.

110. **An important goal of collaborative consultation is:**
     (Easy) (Skill 14.01)

     a. Mainstream as many ESE students as possible
     b. Provide guidance on how to handle ESE students from the ESE teacher
     c. Mutual empowerment of both the mainstream and the ESE teacher
     d. Document progress of mainstreamed students

Correct answer is "c."
Rationale: Empowerment of these service providers is extremely important.

111. **Knowledge of evaluation strategies, program interventions, and types of data are examples of which variable for a successful consultation program?**
     (Average Rigor) (Skill 14.01)

     a. People
     b. Process
     c. Procedural implementation
     d. Academic preparation

Correct answer is "b."
Rationale: Consultation programs cannot be successful without knowledge of the process.

112. **Skills as an administrator and a background in client consultation skills are examples of which variable in a successful consultation program?**
     (Average Rigor) (Skill 14.01)

     a. People
     b. Process
     c. Procedural implementation
     d. Academic preparation

Correct answer is "a."
Rationale: Consultation programs cannot be successful without people skills.

113. **The ability to identify problems, the generation of solutions, and knowledge of theoretical perspectives of consultation are examples of which variable in a successful consultation program?**
(Average Rigor) (Skill 14.01)

    a. People
    b. Process
    c. Procedural implementation
    d. Academic preparation

Correct answer is "c."
Rationale: Consultation programs cannot be successful without implementation skills.

114. **The key to success for the exceptional student placed in a regular classroom is:**
(Easy) (Skill 14.01)

    a. Access to the special aids and materials
    b. Support from the ESE teacher
    c. Modification in the curriculum
    d. The mainstream teacher's belief that the student will profit from the placement

Correct answer is "d."
Rationale: Without the regular teacher's belief that the student can benefit, no special accommodations will be provided.

115. **Mrs. Taylor takes her students to a special gymnastics presentation that the P.E. coach has arranged in the gym. She has a rule against talk-outs and reminds the students that they will lose five points on their daily point sheet for talking out. The students get a chance to perform some of the simple stunts. They all easily go through the movements except for Sam, who is known as the class klutz. Sam does not give up and finally completes the stunts. His classmates cheer him on with comments such as, "Way to go!" Their teacher, however, reminds them that they broke the no talking rule and will lose the points. What mistake was made here?**
(Average Rigor) (Skill 14.01)

a. The students forgot the no talking rule
b. The teacher considered talk-outs to be maladaptive in all school settings
c. The other students could have distracted Sam with talk-outs and caused him to get hurt
d. The teacher should have let the P.E. coach handle the discipline in the gym

Correct answer is "d."
The gym environment is different from a classroom environment. The gym teacher should have been in control of a possibly hazardous environment.

116. **The integrated approach to learning utilizes all resources available to address student needs. What are the resources?**
(Rigorous) (Skill 14.01)

a. The student, his or her parents, and the teacher
b. The teacher, the parents, and the special education team
c. The teacher, the student, and an administrator to perform needed interventions
d. The student, his or her parents, the teacher, and community resources

Correct answer is "d."
The integrated response encompasses all possible resources, including the resources in the community.

117. The following words describe an IEP objective *except*: (Average Rigor) (Skill 14.02)

a. Specific
b. Observable
c. Measurable
d. Criterion-referenced

Correct answer is "d."
Rationale: An IEP should be specific, observable, and measurable.

118. A serious hindrance to successful mainstreaming is: (Average Rigor) (Skill 14.02)

a. Lack of adapted materials
b. Lack of funding
c. Lack of communication among teachers
d. Lack of support from administration

Correct answer is "c."
Rationale: All four choices are hindrances, but lack of communication and consultation between the service providers is serious.

119. Which one of the following is *not* a primary purpose of an IEP? (Rigorous) (Skill 14.02)

a. To outline instructional programs
b. To develop self-advocacy skills
c. To function as the basis for evaluation
d. To facilitate communication among staff members, teachers, parents, and students

Correct answer is "b."
While self-advocacy should be encouraged, it is not one of the primary purposes of an IEP.

120. **Teachers have a professional obligation to do all of the following** *except*:
(Average Rigor) (Skill 14.02)

   a. Join a professional organization such as CEC or LDA
   b. Attend in-services or seminars related to your position
   c. Stay after school to help students
   d. Run school clubs

Correct answer is "d."
Teachers are not obligated to run a school club. It is often considered a volunteering position.

121. **The ability to supply specific instructional materials, programs, and methods, as well as the ability to influence environmental learning variables, are advantages of which service model for exceptional students?**
(Average Rigor) (Skill 14.03)

   a. Regular classroom
   b. Consultant teacher
   c. Itinerant teacher
   d. Resource room

Correct answer is "b."
Rationale: Consultation is usually done by specialists.

122. **Which is not a goal of collaboration for a consult teacher?**
(Average Rigor) (Skill 14.03)

   a. To have the regular education teacher understand the student's disability
   b. Review content for accuracy
   c. Review lessons for possible necessary modifications
   d. Understanding the reasons for the current grade

Correct answer is "b."
The regular education teacher is responsible for the content. A consult teacher is responsible for seeing that the child's necessary modifications are adapted.

123. **A consultant teacher should be meeting the needs of his or her students by:**
(Easy) (Skill 14.03)

   a. Pushing in to do small group instruction with regular education students
   b. Asking the student to show his or her reasoning for failing
   c. Meeting with the teacher before class to discuss adaptations and expectations
   d. Accompanying the student to class

Correct answer is "a."
Students who receive consult services are receiving minimum instructional services. They require little modification to their educational programs.

124. **You are having continual difficulty with your classroom assistant. A good strategy to address this problem would be:**
(Rigorous) (Skill 14.05)

   a. To address the issue immediately
   b. To take away responsibilities
   c. To write a clearly established role plan to discuss
   d. To speak to your supervisor

Correct answer is "c."
If you are having difficulty with your classroom assistant, it is most likely over an issue or issues that have happened repeatedly and that you have already attempted to address. Establishing clear roles between the two of you will provide a good step in the right direction. This may also provide you with the ability to state that you have made an attempt to address the issue or issues to an administrator, should the need arise.

125. **Related service providers include all of the following *except*: (Average Rigor) (Skill 14.05)**

    a. General education teachers
    b. Speech and language therapists
    c. Occupational therapists
    d. Physicians

Correct answer is "a."

General education teachers are important collaborators with teachers of exceptional students; however, they are not related service providers. Related service providers offer specialized skills and abilities that are critical to an exceptional education teacher's ability to advocate for his or her student and to meet a school's legal obligations to the student and his or her family. Related service providers—speech, occupational, and language therapists, as well as psychologists and physicians—offer expertise and resources unparalleled in meeting a child's developmental needs.

126. **Kareem's father sounds upset and is in the office demanding to see his son's cumulative record. You should: (Rigorous) (Skill 14.07)**

    a. Tell him that he will have to make an appointment.
    b. Bring the record to a private room for him to review with either an administrator or yourself.
    c. Take the record to the principal's office for review.
    d. Give the record to the parent.

Correct answer is "b."

Parents have the right to see their children's cumulative record. You do not have the right to remove something from the record so that the parent may not see it. However, it is important to remember that the documents should remain in the folder, and that the parent may need information explained or interpreted; therefore, someone should be present.

127. Educators who advocate educating all children in their neighborhood classrooms and schools, propose the end of labeling and segregation of special needs students in special classes, and call for the delivery of special supports and services directly in the classroom may be said to support the:
(Rigorous) (Skill 15.01)

   a. Full-service model
   b. Regular education initiative
   c. Full-inclusion model
   d. Mainstream model

Correct answer is "c."
Rationale: In the full inclusion model, all students must be included in the regular classroom.

128. The movement towards serving as many children with disabilities as possible in the regular classroom with supports and services is known as:
(Average Rigor) (Skill 15.01)

   a. Full-service model
   b. Regular education initiative
   c. Full-inclusion model
   d. Mainstream model

Correct answer is "c."
Rationale: The full inclusion model is the movement to include all students in the regular classroom.

129. Which of the following statements was not offered as a rationale for (Regular Education Intervention) REI?
(Rigorous) (Skill 15.02)

   a. Special education students are not usually identified until their learning problems have become severe.
   b. Lack of funding will mean that support for the special needs children will not be available in the regular classroom.
   c. Putting children in segregated special education placements is stigmatizing.
   d. There are students with learning or behavior problems who do not meet special education requirements but who still need special services.

Correct answer is "b."
Rationale: All except lack of funding were offered in support of REI or inclusion.

130. **Which of these would not be considered a valid attempt to contact a parent for an IEP meeting?**
(Average Rigor) (Skill 15.02)

   a. Telephone call
   b. Copy of correspondence
   c. Message left on answering machine
   d. Record of home visits

Correct answer is "c."
Rationale: A message left on an answering machine is not direct contact.

131. **Guidelines for an Individualized Family Service Plan (IFSP) would be described in which legislation?**
(Rigorous) (Skill 15.02)

   a. Public Law 94-142
   b. Public Law 99-457
   c. Public Law 101-476
   d. ADA

Correct answer is "b."
Rationale: Public Law 99-457 (1986) provides services for children ages 3 to 5 and for their families; Public Law 101-476 is IDEA; and Public Law 94-142 (Education for All Handicapped Children Act) was passed in the civil rights era. ADA is the Americans with Disabilities Act.

132. **Cheryl is a 15-year-old student receiving educational services in a full-time EH classroom. The date for her IEP review is planned for two months before her 16th birthday. According to the requirements of IDEA, what must additionally be included in this review?**
(Rigorous) (Skill 15.02)

   a. Graduation plan
   b. Individualized transition plan
   c. Individualized Family Service Plan
   d. Transportation planning

Correct answer is "b."
Rationale: This is necessary, as the student should be transitioning from school to work.

133. **Hector Is a 10th grader in a program for the severely emotionally handicapped. After a classmate taunted him about his mother, Hector threw a desk at the other boy and attacked him. A crisis intervention team tried to break up the fight, and one teacher hurt his knee. The other boy received a concussion. Hector now faces disciplinary measures. How long can he be suspended without the suspension constituting a change of placement?**
(Rigorous) (Skill 15.02)

   a. 5 days
   b. 10 days
   c. 10 + 30 days
   d. 60 days

Correct answer is "b."
Rationale: According to Honig versus Doe (1988), "Where the student has presented an immediate threat to others, that student may be temporarily suspended for up to 10 school days to give the school and the parents time to review the IEP and discuss possible alternatives to the current placement."

134. **The concept that a handicapped student cannot be expelled for misconduct that is a manifestation of the handicap itself is not limited to students which are labeled "seriously emotionally disturbed." Which reason does *not* explain this concept?**
(Easy) (Skill 15.02)

   a. Emphasis on individualized evaluation
   b. Consideration of the problems and needs of handicapped students
   c. Right to a free and appropriate public education
   d. Putting these students out of school will just leave them on the streets to commit crimes

Correct answer is "d."
Rationale: A, B, and C are tenets of IDEA and should take place in the least restrictive environment. D does not explain this concept.

135. **The minimum number of IEP meetings required per year is:**
(Rigorous) (Skill 15.02)

   a. As many as necessary
   b. One
   c. Two
   d. Three

Correct answer is "b."
Rationale: Public Law 99-457 (1986) grants an annual IEP.

136. **Satisfaction of the LRE requirement means:**
(Rigorous) (Skill 15.02)

   a. The school is providing the best services it can offer.
   b. The school is providing the best services the district has to offer.
   c. The student is being educated with the fewest special education services necessary.
   d. The student is being educated in the least restrictive setting that meets his or her needs.

Correct answer is "d."
Rationale: The legislation mandates LRE, the Least Restrictive Environment.

137. **A review of a student's eligibility for an exceptional student program must be done:**
(Rigorous) (Skill 15.02)

   a. At least once every three years
   b. At least once a year
   c. Only if a major change occurs in academic or behavioral performance
   d. When a student transfers to a new school

Correct answer is "a."
Rationale: This is done in accordance with Public Law 95-56 (1978), the Gifted and Talented Children's Act.

138. **Section 504 differs from the scope of IDEA because its main focus is on:**
(Rigorous) (Skill 15.02)

   a. Prohibition of discrimination on the basis of disability
   b. A basis for additional support services and accommodations in a special education setting
   c. Procedural rights and safeguards for the individual
   d. Federal funding for educational services

Correct answer is "a."
Rationale: Section 504 prohibits discrimination on the basis of disability.

139. **Public Law 99-457 amended the EHA to make provisions for:**
(Easy) (Skill 15.02)

    a. Education services for "uneducable" children
    b. Education services for children in jail settings
    c. Special education benefits for children birth to 5 years
    d. Education services for medically fragile children

Correct answer is "c."
Rationale: Public Law 99-457 amended EHA to provide special education programs for children aged 3 to 5 years, with most states offering outreach programs to identify children with special needs from birth to age 3.

140. **Under the provisions of IDEA, the student is entitled to all of these except:**
(Average Rigor) (Skill 15.02)

    a. Placement in the best environment
    b. Placement in the least restrictive environment
    c. Provision of educational needs at no cost
    d. Provision of individualized, appropriate educational programs

Correct answer is "a."
Rationale: IDEA mandates a least restrictive environment, an IEP, and a free public education.

141. **What legislation started FAPE?**
(Rigorous) (Skill 15.02)

    a. Section 504
    b. EHCA
    c. IDEA
    d. Education Amendment 1974

Correct answer is "a."
FAPE stands for Free Appropriate Public Education. Section 504 of the Rehabilitation Act in 1973 is the legislation, which enacted/created FAPE.

142. **Taiquan's parents are divorced and have joint custody. They both have requested to be present at the CSE. You call to make sure that they received the letter informing them of the coming CSE. Taiquan's father did not receive the notification and is upset. You should:**
(Average Rigor) (Skill 15.02)

   a. Tell him that you could review the meeting with him later.
   b. Ask him if he can adjust his schedule.
   c. Tell him you can reschedule the meeting.
   d. Ask him to coordinate a time for the CSE to meet with his ex-wife.

Correct answer is "c."
A parent should be informed if he or she is divorced, has joint custody, and has expressed a desire to be present at the CSE. In this case, if the one of the parents wants to be at the meeting but is unable to attend, it should be rescheduled.

143. **NCLB (No Child Left Behind Act), was signed on January 8, 2002. It addresses what?**
(Rigorous) (Skill 15.02)

   a. Accessibility of curriculum to the student
   b. Administrative incentives for school improvements
   c. The funding to provide services required
   d. Accountability of school personnel for student achievement

Correct answer is "d."
NCLB, Public Law 107-110, was signed on January 8, 2002. It addresses accountability of school personnel for student achievement with the expectation that every child will demonstrate proficiency in reading, math, and science. The first full wave of accountability will be in 12 years, when children who first attended school under NCLB graduate; however, the process to meet that accountability begins now. In fact, as students progress through the school system, testing will show if an individual teacher has effectively met the needs of his or her students. Through testing, each student's adequate yearly progress or lack thereof is tracked.

144. **NCLB changed:**
    (Rigorous) (Skill 15.02)

    a. Special education teacher placement
    b. Classroom guidelines
    c. Stricter behavioral regulations
    d. Academic content

Correct answer is "a."
Special education teachers are now required to meet the same criteria as those of the content teachers in their area to be *highly qualified.*

145. **Which law specifically states that "Full Inclusion is not the only way for a student to reach his/her highest potential?"**
    (Rigorous) (Skill 15.02)

    a. IDEA
    b. IDEA 97
    c. IDEA 2004
    d. Part 200

Correct answer is "c."
In IDEA 2004, it was stated that full inclusion was not always best for the individual student. This allows for students who need more restrictive services to be served appropriately when people who push full inclusion are confronted.

146. **If a child does not qualify for classification under special education, the committee shall:**
    (Average Rigor) (Skill 15.02)

    a. Refer the parental interventions to the 504 Plan
    b. Provide temporary remedial services for the student
    c. Recommend to the parent possible resources outside of the committee for which the child may qualify
    d. Give the parents the information about possible reviews by an exterior source

Correct answer is "c."
A student may or may not qualify for a 504 Plan. However, the student may be in need of additional resources (such as outside counseling with an agency) or a mentor situation (similar to what Big Brothers/Sisters provides).

147. **According to IDEA 2004, students with disabilities are to do what?**
(Average Rigor) (Skill 15.02)

a. Participate in the general education program to the fullest extent that it is beneficial for them
b. Participate in a vocational training within the general education setting
c. Participate in a general education setting for physical education
d. Participate in a modified program that meets his or her needs

Correct answer is "a."
Answers B, C, and D are all possible settings related to participating in the general education setting to the fullest extent possible. This still can mean that a student's LRE may restrict him or her to a 12:1:1 for the entire school day.

148. **John has attention deficit hyperactivity disorder (ADHD). He is in a regular classroom and appears to be doing okay. However, his teacher does not want John in her class because he will not obey her when she asks him to stop doing a repetitive action such as tapping his foot. The teacher sees this as distractive during tests. John needs:**
(Easy) (Skill 15.04)

a. An IEP
b. A 504 Plan
c. A VESID evaluation
d. A more restrictive environment

Correct answer is "b."
John is exhibiting normal grade-level behavior with the exception of the ADHD behaviors, which may need some acceptance for his academic success. John has not shown any academic deficiencies. John needs a 504 Plan to provide small adaptations to meet his needs.

149. **Kara's mother has requested a computer for her child to do class work and homework, but the CSE does not agree. Kara complains to you. You should:**
(Easy) (Skill 15.06)

    a. Tell her you agree with her
    b. Recommend an outside source that may provide a free laptop computer
    c. Tell Kara's mother she can still fight the CSE's decision by requesting a due process hearing
    d. Tell the parent to call a lawyer

Correct answer is "c."
It is your legal obligation to let Kara's mother know that she does not have to accept the CSE decision if she does not like it and that she can request a due process hearing.

150. **What is required of a special education teacher when approaching an administrator regarding a request to change placement of a student?**
(Rigorous) (Skill 16.01)

    a. Observation
    b. Objectivity
    c. Assessments
    d. Parent permission

Correct answer is "b."
Presenting a case for change of placement to your supervisor does not require parental permission. It requires your ability to objectively analyze the needs of the student versus current placement.

References

Ager, C. L. and C. L. Cole. 1991. A review of cognitive-behavioral interventions for children and adolescents with behavioral disorders. *Behavioral Disorders,* 16(4), 260–275.

Aiken, L. R. 1985. *Psychological testing and assessment* (5th ed.). Boston: Allyn and Bacon.

Alberto, P. A. and A. C. Trouthman. 1990. *Applied behavior analysis for teachers: Influencing student performance.* Columbus, Ohio: Charles E. Merrill.

Algozzine, B. 1990. *Behavior problem management: Educator's resource service.* Gaithersburg, MD: Aspen Publishers.

Algozzine, B., K. Ruhl, and R. Ramsey. 1991. *Behaviorally disordered: Assessment for identification and instruction CED mini-library.* Renson, VA: The Council for Exceptional Children.

Ambron, S. R. 1981. *Child development* (3rd ed.). New York: Holt, Rinehart and Winston.

Anerson, V., and L. Black, eds. 1987, Winter. National news: U.S. Department of Education releases special report (Editorial). *GLRS Journal* [Georgia Learning Resources System].

Anguili, R. 1987, Winter. The 1986 amendment to the education of the handicapped act. *Confederation* [A quarterly publication of the Georgia Federation Council for Exceptional Children].

Ashlock, R. B. 1976. *Error patterns in computation: A semi-programmed approach* (2nd ed.). Columbus, Ohio: Charles E. Merrill.

Association of Retarded Citizens of Georgia. 1987. *1986–87 Government report.* College Park, GA: Association of Retarded Citizens of Georgia.

Ausubel, D. P. and E. V. Sullivan. 1970. *Theory and problems of child development.* New York: Grune and Stratton.

Banks, J. A., C. A. McGee Banks. 1993. *Multicultural education* (2nd ed.). Boston: Allyn and Bacon.

Barrett, T. C., ed. 1967. The evaluation of children's reading achievement. *perspectives in reading, No. 8.* Newark, Delaware: International Reading Association.

Bartoli, J. S. 1989. An ecological response to Cole's interactivity alternative. *Journal of Learning Disabilities*, 22 (5), 292–297.

Basile-Jackson, J. *The exceptional child in the regular classroom*. Augusta, GA: East Georgia Center, Georgia Learning Resources System.

Bauer, A. M., and T. M. Shea. 1989. *Teaching exceptional students in your classroom*. Boston: Allyn and Bacon.

Bentley, E. L. Jr. 1980. *Questioning skills* (Videocassette and manual series). Northbrook, IL: Hubbard Scientific Company. (Project STRETCH [Strategies to Train Regular Educators to Teach Children with Handicaps], Module 1, ISBN 0-8331-1906-0).

Berdine, W. H., and A. E. Blackhurst.1985. *An introduction to special education*. (2nd ed.) Boston: Little, Brown and Company.

Blake, K. 1976. *The mentally retarded: An educational psychology*. Englewood Cliff, NJ: Prentice-Hall.

Bohline, D. S. 1985. Intellectual and affective characteristics of attention deficit disordered children. *Journal of Learning Disabilities*, 18 (10), 604–608.

Boone, R. 1983. Legislation and litigation. In R. E. Schmid and L. Negata, eds. *Contemporary Issues in Special Education*. New York: McGraw Hill.

Brantlinger, E. A., and S. L. Guskin.1988. Implications of social and cultural differences for special education. In E. L. Meten, G. A. Vergason, and R. J. Whelan. *Effective Instructional Strategies for Exceptional Children*. Denver, CO: Love Publishing.

Brewton, B. 1990. Preliminary identification of the socially maladjusted. In Georgia Psycho-educational Network, Monograph #1. *An Educational Perspective On: Emotional Disturbance and Social Maladjustment*. Atlanta, GA Psychoeducational Network.

Brolin, D. E., and C. J. Kokaska. 1979. *Career education for handicapped children approach*. Renton, VA: The Council for Exceptional Children.

Brolin, D. E., ed. 1989. *Life centered career education: A competency based approach*. Reston, VA: The Council for Exceptional Children.

Brown, J. W., R. B. Lewis, and F. F. Harcleroad. 1983. *AV instruction: Technology, media, and methods* (6th ed.). New York: McGraw-Hill.

Bryan, T. H., and J. H. Bryan. 1986. *Understanding learning disabilities* (3rd ed.). Palo Alto, CA: Mayfield.

Bryen, D. N. 1982. *Inquiries into child language.* Boston: Allyn & Bacon.

Bucher, B. D. 1987. *Winning them over.* New York: Times Books.

Bush, W. L., and K. W. Waugh. 1982. *Diagnosing learning problems* (3rd ed.). Columbus, OH: Charles E. Merrill.

Campbell, P. 1986. *Special needs report* [Newsletter]. 1 (1), 1–3.

Carbo, M., and K. Dunn. 1986. *Teaching students to read through their individual learning styles.* Englewood Cliffs, NJ: Prentice Hall.

Cartwright, G. P., C. A. Cartwright, and M. E. Ward. 1984. *Educating special learners* (2nd ed.). Belmont, CA: Wadsworth.

Cejka, J. M. cons., and F. Needham, sr. ed. 1976. *Approaches to mainstreaming.* (Filmstrip and cassette kit, units 1 and 2). Boston: Teaching Resources Corporation. (Catalog Nos. 09-210 and 09-220).

Chalfant, J. C. 1985. Identifying learning disabled students: A summary of the national task force report. *Learning Disabilities Focus*, 1, 9–20.

Charles, C. M. 1976. *Individualizing instructions.* St Louis: The C. V. Mosby Company.

Chrispeels, J. H. 1991. *District leadership in parent involvement: Policies and actions in San Diego.* Phi Delta Kappa, 71, 367–371.

Clarizio, H. F. 1987. Differentiating characteristics. In Georgia Psychoeducational Network, Monograph #1, *An educational perspective on: Emotional disturbance and social maladjustment.* Atlanta, GA: Psychoeducational Network.

Clarizio, H. F. and G. F. McCoy. 1983. *Behavior disorders in children* (3rd ed.). New York: Harper and Row.

Coles, G. S. 1989. Excerpts from the learning mystique: A critical look at disabilities. *Journal of Learning Disabilities*, 22 (5), 267–278.

Collins, E. 1980. *Grouping and special students.* (Videocassette and manual series). Northbrook, IL: Hubbard Scientific Company. (Project STRETCH [Strategies to Train Regular Educators to Teach Children with Handicaps], Module 17, ISBN 0-8331-1922-2).

Craig, E., and L. Craig. 1990. *Reading in the content areas.* (Videocassette and manual series). Northbrook, IL: Hubbard Scientific Company. (Project STRETCH [Strategies to Train Regular Educators to Teach Children with Handicaps], Module 13, ISBN 0-8331-1918-4).

Compton, C. 1984. *A guide to 75 tests for special education.* Belmont, CA: Pitman Learning.

Council for Exceptional Children. 1976. *Introducing P.L. 94-142.* [Filmstrip-cassette kit manual]. Reston, VA: Council for Exceptional Children.

————. 1987. *The council for exceptional children's fall 1987. Catalog of products and services.* Renton, VA: Council for Exceptional Children.

Council for Exceptional Children Delegate Assembly. 1983. *Council for exceptional children code of ethics* (adopted April 1983). Reston, VA: Council for Exceptional Children Delegate Assembly.

Czajka, J. L. 1984. *Digest of data on person with disabilities* (Mathematics Policy Research, Inc.). Washington, DC: U.S. Government Printing Office.

Dell, H. D. 1972. *Individualizing instruction: Materials and classroom procedures.* Chicago: Science Research Associates.

Demonbreun, C., and J. Morris. *Classroom management* [Videocassette and Manual series]. Northbrook, IL: Hubbard Scientific Company. Project STRETCH (Strategies to Train Regular Educators to Teach Children with Handicaps]. Module 5, ISBN 0-8331-1910-9).

Department of Education. 1981. *Education for the handicapped law reports.* Supplement 45 (102) 52, Washington, DC: U.S. Government Printing Office.

Department of Health, Education, and Welfare, Office of Education. August 23, 1977. *Education of Handicapped Children.* Federal Register 42 (163).

Diana vs. State Board of Education, Civil No. 70-37 R.F.P. (N. D. Cal. January 1970).

Digangi, S. A., P. Perryman, and R. B. Rutherford, Jr. 1990. Juvenile offenders in the 90's a descriptive analysis. *Perceptions,* 25 (4), 5–8.

Division of Educational Services, Special Education Programs. 1986. *Fifteenth annual eeport to Congress on implementation of the education of the handicapped act.* Washington, DC.: U.S. Government Printing Office.

Doyle, B. A. 1978. Math readiness skills. Paper presented at National Association of School Psychologists. *Teaching students through their individual learning styles.* New York. K.J. Dunn.

Dunn, R. S., and K. J. Dunn, 1978. *Teaching students through their individual learning styles: A practical approach.* Reston, VA: Reston.

Epstein, M.H., J. R. Patton, E. A. Polloway, and R. Foley. 1989. Mild retardation: Student characteristics and services. *Education and Training of the Mentally Retarded,* 24, 7–16.

Ekwall, E. E., and J. L. Shanker. 1983. *Diagnosis and remediation of the disabled reader* (2nd ed.) Boston: Allyn and Bacon.

Firth, E. E. and I. Reynolds.1983. Slide tape shows: A creative activity for the gifted students. *Teaching Exceptional Children.* 15 (3), 151–153.

Frymier, J., and B. Gansneder. 1989. *The Phi Delta Kappa study of students at risk.* Phi Delta Kappa. 71 (2) 142–146.

Fuchs, D., and S. L. Deno. 1992. Effects of curriculum within curriculum-based measurement. *Exceptional Children* 58: 232–242.

Fuchs, D., and L. S. Fuchs.1989. Effects of examiner familiarity on black, caucasian, and Hispanic children. A meta-analysis. *Exceptional Children* 55: 303–308.

Fuchs, L. S., and M. R. Shinn. 1989. Writing CBM IEP objectives. In M. R. Shinn, *Curriculum-based measurement: Assessing special students.* New York: Guilford Press.

Gage, N. L. 1990. *Dealing with the dropout problems?* Phi Delta Kappa. 72 (4): 280–285.

Gallagher, P. A. 1988. *Teaching students with behavior disorders: Techniques and activities for classroom instruction* (2nd ed.). Denver, CO: Love Publishing.

Gearheart, B. R. 1980. *Special education for the 80s.* St. Louis, MO: The C. V. Cosby Company.

Gearhart, B. R. and M. W. Weishahn. 1986. *The handicapped student in the regular classroom* (2nd ed.). St Louis, MO: The C. V. Mosby Company.

Gearhart, B. R. 1985. *Learning disabilities: Educational strategies* (4th ed.). St. Louis: Times Mirror/ Mosby College of Publishing.

Georgia Department of Education, Program for Exceptional Children. 1986. *Mild mentally handicapped* (Vol. II), Atlanta, GA: Office of Instructional Services, Division of Special Programs, and Program for Exceptional Children. Resource Manuals for Program for Exceptional Children.

Georgia Department of Human Resources, Division of Rehabilitation Services. February 1987. Request for Proposal [Memorandum]. Atlanta, GA: Georgia Department of Human Resources.

Georgia Psychoeducational Network 1990. *An educational perspective on: Emotional disturbance and social maladjustment.* Monograph #1. Atlanta, GA Psychoeducational Network.

Geren, K. 1979. *Complete special education handbook.* West Nyack, NY: Parker.

Gillet, P. K. 1988. Career development. In G. A. Robinson, J. R. Patton, E. A. Polloway, and L. R. Sargent, eds. *Best practices in mild mental disabilities.* Reston, VA: The Division on Mental Retardation of the Council for Exceptional Children.

Gleason, J. B. 1993. *The Development of Language* (3rd ed.). New York: Macmillan Publishing.

Good, T. L., and J. E. Brophy. 1978. *Looking into classrooms* (2nd ed.). New York: Harper and Row.

Hall, M. A. 1979. Language-centered reading: Premises and recommendations. *Language Arts*, 56: 664–670.

Halllahan, D. P. and J. M. Kauffman. 1988. *Exceptional children: Introduction to special education.* (4th ed.). Englewood Cliffs, NJ; Prentice-Hall.

———. 1994. *Exceptional children: Introduction to special education* (6th ed.). Boston: Allyn and Bacon.

Hammill, D. D., and N. R. Bartel. 1982. *Teaching children with learning and behavior problems* (3rd ed.). Boston: Allyn and Bacon.

———. 1986. *Teaching students with learning and behavior problems* (4th ed.). Boston and Bacon.

Hamill, D. D., L. Brown, and B. Bryant. 1989 *A consumer's guide to tests in print.* Austin, TX: Pro-Ed.

Haney, J. B. and E. J. Ullmer. 1970. *Educational media and the teacher.* Dubuque, IA: Wm. C. Brown Company.

Hardman, M. L., C. J. Drew, M. W. Egan, and B. Wolf. 1984. *Human exceptionality: Society, school, and family.* Boston: Allyn and Bacon.

————. (1990). *Human exceptionality* (3rd ed.). Boston: Allyn and Bacon.

Hargrove, L. J., and J. A. Poteet. 1984. *Assessment in special education.* Englewood Cliffs, NJ: Prentice-Hall.

Haring, N. G., and B. Bateman. 1977. *Teaching the learning disabled child.* Englewood Cliffs, NJ: Prentice-Hall.

Harris, K. R., and M. Pressley. 1991. The nature of cognitive strategy instruction: Interactive strategy instruction. *Exceptional Children* 57:392–401.

Hart, T., and M. J. Cadora. 1980. The exceptional child: Label the behavior [Videocassette and manual series], Northbrook, IL: Hubbard Scientific Company. (Project STRETCH [Strategies to Train Regular Educators to Teach Children with Handicaps], Module 12, ISBN 0-8331-1917-6).

HART, V. 1981. *Mainstreaming children with special needs.* New York: Longman.

Henley, M., R. S. Ramsey, B. Algozzine. 1993. *Characteristics of and strategies for teaching students with mild disabilities.* Boston: Allyn and Bacon.

Hewett, F. M., S. R. Forness. 1984. *Education of exceptional learners.* (3rd ed.). Boston: Allyn and Bacon.

Howe, C. E. 1981. *Administration of special education.* Denver: Love.

Human Services Research Institute. 1985. *Summary of data on handicapped children and youth* (Digest). Washington, DC: U.S. Government Printing Office.

Johnson, D. W. 1972. *Reaching out: Interpersonal effectiveness and self-actualization.* Englewood Cliffs, NJ: Prentice-Hall.

————. 1978. *Human relations and your career: A guide to interpersonal skills.* Englewood Cliffs, NJ: Prentice-Hall.

Johnson, D. W. and R. T. Johnson. 1990. Social skills for successful group work. *Educational Leadership 47* (4): 29–33.

Johnson, S. W. and R. L. Morasky. *Learning Disabilities* (2nd ed.) Boston: Allyn and Bacon.

Jones, F. H. 1987. *Positive classroom discipline.* New York: McGraw-Hill Book Company.

Jones, V. F. and L. S. Jones. 1981. *Responsible classroom discipline: Creating positive learning environments and solving problems.* Boston: Allyn and Bacon.

———. 1986. *Comprehensive classroom management: creating positive learning environments.* (2nd ed.). Boston: Allyn and Bacon.

Kauffman, J. M. 1981. *Characteristics of children's behavior disorders.* (2nd ed.). Columbus, OH: Charles E. Merrill.

———. 1989. *Characteristics of behavior disorders of children and youth.* (4th ed.). Columbus, OH: Merrill Publishing.

Kerr, M. M. and M. Nelson, 1983. *Strategies for managing behavior problems in the classroom.* Columbus, OH: Charles E. Merrill.

Kirk, S. A. and J. J. Gallagher. 1986. *Educating exceptional children* (5th ed.). Boston: Houghton Mifflin.

Kohfeldt, J. 1976. Blueprints for construction. *Focus on Exceptional Children.* 8 (5): 1–14.

Kokaska, C. J. and D. E. Brolin. 1985. *Career education for handicapped individuals* (2nd ed.). Columbus, OH: Charles E. Merrill.

Lambie, R. A. 1980. A systematic approach for changing materials, instruction, and assignments to meet individual needs. *Focus on Exceptional Children,* 13(1): 1–12.

Larson, S. C. and M. S. Poplin. 1980. *Methods for educating the handicapped: An individualized education program approach.* Boston: Allyn and Bacon.

Lerner, J. 1976. *Children with learning disabilities.* (2nd ed.). Boston: Houghton Mifflin.

———. 1989. *Learning disabilities: Theories, diagnosis and teaching strategies* (3rd ed.). Boston: Houghton Mifflin.

Levenkron, S. 1991. *Obsessive-compulsive disorders.* New York: Warner Books.

Lewis, R. B. and D. H. Doorlag. 1991. *Teaching special students in the mainstream.* (3rd ed.). New York: Merrill.

Lindsley, O. R. 1990. Precision teaching: By teachers for children. *Teaching Exceptional Children, 22.* (3): 10–15.

Linddberg, L. and R. Swedlow. 1985. *Young children exploring and learning.* Boston: Allyn and Bacon.

Long, N. J., W. C. Morse, R. G. Newman. 1980. *Conflict in the classroom: The education of emotionally disturbed children.* Belmont, CA: Wadsworth.

Losen, S. M., and J. G. Losen. 1985. *The special education team.* Boston: Allyn and Bacon.

Lovitt, T. C. 1989. *Introduction to learning disabilities.* Boston: Allyn and Bacon.

Lund, N. J. and J. F. Duchan. 1988. *Assessing children's language in naturalist contexts.* Englewood Cliffs, NJ: Prentice Hall.

Male, M. 1994. *Technology for inclusion: Meeting the special needs of all children.* (2nd ed.). Boston: Allyn and Bacon.

Mandelbaum, L. H. 1989. "Reading." In G. A. Robinson, J. R. Patton, E. A. Polloway, and L. R. Sargent, eds. *Best practices in mild mental retardation.* Reston, VA: The Division of Mental Retardation, Council for Exceptional Children.

Mannix. D. 1993. *Social skills for special children.* West Nyack, NY: The Center for Applied Research in Education.

Marshall, et al., vs. Georgia U.S. District Court for the Southern District of Georgia. C.V. 482-233. June 28, 1984.

Marshall, E. K., P. D. Kurtz, and Associates. *Interpersonal helping skills.* San Francisco, CA: Jossey-Bass Publications.

Marston, D. B. 1989. "A curriculum-based measurement approach to assessing academic performance: What it is and why do it." In M. Shinn ed. *Curriculum-based measurement: Assessing special children.* New York: Guilford Press.

McDowell, R. L., G. W. Adamson, and F. H. Wood. 1982. *Teaching emotionally disturbed children.* Boston: Little, Brown and Company.

McGinnis, E. and A. P. Goldstein. 1990. *Skill streaming in early childhood: Teaching prosocial skills to the preschool and kindergarten child.* Champaign, IL: Research Press.

McLoughlin, J. A. and R. B. Lewis. 1986. *Assessing special students* (3rd ed.). Columbus, OH: Charles E. Merrill.

Mercer, C. D. 1987. *Students with learning disabilities.* (3rd ed.). Merrill Publishing.

Mercer, C. D. A. R. Mercer. 1985. *Teaching children with learning problems* (2nd ed.). Columbus, OH: Charles E. Merrill.

Meyen, E. L., G. A. Vergason, and R. J. Whelan. eds. 1988. *Effective instructional strategies for exceptional children.* Denver, CO: Love Publishing.

Miller, L. K. 1980. *Principles of everyday behavior analysis* (2nd ed.). Monterey, CA: Brooks/Cole Publishing Company.

Mills vs. the Board of Educaton of the District of Columbia, 348F. Supplement 866. 1972.

Mopsick, S. L. and J. A. Agard. eds. 1980. Cambridge, MA: Abbott Associates.

Morris, C. G. 1985. *Psychology: An introduction* (5th ed.). Englewood Cliffs, NJ: Prentice-Hall.

Morris, J. 1980. *Behavior modification.* [Videocassette and manual series]. Northbrook, IL: Hubbard Scientific Company. (Project STRETCH [Strategies to Train Regular Educators to Teach Children with Handicaps,] Module 16, Metropolitan Cooperative Educational Service Agency.).

Morris, J. and C. Demonbreun. 1980. *Learning styles* [Videocassettes and Manual series]. Northbrook, IL: Hubbard Scientific Company. (Project STRETCH [Strategies to Train Regular Educators to Teach Children with Handicaps], Module 15, ISBN 0-8331-1920-6).

Morris, R. J. 1985. *Behavior modification with exceptional children: Principles and practices.* Glenview, IL: Scott, Foresman and Company.

Morsink, C. V. 1984. *Teaching special needs students in regular classrooms.* Boston: Little, Brown and Company.

Morsink, C. V., C. C. Thomas, and V. L Correa. 1991. *Interactive teaming, consultation and collaboration in special programs.* New York: MacMillan Publishing.

Mullsewhite, C. R. 1986. *Adaptive play for special needs children: Strategies to enhance communication and learning.* San Diego: College Hill Press.

North Central Georgia Learning Resources System/Child Serve. 1985. *Strategies handbook for classroom teachers.* Ellijay, GA.

Patton, J. R., M. E. Cronin, E. A. Polloway, D. Hutchinson, and G. A. Robinson. 1988. "Curricular considerations: A life skills orientation." In G. A. Robinson, J. R. Patton, E. A. Polloway, and L. R. Sargent, eds. *Best*

Practices in mental disabilities. Des Moines, IA: Iowa Department of Education, Bureau of Special Education.

Patton, J. R., J. M. Kauggman, J. M. Blackbourn, and B. G. Brown. 1991. *Exceptional children in focus* (5th ed.). New York: MacMillan.

Paul, J. L. ed. 1981. *Understanding and working with parents of children with special needs.* New York: Holt, Rinehart and Winston.

Paul, J. L. and B. C. Epanchin. 1991. *Educating emotionally disturbed children and youth: Theories and practices for teachers.* (2nd ed.). New York: MacMillan. *Pennsylvania Association for Retarded Children vs. Commonwealth Of Pennsylvania,* 334 F. Supplement 1257 (E.D., PA., 1971), 343 F. Supplement 279 (L.D. PA., 1972).

Phillips, V. and L. Mccullough. 1990. Consultation based programming: Instituting the collaborative work ethic. *Exceptional Children. 56* (4): 291–304.

Podemski, R. S., B. K. Price, T. E. C. Smith, and G. E. Marsh, illus. 1984. *Comprehensive administration of special education.* Rockville, MD: Aspen Systems Corporation.

Polloway, E. A., and J. R. Patton. 1989. *Strategies for teaching learners with special needs.* (5th ed.). New York: Merrill.

Polloway, E. A., J. R. Patton, J. S. Payne, and R. A. Payne. 1989. *Strategies for teaching learners with special needs.* (4th ed.). Columbus, OH: Merrill Publishing.

Pugach, M. C. and L. J. Johnson. 1989a. The challenge of implementing collaboration between general and special education. *Exceptional Children, 56* (3): 232–235.

———. 1989b. Pre-referral interventions: Progress, problems, and challenges. *Exceptional Children, 56* (3): 217–226.

Radabaugh, M. T. and J. F. Yukish. 1982. *Curriculum and methods for the mildly handicapped.* Boston: Allyn and Bacon.

Ramsey, R. S. 1981. Perceptions of disturbed and disturbing behavioral characteristics by school personnel. Doctoral dissertation, University of Florida. Dissertation Abstracts International, 42(49): DA8203709.

———. 1986. Taking the practicum beyond the public school door. *Journal of Adolescence.* 21(83): 547–552.

———. 1988. *Preparatory guide for special education teacher competency tests.* Boston: Allyn and Bacon, Inc.

Ramsey, R. S., M. J. Dixon, and G. G. B. Smith. 1986. *Eyes on the special education: Professional knowledge teacher competency test.* Albany, GA: Southwest Georgia Learning Resources System Center.

Ramsey R. W. and R. S. Ramsey. 1978. Educating the emotionally handicapped child in the public school setting. *Journal of Adolescence.* 13(52): 537–541.

Reinheart, H. R. 1980. *Children I conflict: Educational strategies for the emotionally disturbed and behaviorally disordered.* (2nd ed.). St Louis, MO: The C. V. Mosby Company.

Robinson, G. A., J. R. Patton, E. A. Polloway, and L. R. Sargent, eds. 1989a. *Best practices in mental disabilities.* Des Moines, IA Iowa Department of Education, Bureau of Special Education.

———. 1989b. *Best practices in mental disabilities.* Renton, VA: The Division on Mental Retardation of the Council for Exceptional Children.

Rothstein, L. F. 1995. *Special education law* (2nd ed.). New York: Longman Publishers.

Sabatino, D. A., A. C. Sabation, L. Mann. 1983. *Management: A handbook of tactics, strategies, and programs.* Aspen Systems Corporation.

Salvia, J. and J. E. Ysseldyke. 1985. *Assessment in special education* (3rd ed.). Boston: Houghton Mifflin.

———. 1991. *Assessment* (5th ed.). Boston: Houghton Mifflin.

———. 1995. *Assessment* (6th ed.). Boston: Houghton Mifflin.

Sattler, J. M. 1982. *Assessment of children's intelligence and special abilities* (2nd ed.). Boston: Allyn and Bacon.

Schloss, P.J., N. Harriman, and K. Pfiefer. (forthcoming[TAR4]). Application of a sequential prompt reduction technique to the independent composition performance of behaviorally disordered youth. *Behavioral Disorders.*

Schloss, P.J. and R. A. Sedlak.1986. *Instructional methods for students with learning and behavior problems.* Boston: Allyn and Bacon.

Schmuck, R.A. and P. A. Schmuck. 1971. *Group processes in the classroom.* Dubuque, IA: William C. Brown Company.

Schubert, D. G. 1978. Your teaching - the tape recorder. *Reading Improvement,* 15(1): 78–80.

Schulz, J. B., C. D. Carpenter, and A. P. Turnbull. 1991. *Mainstreaming exceptional students: A guide for classroom teachers.* Boston: Allyn and Bacon.

Semmel, M. I., T. V. Abernathy, G. Butera, and S. Lesar. 1991. Teacher perception of the regular education initiative. *Exceptional Children*, 58 (1): 3–23.

Shea, T. M., and A. M. Bauer. 1985. *Parents and teachers of exceptional students: A handbook for involvement.* Boston: Allyn and Bacon.

Simeonsson, R.J. 1986. *Psychological and development assessment of special children.* Boston: Allyn and Bacon.

Smith, C. R. 1991. *Learning disabilities: The interaction of learner, task, and setting.* Boston: Little, Brown, and Company.

Smith, D. D., and R. Luckasson. 1992. *Introduction to special education: Teaching in an age of challenge.* Boston: Allyn and Bacon.

Smith, J. E., and J. M. Patton. 1989. *A resource module on adverse causes of mild mental retardation.* Prepared for the President's Committee on Mental Retardation.

Smith, T. E. C., D. M. Finn, and C. A. Dowdy. 1993. *Teaching students with mild disabilities.* Fort Worth, TX: Harcourt Brace Jovanovich College Publishers.

Smith-Davis, J. April 1989. *A national perspective on special education.* Keynote presentation at the GLRS/College/University Forum, Macon, GA.

Stephens, T. M. 1976. *Directive teaching of children with learning and behavioral disorders.* Columbus, OH Charles E. Merrill.

Sternburg, R. J. 1990. *Thinking styles: Key to understanding performance.* Phi Delta Kappa, 71(5): 366–371.

Sulzer, B., and G. R. Mayer. 1972. *Behavior modification procedures for school personnel.* Hinsdale, IL: Dryden.

Tateyama-Sniezek, K. M. 1990. Cooperative learning: Does it improve the academic achievement of students with handicaps? *Exceptional Children,* 57(2): 426–427.

Thiagarajan, S. 1976. Designing instructional games for handicapped learners. *Focus on Exceptional Children* 7(9): 1–11.

Thomas, O. 1980. *Individualized instruction* [Videocassette and manual series]. Northbrook, IL: Hubbard Scientific Company. (Project STRETCH [Strategies to Train Regular Educators to Teach Children with Handicaps]. Module 14, ISBN 0- 8331-1919-2).

Thomas, O. 1980. *Spelling* [Videocassette and manual series]. (Project STRETCH [Strategies to Train Regular Educators to Teach Children with Handicaps]. Module 10, ISBN 0-83311915-X).

Thornton, C. A., B. F. Tucker, J. A. Dossey, E. F. Bazik. 1983. *Teaching mathematics to children with special needs.* Menlo Park, CA: Addison-Wesley.

Turkel, S. R. and D. M. Podel. 1984. Computer-assisted learning for mildly handicapped students. *Teaching Exceptional Children* 16(4): 258–262.

Turnbull, A.P., B. B. Strickland, and J. C. Brantley. 1978. *Developing individualized education programs.* Columbus, OH: Charles E. Merrill.

U.S. Department Of Education. 1993. *To assure the free appropriate public education of all children with disabilities.* (Fifteenth annual report to Congress on the implementation of the Individuals with Disabilities Education Act.). Washington, D.C.

Walker, J. E. and T. M. Shea. 1991. *Behavior management: A practical approach for educators.* New York: MacMillan.

Wallace, G. and J. M. Kauffman. 1978. *Teaching children with learning problems.* Columbus, OH: Charles E. Merrill.

Wehman, P. and P. J. Mclaughlin. 1981. *Program development in special education.* New York: McGraw-Hill.

Weintraub, F.J. March 1987. Interview.

Wesson, C. L. 1991. Curriculum-based measurement and two models of follow-up consultation. *Exceptional Children.* 57(3): 246–256.

West, R. P., K. R. Young, and F. Spooner. 1990. Precision teaching: An introduction. *Teaching Exceptional Children.* 22(3): 4–9.

Wheeler, J. 1987. *Transitioning persons with moderate and severe disabilities from school to adulthood: What makes it work?* Materials Development Center, School of Education, and Human Services. University of Wisconsin-Stout.

Whiting, J. and L. Aultman. 1990. *Workshop for parents.* Workshop materials. Albany, GA: Southwest Georgia Learning Resources System Center.

Wiederholt, J. L., D. D. Hammill, and V. L. Brown. 1983. *The resource room teacher: A guide to effective practices* (2nd ed.). Boston: Allyn and Bacon.

Wiig, E. H., E. M. Semel. 1984. *Language assessment and intervention for the learning disabled.* (2nd ed.). Columbus, OH: Charles E. Merrill.

Wolfgang, C. H. and C. D. Glickman.1986. *Solving discipline problems: Strategies for classroom teachers* (2nd ed.). Boston: Allyn and Bacon.

Ysselkyke, J. E., and B. Algozzine. 1990. *Introduction to special education* (2nd ed.). Boston: Houghton Mifflin.

Ysseldyke, J. E., B. Algozzine, and M. L. Thurlow. 1992. *Critical issues in special education* (2nd ed.). Boston: Houghton Mifflin Company.

Yssedlyke, J. E., M. L. Thurlow, J. W. Wotruba, and P. A. Nania. 1990. Instructional arrangements: Perceptions from general education. *Teaching Exceptional Children, 22*(4): 4–8.

Zargona, N., S. Vaughn, and R. Mcintosh. 1991. Social skills interventions and children with behavior problems: A review. *Behavior Disorders,* 16(4): 260–275.

Zigmond, N. and J. Baker. 1990. Mainstream experiences for learning disabled students (Project Meld): Preliminary report. *Exceptional Children,* 57(2): 176–185.

Zirpoli, T.J., and K. J. Melloy. 1993. *Behavior management.* New York: Merrill.

XAMonline, Inc.
25 First Street, Suite 106
Cambridge, MA 02141
P. 1-800-509-4128
F. 617-583-5552
www.XAMonline.com

2010

Georgia Assessments for the Certification of Educators (GACE)

PO#:		Store/ School:
Address 1:		
Address 2:		
City, State, Zip:		
Credit Card #:		Exp:
Phone:		Fax:
Email		

Titles	Paperback Information				eBook Information				
Titles	Paperback ISBN	Retail	Qty.	Paperback Subtotal	eISBN	Retail	Qty.	eBook Subtotal	Title Subtotal
Art Education Sample Test 109, 110	978-1-58197-531-4	$15.00			978-1-60787-783-7	$12.00			
Basic Skills 200, 201, 202	978-1-60787-017-3	$28.95			978-1-60787-669-4	$25.95			
Biology 026, 027	978-1-58197-773-8	$59.95			978-160787-778-3	$56.95			
Chemistry 028, 029	978-1-58197-540-6	$59.95			978-1-60787-786-8	$56.95			
Early Childhood Education 001, 002	978-1-60787-064-7	$39.95			978-1-60787-679-3	$36.95			
Early Childhood Special Education 003	978-1-60787-065-4	$39.95			978-1-60787-678-6	$36.95			
Early Childhood Special Education 004	978-1-60787-061-6	$59.95			978-1-60787-692-2	$56.95			
Educational Leadership 173, 174	978-1-60787-060-9	$59.95			978-1-60787-781-3	$56.95			
English 020, 021	978-1-60787-062-3	$59.95			978-1-60787-680-9	$56.95			
English to Speakers of Other Languages (ESOL) 119, 120	978-1-60787-063-0	$59.95			978-1-60787-693-9	$56.95			
French Sample Test 143, 144	978-1-58197-530-7	$15.00			978-1-60787-802-5	$12.00			
Health and Physical Education 115, 116	978-1-58197-774-5	$59.95			978-1-60787-785-1	$56.95			
History 034, 035	978-1-58197-685-4	$59.95			978-1-60787-784-4	$56.95			
Mathematics 022, 023	978-1-58197-346-4	$59.95			978-1-60787-794-3	$56.95			
Media Specialist 101, 102	978-1-58197-724-0	$59.95			978-1-60787-788-2	$56.95			
Middle Grades Language Arts 011	978-1-58197-598-7	$59.95			978-1-60787-793-6	$56.95			
Middle Grades Mathematics 013	978-1-58197-345-7	$59.95			978-1-60787-791-2	$56.95			
Middle Grades Reading 012	978-1-58197-535-2	$59.95			978-1-60787-789-9	$56.95			
Middle Grades Science 014	978-1-58197-591-8	$59.95			978-1-60787-790-5	$56.95			
Middle Grades Social Science 015	978-1-58197-686-1	$59.95			978-1-60787-792-9	$56.95			
Paraprofessional Assessment 177	978-1-58197-588-8	$59.95			978-1-60787-796-7	$56.95			
Physics 030, 031	978-1-58197-569-7	$59.95			978-1-60787-782-0	$56.95			
Political Science 032, 033	978-1-58197-549-9	$59.95			978-1-60787-795-0	$56.95			
Professional Pedagogy Assessment 171, 172	978-1-58197-589-5	$28.95			978-1-60787-797-4	$25.95			
Reading 117, 118	978-1-58197-534-5	$59.95			978-1-60787-787-5	$56.95			
School Counseling 103, 104	978-1-58197-587-1	$59.95			978-1-60787-799-8	$56.95			
Science 024, 025	978-1-58197-584-0	$59.95			978-1-60787-779-0	$56.95			
Spanish 141, 142	978-1-58197-720-2	$59.95			978-1-60787-800-1	$56.95			
Special Education General Curriculum 081, 082	978-1-58197-610-6	$73.50			978-1-60787-801-8	$70.50			

	Order Subtotal	
	Discount	
1 book $8.70, 2 books $11.00. 3+ books $15.00	Shipping	
	TOTAL	

CPSIA information can be obtained at www.ICGtesting.com
Printed in the USA
LVOW032130300512

283960LV00005B/6/P